Group Counseling

Strategies and Skills

SEVENTH EDITION

ED E. JACOBS
West Virginia University

ROBERT L. MASSON
West Virginia University (retired)

RILEY L. HARVILL
The HarBeck Company

CHRISTINE J. SCHIMMEL
West Virginia University

BROOKS/COLE
CENGAGE Learning

Australia • Brazil • Japan • Korea • Mexico • Singapore • Spain • United Kingdom • United States

BROOKS/COLE
CENGAGE Learning™

Group Counseling: Strategies and Skills, Seventh Edition

Ed E. Jacobs, Robert L. Masson, Riley L. Harvill, Christine J. Schimmel

Sr. Publisher: Linda Schreiber-Ganster

Acquisition Editor: Seth Dobrin

Assistant Editor: Alicia McLaughlin

Editorial Assistant: Suzanna Kincaid

Media Editor: Elizabeth Momb

Marketing Manager: Christine Sosa

Marketing Assistant: Gurpreet Saran

Marketing Communications Manager: Tami Strang

Content Project Management: PreMediaGlobal

Design Director: Rob Hugel

Senior Art Director: Caryl Gorska

Print Buyer: Karen Hunt

Rights Acquisitions Specialist: Dean Dauphinais

Production Service: PreMediaGlobal

Cover Designer: Gia Giasullo

Cover Image: Gia Giasullo, Studio eg

Compositor: PreMediaGlobal

For product information and technology assistance, contact us at **Cengage Learning Customer & Sales Support, 1-800-354-9706.**

For permission to use material from this text or product, submit all requests online at **www.cengage.com/permissions.** Further permissions questions can be e-mailed to **permissionrequest@cengage.com.**

Library of Congress Control Number: 2010938804

ISBN-13: 978-0-8400-3393-2

ISBN-10: 0-8400-3393-1

Brooks/Cole
20 Davis Drive
Belmont, CA 94002-3098
USA

Cengage Learning is a leading provider of customized learning solutions with office locations around the globe, including Singapore, the United Kingdom, Australia, Mexico, Brazil, and Japan. Locate your local office at **www.cengage.com/global**.

Cengage Learning products are represented in Canada by Nelson Education, Ltd.

To learn more about Brooks/Cole, visit **www.cengage.com/Brooks/Cole**

Purchase any of our products at your local college store or at our preferred online store **www.cengagebrain.com**.

Printed in the United States of America
2 3 4 5 6 7 14 13 12 11

About the Authors

Ed Jacobs is the coordinator of the master's program in the Counseling, Counseling Psychology, and Rehabilitation Counseling Department at West Virginia University. He is also the founder and director of Impact Therapy Associates. He teaches courses in techniques, theories, group, and addictions and conducts workshops throughout the United States and Canada on group counseling and Impact Therapy. Ed has written three other counseling books: *Leading Groups in Corrections,* *Impact Therapy,* and *Creative Counseling Techniques: An Illustrated Guide.* In addition, he enjoys traveling, biking, skiing, and visiting with friends all over the country.

Bob Masson is Professor Emeritus at West Virginia University and remains active in the counseling field by teaching courses at various universities and by serving on the counselor licensure board for the State of West Virginia. He was a professor for more than 30 years at West Virginia University in the Counseling, Counseling Psychology, and Rehabilitation Counseling Department. He taught courses in techniques, theories, group, and rehabilitation counseling. Bob enjoys bicycling and sailing with his wife, Kathy.

Riley Harvill is the co-founder of The HarBeck Company, a human resource training and consulting firm located in Dallas, Texas. Before co-founding The HarBeck Company, Riley was an associate professor at University of North Texas in the Counselor Education Department, where he taught courses in individual and group counseling. His latest venture is LearningCast.net, a web-based organizational training company.

Christine Schimmel is the coordinator of the school counseling program in the Department of Counseling, Rehabilitation Counseling and Counseling Psychology program at West Virginia University. She has been a counselor educator for over 15 years and has taught courses in school counseling, counseling techniques, group counseling, and counseling children and adolescents. Chris currently serves as the secretary for the WV Board of Examiners in Counseling, the licensure board for professional counselors in WV. She is a former school counselor whose teaching and research interests remain in the field of school counseling.

Contents

DVD Menu

Preface

G*roup Counseling: Strategies and Skills*, Seventh Edition, provides an in-depth look at group counseling with an emphasis on practical knowledge and techniques for effective group leadership. For this edition, we are excited to include an accompanying DVD that brings to life the skills presented in this textbook. The book is written for counselors, social workers, psychologists, and others who are leading groups in a variety of settings. Our active approach to group leadership reflects a belief that the leader is primarily responsible for the planning and implementing of the group. We have found that in most settings—schools, hospitals, rehabilitation facilities, and mental health centers—the leader must take a very active part in facilitating the group. In this book, we offer a reader-friendly, practical, how-to group text. This book is written for students.

Throughout the book and in the DVD we discuss and demonstrate many different kinds of groups. The examples offered in the book and on the DVD help the reader understand how an effective leader utilizes both basic and advanced leadership skills. We integrate the skills and examples described in the text with the role-play demonstrations presented in the DVD.

We recognize that group leadership is one of the most difficult forms of counseling performed by therapists, school counselors, drug and alcohol counselors, correctional counselors, nurses, and others in the helping professions. Our goal is to bridge the gap between theory and practice. We present a sophisticated how-to approach for both beginning students and experienced practitioners. In each chapter we address the needs of counselors, social workers, correctional officers, ministers, nurses, and others who may be reading this book. The purpose of the text and DVD is to integrate traditional theories and concepts of group process with thoughtful strategies and specific skills.

Other Changes and Additions to this Edition

In this Seventh Edition we have also made the following changes and additions:

1. We have moved the section on ethical issues from Chapter Eighteen to Chapter One. This change is in response to feedback from a number of consumers and reviewers who felt that learning about ethical considerations regarding group work should come at the beginning of the book.

2. We have updated references throughout the text to reflect current concepts and research findings relevant to group process.

3. In Chapter Eighteen, we now address the importance of social justice and consumer/client advocacy as relevant to the work of the group leader. These are particularly important concepts as group membership grows more diverse and social and political issues have the potential for impacting the success of our consumers and clients in the "real world."

4. We continue to expand our discussions of multicultural issues as related to group work. We strongly encourage our readers to blend the concepts and skills presented in this text with the excellent material now in print regarding effective techniques for incorporating multicultural considerations in everyday practice.

5. The original test bank for the instructor's use has been expanded by nearly a third, providing a large reservoir of questions in the form of matching, sentence completion, multiple choice, true or false, and short essay/answer. The questions are organized by chapters, allowing the instructor to test the content of each chapter and/or construct a comprehensive midterm or final examination for students. The correct responses to each question are provided, along with the appropriate page designations for reference.

6. The Web-Based Test Bank for students has been completely revised. The entire bank of questions is new and distinct from any questions appearing on the test bank accessible to the instructor. The Web-Based Test Bank allows the student to independently test his or her information level. The feedback system is immediate and provides an analysis of correct/incorrect responses and page locations of the relevant explanations.

Organization

Our readers, from time to time, have suggested a reorganization of the chapters to flow more with their individual teaching or learning styles. We have considered such changes with each revision, but have concluded that instructors vary in their use of the text based on their previous experience with teaching the group course. It would be nice if we could offer various arrangements to the chapters depending on how the book is going to be utilized; but because we cannot, we chose the order that seems to work well for many. Readers who are currently leading groups usually go to the chapters that are relevant for their immediate needs.

Our own approach has been to teach an overview that includes basic skills, planning, beginning groups, advanced skills and techniques, and finally approaches for closing a group. The last two chapters cover special populations and issues, although many educators have students read these chapters during the first couple of weeks of the semester.

Specifically, the three opening chapters provide an overview of group leadership. In these chapters, we examine various kinds of groups, leadership styles, uses of current theories, group dynamics, therapeutic forces in groups, group process, and the purpose of groups. In Chapter 1, we introduce our approach to group leadership based on the principles of impact therapy, which is an active, multisensory approach to counseling. Also in Chapter 1 we present a clear picture of different approaches to leading groups and discuss in detail the differences between the interpersonal and intrapersonal approaches to leading. We have also moved the section on ethics in group counseling to this chapter so that the reader becomes grounded in the importance of following ethical guidelines. Chapter 2 focuses on the importance of understanding therapeutic forces, including those presented by Yalom (2005). Chapter 3 emphasizes the importance of clarity of purpose which is a key element in the successful outcome of nearly any kind of group. We have on the DVD three segments on clarity of purpose.

Chapters 4, 5, and 6 cover a range of both basic and advanced leadership skills for planning and implementing a group, as well as specific strategies and skills for initiating the first and second sessions of a group. Chapter 4 is on planning groups. Included in the chapter on planning are sample plans with a detailed discussion of each plan. Chapter 5, which focuses on the first and second sessions of a group, describes the many different things a leader must consider in the first sessions. We provide numerous examples of how to begin various kinds of groups. We also present techniques for the introduction of members and the introduction of a new member during the second or subsequent sessions. Three DVD segments on beginning groups are provided. Chapter 6 focuses on basic skills of group leading. Summarizing, clarifying, and using one's eyes in effective ways are among the skills discussed. Three segments of the DVD are on basic skills.

Chapter 7 affirms the importance of establishing, holding, and deepening the focus in a group. We present creative ways to "get the focus" and a discussion of the depth chart, which is a tool for monitoring the depth of a session. Six DVD segments are presented regarding the focus of the group. Chapter 8 offers techniques for skillfully drawing out quiet members and cutting off members who ramble or otherwise diffuse the focus of the group. We provide seven DVD segments on these two concepts.

The essential uses of rounds and dyads are outlined and illustrated by numerous examples in Chapter 9. Three segments of the DVD focus on different kinds of rounds. Other exercises are discussed extensively in Chapters 10 and 11. Written, movement, fantasy, and creative exercises are among those reviewed in these chapters. Techniques are presented for introducing and processing the exercises, along with ethical considerations and specific cautions for using them. We provide four segments on the DVD that show effective use of exercises.

Chapter 12 is devoted to the strategies and skills important to the critical middle sessions of a group. We offer a way for the leader to prepare for dealing with topics during the middle sessions. We discuss four topics in detail: sex, need for approval, religion, and self-esteem. We also address issues of trust and commitment, common mistakes some leaders make during this period, and various strategies for increasing the group's effectiveness. Chapter 13 is on the use of counseling theories in groups. We offer brief descriptions of seven theories and many examples on how the theories can be used in groups. The coverage of theories is different from that in any other group book that we have seen and we provide three DVD segments that show the effective use of theories in a group.

Chapter 14 focuses specifically on skills and techniques essential for leading therapy groups. We discuss the role and responsibilities of the leader, the process of therapy, specific techniques, and common mistakes. We also outline ways of conducting therapy with a member while involving all the other members. Three DVD segments relate to Chapter 14.

Chapter 15 contains techniques for closing sessions and groups. We have three examples of closing on the DVD. Chapter 16 offers strategies for handling problem members (the chronic talker and the negative member, for example) and situations (such as resistance, sexual feelings, and conflicts between members). Chapter 17 deals with issues specific to certain populations, such as children, adolescents, couples, older people, and those who are chemically dependent, divorced, survivors of sexual abuse, and adult children of alcoholics. On the DVD we varied the kinds of groups so there are segments with kids, teenagers, and those in treatment centers. Chapter 18 offers thoughts on coleading, social justice and consumer/client advocacy, research, and evaluation techniques. We also discuss the training of group counselors and the future of group work.

To simplify the presentation, we use *he* and *she* alternately to represent the leader and group members. We also use the terms *counseling* and *therapy* interchangeably.

Supplements for Students and Instructors

In addition to the core book, the Seventh Edition of *Group Counseling: Strategies and Skills* can now be bundled with the DVD that demonstrates many different group leadership skills. The same videos found on the DVD are also available online through the *Group Counseling: Strategies and Skills* CourseMate website found at www.cengagebrain.com/shop/ISBN/0840033931, where students can also access a complete eBook and free Web quizzes to help self-assess their knowledge.

Also available on the CourseMate website, instructors will find an Online Instructor's Manual. An eBank Test Bank is also available.

Acknowledgments

We wish to express our appreciation to our many friends and students who contributed ideas and insights to the Seventh Edition of this book. We also in particular wish to thank those who participated in the role-plays for the DVD, both as leaders and as members. Although the authors provided guidelines regarding the issues to explore in each role-play, the participants presented these roles in such a way as to create very realistic scenarios.

We also want to express our appreciation to the many workshop participants who shared with us the difficulties inherent in leading groups in the field. Their insights have done much to guide the development of our thinking through these seven editions.

We also welcome a fourth author to this edition, Dr. Christine Schimmel, Assistant Professor at West Virginia University. Chris brings a freshness of perspective regarding group leadership and a strong background in the area of groups in schools. You will see Chris in action as a leader of several role play situations on the DVD. Chris has offered presentations at national conferences and will continue to contribute to the field of group counseling and to this textbook.

We want to also thank the reviewers who encouraged us to assess various sections of the book. We continue to try to make each edition better based on the different suggestions of the reviewers. Our sincere thanks go to: Darlene Daneker, Marshall University; Maureen C. Kenny, Florida International University; Diane Frey, Wright State University; Barbara Sheffield, Antioch University Santa Barbara; Lorraine R Barber, Community College of Philadelphia; Yvonne Callaway, Eastern Michigan State University; and Lisa Schmidt, Drexel University.

We also want to thank Seth Dobrin, our editor, for his help in seeing that the book got published in a timely fashion and for being such a helpful person to work with. Special thanks goes to Seth for seeing the value of having a DVD as a supplement to text and then doing all the hard work to see that the DVD project happened. Thanks also to Dennis Fitzgerald who worked with us specifically on the DVD. Without his help, the project would not have happened. And thanks to Brian Peterson and those at MotionMasters for doing such a professional job with the DVD. Thanks go to Rebecca Francescatti whose hard work as the copy editor made the book more readable. Thanks also to Rathi Thirumalai, the production editor. She was great to work with—very cooperative, professional, and dedicated. We felt she sincerely cared about this project. Finally, we want to thank all the people at Brooks/Cole who worked on this project—you are a great group of people to work with.

Ed E. Jacobs
Robert L. Masson
Riley L. Harvill
Christine Schimmel

Chapter 1

Introduction

If you are a new group leader or a student studying group leadership, you may be thinking that you know very little about groups, especially if you believe you have never been in one. Actually, everyone has had some kind of group experience, be it in classes, orientation sessions, job-training sessions, Sunday-school meetings, staff meetings, or counseling or support groups. Depending on the leader's ability, some of these experiences have been valuable and some have not.

If studying group counseling is new for you, you may be asking yourself several questions:

- What are the advantages of leading groups?
- What kinds of groups are there?
- What happens in groups?
- How do I prepare for leading my group?
- What do I do if nobody talks?
- What should I do if someone talks too much?
- What leadership style should I use?

This book was written to answer these questions. In this book, we provide a wealth of information and practical examples, hints, and techniques that will increase your understanding of group dynamics and enhance your effectiveness as a group leader. We believe that reading this book will improve your ability to lead all kinds of groups, trainings, and meetings. Our emphasis is on skills, techniques, and the art of leading.

In this chapter, we discuss a number of basic considerations: who should lead groups, reasons for leading groups, kinds of groups, group versus individual counseling, use of theories, group counseling in a multicultural context, group

1

leadership styles, leadership functions, what makes an effective leader, ethical considerations regarding group leading, and potential group problems.

GROUP COUNSELING SKILLS: Introduction

If you purchased the DVD, we encourage you to take a few minutes and watch video clips 1.1 and 1.2 ("Introduction") where we show two brief segments of a group: one being led by a leader without skills, and one being led by a leader with the skills that are highlighted throughout this book. In the DVD introduction, you will hear about our model of leadership and get a preview of what you will be learning in this book and what is included in the DVD.

Who Should Lead Groups?

Knowing how to lead groups is beneficial to anyone in a helping, teaching, or supervisory role. Professionals such as counselors, psychologists, social workers, psychiatrists, ministers, managers, and teachers can all use groups to enhance their work with people. Any helping professional who is looking for an economical and effective means of helping individuals who share similar problems and concerns should use groups. Many counselor educators talk about how counselors no longer have the option of just doing individual counseling (Bauman, 2009; Corey, 2008; Gladding, 2008; Jacobs & Schimmel, 2004). Currently, more and more administrators in schools and agencies are requiring their counselors to lead groups. In correctional settings, there is much more demand for groups (Jacobs & Spadaro, 2003).

Reasons for Leading Groups

Corey (2008) opens his text on group counseling by saying, "Although there is still a place in a community agency for individual counseling, limiting the delivery of services to this model is no longer practical, especially in these tight financial times. Not only do groups let practitioners work with more clients, but the group process also has unique learning advantages" (p. 3). The American School Counselor Association (ASCA) has recognized the importance of groups. In the ASCA National model leading groups in schools is promoted (ASCA, 2003; Campbell & Dahir, 1997).

There are many valid reasons for using a group approach. Two reasons are common to all groups: Groups are more efficient and groups offer more resources and viewpoints. Other reasons for using a group approach include the feeling of commonality, the experience of belonging, the chance to practice new behaviors, the opportunity for feedback, the opportunity for vicarious learning by listening and observing others, the approximation to real-life encounters, and the pressure to uphold commitments.

Efficiency

Having several clients meet as a group for a common purpose can save considerable time and effort. For instance, a school counselor who is responsible for 300 students will barely be able to see each student once during a school year using only one-to-one counseling. However, school counselors can meet the needs of many more students by having groups for advising, values clarification, personal growth, support, and problem solving. Groups provide a framework that promises to deliver services to the largest number of students with the most efficient use of time (ASCA, 2003; Bauman, 2009; Day, 2007; Jacobs & Schimmel, 2004; Van Velsor, 2009). Groups can certainly save time in situations where there is a need to orient residents, patients, or prisoners to policies and procedures (Stohr & Walsh, 2009). If a supervisor finds that her staff members have different opinions about an issue, bringing the people together for one meeting is more efficient than having individual meetings. In most agencies and schools, professionals are incorporating groups into their overall program to help handle the increasing caseloads. They no longer have the luxury of just working with individuals.

Experience of Commonality

Many people have feelings they believe to be unique. Having people get together in a group allows them to discover that they are not the only ones having similar thoughts and feelings. As group members share personal concerns, thoughts, and feelings, they are often amazed that others in the group have similar concerns. Yalom (2005) uses the term *universality* when he discusses the value of people getting together. Following are some examples of groups where the experience of commonality can be helpful:

- Parents whose children have died
- Pregnant teenagers
- Children new to a school
- Recently divorced persons
- AIDS patients
- Soldiers who have returned from war

Greater Variety of Resources and Viewpoints

Whether they are sharing information, solving a problem, exploring personal values, or discovering they have common feelings, a group of people can offer more viewpoints and, hence, more resources. Group members often relate that one of the most helpful aspects of being in a group is the variety of viewpoints expressed and discussed. When only two people get together, it is possible they will possess similar information, values, or ways of seeing the world. Usually this is not the case in a group setting—members will have a variety of opinions and ideas, thus making the experience interesting and valuable.

Sense of Belonging

Writers in counseling and psychology have pointed out the powerful human need to belong (Adler, 1927; Berne, 1964; Glasser, 2000; Maslow, 1962). Being in a group can satisfy this need in part (Steen, 2009; Trotzer, 2006; Yalom, 2005). Members will often identify with one another and then feel part of a whole. A sense of belonging has proven beneficial in such groups as those for veterans, women, men, ex-convicts, addicts, addicted teenagers, people with disabilities, and the elderly. Members of these groups report that the experience of being accepted was one of the most important features of the group.

Skills Practice

Groups provide an arena for safe practice (Capuzzi & Gross, 2009; Johnson & Johnson, 2009). Members can practice new skills and behaviors in a supportive environment before trying them in real-world situations. The range of new behaviors to explore is nearly infinite; members can practice interviewing for jobs, learning how to make friends, being more assertive, asking for a raise, or talking to significant people in their lives. They may share personal facts about themselves, confront others, talk about difficult subjects, look at others when they talk, cry in front of others, laugh with others, sing with others, or disagree with others. Assertiveness, communication, parenting, marital enrichment, employer–employee relations training, and police riot-training groups are all examples of groups where members might experiment with new behaviors.

Feedback

Groups provide an opportunity for members to receive feedback. Group feedback is often more powerful than individual feedback because when only one person is giving feedback, the receiver can dismiss that person's viewpoint. When six or seven people are saying the same thing, it is difficult to deny the accuracy of what is being said. In groups where behavior rehearsal is a major component, the suggestions, reactions, and perceptions of others can be valuable.

There are many kinds of feedback and ways of giving feedback in a group. Frequently, members will have the opportunity to hear both first impressions and updated impressions. Because feedback can be such a valuable part of group counseling, we have devoted an entire section to feedback exercises and how to deliver effective feedback (see Chapter 10).

Vicarious Learning

A number of authors have discussed the positive value of vicarious learning in groups (Day, 2007; Lefly, 2009; Steen, Bauman, & Smith, 2008; Van Velsor, 2009). Members frequently have the opportunity to hear concerns similar to their own. On countless occasions members have said such things as, "That's exactly the same problem I have." Other members have said, "Listening to you has really made me aware of the fears and hang-ups I have."

Real-Life Approximation

Groups replicate real-life situations better than one-to-one counseling. Different writers have discussed the idea of groups as a microcosm or reflection of society (Hagedorn & Hirshhorn, 2009; Yalom, 2005). Trotzer (2006) calls groups "minisocieties." Sometimes the group setting becomes a temporary substitute for the community, family, work site, or organization. In the comparatively safe atmosphere of the group, emotions, human behaviors, and attitudes such as confrontation, rigidity, fear, anger, doubt, worry, and jealousy can be identified and discussed. Being exposed to these in a group environment enables individuals to learn methods of relating and coping that may extend into their everyday living.

The social context of the group experience is valuable in many other ways. Not only are maladaptive emotions and behaviors scrutinized and worked on, but members also are given the opportunity to discover how people honestly react to them over a period of weeks or months.

Commitment

Commitment to work on specific concerns often has more strength when made in a group setting. Although people often make such commitments in one-to-one situations (counselor–client, nurse–patient, supervisor–supervisee), the motivation to honor them seems to be stronger when they are made to a number of people. This is one of the most helpful aspects of groups such as Alcoholics Anonymous, Weight Watchers, and groups that help people stop smoking, find a job, or become more assertive. In these groups, members make at least an implied commitment to stop, start, or change certain behaviors. The combination of support, subtle expectations, and the desire not to let down the group is often a powerful motivation for behavioral change.

Kinds of Groups

Some people think the term *group* refers exclusively to a counseling or therapy group for troubled individuals. In fact, there are many different kinds of groups, with a variety of purposes. A leader may form a group to discuss or decide something, to explore personal problems, or to complete a specific task or achieve a specific goal. During your professional career, you will most likely have the opportunity to lead many different kinds of groups. The techniques discussed in this book can apply to all kinds of groups and also to meetings, workshops, classes, and family counseling.

Educators have classified groups differently. The Association for Specialists in Group Work (ASGW), which is a division of the American Counseling Association, sets forth training standards for four kinds of groups: guidance/psychoeducational, counseling/interpersonal problem-solving, psychotherapy/personality reconstruction, and task/work groups. Gladding's (2008) list of kinds of groups includes group guidance, group counseling, and group psychotherapy, along with some additional traditional and historical categories. Don Ward (2006), former editor of *The Journal for Specialists in Group Work*, has an excellent article that gives the history and evolution of the different kinds of groups. He states "… it also seems that overlapping and blending of group types in the same group experience often best represents the reality of the evolving practice of group work" (p. 95).

We have created seven categories of groups, based upon their different goals. Some goals reflect what the members gain from the group and others what the members will do in the group.

Categories of Groups

1. Education
2. Discussion
3. Task
4. Growth and experiential
5. Counseling and therapy
6. Support
7. Self-help

Education Groups

Often, helping professionals are asked to provide clients with information on various topics. The following are examples:

- Rehabilitation clients learning how to use a wheelchair
- Students learning study skills
- People with diabetes acquiring information on nutrition
- Women learning how to protect themselves from being raped
- Managers learning how to better supervise employees
- Fifth-graders learning about the harmful effects of drug use

In each of these groups, the leader provides information and then elicits reactions and comments from the members, thereby serving sometimes as an educator and other times as a facilitator of discussion. It is very important for the leader to conceptualize this dual role. There is no set formula for how much one should be in each role—it depends on the amount of information to be covered, the amount of knowledge the members already have, and the amount of time available. Likewise, there is no set format for the number of sessions or length of meetings. Often, education groups are held just once for 2 to 8 hours. Others meet for a number of weeks, 1 or 2 hours per week.

■ EXAMPLES

This group is composed of eight students who want tips on how to study more efficiently. It is 20 minutes into the first session.

LEADER: Okay, let's talk about the different ways of going about studying a chapter in a text. What are the ways that you do it?

JERRY: Well, I just read the chapter and underline.

BILL: I do the same thing.

KEVIN: I try to outline 'em, but it takes me too long.

BOBBI: I just read it twice and hope for the best.

LEADER: Let me give you some ideas. One of the best things you can do is to sit down and skim the chapter for the main idea of what you are going to read. Often, there is a summary at the end of each chapter. Then decide the kinds of questions that the professor might ask. If you can, look over your other tests and try to get a sense of the kind of questions you have been asked before. How does that sound?

BECKY: Well, I never thought of skimming the chapter.

JIM: I like that idea.

CHU: Me, too. Would you suggest underlining or taking notes or what?

LEADER: I would suggest writing a question that summarizes the topic and then underlining the answer. Most people, however, don't learn from underlining alone.

KEVIN: That's true for me. It's not helpful for me to underline. But when I take notes as I read, I remember.

JIM: Yeah, I like that idea. I've been underlining too, but it hasn't helped. I think I'd better take notes.

The leader's role in this group is to offer helpful suggestions and ideas concerning ways of studying and to get members to share methods of studying that do and do not work for them.

■ ■ ■

This group is composed of five women who weigh more than 200 pounds. The purpose of the group is to educate the women about behavior modification methods of losing weight. It is the second meeting, and it is 10 minutes into the session.

LEADER: Get out your list of things other than food that are reinforcing for you—let's talk about them.

RHONDA: I realize that I do like to read, although I don't do it, and there are three or four TV shows that I like. I also put on my list that I have two friends who live back in Missouri that I would like to call but don't.

PHYLLIS: Gosh, that's strange. I also put down that I have some friends who live in California that I would like to call. The other thing I like to do that would be good for weight control is walking early in the morning. I'll bet I haven't gone for a good walk in the morning for over a year.

SALLY: Oh, I'd go with you! I get up early, but I just sit around and watch the news.

LEADER: I hope the two of you will talk after the meeting about doing that. How about others? Margie, what about you?

MARGIE: My list doesn't make sense.

LEADER: Do you mean that the activities you listed are strange or that you did not do it exactly right? I'm not sure what you mean.

MARGIE: Well, I've got things like sleeping, exercising, washing my car, cleaning my house—you know, dumb things like that.

LEADER: I don't really see those as dumb. In fact, let's talk more about how you can use your "reinforcer list" to help you. Let me go into a little more theory....

In this example, the leader is both educating by providing information and facilitating interaction by bringing up topics, clarifying comments, and getting members to share.

■ ■ ■

Discussion Groups

In discussion groups, the focus is usually on topics or issues rather than any member's personal concerns. The purpose is to give participants the opportunity to share ideas and exchange information. The leader serves mainly as a facilitator because he does not necessarily have more knowledge than the members do about the subject. Following are some possible examples of discussion groups:

- Book club
- Current events group
- Bible study group
- Lifestyle group

■ EXAMPLES

This group is composed of students discussing "how the family is changing."

LEADER: Let's list all the different forms in which families exist in our town. Each of you make a list. (*After a couple of minutes*) In looking at your list, what stands out to you?

LYNN: I never realized how many families aren't just the regular kind—that is, a mom, a dad, and some kids.

DON: You know, I think we need to be more accepting of all these kinds of families.

HECTOR: I agree, because I'm currently living with just my mom, and I remember that last year I was kidded about it.

LEWIS: Yeah, I think there is too much bullying of other kids. How do we stop bullies from having so much power?

LEADER: (*Intervening*) Wait, let's discuss the different kinds of families today. Maybe some other time we can talk about the bully problem.

BILLY: The thing I wonder about is all those single fathers. What do they know about babies?

The leader's role in this group is to generate discussion on the topic of the changing family. Because it is a discussion group, the leader did not let Lewis shift the focus of the group to dealing with bullies.

■ ■ ■

It is the monthly meeting of the Reading Club. The book being discussed is titled *Love and Addiction*.

LEADER: Let's do a quick round of 1 to 10. If you liked the book a whole lot, give it a 10; a 1 means you did not like it at all.

LESLIE: I'd give it a 7.

RALPH: 9.

STEVE: 10.

TUYEN: 7.

CINDY: 8.

LENDON: 9.

LEADER: Because most people did like it, let's talk about what stood out for you. What were two or three points that really hit you?

STEVE: There was just so much in there that helped me to understand the crazy relationship I'm currently in. I felt the authors were talking directly to me. I thought it was really interesting the way they described how people get into bad relationships.

TUYEN: It reminded me of the Bible and some of its passages. Don't you think the Bible is good for learning about relationships?

LEADER: Let's save that discussion for the end or later. Let's, for now, focus on this book.

RALPH: I thought the description of kinds of relationships was excellent. It really helped me to think through an old relationship that I'd had. On page 27—everyone look at that for a minute....

In this group, the leader used the 1 to 10 ratings to generate discussion. Once the discussion got going, she kept members involved and did not let the discussion shift off the main topic, the book the members had read.

■ ■ ■

Task Groups

The task group is one in which a specific task is to be accomplished, such as discussing a patient on a psychiatric ward, resolving conflicts among house residents, or deciding policies for a school. This kind of group usually meets once or just a few times and ends when the task is completed. Staff meetings, faculty meetings, organizational meetings, planning sessions, or decision-making meetings are examples of task groups. In the field of business, a *focus group* is a kind of task group that is used to evaluate products or perceptions of products.

The following list should give you a better idea of task groups:

- Members of a club choosing a slate of officers
- Houseparents deciding rules and policies
- Professionals involved in the treatment of one student (for example, a counselor, two teachers, a social worker, and a special-education coordinator)
- Professionals collaborating on a year-end report
- Committee deciding on location of a new highway
- Citizens wanting to do something for returning soldiers
- Students or teachers talking about ways to curb violence on the playground
- Students or teachers trying to change some policies at their school

The leader's role in a task group is to keep the group on task and to facilitate discussion and interaction. In some task groups, the members stay focused with little intervention by the leader; thus, the leader's role is more facilitative. In other task groups, discussion becomes unfocused or conflict breaks out among members. In such instances, the leader intervenes and brings the group back to the task. Stanley (2006) points out the importance of training for task group leaders of groups where important decisions are made.

■   EXAMPLES

The purpose of the group is to discuss Oswaldo's living situation. (The child is currently residing in an emergency crisis shelter.) A houseparent, Oswaldo's mother, a social worker, and a counselor have been brought together. The leader of the group is the social worker.

MOTHER: I want Oswaldo at home! He's my boy, and that's where he should be!

HOUSEPARENT: Oswaldo has not been cooperative here, and I don't think he's ready to go home.

MOTHER: *(In a condescending voice)* I don't care what you think. I think the program here is terrible. He should be allowed to call home whenever he wants. And the policy about visitations should absolutely be changed. Let's talk about that!

LEADER: *(Seeing that they're off the task)* Wait a minute. Let's get back to our task, which is deciding whether Oswaldo is ready to go home.

COUNSELOR: I have seen Oswaldo for five sessions, and he's still a very angry kid. My own opinion is he will not do well at home.

LEADER: Why don't you elaborate on why you feel that way and what you think would be helpful for Oswaldo?

■ ■ ■

The purpose of this group is to select one of three applicants to fill a vacant position in a small community agency. To make the decision, the director has brought together her staff of six to discuss the interviews.

MONTEL: I feel that we need a female, so I think we should hire Sarah.

SHERI: I agree we need another female.

TOM: *(Angrily)* Hold on just a minute! That's a bunch of crap. Why did we interview two guys if we were going to hire a woman? We never said anything about hiring a woman.

DIRECTOR: *(Recognizing a potentially volatile situation)* Let's talk about what we do need. I think both points are well taken. We never did decide we needed a woman. However, all things being equal, I think hiring a woman would be in our best interest. Let's go over each candidate's strengths and weaknesses.

FILIP: I didn't like the fact that Sarah smokes. None of us smokes. In fact, I think we should get the secretary to stop smoking.

TOM: Oh, I agree. Let's do that. Let's make a policy about smoking. *(Turns to the director)* How do we pass such a policy? I would like to make a motion.

DIRECTOR: *(Realizing that the group is off the intended task)* Wait! We're here to decide on the three candidates. We need to choose one of them. At the next meeting, we can set policies on smoking or whatever. Let's go over each candidate, listing strengths and weaknesses.

In each of these groups, the leader made clear what the task was and kept the group working on that task.

■ ■ ■

For anyone interested specifically in task groups, *Making Task Groups Work in Your World*, by Hulse-Killacky, Killacky, and Donigian (2001), is excellent. Also Van Velsor (2009) has an article on task groups in a school setting.

Growth Groups and Experiential Groups

Members who want to experience being in a group and who are motivated to learn more about themselves often benefit from growth groups. T-groups, or *training* groups, were the first popular kind of growth group; the first one was held in Bethel, Maine, in 1947. Sensitivity groups, awareness groups, and encounter groups would all be considered growth groups. Growth groups are conducted in settings such as schools, colleges, community centers, and retreat centers. In these groups, members are given the opportunity to explore and develop personal goals and better understand themselves and others. Goals may include changes in lifestyle, a greater awareness of oneself and others, improved interpersonal communications, and an assessment of values—all accomplished in an atmosphere of sharing and listening. Quite often in growth groups, considerable counseling will take place as different issues come to the surface.

One form of growth group is the experiential group, where the leader designs experiential activities for the members. Often these are conducted outdoors and involve physical challenges, risk taking, and cooperation among members. Perhaps the best known is the "ropes course," where members are challenged on a number of activities that involve ropes. If you are unfamiliar with ropes courses, we suggest you do an Internet search of the term and read about the different kinds of ropes courses.

■ EXAMPLES

This group is composed of 10 teenagers who are out on the ropes course. They have just completed two activities.

LEADER: What have you learned so far?

BUZ: That fear is more in the mind!

EDEN: I agree. I never thought I could do the "Pamper Pole," but when I saw Amiel do it, I thought, "I can do it."

STEVE: The group support has been what stood out for me. I was really scared, but everyone kept telling me I could do it. That really helped.

LEADER: I want us to talk about the value of group support, but first let me pick up on what Buz is saying about fear often being in the mind.

■ ■ ■

The purpose of this group is to examine values. (This kind of group could meet in a school, a church, or a community center.)

LEADER: Today we are going to take a look at some of the things you value. First, let me have everyone stand up and get in a line behind Serj. *(Everyone is now standing in the center of the room in a straight line, with the leader standing in front where everyone can see him.)* On the count of three, I am going to ask you to move to the position that is most like the way you are. Toward the wall to your left is "spender," and toward the wall to your right is "saver." That is, if any time you have money you spend it, you would move all the way to the wall to your left. If you spend some and save some, you may want to position yourself in the middle, and so on. Everyone understand? *(Everyone nods.)* Okay, on three: one, two, three. *(Everyone moves.)*

LEADER: Any comments?

DOUG: I am glad to see I am not the only spender because my mom says I spend, spend, spend.

TONI: I wish I could spend. I always feel like I must save my money. That's why I'm up against this wall. Have you spenders always been able to spend?

LEADER: *(After letting several members comment)* The main point of doing this is to see that people are different and to help each of you get a better understanding of why you are the way you are. Let's now talk about why you are the way you are and whether you want to change.

In each of these examples, the leader initiated activities that focused members on relevant self-exploration and personal growth.

■ ■ ■

Counseling and Therapy Groups

Counseling and therapy groups are different from growth groups in that the members come to the group because of certain problems in their lives. School counselors often lead counseling groups for students who have various problems at home, at school, or with friends. The leader focuses the group on different individuals and their problems; then, members try to help one another with the leader's guidance. The leader will, at times, play a dominant role by directing the session to make it more productive.

Therapy groups are for members who have more severe problems. Examples of therapy groups include the following:

- Patients diagnosed as having emotional disorders
- Teenagers in an institutional setting
- People with an eating disorder or some other addiction
- People who suffer from panic attacks
- People who were sexually abused

It is important to realize that group experts do not agree on how counseling and therapy groups should be conducted. Opinions vary widely on the role of the members, the role of the leader, the appropriate tone, and the use of theory in the group. Some believe that members should be responsible for the majority of the therapy, with supportive probing and encouragement from the leader (Rogers, 1970; Yalom, 2005). Others feel that a confrontational, aggressive approach works best, such as in positive peer culture groups (Vorrath, 1974). Some believe that individual therapy by the leader, while the majority of the group observes, is very beneficial (Dyer & Vriend, 1980; Perls, 1969). Some leaders strictly follow one of the theoretical models, such as rational emotive behavior therapy (REBT), transactional analysis (TA), or behavioral theory. Others use none of the individual counseling theories as their theoretical base: instead, they believe it is the power of the group interaction—sharing, involvement, and belonging—that serves as the main agent for change (Yalom, 2005).

Our leadership model for counseling and therapy groups is based on impact therapy (Jacobs, 1994), which is an active, creative, multisensory, theory-driven approach to counseling. In our approach, the leader is primarily responsible for making sure that individuals working on issues get the best help possible. The leader will do whatever is most helpful—sometimes using other members' input and sometimes conducting therapy while the other members listen, watch, and periodically share. Later in this chapter and throughout the book, we discuss how to use an impact therapy approach and why this approach is well suited for most group counseling situations.

■ **EXAMPLES**

This group consists of five women whose husbands routinely physically abuse them. It is 20 minutes into the second session.

LEADER: A number of you have talked about your poor self-concept. Rather than us just talking about self-concept, I'd like for someone to volunteer to work on her self-concept. The rest of us will listen and try to be helpful.

KATELYN: I will because I feel terrible about myself, but I'm sort of scared.

LEADER: I think all of us understand your fear. Why don't you start by telling us more about how you felt growing up?

KATELYN: I always felt like a nothing. My parents definitely favored my brother and sister. They even told me that if they'd known I was going to be so much trouble, they would have never had me. *(Starts to cry)*

JODI: My cousin who lives in Cleveland told me she felt the same way. The other day she told me this story. She said ...

LEADER: *(With a kind voice)* Jodi, let's stay with Katelyn. How many of you have felt like Katelyn? *(All four raise their hands.)*

SUE LIN: Katelyn, I cried myself to sleep every night, it seemed like, when I was growing up.

KATELYN: You did? So did I. I always felt everything was my fault....

■ ■ ■

This group consists of five teenagers who all recently attempted suicide. It is 15 minutes into the third session, and the members have been discussing their relationship with their parents.

CARL: At least your parents care! Hell, my old man hasn't been to see me since he brought me here. When he left, he said to me, "I'm done with you!"

DIONE: At least you have a dad. My mom has all these men over all the time. I can't stand it.

LEADER: *(In a caring tone)* Look, we could sit here and talk about how bad things are, but I am not sure that is the most helpful thing. What do the rest of you think?

TRUDY: I think we have to learn to feel good about ourselves no matter what our parents say and do. Like you said last time, we all need to learn how to cope with our feelings.

LEADER: Let's focus on the feelings you have about yourself and talk about how you can change your feelings by changing some of the negative "self-talk" that is in your head. I want each of you to think of the negative things you tell yourself throughout the week. I am going to write your thoughts here on the whiteboard and then show you how you tell yourselves all kinds of negative things that are not true.

In the first example, no specific theory was demonstrated, although the leader was most likely thinking in terms of Adlerian, rational emotive behavior therapy, or transactional analysis. In the second example, the leader was using impact therapy (writing on the whiteboard) and rational emotive behavior therapy to help these teenagers examine their poor self-concepts. (If you are a beginning student, you may not be familiar with the approaches mentioned. This is not important at this point. The crucial point is that the leaders of counseling or therapy groups use some kind of theory and do not just "wing it.")

■ ■ ■

Support Groups

A support group, which consists of members with something in common, meets on a regular basis—every day, once a week, once a month, or twice a month. In this type of group, members share thoughts and feelings and help one another examine issues and concerns. Support groups enable members to learn that other people struggle with the same problems, feel similar emotions, and think similar thoughts. The following are examples of support groups:

- Victims of a natural disaster, such as a flood or tornado, who share feelings about the loss of loved ones, loss of property, or survivor's guilt
- Elderly people confined to convalescent centers
- Those whose loved ones are dying
- Individuals with a disability coming together to share their feelings and fears
- People with AIDS, hepatitis C, cancer, herpes, or some other disease
- Stepparents who find it helpful to share the specific difficulties experienced in a stepfamily
- Teenage mothers who are still in high school

The role of the leader in a support group is to encourage sharing among participants. Ideally, the interactions are personal, and members speak directly to one another. It is important for leaders of these groups to keep in mind that sharing is the group's purpose and goal. It cannot be achieved if the leader or any one member dominates.

■ EXAMPLES

This group is composed of community members who have recently experienced a disaster. A fire in a local movie theater killed 50 people. Of the 10 members present in the group, some were in the theater and managed to escape, and some lost loved ones in the fire. It is 45 minutes into the third session.

LEADER: How are you sleeping?

JOE: I'm still not sleeping through the night. I have this anger at God, and I don't know what to do with it.

SHERITA: I have the same feeling. I haven't been to church since the fire, and I don't know if I'll ever go back.

LEADER: *(Seeing that Bill is shaking his head "no")* Bill, you seem troubled by what Sherita and Joe said.

BILL: *(In a tentative, gentle manner)* Well, I am troubled. I guess my faith in God has been the thing that has pulled me through this. I don't know why it happened, but I guess He had a reason. I wish Sherita and Joe could see their ways clear to go back to church.

LEADER: Does anyone else want to comment on that?

JACK: A priest gave me a book to read that helped me cope. The main point in the book was that you just have to go on and not ask "why." I guess that book really has helped, and I did sleep last week for the first time.

At this point, the leader's purpose is not to work therapeutically with the members' anger toward God, but rather to facilitate interaction and let people hear how others are coping. Now the leader invites another member into the discussion.

LEADER: Zach, what has helped you the most?

ZACH: I'm staying busy. I'm back at work, and at night I've made it a point not to be alone, at least in the early evening. I've arranged to eat meals with friends and family. I've also planned weekends well, and I'm making myself do things even though they don't seem to have much meaning. A friend of mine said, "Zach, you've just gotta start living again." He was right!

JOE: You know, hearing you say that is helpful. I think that's what I need to start doing. I guess I haven't really thought about it, but I'm not trying to live in the present; I'm just staying in the past.

HEIN: Joe, I hope you'll start living now because it's true for me, too. Just a week or so ago, I started living again, and it really made all the difference. I really do believe that as long as we're here on earth we've got to focus on our life and not on why it was our husband or son or loved one who died. *(Pauses and says with pain)* But believe me, it's not easy.

LEADER: You know, I do have to agree with Hein and Zach that focusing on the present and future is really the way to go. Does anyone else want to comment?

The leader is doing an excellent job of leading the group by allowing members to share and learn from each other. *Notice that the leader is not overly involved in the discussion. Many leaders make the mistake of talking too much, which prevents members from sharing.*

■ ■ ■

This third session is composed of eight elderly people living in a convalescent center.

CARL: Nobody came to visit me this weekend.

THREE MEMBERS SIMULTANEOUSLY: They didn't?

CARL: *(Dejectedly)* They called at the last minute and said something else came up and they weren't going to be able to come.

CLAUDE: That's too bad. I didn't check on you this weekend because I thought you were gone.

WAYNE: I wish you had come down to my room. I certainly would have spent time with you.

BOB: We oughta set up a system to check on each other during the weekends. You know, they're the hardest.

BERTHA: Boy, that's for sure.

JIM: I guess I'm beginning to count on this group more than on my family.

CLAUDE: I enjoy this group because you all care. It's not that my family doesn't care; it's just that it's a burden for them to come here. Yeah, I do like this group.

LEADER: *(Realizing that Leona hasn't talked)* How about you, Leona? Are you feeling better about the group? I know the first couple of times you weren't sure if you were going to like it.

LEONA: Oh, I think I like it. We just talk. I guess I was afraid people were going to tell me what to do. It feels good here.

The leader understands that the purpose of this group is to generate member-to-member interaction so that they feel cared for by other members. Because this appears to be happening, he is staying out of the discussion except to draw out comments from quiet individuals or generate discussion if the interaction starts to decline. Eventually the leader may initiate discussion of Bob's suggestion that they develop a system to check on each other during weekends.

■ ■ ■

This second session is composed of eight teenage girls who all are at least 6 months pregnant.

LEADER: Let's talk about two things today. First, the reaction you're getting from peers and family; second, any decisions you have

made regarding keeping the baby or giving it up for
adoption.

JULIE: Can I start?

LEADER: Sure.

JULIE: Well, the decision is so hard. I thought I knew for sure that I was
going to keep the baby, and then I saw a show on TV about a
teenager giving up her baby. Did anyone see that movie?

PAIGE, LINDA,
AND REBECCA: I did.

JULIE: The movie got me thinking about giving up the baby.

LINDA: I want to give up the baby, but my mom is like the mom in
the movie. She doesn't want me to give it up. She thinks
giving up the baby would be a horrible thing to do. *(Turns to
leader)* What do you think?

LEADER: No doubt the decision is a tough one, especially when your
family is putting pressure on you one way or another. I hope
that what we can do is take a look at all the forces that come
into play in this decision and then try to help each one of you. I
hope you realize that although each of you is in the same situation, you must make your own decision. I hope what we do in
the group will be helpful and supportive.

CINDY: But what do you do when you have pressure from your mom
and dad? They want me to keep the baby, but I really don't
want to be reminded of this period of my life. This has been
horrible for me. There are lots of people wanting to adopt babies, and I don't want a baby.

LEADER: *(Knowing that Cindy is a fairly strong person, she decides to spend a
little time with her, believing the others will benefit.)* Cindy, what is
the thing you are most afraid of if you give up the baby?

CINDY: I'm afraid of how mad my parents are going to be. Other than that,
I see it as a good idea for me. I'm not saying you all should do this.

LEADER: Okay, can you deal with your parents being mad at you—and
how mad would they be?

CINDY: Well, they would be real mad, and I am not sure if I could
handle their anger. I feel so bad when they are mad at me.

LEADER: Cindy, I want to help you and everyone understand more about
where feelings come from. *(Leader teaches Cindy and the rest of the
group that thoughts can cause feelings.)*

This vignette is an example of how one kind of group will sometimes overlap
with another kind. Even though some education and counseling is taking place,
it is mainly a support group.

■   ■   ■

Self-Help Groups

The last kind of group we want to discuss is the self-help group, which is now very popular. Laypeople with similar concerns as those at the meeting generally lead self-help groups. Millions feel that attending meetings for Alcoholics Anonymous, which is the most well-known self-help group, has changed their lives. Many other self-help groups follow the AA model, using the Twelve Steps. We realize that these groups cannot help everyone, but we do believe that all counselors should be aware of these groups, because they have been of tremendous value to so many people throughout the world. Students of ours are required to attend AA meetings as part of a course on addictions. They report that the experience was one of the best learning activities of their entire master's program.

Because these groups have no permanent, professional leader, and the purpose of this text is to improve group leadership, we will not focus on self-help groups. However, if you are not familiar with these groups, we encourage you to attend some meetings and read about them.

Group Versus Individual Counseling

Many people ask us, "Which is better, group counseling or individual counseling?" This is difficult to answer because people and situations are so different. Sometimes one or the other is best, and sometimes the combination of individual and group counseling produces the most benefit. For most people, groups can be quite valuable. For some people, group counseling is better because members need the input from others, plus they learn more from listening than talking. In many instances with teenagers, group counseling is better than individual counseling because teenagers often will talk more readily to other teenagers than with adults. For those stuck in the grief process, groups have been found to be very valuable (Humphrey; 2009; Worden, 2009).

Although there are many advantages to group counseling, it is important to realize that group counseling is not for everyone (Corey, 2008; Yalom, 2005). Administrators often do not understand this and, consequently, force members into groups. Individuals who do not want to be or are not ready to be in a group can disrupt it or be harmed because group pressure may cause them to take some action or self-disclose before they are ready. Also, sometimes an individual's problems are not addressed adequately in a group setting due to constraints of time. When group leaders recognize that a member needs more than group counseling can provide or that the member is going to be disruptive, they should encourage the member to consider the option of individual counseling instead of group counseling.

Use of Theories

Many of our students have asked us if there are any specific group counseling theories. The answer is no. Although labels have been given to many groups—

encounter, T, sensory awareness, here-and-now, psychodrama—these names simply describe what takes place in the groups and are not specific group counseling theories. However, this does not mean that a leader does not use theory when working with growth, support, or counseling/therapy groups. Theories originally developed for individual counseling—such as rational emotive behavior therapy (REBT), transactional analysis (TA), client-centered, Adlerian, or reality therapy—have been successfully adapted for groups.

Throughout this text, we mention various counseling theories in many of the examples. In the chapter on counseling and therapy, we discuss how theory can be used and we devote an entire chapter, Chapter 13, to the use of counseling theories in groups. If you desire further information about specific theories as they apply to group work, see Corey (2008) or Gladding (2008).

We cannot stress enough the importance of being able to use counseling theory when leading counseling, therapy, or growth groups. Those who do not have a good working knowledge of at least one theoretical perspective often lead a very shallow group; that is, the group never goes below surface interaction and sharing. If the members do become more involved, the leader who does not have a theoretical base is usually overwhelmed. Ideally, group therapy leaders will have multiple theoretical models in order to provide richness and diversity for conducting groups (Gladding, 2008).

On the other hand, certain kinds of groups do not require the use of counseling theory. Discussion, education, and task groups require that the leader possess a variety of basic leadership skills to monitor and direct the flow of conversation and interaction. For human relationship–training groups, there are some organization and development theories that may apply. Johnson and Johnson (2009) discuss these and present a strong argument for the use of theory with training groups.

Our Approach to Groups: Impact Therapy

Our approach to groups is based on the principles of *impact therapy*, which is a multisensory approach that recognizes that change or impact comes not only from verbal, but also visual and kinesthetic exchanges (Jacobs, 1994). "Impact therapy is an approach to counseling that shows respect for the way clients learn, change, and develop. The emphasis is on making counseling clear, concrete, and thought provoking, rather than vague, abstract, and emotional" (p. 1).

Impact therapy is a theory-driven approach using primarily rational emotive behavior therapy (REBT), transactional analysis (TA), Gestalt, Adlerian, reality therapy, and many creative techniques from *Creative Counseling Techniques: An Illustrated Guide* (Jacobs, 1992). The following are four core beliefs of impact therapy:

- People don't mind being led when they are led well.
- Counseling should never be boring.

- Counseling should be clear and concrete.
- The counselor is primarily responsible for the therapy but not ultimately responsible for the outcome.

The impact therapy model encourages leaders to be active, creative, and multisensory.

As we do workshops all over the country, many participants express how relieved and thankful they are to hear that it is okay to be active when leading groups. We believe the counselor should feel in charge and actively lead most groups using theories and techniques that make the sessions interesting and productive. Also, by being creative and multisensory, the leader has a much better chance of engaging more members. Throughout the book, we use many theory-driven, multisensory examples to give you a good idea of the impact therapy model and to give you permission to use your own personality and creativity to make your groups enjoyable and beneficial.

Group Counseling in a Multicultural Context

More counseling programs are emphasizing multicultural counseling; many are requiring courses on the subject. Certainly in today's society, understanding cultural differences is a must, especially for counselors who are leading groups with diverse populations. Corey (2008) states, "Multicultural group work involves strategies that cultivate understanding and appreciation of diversity in such areas as culture, ethnicity, race, gender, class, religion, and sexual orientation" (p. 17).

Because this book is about an active leadership approach, we want to emphasize that the leader must always consider the different cultural backgrounds of the members. For instance, counselors working with Asian students and students from many other cultures will need to be aware that these members may be quiet at first out of deference to authority figures. Using non-threatening questions in the beginning may be very helpful (Anderson, 2007). The leader needs to be aware of issues pertaining not only to cultural matters, but also to gender, age, and sexual orientation. Ethically, we have an obligation to acquire the knowledge and skills necessary to work in a multicultural context (Corey, 2008; DeLucia-Waack & Doingian, 2004; Sue & Sue, 2003).

The Association for Specialists in Group Work has an approved set of guidelines—"Principles for Diversity-Competent Group Workers"—that can be found online at the ASGW Web site. These guidelines outline what a group leader needs to know in regard to counseling diverse populations. If you feel you are not well versed in multicultural issues and counseling considerations, we strongly encourage you to seek out coursework, workshops, readings, and life experiences that will broaden your understanding. Two excellent books with which to start are DeLucia-Waack and Donigian's book *The Practice of Multicultural Group Work* (2004) and Salazar's *Leading Multicultural Groups* (2009). Also, several excellent articles on multicultural counseling can be found in *The*

Journal for Specialists in Group Work. In Chapter 17 on special populations, we address many of the issues regarding group work with a multicultural population.

Group Leadership Styles

Much has been written regarding leadership style (Capuzzi & Gross, 2009; Corey, Corey, & Corey, 2009; Johnson & Johnson, 2009; Posthuma, 2002). The style or role of the leader will always depend on the purpose of the group. As Gladding (2008) states, "Most effective group leaders show versatility" (p. 76). However, some people are taught only one style of leadership, regardless of the kind of group they are leading. Many model their group leadership style after the style of a group leader they had in graduate school. This may not be a good idea because the groups in graduate programs may differ greatly from those in a public school, rehabilitation, prison, or mental-health setting.

The major leadership debate seems to center on how active, directive, and structured the leader should be. Until recently, many group educators were hesitant to tell students to be active and directive. A similar situation existed in the 1960s regarding individual counseling, when educators debated the relative merits of directive and nondirective counseling. Now most educators encourage their students to be active and reasonably directive in their individual counseling.

For group counseling, our position is that an active style of leadership works best for most groups. We strongly believe what we stated earlier: *People don't mind being led when they are led well.* Most members of most groups need some structure, organization, and direction. In fact, most members expect and want the leader to lead. This is especially true in schools, hospitals, prisons, mental-health facilities, and rehabilitation centers and with issue-focused groups such as those concerning divorce, abuse, incest, or addiction.

Leader-Directed Versus Group-Directed Approaches

A related question regarding leadership style is whether it should be a leader-directed or group-directed approach. Many writers express concern regarding the leader-directed approach (Capuzzi & Gross, 2009; Posthuma, 2002). One concern is that the members will have to cater to the leader. The opposite is actually true. Effective leaders who follow the leader-directed model never demand that the members follow them as if they were gurus; rather, they lead in a manner that is valuable for the members. The leader-directed style of leadership does not mean that the leader is on an ego trip or that the group has to serve the personality of the leader. It simply means that the leader has an understanding of the members' needs and structures the group to meet those needs.

Leaders using the group-directed approach often turn the group over to the members and have the members determine the direction and content. This can be quite valuable for some groups. However, there are times when this approach wastes much time, especially for a group that is meeting only once or for only a few sessions. Often the members don't know what they need. For example, parents of teens in a drug-treatment center or victims of some kind of disaster often attend a group to find help, but they are not at all clear as to how the group can be helpful. A leader-directed style can be of great benefit by providing structure, thought-provoking questions, and group exercises.

The question is not really whether the approach is group-directed or leader-directed, but rather who is primarily responsible for the group—the leader or the members? We believe the leader is responsible for the group. As Trotzer (2006) states,

> Leaders, because of their training and professional commitment, are remiss if they do not exercise their responsibility to prevent negative consequences in the group. Leaders can share responsibility to a very large degree, but they can never abdicate their responsibility. Doing so completely undermines the nature of the helping profession and is detrimental to positive therapeutic intervention. Leaders must be willing to divert topic and conversational trends that seem to be shaping into negative and damaging content (Blaker & Samo, 1973). They must be willing to intervene to protect members and to serve as a reality check if the group does not do so. As Lakin (1969) noted, responsibility must be consciously exercised and modeled by the leader if the group is to qualify as a professional therapeutic venture (p. 218).

Even though the leader is responsible, the amount of leading will depend on the kind of group and the composition of its members. For certain groups, the leader may primarily want the members to direct the group; for other groups, the leader will want to assume much of the directing. It is important for the leader to remember that the amount of active leading can vary according to the stage of the group. In the middle stage of many kinds of groups, the members are fully aware of how the group should flow and, therefore, should be actively involved in choosing the topics and the direction.

Interpersonal Versus Intrapersonal Leadership Styles

Another way to view leadership style is as a continuum; some styles focus on the group as a whole and some styles focus on the individuals in the group. Corey (2008) states that the *interpersonal oriented* leader "emphasizes the here and now, the interactions among the members, the group as a whole, the ongoing group dynamics, and the obstacles to the development of effective interpersonal relationships within the group" (p. 82). The *intrapersonal oriented* leader focuses primarily on the needs and concerns of the individual members.

Understanding both styles of leadership is very important. Leaders must be able to adapt a style along this continuum, depending on the kind of group, the needs of the members, and the dynamics occurring within the group. You might want to think of the continuum as a 1–10 scale:

Interpersonal									*Intrapersonal*
Focus on group process							Focus on personal issues		
1	2	3	4	5	6	7	8	9	10

When the purpose of the group is to improve relationships among members or to accomplish a task, the leader will probably use an interpersonal leadership style within the 2–5 range. For growth groups, the leadership style will depend on the purpose of the group—some growth groups benefit from a 2–5 range and others benefit from a 6–8 range.

On the continuum, for most counseling and therapy groups, leaders should use a style that falls between a 6 and an 8. The intrapersonal model (6–8 on the continuum) is better because members in most of these groups have intrapersonal conflicts (conflicts within themselves) they need to deal with. In most therapy groups, the members need to address issues such as unfinished business from the past, problems with parents or lovers, sexual abuse, abandonment, low self-esteem, fear of failure, guilt, shame, or need for approval. The intrapersonal perspective seems better suited for helping clients obtain a better understanding of these issues. The intrapersonal oriented leader will address these issues directly, whereas the interpersonally oriented leader will wait until the issues emerge and then may focus on them only as they apply to the here-and-now experience within the group. For these reasons, we find the interpersonal leadership style somewhat limited.

In using a style ranging from 6 to 8 on the continuum, the leader will primarily encourage members to share with the group their personal issues, concerns, and feelings. Once a member discloses a concern, the leader would use techniques and theories to help the disclosing member. She would involve the other members in many different ways when focusing on a member or an issue. Those leaders operating at a 9 or 10 on the continuum usually do only one-on-one counseling while other members watch (Perls, 1969). Leaders using a style in the 2–4 range focus more on what is happening in the group in the present moment and less on pressing personal issues or the past. The following would be an example of this:

JOE: *(angrily)* Mary, you always contradict what I say. My parents used to always do that to me! I always felt put down by them and by teachers and other kids in the school.

LEADER: Joe, you seem angry now here in the group.

There are times when this leadership style is helpful; however, for most counseling and therapy groups a style of 6 to 8 on the continuum is best. We say this with caution because *at all times the leader must be flexible.* There will be times when the leader will need to focus on the group dynamics and interaction rather than on an individual's personal problem.

It should also be pointed out that some experts (Carroll, 1986; Rogers, 1970; Yalom, 2005) believe strongly in the interpersonal model (1–3 on the continuum) for counseling and therapy groups. Group leaders who follow this model place strong emphasis on the stages of the group and on the members being the primary agents of change.

Another important point is that, for some groups, the leadership continuum will be of little importance. For instance, leaders of education and discussion groups will primarily use various leadership skills and techniques to generate discussion and not be concerned about the group having either an interpersonal or intrapersonal focus.

Leadership Functions

Another way to view leadership style is to consider leadership functions. Yalom (2005) states that the leader may provide emotional stimulation, caring, praise, protection, acceptance, interpretations, and explanations. The leader also may serve as a model through self-disclosure and as a person who sets limits, enforces rules, and manages time. In other words, depending on the kind of group, the leader may perform many different roles and functions. In a middle-school group on transitioning to high school, the leader serves as the person with information and ideas on how to make the transition easier. In a crisis group after a suicide, the leader's function is to be very supportive, reassuring, and facilitative. In a group for going over rules in a residential setting, the leader is the authority on what is expected of the residents. In a group on information for cancer patients, the leader is the expert.

What Makes an Effective Leader?

Numerous writers have described what makes an effective counselor and group leader (Brown, 2009; Corey, Corey, & Corey, 2009; Egan, 2010). Among the characteristics discussed are caring, openness, flexibility, warmth, objectivity, trustworthiness, honesty, strength, patience, and sensitivity. Each of these characteristics is important, and we suggest you refer to the works cited or to any other beginning counseling text if you desire further clarification of ideal helper characteristics.

Additional leadership characteristics include comfort with oneself and others; a liking for people; comfort in a position of authority; confidence in one's ability to lead; and the ability to tune in to others' feelings, reactions, moods, and words. Another very important characteristic of an effective leader is sound psychological health. Leading is so demanding that personal issues are likely to surface if they have not been resolved. Corey (2008) and Yalom (2005) both strongly suggest that leaders be actively involved in their own personal growth (outside the group they are leading).

Leading groups successfully requires a great deal from the leader. Often people lead groups when they simply do not possess the necessary leadership characteristics. Aside from those already mentioned, six other traits warrant further discussion.

Experience with Individuals Effective leaders have spent considerable time talking with all kinds of people, not just those like themselves. The broader the leader's range of life experiences, the greater the chances for understanding the diverse members of a group. More and more groups have a multicultural membership for which the leader should be prepared (Day, 2007; DeLucia-Waack & Donigian, 2004).

The effective counseling or therapy group leader has not only general experience with people, but also considerable experience in one-to-one counseling. This is necessary because all types of situations arise while leading these groups, and the more experience the leader has working with individuals, the easier it will be to work with an individual and the group simultaneously. Without individual counseling experience, one would very likely find leading counseling and therapy groups very difficult.

Experience with Groups In the development of any skill, practice and experience increase one's effectiveness. Effective leaders have led many groups. Beginning leaders can learn from their mistakes with each group experience and should not be overly self-critical. When possible, it is advisable to begin by leading education, discussion, support, or task groups, restricting the number of members to four or five. Once comfortable, beginning leaders can increase the number of members or try a growth group centered on topics familiar to them. When novice leaders feel they can comfortably facilitate growth groups, they might try co-leading several counseling or therapy groups before leading one on their own.

Planning and Organizational Skills Effective leaders are good planners. They can plan a session or a series of sessions in such a way that the group is interesting, beneficial, and personally valuable. When leading discussion, education, task, or growth groups, effective leaders give considerable thought to relevant topics and to activities and exercises that pertain to those topics. Effective leaders organize sessions in such a way that the topics are covered and there is a flow from topic to topic.

Knowledge of the Topic In almost any kind of group, the leader who is well informed will naturally do a better job of leading than the one who lacks information. The leader can use information to stimulate discussion, clarify issues, and share ideas. Too often, unfortunately, leaders are asked to lead groups on topics for which they have very little knowledge or understanding.

A Good Understanding of Basic Human Conflicts and Dilemmas A group leader must be prepared to deal with a number of human problems and multicultural issues (Brown, 2009; Corey, 2008; Salazaar, 2009). This is especially true in growth, counseling, and therapy groups—issues such as guilt, fear of failure, self-worth, parents, anger, love relationships, and death often emerge in such groups. Effective leaders have an understanding of these issues and know several ways to help those who are struggling with them.

A Good Understanding of Counseling Theory   Even though we discussed this earlier, it is important enough to briefly comment again on the importance of knowing a theory. Knowledge of counseling theory is the key to understanding people and the world in which we live. Theories of therapy—such as rational emotive behavior therapy, transactional analysis, reality therapy, Adlerian, and behavioral therapy—help counselors understand why people behave the way they do in their lives and in groups. Theories offer group leaders a variety of ways to comprehend what people are saying and doing. Corey, Corey, and Corey (2009) state, "Group leaders without any theory behind their interventions will probably find that their groups never reach a productive stage" (p. 7).

Ethical Considerations

Along with all of the above, an effective leader must be aware of ethical considerations. Over the last 20 years, much has been written about ethics in counseling and ethical behavior in group work (Corey, 2008; Gladding, 2008). Most ethical problems and situations deal with therapy and growth groups, although ethical standards apply to leaders of all kinds of groups. Unethical behavior on the part of leaders usually consists of leaders not being competent to lead the groups they are leading or leaders not caring properly for their members.

Ethical Standards

All professional associations, such as the American Counseling Association, the National Association for Social Workers, and the American Psychological Association, have ethical standards regarding working with clients in groups. Aside from these organizations, there are special organizations that consist of professionals who do group work—the American Group Psychotherapy Association (AGPA) and the Association for Specialists in Group Work (ASGW). These associations have their own codes of ethics. It is very important that you become familiar with the standards of any organization with which you affiliate. We have found that many people who lead groups are unfamiliar with these organizations and therefore do not realize that any ethical standards exist. The *Best Practice Guidelines* of the Association for Specialists in Group Work can be found at www.asgw.org.

Lanning (1992) discusses ethical codes as guidelines for responsible decision making. He talks about counselors using a "systematic process of ethical reasoning" (p. 21). We agree with Lanning that many ethical situations are not so cut-and-dried as some make them out to be. In the following discussion, we try to present a realistic view of ethical behavior and situations that occur for group leaders.

Leader Preparation and Qualifications

The fundamental ethical principle for leading groups is found in ASGW's *Best Practice Guidelines* (2008): "Group counselors do not attempt any technique unless thoroughly trained in its use or under supervision by a counselor familiar with the intervention." Just as it is unethical to practice dentistry or surgery without training, it is unethical to practice any kind of counseling without proper preparation. Helpers must realize that it is unethical to lead groups, especially therapy groups, without proper preparation. ASGW spells out excellent standards for the training of group leaders in great detail. If every group counselor had this kind of preparation, there would be no question as to whether the person had been properly trained. Unfortunately, most group leaders are not prepared at this level; yet many feel qualified to lead groups because they have a degree in one of the helping professions.

We want to emphasize that an advanced college degree alone does not make one qualified to lead groups. We have talked with many therapists with master's or doctorate degrees who are leading groups but have no understanding of what it takes to lead an effective group. It is the ethical responsibility of any group leader to understand group dynamics, group process, group leadership skills, and group development. Also, the leader needs to have thorough knowledge of the subjects being discussed in the group. So often we have heard leaders at our workshops say they did not realize there was so much to leading groups. They thought you just "went in and did a group—just let the members take charge and go with the flow." This is unethical leadership!

Leaders in private practice should understand that they must have the necessary skills for conducting any group they establish. Although the same standard applies in agencies, this is not as clear as it may first seem. Confusion results because administrators in agencies, hospitals, schools, and prisons force their employees (the helpers) to violate the ethical standard of being properly prepared by mandating that the helpers conduct group counseling even though they lack the qualifications and knowledge to do so. Often, the helpers have never been trained in group work or have had only minimal training. Every day, counselors, nurses, social workers, and drug and alcohol therapists are required to conduct groups even though they are not qualified. This is unethical according to the standards of all the professions mentioned above.

If you are asked to lead groups and do not feel qualified, you should make sure you get training before you start. If you are currently leading groups without proper training, it is important that you seek training immediately. Also, if you are not properly trained, you need to be aware that you and your agency are at risk of being charged with an ethics violation. More and more clients are becoming aware that therapists have ethical standards by which they should abide; thus, an increasing number of clients are challenging the ethical behavior of professional helpers.

Knowledge

It is unethical to lead a group without having a good grasp of the material being discussed. Too often, we hear of leaders who have little or no knowledge of the subject of the group they are leading, such as groups on eating disorders, panic attacks, anger, or grief. In each of these groups, there exists the potential for members to get into some deeply emotional material: It is the leader's ethical responsibility to know how to deal with such material. The leader cannot count on the members to know how to help other members with such complex issues as these.

Another area of knowledge that is crucial is the understanding of the cultural and gender issues of the members. It is unethical for a helper to lead a group when she is not familiar with issues that may be unique to the members due to their cultural background.

Personal Growth

Leaders should not use groups for their own personal growth. We see the need and value for therapists to experience personal growth through groups, but this should not be done in the group that the person is leading. We have heard of numerous instances of leaders drawing attention to themselves and using the group for their own therapy. This is unethical.

Dual Relationships

Even though ACA no longer uses the term "dual relationships" in the Code of Ethics, we did want to address this since it has been a concern of group leaders. For group work, we define a dual relationship as a relationship that exists in addition to the therapeutic relationship established between the leader and the members. Dual relationships are not harmful in and of themselves; many dual relationships can be very beneficial to group members. We feel that dual relationships often cannot be avoided because helpers have more than one relationship with their clients. For instance, a group leader may also be the group members' residential house counselor or the staff person who takes residents to the movies, on hikes, or on bike trips, or plays on the same sports team. There are times, especially in small towns, when group leaders find themselves at the same party as members of their group. We do not feel that the leader is being unethical if he socializes with a member of his group as long as the leader is aware that potential problems could arise. *It is the leader's responsibility to make sure that the therapeutic relationship is not being jeopardized.*

Any dual relationship should be entered into with caution, and any exploitative dual relationship is unethical and should be avoided. By *exploitative*, we mean any relationship where the group leader exploits a group member in any way. The dual relationship that creates the most concern is that of a sexual or romantic nature. Other dual relationships that can be exploitative involve social or business relationships between the leader and group members. Any time a leader enters into a dual relationship, the leader must proceed with great caution to ensure that it is not harmful to the member or the group.

A different kind of dual relationship exists when the group leader sees a member for individual counseling. Some argue that group leaders should not conduct individual counseling with members of their therapy groups. We disagree with this position; in fact, we think it is unethical not to provide therapy if it would be in the best interest of the member. The purpose of group therapy is to help clients get better, and if individual therapy aids in the client's improvement, then it should be seen as a valuable tool in the therapeutic process. Many times groups are formed as a result of clients being in individual counseling with the leader and the leader deciding that a group would be beneficial. For a more detailed discussion of dual relationships as they relate to group work, see Herlihy and Corey (1997).

Confidentiality

There are two issues regarding confidentiality that any group leader should understand: the leader's ethical responsibility for keeping material confidential and the leader's lack of total control regarding members keeping matters confidential.

It is unethical for the leader to divulge information to anyone about any member of the group except in the cases of child and adolescent group members. Leaders must be very careful not to give a member's friends, family members, or business associates any information, including whether or not the person is a member of the group. There are exceptions to this rule. Breaching confidentiality is required by law when a member is threatening harm to himself or others. Also, in certain institutional settings, the leader may be required to write notes in a file that is open to other staff members. The best way to deal with such a situation is to inform the members of what is required of you by the law and the administration so that the members understand from the beginning what your requirements are regarding confidentiality. Corey (2008) states, "Generally speaking, you will find that you have a better chance of gaining the cooperation of group members if you are candid about your situation than if you hide your disclosures and thereby put yourself in the position of violating their confidences" (p. 58).

Regarding members keeping what is said confidential, it must be understood that leaders cannot guarantee complete confidentiality because they have no control over what members say once they leave the session. The best way to prevent any breach of confidentiality is to stress its importance and discuss the subject whenever it seems necessary (Corey, 2008). In cases where one member is found to repeatedly discuss group material outside of the group setting, it will be necessary to ask that member to leave the group if possible.

Informing Members About the Group

Prospective members have the right to know the purpose of the group and how it will be conducted. The *Best Practice Guidelines* (ASGW, 2008) clearly state that members should be informed of any possible risks they might encounter, such as a heightened awareness of unpleasant events from their past or the desire to make decisions that could lead to stressful consequences, such as getting a divorce. For voluntary groups, informing the potential members will give them a chance to decide if they want to join a group where such activities and explorations will occur. It is best, whenever possible, for the leader to use a screening interview to determine if a person should be a member of the group and to have an open exchange about the risks involved. For non-volunteers, explaining what is going to happen and what is minimally expected prevents any disgruntled member from saying he was never told how the group was going to be conducted or what was expected of him.

During the first session of therapy groups or any groups where emotional material is going to be discussed, leaders should discuss the various potential risks. Members should be warned about the danger of disclosing too much too soon and the tendency to feel pressure to disclose. Members should be reassured that they do not have to disclose anything that they are uncomfortable talking about. Members should also be warned about the danger of demanding that significant people in their world act like the group members who may be warm, accepting, caring, open, or attentive. In other words, it is unethical not to inform the members about how the group will affect them both during the session and in their daily lives. Any concerns about these matters should be thoroughly discussed during the early sessions.

The Ethical Use of Exercises

Leaders should keep several ethical considerations in mind when using structured activities or exercises during a group session. Most ethical problems involving exercises result from a lack of expertise or sensitivity on the part of the leader. Leaders may use exercises that generate reactions they are unable to handle because of their lack of experience and theoretical background. Any leader who goes beyond his skill level in this respect is operating unethically.

The following are examples of operating without adequate skills:

- Conducting an exercise on death, such as writing your own epitaph, and then not being able to deal with the pain and other emotions that arise
- Conducting an exercise on guilt and shame and then not being able to deal with the material that surfaces, such as incest, child abuse, or affairs
- Conducting a feedback exercise and allowing one member to be viciously attacked by the rest of the group

Additional leader behavior that is considered unethical includes the following:

- Not informing members of what they are about to experience if they participate in any group exercise. Any potential risk must be pointed out.
- Forcing a member to participate in any exercise. If, for whatever reason, a member states she does not want to take part in a given activity, the leader must allow the member this right. (It is not unethical to encourage participation.)
- Demanding continued participation. Members must be allowed to stop participation at any time. For agencies that require members be present in the room, it should be recognized that these members should not be forced to participate.

- Tricking a member into revealing something personal that the member might not want to reveal. For example, an exercise called "Secrets" involves members anonymously writing on an index card a secret that might be hard for them to tell others. These cards are then shuffled, and the leader or each member picks a card and presents the issue as if it were her own. If the leader lets members identify their secrets, by elimination, everyone can figure out a member's secret.

- Using exercises that lead to heavy emotional material without leaving adequate time for processing. In other words, it is unethical to "unzip" members and leave them hanging.

The Leader's Role in Making Referrals

It is the ethical responsibility of the group leader to make sure members are made aware of proper follow-up treatment possibilities. The leader may see members for follow-up counseling or refer members to other therapists. Follow-up is important because very often in therapy groups, members need additional individual, group, or family counseling. Too often, this ethical standard is violated in that no follow-up treatment is outlined.

Closing Comment on Ethics

We close this section by saying that, without a doubt, the most frequent unethical practice in group counseling occurs when untrained or ill-trained leaders conduct groups. We often hear from workshop participants and from our students who are observing groups in their internship sites about very poorly run groups. We hope this book is helpful in giving you the skills you need to lead groups, and we strongly suggest that you do not lead groups unless you feel you have the skills and knowledge to do so.

Potential Group Problems

So far, we have discussed basic issues that pertain to the general field of group work. Groups offer complex dynamics: you saw some in the first introductory segment of the DVD. Also, we have compiled a partial list of challenges. Some of these challenges occur in certain kinds of groups; others, in all kinds of groups. This list of problematic member behaviors and situations further illustrates the need for learning effective leadership skills. Group members might do any of the following:

- Skip from topic to topic
- Dominate the discussion
- Be "chit-chatty" rather than personal and focused
- Attend sporadically

- Be shy and withdrawn
- Get angry at the leader
- Get angry at one another
- Pressure (force) others to speak
- Preach their personal morality
- Be resistant because forced to attend
- Dislike other members
- Stop attending the group

As you can see, leaders must be able to deal with all kinds of members and situations. In the remainder of this book, we teach ways of approaching not only these situations, but many more.

Concluding Comments

Counselors, psychologists, social workers, ministers, teachers and others who work with people should learn to lead groups. The advantages of group work include efficiency, viewpoint variety, belonging, feedback, vicarious learning, and practicing in a setting that is close to real life. There are seven kinds of groups: education, discussion, task, support, growth, counseling/therapy, and self-help. It is important for leaders to identify what kind of group they are leading so that the purpose is clear. There are many approaches to leading groups but no actual group theories. Understanding leadership style is very important. It is essential to understand the difference between an interpersonal and intrapersonal group leadership style. A leader should be flexible because different kinds of groups have different purposes and require leaders to adjust their style accordingly. Our approach to group counseling is very much in line with the impact therapy approach to counseling, which is an active, multisensory, theory-driven approach. We included a portrait of the effective leader and concluded with ethical considerations and a list of difficult situations that typically arise in groups. Throughout the book, many of the topics covered in this chapter will be elaborated on, so if you are feeling overwhelmed by the material, relax and enjoy the rest of the book. By the end, you will have a good understanding of kinds of groups, leadership styles, and group leadership skills and techniques.

■ ACTIVITIES

1. Think of a setting in which you plan to work. List the different kinds of groups you might lead in that setting.
2. Within the different kinds of groups generated from Activity 1, list names of groups that would fall under each kind, such as an anger-management group, which could be education or therapy or both. A group for

children of divorce could be supportive or counseling. Compare your list with those of fellow students. You'll find that the lists can be almost endless.

3.   On pages 26-27 there are six skills listed. On a 1–10 scale, rate yourself on these skills (10 being excellent at the skill). If you are not an 8, 9, or 10, what is your plan for improving on the given skill? (You may want to skip the skill of knowledge of the topic because that will depend on the topic.)

GROUP COUNSELING SKILLS

1.   Review video segments 1.1 and 1.2.
    a.   List the mistakes that the "bad" leader made.
    b.   What skills did the second leader use to make the group go much better?
    c.   What differences did you notice between the groups? How were the body language and energy of the group different?
2.   Although the DVD was created for you to view as you read through the chapters, you may want to watch the entire DVD now, and then view again different segments as they are mentioned in subsequent chapters.

Chapter 2

Stages of Groups, Group Process, and Therapeutic Forces

The literature on group counseling frequently addresses three aspects: stages of group, group dynamics or group process, and therapeutic forces. In this text, the terms *group process* and *group dynamics* refer to the attitudes and interaction of group members and leaders. Writers sometimes define these terms differently, but all agree that they are similar. We agree with Posthuma (2002) who states, "Because of this concurrent, intimate, and ongoing relationship between the two, the two terms can be used interchangeably to mean the same thing" (p. 7). *Therapeutic forces* are the factors that influence the group dynamics. In this chapter, we discuss the importance of understanding each of these aspects of group counseling and how they are interrelated.

Stages of Groups

Much has been written regarding the stages of groups, the characteristics of each stage, and how much time each stage takes (Corey, 2008; Gladding, 2008; Yalom, 2005). However, some of the literature can become confusing when the more detailed description of stages is applied to certain groups, such as discussion, education, or task groups. Our description of stages applies to any kind of group.

All groups go through three stages, regardless of the type of group or style of leadership: the *beginning* stage; the *middle*, or *working*, stage; and the *ending*, or *closing*, stage. Whether a group meets for one session or fifteen sessions, it will go through these stages; it is important that the leader attend to each.

The Beginning Stage

The *beginning* stage refers to the time period used for introductions and for discussion of such topics as the purpose of the group, what to expect, fears, group rules, comfort levels, and the content of the group. In this stage, members are checking out other members and their own level of comfort with sharing in the group. For some groups, such as certain task, education, and discussion groups whose topics or agendas have not been predetermined, this is the period when the members determine the focus of the group.

The beginning stage may last part of the first session, the entire first session, or the first couple of sessions. It is not uncommon for the members of certain groups to take more than two sessions to feel enough trust and comfort to share beyond the surface level. For instance, it may take groups in a prison or residential treatment center for teenagers as many as three sessions to develop an atmosphere that lends itself to productive group work. For groups in a residential setting, "agendas" between members must sometimes be resolved before the group can proceed to the working stage. School counselors leading groups in educational settings may find that the beginning stage moves more quickly because students know each other. For groups with a culturally diverse membership, the beginning stage may need to last a couple of sessions or even longer because members may initially be very uncomfortable and awkward when sharing in front of others.

For some groups, the beginning stage lasts only a few minutes because the purpose is clear and the trust and comfort levels are already high. For example, members who meet to share feelings about a recent suicide, death, or disaster can move through the beginning stage in just a few minutes if the leader structures the group so members can share their feelings. Additionally, school counselors leading groups in an educational setting may find that because of the students' comfort levels with the school counselor, the beginning stage can move more quickly. Oftentimes, leaders spend far too long on this stage, conducting icebreakers and talking about group rules and the purpose of the group. A leader who provides very little structure tends to create a group that stays in the beginning stage for several sessions, creating dynamics that could be avoided. On the other hand, we have seen leaders move too quickly into the working stage, causing members to feel uncomfortable and even become angry.

 GROUP COUNSELING SKILLS

If you watched the two DVD introductory segments, you saw a bad and then a good opening of the beginning stage. You may want to view segments 1.1 and 1.2 again.

The Working Stage

The *middle*, or *working*, stage is the stage of the group when the members focus on the purpose. In this stage, the members learn new material, thoroughly discuss various topics, complete tasks, or engage in personal sharing and therapeutic work. This stage is the core of the group process; it is the time when members benefit from being in a group.

During this stage, many different dynamics can occur, because the members are interacting in several different ways. The leader must pay particular attention to the interaction patterns and attitudes of the members toward each other and the leader. This is the time when members decide how much they want to get involved or share. If multicultural issues exist in the group, the leader needs to pay close attention to group dynamics because the members may be acting and reacting in very different ways, which can be misunderstood by others in the group.

The Closing Stage

The *closing*, or *ending*, stage is devoted to terminating the group. During this period, members share what they have learned, how they have changed, and how they plan to use what they have learned. Members also say goodbye and deal with the ending of the group. For some groups, the ending will be an emotional experience, whereas for others the closing will simply mean that the group has done what it was supposed to do. The length of the closing stage will depend on the type of group, the length of time it has been meeting, and its development. Most groups need only one session for this stage.

Other Models of Sequential Stages of Group Development

In the literature, a number of writers have conceptualized the stages of group in different ways. As outlined earlier, our model is a three-stage model: beginning, working, and closing. Corey (2008) offers a six-stage model: formation, orientation, transition, working, consolidation, and follow-up. Corey's first and last stages have to do with leadership functions such as preplanning, screening, and giving follow-up questionnaires to monitor members' development within the group. We agree with Corey that in many groups, there is a transition stage. According to Corey, the transition stage is the period when the beginning stage is over, but members are not yet ready to share on a highly personal level. Members contribute and interact, but they are still checking things out. Many counseling, therapy, support, and growth groups go through a transition stage. It is important for a leader to recognize that the group is going through a transition stage and refrain from pushing the group ahead too quickly, thereby causing discomfort. An example of the transition stage would be any group in the second or third session where the members are still feeling out the other members. During the transition stage, members talk and share but nothing goes very deep or personal. We call the sharing done during the transition stage "safe sharing."

The transition stage is important in most counseling and therapy groups. A good example of the leader not recognizing the need for the transition stage is bringing up the topic of sex in the second or third session, when the members are still getting comfortable being in a group and sharing personal matters. This topic would be much better received once the members are in the working stage.

Johnson and Johnson (2009) suggest a seven-stage model that explains members' development within a group:

1. Defining and structuring procedures
2. Conforming to procedures
3. Recognizing mutuality and building trust
4. Rebelling and differentiating
5. Committing to and taking ownership for the goals, procedures, and other members
6. Functioning maturely and productively
7. Terminating

The Johnson and Johnson model is an expansion of probably the most well-known sequential stage theory, which is put forth by Tuckman (Tuckman, 1965; Tuckman & Jensen, 1977). Tuckman reviewed studies of group development and found that there were five stages: forming, storming, norming, performing, and adjourning. It is important to point out that almost all the studies reviewed by Tuckman were studies where the leader was mainly using an interpersonal, passive leadership model (Johnson & Johnson, 2009). We agree that in groups where leaders offer little structure, groups most likely will go through these stages, but we want to emphasize that most groups should have enough structure to eliminate the need for going through a storming stage.

The *forming* and *norming* stages that Tuckman describes fall within what we are calling the beginning stage—the period where members get comfortable with being in a group and figure out what is expected and what is going to happen. Cohesion and commitment increase during the norming stage (Johnson & Johnson, 2009). The *storming* stage (which is also in our beginning stage and in Corey's transition stage) occurs in groups where there is tension due to the makeup of the group, the commitment of the members, the purpose of the group, and/or the approach of the leader (Gladding, 2008). Many education, discussion, growth, and counseling groups do not have this kind of tension, so there is no need for a storming stage. Leaders who provide too little structure often see their groups go through a storming stage because the members are frustrated due to lack of leadership on the part of the leader. In our view, the more skilled the leader, the less likely there will be a storming stage, because the leader will do what is necessary to reduce the tension in the group. However, in groups where members are forced to come or in groups where the goal may be team building or learning to get along, the storming stage will most definitely be present. Sometimes leaders want the members to learn to work together, such as in certain task groups and some residential groups, so they more or less precipitate a storming stage by not providing much direction during the early stage of the group.

Corey (2008) and Gladding (2008) describe in detail some of the dynamics that occur during the storming stage. One sign of the storming stage is a lot of conflict between members. Testing the leader is often a characteristic of the storming stage. Resistance is another sign that the group is going through a storming stage. The key for leaders is to recognize what is happening. Leaders who use an active, creative approach to groups usually do not create a storming stage. Skilled leaders curtail many of these occurrences by making sure the members clearly understand the purpose of the group, and by making the group valuable, relevant, interesting, and meaningful.

In certain kinds of groups, particularly task groups, there are times when storming is a desired or necessary stage, especially when there are powerful personalities and some disagreement as to how things should be done. Great skill is required to guide the unpredictable interactions among members through the storming period, bringing members to a point where they can work together.

Group Process

Group process refers to the interaction and energy exchange between members and leaders, how the leader reacts to the members, and how the members talk to one another and the leader. Sociologists, social psychologists, therapists, and researchers have studied group process. If you are interested in a discussion of the sociological view of group dynamics and a brief history of the study of group dynamics, see Johnson and Johnson (2009).

Dynamics of Interaction Patterns

One of the most important group dynamics to observe is who talks to whom and how often each member speaks. It is not unusual in the beginning stage of a group for a couple of members to try to dominate. If this occurs, the leader should alter the pattern by using cutting-off and drawing-out skills. Sometimes members fall into the habit of talking only to the leader or selected members instead of to the entire group. The leader will usually want to change this dynamic and get members to address the entire group, because talking only to the leader or a few other members will not lead to group cohesion.

Silent members may or may not create negative group dynamics. In most groups, participation of all members is desirable. When a member is almost totally silent, some of the others usually become uncomfortable, especially if this pattern continues for several weeks and the group is a counseling, therapy, or support group. In certain education, discussion, and task groups, the silent member may not produce a negative dynamic because in these groups the members are not usually as sensitive to the silence.

Another pattern for which the leader should watch is that of one member speaking, followed by the leader, then a second member, then the leader, then a third member, then the leader—rather than member-to-member interaction. The leader should avoid establishing a pattern of responding after each member's comment. Group dynamics may also be affected by members' expectations. If members have been in other groups, it is always a good idea to get some sense of how their groups were conducted because they may expect the current group to be the same as their previous one. Also, the leader should be aware at all times of any cultural or gender issues that may be affecting group dynamics.

■ E X A M P L E

In this example the leader makes the mistake of responding to each member's comment. A more skilled leader would have let more members comment before commenting herself.

SAM: I like my mother, but I don't feel close to her.

LEADER: I hope that gets better for you.

BILL: My mom and I fight all the time. I can't talk to her about anything.

LEADER: So it is hard for you to talk to her.

NAN: I feel that my mom favors my brother but she won't admit it. We have a terrible relationship.

LEADER: So you feel hurt by your mom's favoritism.

■ ■ ■

Other patterns that the leader wants to look for include the following:

- Members "ganging up" on other members
- Members arguing with each other
- Members discounting each other's suggestions
- Members presenting problems and others trying to rescue them
- Members presenting a problem and the rest of the group giving advice (It is important for the leader to realize that groups are not advice-giving sessions.)

■ E X A M P L E

The following example demonstrates how allowing members to give advice from their own frame of reference is often not helpful. Sometimes advice and suggestions are beneficial, but often leaders mistakenly let the group turn into an advice-giving session. In this example, the leader should intervene and redirect the discussion.

LARRY: … so I don't know whether to call her or not.

STEVE: I don't think you should call her for at least a week.

NANCY: I don't know. I think you could wait a week and then send her a nice card.

SANDY: Why not a funny card?

CRAIG: I personally think you should let her make the next move. Let me tell you what happened to me.…

■ ■ ■

Group Dynamics of Different Kinds of Groups

Any discussion of group dynamics has to take into consideration the kind of group and the leadership style. If the leader does not play an active role, someone in the group will usually try to take the leadership role. Even with an active leader, there can be a bid for control by one or more members. Members may challenge the leader's authority or competency. Throughout the book, we discuss skills for handling these dynamics if they arise. In this section, we discuss dynamics unique to the seven kinds of groups described in Chapter 1.

Education Groups

In an education group, the leader is usually presenting some information. Although the members will probably interact with each other, this is not the most important dynamic. Often, those attending education groups are eager to learn the material being presented. In some education groups, however, the members are not interested in the topic because they have been forced to attend, such as those attending a DUI (driving under the influence) group. In these groups, if the leader does not plan well or is not energetic, the group will, more than likely, not go well.

The dynamics for an education group become difficult when members are at different levels of understanding regarding the subject matter or when some are much more comfortable with the topic than others. The leader of a sex education group must be aware that some members will be more open and comfortable than others. In a group with a diverse population, multicultural issues may create some powerful group dynamics. It is important for the leader to observe how the members are relating to the material and devote extra time if necessary to process any cultural issues.

Education groups usually will not go through long beginning or closing stages. The leader does, however, have to plan for these stages. Although this may seem obvious, we have observed beginning leaders who pay no attention to group process in their planning. The middle stage of an education group includes delivery of the content and discussion of the material. As members get to know each other, they usually become more comfortable and willing to share their reactions, questions, and feelings. The closing stage of an education group usually includes a summary of the material covered and sometimes questions about and reactions to the information.

Discussion Groups

Discussion group leaders primarily need to be aware of any member who tries to dominate or distract the group. Leaders also should pay attention to how comfortable members are in sharing, because if many are not comfortable, only a few members will contribute and a good discussion will not occur. Discussion groups are often led in conjunction with a workshop or class and are, therefore, one-time experiences that last anywhere from 15 minutes to an hour. The tone set at the beginning of a discussion group is usually crucial—the leader should try to set a positive, interactive tone. If possible, the leader should try to get everyone to share something in the first few minutes. This gets members involved and gives the leader an idea of each member's energy for the topic. The closing usually consists of a summary of what was said.

Task Groups

In a task group, the ways in which members interact may be the most important dynamic to monitor. This is especially true if the leader's task is one of team building. Often, task groups accomplish little because the members cannot get along well enough to work together. If this is the case, the leader must do some conflict resolution work or team building before getting to the task of the group. The leader must also be aware of the formation of cliques and plays for power and control.

The beginning stage of task groups is usually brief—the task is clarified and the members move to the working stage. Ideally, most of the group's time is spent in the middle stage—working on the task. When a task group experiences power plays or tension between members, or the members disagree with the stated task, the leader must be skillful in getting the members through the storming stage. The leader may need to use cutting off, structured activities, and maybe sit in on some pairs of members who are in conflict to help ease the tension. The closing stage of a task group can be very brief, sometimes coinciding with accomplishment of the task. However, some task groups require a longer closing stage.

Growth and Experiential Groups

Growth and experiential groups vary greatly. In groups whose purpose is values clarification or self-exploration, the most important dynamic is how the members feel about one another, because they will be sharing their thoughts and feelings. Also, members might become jealous of other members' growth or become angry with the leader and blame her for what they are learning about themselves.

In some growth and experiential groups, individual members' needs and expectations can vary so widely that negative forces are created. If this occurs, the leader should focus on issues and concerns that are relevant to the majority of the members. The leader should also look for members who are not appropriate for the group—members who would be better served in some other group experience or individual counseling.

Struggles for leadership can occur in some experiential groups where the purpose is team building and cooperative interaction. Also, members may form cliques that create antitherapeutic forces. Competition among members may arise and can be a detrimental dynamic. If these dynamics occur, the leader may want to talk to members privately or bring it up in the group. The proper method of dealing with this depends on the dynamics, the intensity, and the purpose of the group. When conducting group exercises, members will sometimes angrily turn on other members or on the leader as a result of frustration with the activity.

The beginning stage of a growth or experiential group usually lasts only one or two sessions, because the leader will probably engage the members in some activities during one or both of these sessions. Most members will get more comfortable as the group progresses, and the working stage will be reached fairly quickly. The closing stage usually lasts no more than one session and consists of people sharing what they have learned about themselves and how they have grown.

Support Groups

In a support group, the leader should create a safe environment where members can share. The leader should also make sure that members feel they have opportunities to share their ideas and concerns with the group and that one member does not dominate. Trust, commitment, and genuine caring of members for one another are important dynamics for this kind of group. When members do not trust one another or there are members who are at odds with each other, the support group is not effective. If these dynamics occur, they must be worked through for the group to succeed, either in private or in front of the group, depending on the nature of the problem. The leader may even need to screen out some members if they are detracting from the supportive purpose of the group.

One other dynamic that is important to watch for is lack of commonality. For instance, a leader might form a group to help students who recently moved to the area and are new to the school. Most of the members probably welcome the support, but a member who is new to the school because she could not get along in her other school and was forced to come to the new school would probably not be a good member of such a support group. A member who is new to the school because he is just returning from a 1-year drug treatment facility may not be good for a support group—his needs may be too great, and individual counseling plus a counseling group or a group for recovering students might be best. For a support group to work, members must feel a common bond.

The beginning stage of a support group usually lasts one to three sessions. During this stage, the sharing is usually not as personal as in the middle stage, when sharing is more intimate and caring is greater because the members now know each other. The closing of a support group can be an emotional experience for its members. Some may even feel frightened by the loss of the group as a support system. Because of this, the leader must allow plenty of time for terminating the group—maybe as much as two entire sessions.

Counseling and Therapy Groups

In counseling and therapy groups, the leader must be keenly aware of how members feel about each other and the leader. Members may resent others for being too quiet, too open, or too "together." Because members of these groups vary in their degree of mental health, the chances for complex dynamics are much higher than in any other group discussed. To prevent the occurrence of some of the complex dynamics, we advocate screening through individual interviews of potential members whenever possible.

Some leaders mistakenly ignore the dynamics and lead the group as if everyone were comfortable with everyone else. This often results in members being not willing to share personally due to their lack of trust in other members, the leader, or both. Also, one negative or hostile member can create impossible dynamics unless the leader does something to neutralize the effect of this member. The leader can do this privately, which is usually best, or in the group if she sees value in this kind of intervention.

Much skill, knowledge, and courage are needed to lead an effective counseling or therapy group. Because members are dealing with personal issues, attacks on the leader are not uncommon. Unfortunately, sometimes the attacks are justified because the leader does not have the knowledge or skills necessary to lead the group but is doing so because it is part of the job. As we say throughout the book, *leaders should not lead groups they are not trained to lead*.

The beginning stage of a counseling or therapy group can last one, two, or three sessions. Although some therapeutic discussion or work will probably be done during these sessions, the members usually will still be warming up to the idea of sharing their problems with others. Depending on the members, the counseling/therapy group may go through a transition stage, in which members are sharing but are still not going into serious personal issues. The leader needs to be aware of these dynamics so that he does not push too much for sharing that is beyond the comfort level of the members; at the same time, the leader will want to make sure the group is productive.

During the working stage, the leader needs to be aware that some members may become uncomfortable because watching others work on personal issues gets them in touch with the pain they are trying to avoid. The leader will want to try to make the group safe but also not so comfortable that members bring up only superficial concerns. Members may also have the tendency to draw attention to other members' issues in order to avoid focusing on themselves.

The closing stage usually lasts one session, although there may be occasions when the leader sees a need to allow more time. The leader should pay careful attention to members' feelings about ending the group, especially if being in the group has been a very emotional, supportive experience for some members.

Self-Help Groups

Many different dynamics can occur in self-help groups, and without a leader to resolve these dynamics, some groups will not be productive and can even be harmful. We strongly believe in the self-help group and feel that generally these groups are very helpful and supportive. However, we recognize that usually few restrictions exist in these groups and that all kinds of dynamics can arise among the members as a result. If you are involved in setting up self-help groups, you should be aware of several dynamics. Members may attack each other or may try to take over the group. Cliques often form, causing other members to feel excluded. Members may need individual therapy in addition to or instead of a self-help group.

Once self-help groups have formed, they usually are ongoing, with new members coming and others leaving constantly. There is usually no trained leader designated in self-help groups. If you are in charge of establishing a self-help group, you may want to attend the first couple of meetings to ensure that the members get off to a good start. We suggest that you then drop in periodically to see if the group is being productive. Sometimes the groups have strayed far from their intended purpose and need to be redirected. Certain self-help groups, such as AA, have a good deal of structure that has evolved over the years.

Therapeutic Forces

It is important for leaders to realize that they must attend to much more than just the verbal exchange among members. Hansen, Warner, and Smith (1980) describe the "group dynamicist" as a person who closely observes the "potent group currents" that influence the members. Some of these currents are lack of trust, lack of commitment, power plays, conflicts between members, strong alliances between members, and attention-seeking behaviors. Awareness of these forces is essential for good leading. Ohlsen, Horne, and Lawe (1988) describe a number of the forces present in almost any group situation. Members want to (1) feel accepted by the group, (2) know what is expected, (3) feel they belong, and (4) feel safe. When these forces are absent, members tend to be negative, hostile, withdrawn, or apathetic. Negative forces create dynamics that require the leader's attention.

The leader can tune in to some of the group dynamics and therapeutic forces by considering the following questions:

How does each member feel about being in the group?

Do the members seem to know what is expected in the group?

Is each member clear about why he or she is in the group?

How does each member deal with being in the group?

Do the members seem to like one another?

Do the members seem comfortable with one another?

Do the members have a sense of belonging to the group?

Do the members seem comfortable with the leader?

The answers to these questions can be very helpful to the group leader in understanding how members are feeling about the group and the leader.

Yalom's Curative Factors

Probably the best-known list of therapeutic forces is set forth by Yalom (2005). He discusses therapeutic forces in terms of *curative factors* operating in groups. Yalom studied counseling and therapy groups based on his interpersonal style of leadership and came up with 11 therapeutic factors that he felt needed to be present for a group to be successful:

1. Instillation of hope (feeling hopeful about one's life)
2. Universality (realizing others have similar concerns)
3. Imparting of information (gaining information about healthy living)
4. Altruism (giving to other members)
5. Corrective recapitulation of the primary family group (opportunity to experience dynamics similar to early childhood experiences)
6. Development of socialization techniques (learning social skills)
7. Imitative behavior (modeling positive behaviors from other members)
8. Interpersonal learning (learning to interact with others)
9. Group cohesiveness (closeness among members)
10. Catharsis (expressing feelings never expressed before)
11. Existential factors (accepting responsibility for one's life)

Of these factors, we agree that most are essential for a therapy group to be productive. The one that may not always occur is the re-creation of early family dynamics. In our more intrapersonal style of leadership this sometimes occurs, but often it does not. Members do, however, work on personal issues pertaining to their childhood. Yalom's groups were more here-and-now groups, so the re-creation of family dynamics often did occur in his groups.

Jacobs, Masson, Harvill & Schimmel's 15 Therapeutic Forces

Following are descriptions of 15 forces that we feel the leader should attend to. These forces can be either positive (therapeutic), neutral, or negative (antitherapeutic).

Groups that are not successful have one or more antitherapeutic forces operating. As a way to understand this, think of any group you have ever led or been a member of; then go through the 15 therapeutic forces, considering if the force was positive, neutral, or negative for that group. You will find that, if the group was successful, most of the forces were positive or neutral. If the group was not successful, one or more of the forces were negative. Sometimes a single antitherapeutic force can destroy a group. The 15 forces are as follows:

1. Clarity of purpose for both the leader and the members
2. Relevance of purpose for the members
3. Size of the group
4. Length of each session
5. Frequency of meetings
6. Adequacy of the setting
7. Time of day for both the leader and the members
8. The leader's attitude
9. Closed or open group
10. Voluntary or nonvoluntary membership
11. Members' level of commitment
12. Level of trust among members
13. Members' attitudes toward the leader
14. The leader's experience and readiness to deal with groups
15. Coleadership harmony

Clarity of Purpose

The single most important therapeutic force is clarity of purpose; that is, the leader and the members must clearly understand the purpose of the group. In unsuccessful groups, the leader often is unclear as to the purpose and, thus, confuses the members. For instance, a leader might say the group is educational but spend most of the time doing therapy, or the leader might say the group is for support but spend the majority of the time focusing on one person or on one topic that is not relevant for most of the members. Unfortunately, groups where members are unsure of the purpose are an all too common occurrence. It is important that both the leader and members clearly understand the purpose of the group. Much of Chapter 3 deals with clarity of purpose.

Relevance of Purpose

Not only should the members and leaders be clear regarding the purpose, but the purpose must be relevant for the members. For members in prison, talking about their future jobs would not be relevant if the members had another

5 years on their prison sentence—a more relevant topic would be getting the most out of prison or getting along with others in prison. For those on the verge of dropping out of school, it would not be relevant to discuss how to study for math and history tests. A better topic would be attitude about school and their plans should they drop out of school. Some leaders have to use prepared materials and there are times when these materials are not relevant for the members.

Group Size

Group size can definitely affect group dynamics, so the leader should pay close attention to the decision of how many members to have in the group. The size of the group will depend in part on its purpose, the length of time of each session, the setting available, and the experience of the leader. We suggest 5 to 8 as the ideal number of members for most groups. For multicultural groups, the leader and members may be more comfortable with groups of no more than 5.

If the group is going to meet for 1 hour or less, the leader should keep the group relatively small (no more than 6), unless it is an education group. Education groups usually have from 5 to 15 members; discussion groups usually have from 5 to 8. Ideally, personal growth, support, and counseling/therapy groups have from 5 to 8 members, although there can be as few as 3 and as many as 12.

The size of the group can definitely be antitherapeutic. If the group is too large, members very often hesitate to share or do not have time to share. Leaders form large groups out of necessity without realizing that an antitherapeutic force is being created. Groups that are too small can cause members to feel too much pressure to participate, creating an equally negative force. On the other hand, some small groups (2 or 3 members) with a specific focus, such as on members who attempted suicide or members who had been raped, can sometimes be quite valuable.

Length of Each Session

For members to feel invested in the group and in one another, enough time must be allotted for each session. If a group session is not long enough, members may feel they did not get their chance to share. Another problem that arises when insufficient time is allowed is that the group never really accomplishes much and the sharing never gets very personal. For education, discussion, and task groups, the usual session lasts from 1 to 2 hours; it can be longer in certain instances. Groups in schools usually last a class period, which is 40 to 50 minutes. For groups composed of children, the length of time may be much shorter; 30 to 45 minutes is usually a good duration for younger children. For therapy, support, and growth groups, at least 1½ hours—and usually not longer than 3 hours—is advisable. However, there may be times when the leader and members decide to meet for a more extended period—5 or 6 hours or for as long as an entire weekend.

Frequency of Meetings

The number of meetings per month depends on many different factors, the most important being the purpose of the group and the composition of the members. Groups in residential settings often meet daily or two to three times a week. Most outpatient groups meet once a week or once every 2 weeks. Support groups usually meet once or twice a month. The key to the frequency of meetings is that they not be so frequent that they become boring and not so infrequent that each meeting is like a first session. A leader should pay attention to the effect of the interval between sessions and, if at all possible, adjust the frequency so that it is a positive rather than negative force.

Adequacy of the Setting

There are a number of things to consider regarding where the group meets. One is convenience. Members will tend to come regularly if the location is easily accessible. Of course, the choice of location is not always within the leader's control; but when it is, the leader should consider the convenience factor.

Another consideration is the privacy of the meeting room. Ideally, the group will meet in a room that is closed to any other traffic during the meeting time. Sometimes, especially in schools and some institutions, this is not possible. When faced with an inadequate setting, the leader must do as much as possible to ensure privacy, recognizing that an antitherapeutic force is operating.

The leader should also continue impressing upon the administration the importance of having a private room for group work. We say this because, unfortunately, the setting for groups is often very poor—be prepared to deal with terrible spaces for conducting groups.

Other things the leader needs to consider about the setting are whether the room is comfortable, what the wall decorations are like, what the lighting is like, and whether the seating arrangements and chairs are comfortable. Any of these can affect the therapeutic forces. The relative size of the chairs must also be considered. It is best when they are approximately the same size, especially in a counseling/therapy group, because members sitting at various heights may create a negative group dynamic. An option in such a case is to have everyone sit on the floor. The leader would want to do this only if there is a comfortable carpet to sit on and the members agree. More than likely, a leader would not use the floor for education, discussion, or task groups. In most group situations, it is best that the chairs not be lounge chairs because members tend to simply relax and not get involved in the process. Another consideration is whether or not to use tables. In most cases, it is better not to, because tables tend to serve as barriers between members. But there will be times when the leader may want to have tables, particularly in certain education and task groups.

Once these details are taken care of, the leader still has some other factors to consider. Usually the best seating arrangement is a circle, so that all members can see one another. The leader will want to make sure that all members can see and are not blocked so that no one feels excluded. A tighter circle often creates a more intimate feeling, and members may tend to share more.

Time of Day

The time the group meets can be a negative force. If the group meets right after lunch or late in the day, the leader and the members may be tired. When setting up a group, the leader should choose a time that seems best for the majority of those involved. This may seem like a simple matter, but often leaders find themselves leading a group where the members have little energy because of the meeting time.

The Leader's Attitude

The leader's feelings about leading a group definitely affect how the group will go. During workshops on group leadership, it is common to hear group leaders express their inability to control negative members, which results in their disliking the group. If the group contains hostile, nonvoluntary members, the leader should try to find a way to get these members involved; however, if the members are completely resistant and negative, the leader may need to remove them from the group. Otherwise, the leader will end up battling or possibly arguing with them each session.

Another possible reason for the leader having a negative attitude is that the leader is being required to lead a group with people he does not like or on a topic in which he has little or no interest. If the leader cannot avoid leading the group and cannot change his feelings about the members or topic, he may try adding a coleader. If that is not possible, the leader should spend extra time planning the sessions in the hope that the exercises and activities will help make the group more interesting for both the members and leader. If the leader does not do this, the group surely will go poorly. If you ever find yourself in this situation, remember that trying to make it interesting is certainly to your advantage.

Closed or Open Groups

An important decision for the leader is whether the membership will be *open* or *closed*. Many groups are conducted as closed groups—that is, no new members are admitted once the group is established. Closed groups can be time limited and goal oriented. Groups are also conducted on an open basis—members join and leave periodically. The purpose of the group and the population being served usually dictate the leader's choice. In most cases, especially for support and counseling/therapy groups, a closed group is better because the members develop trust and comfort as the group evolves. The only time a closed group becomes a detriment is when the group is getting stale and additional members would add new life.

In some settings, such as hospitals or residential treatment centers where there are new arrivals weekly, groups with an open membership are mandated. This does not have to constitute a negative force if the leader's style is adjusted for this dynamic. The leader must keep in mind that the group will not evolve through various stages because members will always be at different places in their feelings about the group. When introducing new members, the leader will want to develop methods that do not detract from the flow of the group. Often leaders will spend too much time introducing and orienting new members, thus creating a negative force.

Voluntary or Nonvoluntary Membership

Perhaps the most basic force to consider is whether the members are voluntary or nonvoluntary. Naturally, it would be nice if all groups could be held on a voluntary basis. However, the courts and settings such as correctional institutions, residential treatment centers, and schools often mandate group participation. When a leader must conduct a group where there are nonvolunteers, it is important to adapt to this dynamic. Both Yalom (2005) and Corey (2008) state that negative attitudes about being in a group can be transformed by the leader's ability to prepare members for the group. Corey further states that the leader also has to *believe* in the group process. Often some nonvoluntary members change their negative attitude if the first couple of sessions go well. To make the first sessions successful, the leader must plan the group on the assumption that there will be negative attitudes. The following are three examples of what a leader might say to nonvoluntary members during the first session.

■ EXAMPLES

LEADER: I realize many of you do not want to be here and probably are thinking this is going to be a big waste of time. All I can say is that I hope you will at least give it a chance. I think I have some things planned that should be of interest to all of you.

■ ■ ■

LEADER: Because you did not volunteer for this group, I imagine you may have some strong negative feelings about being here. You will have a chance to air those feelings in a few minutes, but first I want to tell you a little about what we will be doing in the hope that you will see that the group can be interesting and may be helpful to you.

■ ■ ■

LEADER: Every time I lead one of these groups, there are members who fight being here at the beginning, but by the end they thank me for providing a place for them to share their thoughts and feelings. I know that some of you right now are angry about being forced to be in this group. All I can say is that these groups have helped some people, and they can help you if you let them. If you will give the group a chance for a couple of weeks, I will do all I can to make it a good experience.

■ ■ ■

There will be times when, no matter what the leader does, some members remain negative and antitherapeutic. When faced with this situation, the leader should accept that the group will not go as well as desired. It is sometimes a good idea, when possible, to divide the group and let those who are totally negative sit out of the circle of the group and do something else, such as read, rest, or sit quietly. Another strategy is to meet with the entire group for less time and then excuse the negative members and have those who are really interested remain. If you have nonvoluntary members, remember to plan for the negative group dynamics at the beginning of and perhaps throughout the sessions. Planning interesting and creative sessions is essential!

Members' Level of Commitment

One of the forces to consider when thinking about the group is the members' level of commitment. By commitment, we mean desiring to be cooperative rather than resistant, disruptive, or hostile. A group made up of members with commitment will be much easier to lead than one with members who have little or no commitment. Members lacking commitment are those who are forced to attend, as well as those who want to direct the group or be the center of attention. When commitment is low, members tend to get off track, show little interest, contribute very little, display disruptive behavior, argue with the leader, or attack each other. In other words, all kinds of negative group dynamics occur when there is little commitment.

How do you know if there is commitment? One way to access commitment is to conduct pre-group interviews to gage where the members are in reference to being a member. If screening is not possible, the best way to assess this is simply to observe your members. You can nearly always tell how they feel about being in the group. If you are not sure, bring the topic up for discussion. Simply ask, "What is your feeling about being in the group?"

Level of Trust

In groups whose members have commitment, trust will usually develop over time if the group is moving in a positive direction. Problems of trust often occur when members have very different points of view. If the group consists of members who do not like each other, the leader can try to change this by bringing it up in the group or by meeting with some members privately to see if their differences can be resolved. The leader may even ask one or more members to drop out of the group. If the lack of trust does not change and, because of administrative policy, the members cannot be asked to leave the group, the leader will have to accept the fact that leading the group will be very difficult.

In almost any group, the trust level increases or decreases as the group progresses, and it is important for the leader to pay attention to the evolving trust level. This increase or decrease usually depends on the ways members are reacting to one another. Obviously, if members are being hostile or are saying things that insult other members, the trust level will be low. In counseling/therapy and growth groups, there is always the chance that some members will make some hurtful and judgmental comments to another member after some disclosure of an intimate detail of her life such as an affair, abortion, or sexual orientation. The leader's first concern needs to be for the disclosing member and to show that members will not be attacked for sharing comments or details of their lives. The leader needs to discuss these critical comments in such a way as to be supportive of the member under attack and, at the same time, not alienate the critical member or members.

■ EXAMPLE

JODI: *(With her head down and in a sad voice)* I don't know how this happened. I didn't think this happened to people in their 50s. I thought only young people had affairs. Karl and I have nothing in common, and now with the kids being off at college, I am lonely. This guy at the place I work started eating lunch with me; and over the last six months, we have shared a lot. One thing led to another; and last week, we spent the afternoon at his place. Now, I feel so guilty and confused.

BUD: Jodi, I can't believe you would do that to your husband! You should have controlled yourself and not been so selfish. What about Karl?! I think …

LEADER: *(Using a firm but soft voice)* Bud, I want to stay with Jodi and help her with her pain. I want us to try to help her deal with her feelings and not be judgmental about her behavior. That is not what this group is for. Jodi, why don't you say some more and then we'll hear from others. I know that many can understand your feelings. *(Heads nod indicating they understand)*

■ ■ ■

If the leader allows negative statements to go by without clarification, trust becomes an antitherapeutic force and the members will probably tend not to disclose much personal information for fear of being criticized. Ideally, the leader can address the issue of being judgmental in the group and help members be more open-minded and less critical. Leaders should first help the member who disclosed the personal information. Sometimes, leaders get sidetracked and focus on the "judgmental" member or the topic of not being judgmental instead of focusing on the disclosing member who is in pain.

Members' Attitude Toward the Leader

The attitudes of the members toward the leader have to be considered when leading any group. Do they like him? Do they respect him? Do they trust him? Do they respect his group leadership skills? In most groups, members will have a variety of feelings toward the leader. Sometimes all the members may have negative feelings about the leader. In such a case, the leader needs to examine this dynamic, because it may have something to do with leadership style or ability.

Often only one or two members harbor negative feelings. One person who is out to "get the leader" can definitely interfere with positive group dynamics.

■ E X A M P L E

LEADER: I would like to take a few minutes to discuss how you are feeling about your progress in reaching the goals you set for yourself.

MELVIN: *(Angrily)* Why do you always ask us that? Let's do something different. This isn't helpful.

In this situation, the leader would not want to focus on the negative member, especially if she knows that the member is mainly out to "get" her. The leader can deflect the negative dynamic by saying, in a soft, firm voice, something like this:

LEADER: Melvin, I think most find this helpful and a way to think about their goals. *(Turning to the rest of the group)* How are all of you feeling about your progress?

■ ■ ■

The most important thing for leaders to realize is that negative attitudes about them as leaders definitely affect the interaction and disclosures in the group.

The Leader's Experience in Leading Groups

For those who are just starting out, the therapeutic force of experience needs to be mentioned. A beginning leader may be an antitherapeutic force because the leader lacks skills, may be nervous, and will make mistakes. If the leader is nervous, it is important to recognize this and, if need be, mention it to the group. Along these same lines, in a counseling/therapy group, an antitherapeutic force will be present if the leader does not have much individual counseling experience. For a good therapy group to occur, the leader must be experienced in individual counseling and have knowledge about counseling theories.

Ideally, beginning leaders would work with a more experienced coleader for a few groups before leading by themselves. If you find yourself leading without the benefit of prior experience, do the best you can and learn from the experience by discussing your group with your supervisor or colleague.

Coleadership Harmony

Coleading can be a very positive or negative force when leading a group. If the two leaders are in sync with each other, then it is almost always a positive force. When the leaders view group leading in two different ways, then coleading can serve as an antitherapeutic force. In Chapter 17, we discuss in detail the pros and cons of coleading.

Process and Content

We, along with Corey, Corey, and Corey (2009), Geroski and Kraus (2002), Gladding (2008) and many other writers, stress the importance of paying attention to the group process. Posthuma (2002); Hulse-Killacky, Kraus, and Schumacher (1999); and Sonstegard and Bitter (2004) discuss the need for balancing *process* and *content*. The term *process* includes stages of group, group dynamics, and therapeutic forces. *Content* refers to the purpose or task of the group. The leader always needs to be aware of both the content and process and focus the group on each, depending on the purpose and what is needed at the time. Hulse-Killacky et al. (1999) state, "… process and content are mutually interactive and operate as two threads of one string" (p. 117). Geroski and Kraus (2002) found in their study of psychoeducation groups that experienced group workers were unable to agree on what constitutes process and content in the specific groups studied.

Leaders make mistakes when it comes to how much emphasis should be placed on process and content. Some put too much importance on content and some put too much importance on process. Some leaders focus so much on what is going on and making sure everyone speaks that the group never achieves any meaningful depth. Other leaders focus so much on individual counseling that they miss the tremendous value of members interacting and hearing from others and struggling at times with relationships within the group. Hulse-Killacky, Killacky, and Donigian (2001) discuss the interplay between process and content throughout their book. *The skilled leader is always monitoring the content and the process during any session.*

 GROUP COUNSELING SKILLS: Process and Content

Watch segments 2.1 and 2.2. You will hear a discussion of the balance of content and process and see the leader focusing on process in 2.1, and balancing between content and process on 2.2.

Concluding Comments

In this chapter, we discussed the stages of groups, group process, and therapeutic forces that leaders must be aware of to be effective. All groups go through at least three stages: beginning, working, and closing. Some groups go through additional stages. It is important that leaders be aware that groups go through these stages even though the amount of time for each stage depends on the kind of group and its purpose. *Group process* (also called *group dynamics*) refers to the attitudes and interaction of members and leaders. *Therapeutic forces* are the many different elements operating in a group, such as its size, its setting, the time of day it meets, its member composition, the trust and commitment levels of its members, and its leader's attitude and experience. It is also important for the leader to be aware of both *process* and *content* during any session.

■ ACTIVITIES

1. Think back on groups you have either been in or led and think about mistakes that were made in each of the three stages of the group.
2. Think of two groups that you led or were a member of that were not successful. Now look over the list of the 15 therapeutic forces and mark which ones were antitherapeutic for each of the two groups. Consider what you or the leader could have done differently to change the antitherapeutic forces to make them more therapeutic.

GROUP COUNSELING SKILLS

1. Review video segment 2.1.
    a. Think about the importance of the leader being aware of both content and process.
    b. What would have happened if the leader would have just stayed with the content and had the members get into pairs?
2. Review segment 2.2.
    a. Why did the leader need to think about both content and process?
3. Review the first segment—The Leader Without Skills (1.1).
    a. What group dynamics do you see between members?

Web Sites

If you are interested in specific literature on group dynamics, you may want to check out the APA journal *Group Dynamics: Theory, Research, and Practice* (www.apa.org).

You may also want to do an Internet search of the term "group dynamics" and visit some of the sites that seem most interesting to you.

For more information on the different kinds of groups, you can conduct an Internet search of terms like "task goups" or "therapy groups."

Chapter 3

Purpose of Groups

Being clear about the purpose of the group is perhaps the most important group leadership concept to be learned. All the other skills and tasks discussed in this book—such as planning a group, holding and shifting the focus, and cutting off and drawing out members—are based on the leader's clear understanding of the purpose of the group. Because we consider this concept so important, we discuss clarity of purpose in this separate chapter and continue to mention it throughout the book. *Purpose* refers to why the group is meeting and what the goals and objectives are. (We sometimes use the terms *goals* and *objectives* in place of *purpose.*) When the leader fully understands the purpose of the group, it is easier for him to decide such things as its size, membership, session length, and number of sessions (Brown, 2009).

The purpose of the group serves as a map for the leader. Members and leaders must be clear about both the general purpose of the group and the specific purpose of each session (Hulse-Killacky, Killacky, & Donigian, 2001). Sometimes the purpose is obvious, such as losing weight, quitting smoking, overcoming a phobia, or learning study skills. Often, however, members' needs are not so specific. Leading groups of people with various needs means that the leader must help the group decide which needs are reasonable and possible to address. *Clarity of purpose helps the leader keep the members on course by suggesting relevant activities, asking relevant questions, and cutting off irrelevant discussions.*

When the Leader Is Unclear About the Purpose

As we said, groups are often confusing, boring, or unproductive when the objectives are not well-defined or the leader does not follow the stated objectives. The following examples are examples where the purpose is either unclear or is not adhered to by the leader. We follow each example with a discussion of what the leader could have done to ensure clarity of purpose.

■ EXAMPLES

Purpose: Learning to survive the pain of divorce

It is the first meeting. Members have been talking about their loneliness, self-doubts, and fears. Alan interrupts abruptly and starts talking about his thoughts about changing jobs. The leader says to the group, "What are your thoughts on how Alan should go about making this career decision?" For the next 30 minutes, the group gives Alan suggestions on how to handle the situation, with much of the talk centering on what salary he should request.

This leader made a mistake by asking for comments on what Alan was saying. The stated purpose was support and therapy to survive the pain of divorce, so the leader should not have focused the group on Alan's concern about his career. Rather, the leader should have halted the discussion and redirected the group to a discussion of the members' feelings about their divorces.

Allowing the group to continue the career discussion probably resulted in some members becoming bored and frustrated. Members may also have become angry and left the group or cut in on the discussion and attacked Alan or the group. Such responses could have been prevented had the leader been clear about the purpose and then used her skills to redirect the group. For example, the leader could have said something like, "Alan, that's an important topic; however, it does not fit with the purpose of the group at this time. If you feel the need to talk about this, let's schedule an appointment."

■ ■ ■

Purpose: Orientation to prison life

The group starts with the leader going over the procedures for meals, visits, and weekend passes. One man brings up the prison's policy of no passes for the first month. Another inmate chimes in about the lack of places to be alone when he has visitors. Another asks the group what they think of that situation. Different members offer their opinions and ideas about it. Following this, the leader brings the discussion back to the policies and procedures by discussing mealtime procedures. One inmate mentions that he is a vegetarian and two others ask him a number of questions about why he doesn't eat meat. Another inmate says he thinks the meals are terrible. The leader asks what other members think about the meals. Two inmates then start complaining about the food, the heating in the rooms, and the lack of television sets on the units. The group ends with very little having been said about procedures in the prison.

Because this leader did not stick to the purpose and was more worried about whether people would talk, he let the group wander. There is a good chance that some members will be resistant at the second meeting because the first one was boring and irrelevant. The leader should have halted the discussion on the side issues and brought the group back to its intended purpose by saying kindly but firmly, "The purpose of this group is to discuss the rules and procedures of the prison. I'd be more than happy to arrange a time to discuss these other matters. However, for now let's get back to the topic—let's talk about the procedures for having a visitor."

■ ■ ■

Purpose: Adult Sunday school discussion group on church-related issues
It is the fourth session, and the topic scheduled for discussion this week is "Ways the Church Can Be More Responsive to the Changing Family—The Single-Parent Family and the Stepfamily." The discussion has been interesting and relevant. Then a member asks, "Why is the divorce rate so high now?" The leader mistakenly throws the question open to the group and, for the next 25 minutes, four of the nine members argue about the many reasons. When the group returns to the original topic of the church being responsive, the other members have lost interest and have little energy for the original topic.

Again, the leader's lack of clarity caused this group to go awry. If the leader had been clear about the purpose of this meeting, she would not have let the members discuss the causes of divorce. Rather, she would have said something like, "That might be something we could discuss at a later meeting. However, let's stay with the topic for this week."

■ ■ ■

Purpose: Dealing with fears of going to middle school next year
It is the second session and members are talking about their different fears. One student talked about her fear of changing classes. When the leader asks if others share the same fear, Tommy jumps in and starts to talk about how he is afraid of the dark sometimes. The leader asks members if they are afraid of the dark. Carlos says he is a little. The group then discusses fear of the dark for the rest of the session.

The leader allowed this group to deviate from the purpose of the group. If she had been clear on the purpose, she would not have focused on Tommy's concern because his concern had nothing to do with going to middle school next year.

In each of these examples, the leader does not stick to the purpose, which causes the group to be superficial. *Awareness of the purpose is very important for any group situation.*

■ ■ ■

GROUP COUNSELING SKILLS: Clarity of Purpose

Go to the segments on Clarity of Purpose (3.1, 3.2, and 3.3) on the *Group Counseling Skills* DVD to see how important clarity of purpose can be. Watch a discussion and three clarity of purpose demonstrations, one of a group leader without clarity of purpose, and two demonstrations of a group leader with clarity of purpose.

Determining the Purpose of the Group

When setting up a group, the leader must assess the potential members' needs and then decide which kind of group will be most helpful. For example, a leader working with a group of mentally challenged teenagers might decide on an education group covering such topics as sex, money, and job hunting or a counseling/support group to help them explore their feelings. Gathering information about the members' needs, deciding which needs can be met by the group, and then conceptualizing the kind of group that will ideally meet those needs clarifies the purpose for the leader. The next example illustrates the process of clarifying the purpose by determining the kind of group.

■   E X A M P L E

A therapist has been asked to lead a group for pregnant teenage girls. She gathers information about the members' ages, length of pregnancies, attitudes of their parents, and reasons for wanting to be in a group. She finds that there are five girls ranging in age from 14 to 17. They are all at least 4 months pregnant, and all plan to keep their babies. They've volunteered to be in the group because of conflicts at home and a desire for information. The leader also discovers that their needs range from dealing with their peers, handling guilt associated with religious beliefs, needing nutrition information, parenting skills, coping with pregnancy, planning for the baby, and needing information regarding the effects of drugs, alcohol, and smoking on the fetus.

Given these needs, an education/support group would be beneficial to educate the girls on various aspects of pregnancy, as well as to facilitate personal sharing in an effort to establish support among members.

■ ■ ■

During the first session of any group, the leader needs to clarify the purpose with the members. By doing this, the leader ensures that the purpose is clear and hopefully coincides with what the members want or expect. Sometimes it is the leader who determines exactly what is to happen in the group. This is true for such groups as DUI or certain task groups. Other times it is the members who have much to say about the purpose. No matter who is determining the purpose, the important point is that the purpose is clarified during the first session.

Common Questions About Purpose

Certain questions often arise regarding the purpose of groups. Although some of them may seem similar, each one addresses slightly different issues.

Can the Group Have More Than One Purpose?

Yes. Many groups may have multiple purposes, such as providing support, information, and therapy. The pairing of values clarification with counseling or drug information is compatible and can set the stage for an effective and interesting group experience. For example, a group for people just released from an inpatient psychiatric treatment center could have at least two purposes: to provide support and to provide information on such subjects as budgeting and how to interview for a job. A group for teenagers who are in gangs could also have multiple purposes—conflict mediation, counseling, and providing information about alternatives to gangs.

■ EXAMPLE

The group consists of six teens in an alternative school. The purpose is to help them improve their attitude about school, to focus on problems at home, and to help them get along better with others.

Scott: I didn't do any schoolwork for the last week.

Leader: Is there a reason for that?

Scott: I think algebra is hard and I don't like to read.

Eric: I did what we said about doing the work even if I didn't like it and then rewarded myself by playing some video games.

Leader: What are others of you doing in regard to studying?

Dennis: I get real frustrated when doing those stupid math problems.

Leader: I have a better idea. Instead of talking about studying, let's talk today about something that applies to school and to life in general. It is called *low frustration tolerance*. . . .

In this example the leader shifts from more of an educational purpose to a counseling purpose in teaching low frustration tolerance from REBT theory.

■ ■ ■

Sometimes leaders mix purposes in incompatible ways. For example, an unskilled leader in a group on child rearing might mistakenly use 30 minutes of the group's time to do counseling with a woman complaining about her husband. Ideally, the leader would meet with the woman at the end of the session or the next day, but not during the group because the other members have come for a totally different purpose. In residential settings such as halfway houses, juvenile centers, or prisons, incompatible purposes often emerge. In these settings, leaders sometimes try to deal in a single session with issues such as problems with parents, tensions between residents, house rules, and disciplinary procedures. The issues should be separated into two or three different meetings, because each has a tone and agenda that does not really mesh with the others.

The first session of any group is another example of a multiple-purpose group session. The leader always has at least two purposes in mind. One is introducing the general content of the group (such as study habits, communication skills, increasing marital happiness), and the other is getting members clear about the group and how it will be conducted.

■ EXAMPLES

It is the first session of a cancer support group. The leader has two purposes—one is to help members get comfortable being in the group. The other is to encourage members to share their thoughts and feelings about their illness and to provide valuable information and support for each other.

■ ■ ■

It is the first session of a high school group for gay, lesbian and transgendered students. Given the sensitive nature of this group, the primary purpose is to get members to feel comfortable being in the group, especially if the members are not familiar with each other. The other purpose is to address some of the difficult issues that the members face being gay, lesbian or transgendered.

■ ■ ■

It is the first session bringing two gangs together to resolve their differences. The leader's primary purpose is to make sure things do not heat up and that a positive tone is set. The leader also wants members to begin a dialog about how they can coexist with each other and to break down the rigid boundaries that each gang has set for itself.

■ ■ ■

There are also multiple purposes for the final session: covering content relevant to the group and spending time helping members gain closure since the group is ending.

■ EXAMPLES

It is the last of six sessions of a group at a women's shelter. The leader has three purposes—one is to deal with any unfinished business or issues that are still not resolved. The second purpose is to help members reinforce what they learned and share hope and encouragement with each other. The third purpose is to say goodbye to the other members, have members feel they are not alone, and encourage contact with each other for support.

■ ■ ■

Because it is the end of the school year, it is the last session of a group for teenage loners. One purpose is to try to get members to commit to connecting with people over the summer. The leader would most likely focus on each person's plan to be with other people for the summer. The other purpose is to say good-bye and share what they have learned from the group.

■ ■ ■

The main thing to consider when developing multiple purposes is whether or not they are compatible.

Must Each Session Have a Purpose?

Yes. A good group leader should have in mind the purpose or purposes of each specific session. So far, our discussion of purpose has mostly centered on the content of the group and the overall purpose. Purpose can be looked at more specifically. One purpose might be to clarify what the rest of the sessions will be like. Other purposes can be to give feedback to each other; to get to know each other better; or to discuss a specific topic such as religion, sex, or the need for approval. Sometimes the leader, the members, or both will decide beforehand what the purpose of the next session will be. The following is a list of possible purposes for a session or a part of a session:

- To have fun
- To be informative
- To build trust
- To increase commitment
- To be thought provoking
- To discuss group process—that is, what is happening between members
- To discuss gender, race, or other cultural issues that exist in the group
- To accomplish a task
- To work on personal issues

Each of these may serve either as part of a multiple purpose or the sole purpose for one or more sessions. For instance, a leader who discovers that the group lacks trust or commitment would probably want to focus part of the next meeting on those issues rather than on the overall purpose, such as personal growth, getting out of prison, living with cancer, or learning assertiveness. Following are some examples of the specific purposes of group sessions.

■ EXAMPLES

This is a growth group consisting of three women and five men. The leader starts the session by saying:

LEADER: Tonight I thought it might be helpful to discuss something that I have observed in the group. Ever since Gloria shared that she is a lesbian, there has been an underlying tension or something, and I think the group could benefit from talking about this.

■ ■ ■

In the fifth session of a therapy group, Sandy starts rambling again. The leader decides that the group is far enough along to start giving feedback to one another. He says the following to the group and to Sandy:

LEADER: Sandy, I want to pick up on something that I think will help you and the other members of the group. I want to do a feedback exercise where we tell each other how we experience them in the group. That is, for the next 45 minutes, we are going to give each other feedback. Here's what I'd like you to do.

■ ■ ■

It is the third session of a support group composed of juveniles in a detention center. The leader notices that there is no energy, even though the group began only 10 minutes ago. She decides, therefore, that the best purpose for this session is to work on commitment and trust and says to the group:

LEADER: On a 1 to 10 scale, with 10 being *a lot* and 1 being *none,* how much commitment do you have to this group?

After the information is gathered, the leader focuses the remainder of the session on why members are not committed and what would increase their commitment.

■ ■ ■

It is the third in a series of five sessions of an educational group whose overall purpose is to teach nursing supervisors new ways to deal with their staff. The leader starts by saying:

LEADER: Today, we are going to focus on nonverbal behavior. I want to go over some of the latest research, which I found to be quite useful; then I'll ask for reactions and comments. Jefferson and Smith studied the nonverbal behavior of 22 nursing supervisors and found . . .

■ ■ ■

A therapy group in its third session is composed of mental-health patients. The leader opens the group by saying, "Who has something to bring up tonight?" Two of the seven members respond. Joe says he wants to talk about his mom and her desire to control him. Molly mentions her anxiety at work. The leader says to the group:

LEADER: Tonight, we'll focus on Molly's and Joe's concerns, and then during the last hour we'll spend time talking about learning to control our feelings by paying attention to the things that we tell ourselves.

■ ■ ■

As you can see, a leader can establish the session's purpose in a variety of ways. The simple, direct approach is often a very good way to make the purpose clear.

Can the Purpose Change?

Yes. Groups often start out as education, support, or growth groups; as they develop, the members begin to share on a more personal level. If the leader sees a need to shift to counseling, it is usually valuable for him to discuss this in the group. Perhaps the best way to make the change is for the leader to explain how the group could alter its purpose. If the group decides to switch its emphasis, the leader needs to be aware that it will probably take one or two sessions to completely change the direction. *Often leaders make the mistake of shifting the purpose of the group without informing the members.* As a result, members feel frustrated, confused, fearful, or resentful. As we have said throughout this discussion, it is important that both leaders and members remain clear about the group's purpose, and the leader should reiterate the purpose whenever necessary. If the leader decides to shift the purpose, she must be sure that the members are aware of her intent and that they also desire the shift.

■ **EXAMPLE**

It is the third session of an education/support group for stepfamily living. Four women make up the group. The leader has noticed that all the members have numerous personal concerns that are interfering with effective living.

SHEILA: I can't stand the way their mother treats them. I actually called her up and threatened her. I can't help it!

CELINA: I get so angry when Juan's mom is late all the time in meeting us! But I am just an angry person, or so my husband says. He even told me the other night he could not take my anger much longer.

LEADER: Let me talk about a possible shift here in the group. I know we originally got together because of stepfamily issues, but I have noticed that each of you has some major concerns that aren't necessarily related to stepfamilies. Sheila, you and Celina seem to have some major issues with anger. Dealing with anger seems like a good topic. Another topic could be dealing with guilt because Dana, you and Sharon both mentioned that last week and again this week. Would you like to shift the group to more of a counseling group about these and other issues, still focusing on stepfamily issues as they relate to these?

DANA: I need help in both areas. I don't want to *not* be able to talk about my adjustment in my stepfamily.

LEADER: We will definitely keep talking about stepfamily matters as well, but I just did not want to switch the purpose unless we all agree.

CELINA: I'm for it because I need help or my husband may leave.

■ ■ ■

Can There Be No Purpose?

Not having a purpose is inadvisable. Groups without a purpose usually dissolve because of lack of interest and direction. Although you may choose to bring together a group of people having no predetermined goal in mind, the purpose of the first meeting should be to decide what the purpose should be for the remainder of the meetings. In fact, a group with no purpose cannot really be termed a group; rather, it is a social gathering.

If the Leader Is Clear, Will the Members Be?

Not always. Often, members have their own ideas of what the group should be about, and they try to steer it in that direction. In addition, some members will come to groups for reasons other than the stated purpose; that is, they come to complain, to preach, or to attack and will not follow the leader's direction. Another reason members may not be clear about the group's purpose is that some find it hard to understand what is going on. Because of their anxiety, they are not able to listen well. By reiterating, the leader can do much to clarify the intent of the group for the members. If she sees that some of the members are confused, she will probably want to do one of two things: (1) meet with those members who seem confused or (2) discuss the problem in the group. Often, this clears up the confusion.

■ E X A M P L E

The leader views this group as a support group for those with hepatitis C. Two members want the group to be a more general support group and also a therapy group and continually bring up unrelated personal problems. It is the second session and the leader realizes that the two members may not understand the purpose.

MARY: I am still trying to decide if I want to take the new drug—I am afraid of the side effects.

TONI: I understand. My doctor wants me to try something new and I am scared to death, but I do not like how I have been feeling lately.

HECTOR: I think we can all be supportive of each other, especially when taking one of those powerful drugs. We could meet more often or at least make sure we are in contact by phone or e-mail.

NICOLE: I know I could use the contact during the holidays. I have such problems with my in-laws. They are the hardest people to buy gifts for. Do any of you worry about buying the right gift?

CHERYL: My problem is being disappointed by the gifts my husband buys me. He always . . .

LEADER: Let me talk about something here. During the first session, we talked a lot about being supportive of each other and how this is a support group. However, it really is not a general support group but rather a specific one focusing on issues pertaining to having hepatitis C. I'd rather have us stay focused on those kinds of issues. Cheryl and Nicole, I realize you have concerns that are important to you, and if you would like to talk about those privately with me, that would be fine. Let's go back to what Mary, Toni, and Hector were talking about.

If the two members continue to be unclear as to the purpose of the group, the leader would want to talk with them privately. After talking with them, if they continue to bring up unrelated therapy issues, the leader may decide to ask them not to be in the group and find them a therapy situation that fits their needs—either another group or individual counseling.

■ ■ ■

Purpose in Single-Session Groups

Most of our comments have implied that groups meet for a number of sessions. Many groups meet only once. When leading a single-session group, clarity of purpose is even more essential. The leader needs to be very clear about why this group is meeting and then plan a group that will accomplish the desired objective in the time allotted. The group's purpose may be to discuss and determine a treatment plan for a patient, to resolve a conflict, or to plan an event. Being clear will help the leader use the time effectively and accomplish the desired outcomes. Often at single-session group meetings, little is accomplished because the members keep switching topics and the leader fails to keep the discussion within the boundaries of the purpose. Members may also focus for half the meeting on something that is irrelevant, thus necessitating a second meeting. A good leader should be clear as to the purpose, what needs to be done, and how much time should be spent on introductions, warm-up, background information, and the various topics.

Concluding Comments

Being clear about the purpose is perhaps the most important factor in determining the outcome of a group. It also affects the leader's choice of the kind of group, membership, topics, dynamics, and depth as well as the leader's role. Clarity of purpose is crucial no matter what type of group is being led. The purpose of the group serves as the map for guiding the leader in planning and conducting the session. Many beginning leaders fail to be clear as to the purpose, or they do not stick to the purpose. Sessions have different purposes, sometimes more than one. Also, the purpose of the group can change as the group develops. Once you have mastered the process of clarifying the purpose, the next important aspect of effective group leadership is planning, which is discussed in the next chapter.

■ ACTIVITIES

1. Think about any current groups you are leading or of which you are a member. Is the purpose clear? If so, why? If the purpose is not clear, why? How can you change this situation?
2. Think of three different group situations where the purpose was not clear either due to the members or leader. (If you have not had much group counseling experience, think of classes, family situations, study groups, church groups, or school groups.)
    a. What was the consequence of the confused purpose?
    b. What could the leader have done to improve the group?
3. Discuss with classmates or colleagues why clarity of purpose is so important for groups and staff meetings. (We believe that by discussing this you will have a much greater chance of remembering that this is the most important aspect of group leading. Without clarity of purpose, a group has a good chance of going poorly.)

GROUP COUNSELING SKILLS

1. View again segments 3.1 and 3.2.
    a. What do you see as the difference?
    b. What did the leader do in 3.2 to make sure the group stayed with the purpose?
    c. What would have happened if the leader had not had clarity of purpose?
2. View segment 3.3.
    a. What would have happened if the leader had not had clarity of purpose in this segment?
    b. Would the teachers have talked about teaching or would they have been talking about the hospital and about the member's mom's medical condition?
3. Review the first two segments of the DVD—The Leader Without Skills (1.1) and The Leader With Skills (1.2)—and note the difference regarding clarity of purpose. What skills did the leader in the second group use to clarify the purpose?

Chapter 4

Planning

The importance of carefully planning a group cannot be overemphasized. Corey (2008) states, "If you want a group to be successful, you need to devote considerable time to planning. In my view planning should begin with the drafting of a written proposal" (p. 80). We agree that there are *two aspects of planning: pregroup planning* and *session planning*. Both are very important.

Pregroup Planning

Many groups are not successful due to too little emphasis on pregroup planning. Gladding (2008) points out the necessity of pregroup planning: "The dynamics of a group begin before the group ever convenes" (p. 52). In Chapters 1 and 2, we discussed several considerations for the formation of a group: how large it should be, whether it should have open or closed membership, how long sessions should last, and where it should meet. Four additional decisions to be made when establishing a group include the following:

1. For how many sessions will the group meet?
2. When will the group meet?
3. Who should the members be?
4. How will the members be screened?

For How Many Sessions Will the Group Meet?

Many groups are established for a certain length of time. For instance, parenting, childbirth, assertiveness-training, certain growth and therapy, and many education groups are scheduled to meet for a specified number of sessions. Counseling, therapy, growth, task, and support groups sometimes begin with no set number of sessions planned. Usually it is best to set a limit because it gives members an idea of how long they have to complete any personal work. Another option is to allow members to determine the number of sessions once the group has been meeting for a while. Often, the number of sessions is dictated by other considerations, such as the length of a school term, the leader's availability, the needs of the population being served, or the amount of educational information to be covered.

When Will the Group Meet?

Two factors must be considered: time of day and frequency of meetings. Ideally, the meeting time will not conflict with members' other activities. If the setting for the group is an agency, school, or hospital, the choice of meeting time should cause as little disruption as possible to the daily routine. Choice of meeting time is especially important in a school, where the students come from classes. The leader will want to make sure the same class is not missed on a regular basis by having the group rotate periods each week. For groups in an elementary setting, a counselor may be inclined to always have the group meet during recess. Be cautious of this in that students may not want to always give up their recess time.

The members' schedules also must be considered when setting the time. If the members work, perhaps the evening is best, or maybe even early morning or noon. For groups in a residential center—such as a prison, hospital, or detention center—a careful examination of the daily routine is helpful. Beginning leaders often make the mistake of planning a group without fully considering the many factors that might make the meeting time inconvenient.

The leader's schedule is also important; she must always be available to lead the group, and some times and days are better than others. Days when the leader tends to be very busy with such things as staff meetings, paperwork, or intakes should be avoided. In the case of therapy groups, it is too taxing for the leader to lead one group right after another. Ideally, any therapy group leader would lead no more than one group a day; the maximum should be three.

Besides deciding on the best time to meet, the leader is usually the one to decide how often the group will meet. Some groups meet daily; others meet twice a week, once a week, once every two weeks, or once a month. The frequency of meetings depends on the kind of group, its purpose and the availability of members and the leader. There is no set formula for how often a group should meet, but the leader must ensure that the meetings are properly spaced. It is important that the group neither meet so often nor so infrequently as to defeat the overall purpose.

Who Should the Members Be?

Any time a group is being formed, a number of considerations arise regarding its membership (Corey, 2008). Once the population to be served is determined (schoolchildren, hospital patients, prisoners, clients of a mental-health center, or interested persons in a community), the leader should decide whether the entire population will automatically constitute the membership or whether the members will volunteer or be selected. For example, in an orientation group at a university residence hall, will the group consist of all 15 new students in a wing, or will it include only those who want to be in a group? In a hospital unit for psychiatric patients, will the group be for everyone, or will only selected patients be allowed? There are no absolute guidelines for deciding whom to include; usually the purpose of the group, time constraints, and setting will help the leader decide how to limit membership.

Another consideration is whether to place members who are very different in age or background in the same group. Certainly, multicultural issues need to be considered when selecting members. In schools, counselors have to decide whether to include students from the same grade or from different grades. Also, school counselors need to decide if the groups should consist of the same or mixed gender. In various hospital situations, patients in the same unit often include young and old people or people with varying educational or socioeconomic backgrounds. Sometimes mixing the ages or backgrounds is beneficial; at other times, it can be detrimental. If the leader were planning a group for the unemployed, it would not be beneficial to place college-educated individuals and high school dropouts in the same group because their needs would differ. In a marital-problems group, mixing ages and backgrounds would probably prove beneficial because members might benefit from hearing different views and ideas. Because each group is different, we are not saying that certain groups should have certain members, but it is very important that the leader consider these different variables when selecting members of a group.

How Will the Members Be Screened?

Closely related to questions about composition of membership are decisions about screening members. One of the biggest problems faced by counselors in agencies and institutions is that administrators do not let them select the members; therefore, groups are often conducted with members who should not be in the group. We encourage you to lobby hard for the right to screen your members if the goal is to benefit the participants. *Screening is essential because not everyone is appropriate for every group.*

Sonstegard and Bitter (2004) present a different point of view from most others who write about group counseling:

> Adlerians typically reject the idea of screening. The process seems more designed for the protection of the therapist than the facilitation of the group. Too often, prescreening eliminates from the group the very person or people who could use the group experience: the disruptive, the self-absorbed, and the isolated (p. 19).

Although we see some merit in their point of view, it has been our experience that some members can ruin groups, especially if an inexperienced leader is in charge. Even with experienced leaders, negative, hostile, or inappropriate members can cause other members to stop coming to a potentially beneficial group. We encourage leaders not to sacrifice an entire group trying to help one individual and agree with Corey, Corey, Callahan, and Russell (2010) who write: "Leaders need to keep in mind that all groups are not appropriate for all people" (p. 47).

With some groups, screening is either unnecessary or only slightly beneficial. As Corey (2008) says, "The key point is that screening needs to be done within the context of the type of group that a practitioner is offering. Whether a client is to be included or excluded has much to do with the purposes of the group" (p. 83). For education, discussion, and task groups, screening may not be necessary—it depends on the specific situation. In many situations screening is not possible; when it is both possible and desirable, the leader has several procedural options for screening.

The Personal Interview The best screening method, though the most time consuming, is the personal interview. It allows the leader to assess most easily the appropriateness of the member for the group, and it gives the leader a chance to make contact with potential members. The leader has an opportunity to inform the prospective member about the group's content, process, membership, rules, and so forth. Also, the personal interview gives potential members the chance to ask questions about the group and gives the leader the chance to see if the group is right for them. Listed are a number of questions that can be asked in a personal interview or on a screening form:

- Why do you want to be in this group?
- What are your expectations of the group?
- Have you ever been in a group before? If so, what was it like?
- What concerns do you want help with?
- Is there anyone with whom you would not want to be in group?
- How do you think you can contribute to the group?
- Do you have any questions about the group or the leader?

Individual contact with the potential member Personal interviews permit the leader and member to meet each other before the group actually begins. It is important for the leader to make this experience more than just a question-and-answer session. The leader should realize that the interview is the beginning of his relationship with the member. He will want to use many of the same skills used in an individual counseling session—attending, listening, and some probing—without letting the interview become a counseling session. Too often, leaders alienate candidates by making the interview too formal or by turning it into a therapy session. The interview should be as comfortable as possible while the leader assesses the potential member's needs and goals.

Informing the member about the group During the screening interview, the leader can explain the purpose of the group, how it will be conducted, any rules, and other relevant information. If the group is a counseling or therapy group, the leader can tell the member about the theories that may be used. If it is to be a support group, the leader can give the member examples of what might be shared. Some leaders show a videotape of a group so the prospective member can see what the group will be like.

Assessing appropriateness   By asking questions relevant to the type of group being formed, the leader can determine whether the potential member is appropriate for the group. In the personal interview, the leader can often spot those people whose needs and goals differ from those of the planned group. For educational groups, the leader tries to determine if the individual knows either too much or too little about the subject matter. For support groups, the leader may find that a potential member needs individual or group therapy rather than a support group. Screening for counseling and therapy groups allows the leader to determine if the person's needs can best be met by group or individual counseling.

Written Screening   Another method of screening is to have prospective members complete a written form. This gives the leader information necessary to decide if the person is appropriate for the group. Sometimes, the only information the leader needs is biographical: age, grade level completed, sex, marital status, living situation, age of children, diagnosis, length of illness, and any important medical information. When basing choices on written material only, the leader must remember to include all the pertinent questions. Questions that are sometimes overlooked include the candidate's availability for meetings and whether the candidate needs childcare and transportation.

The questions outlined for the personal interview can be used as part of a written screening form. Naturally, the questions asked depend on the purpose of the group. If the topics to be covered are sensitive ones—such as sex, death, divorce, or religion—the leader may want to list them and ask prospective members to comment on how they feel about talking about those subjects. Some leaders ask members to write a brief autobiography as a way to help with screening. The key to effective screening is to find out the information needed to form a group of members who can share and learn together.

Screening by Referral Sources   Another type of screening occurs when the leader informs possible referral sources, such as teachers or administrators, other therapists, or hospital staff, about the group, its purpose, and the kind of member sought. These people, in a sense, do the screening by telling appropriate potential members of the availability of the group. The leader who uses this method of screening will want to make sure that those making referrals fully understand the purpose of the group and the kind of members desired.

Screening by Using a Comprehensive Group Program   A leader conducting several groups in the same setting—such as in a prison, hospital, company, or school—can "screen" by assigning members to any one of the groups. Assigning members according to their knowledge, age, experience, or some personality characteristic often increases the likelihood of the group being valuable to the members. The leader can also sort members according to their interaction style or level of mental health. The leader may choose to place some highly verbal members in a group with some nontalkers. At times, it is useful to mix certain characteristics in that way. There really are no absolute guidelines for making these decisions because each situation and purpose is so different. The main thing to realize is that these kinds of screening decisions can be instrumental in enhancing positive therapeutic forces.

If the leader does not select a member, she may want to meet with that member and discuss options for other groups or individual counseling. This depends on the setting and the situation, but it is important for the leader to be sensitive to anyone who may feel rejected by the screening process.

Screening After the Group Has Begun   Corey, Corey, Callahan, and Russell (2010) suggest conducting a preliminary group session for potential members, especially in therapy groups, to give participants a chance to see if being in a group is the best decision for them. Also it gives the leader a chance to see the potential members in a group situation. There may be times when a leader needs to screen members even after the group has begun. For groups where screening before the group starts is not possible or thorough enough, the leader may state in the first session that after the group meets for a couple of times, he plans to meet with each member to discuss their ongoing participation in the group. This kind of screening can be an excellent way to handle the formation of groups when pregroup screening is not possible or when there is a need to screen out some members who are not right for the group.

Another kind of screening that can be done after the group has been meeting for a few weeks is to have the members write a couple of pages on why the group is important and what they want to get from the group. The leader stipulates that only those who complete the assignment can be in the group for the remaining sessions. The leader would use this kind of screening only when wanting to weed out those who are not committed to working in the group. In Chapter 12, we discuss further when and how to screen out members during the middle sessions.

Additional Considerations for Pre-group Planning

The leader will want to ascertain whether any additional materials are needed for the group, any resource people must be contacted, or any permission forms must be signed. School policy often requires that school counselors have permission forms signed by parents or guardians. A simple form describing the group and its purpose usually is sufficient. It may also be useful to consider whether any kind of oral or written contract from members is desirable.

Big-Picture Planning

Another part of pre-group planning is what we call *big-picture planning*. By this we mean thinking about all the possible topics that need to be covered and/or could be covered. Too often, leaders think only about the first session and not the overall picture of what needs to be covered during the life of the group. We suggest the leader first list the possible topics and then later put them in some possible order to be covered during the beginning, early middle, and middle stages of the group. A good leader makes an extensive list of possible topics and then prioritizes the topics to gain a better idea of what is important to cover and what can be omitted. The examples below are lists of possible topics that would then be prioritized.

Anger Management Group (Meeting for Six Sessions)

Where anger comes from

Who or what situations members
   think cause them to get angry

How different theories look at anger

REBT self-talk; TA child ego-state

Anger at parents

Guilt in regard to anger

How members currently deal with anger

Current anger

Past anger

Anger at siblings, friends, others

Anger as a habit

Better ways to handle anger

Anger as a cover-up for hurt

What members learned about
   anger as they were growing up

Divorce Group (Meeting for Eight Sessions)

Children

Dating

Sex

Anger

Guilt, hurt, blame/fault

Loneliness

Unfinished business

Self-esteem

Money

Remarriage

History of other relationships

What can be learned from the
   marriage experience

Fears

Feelings of failure

After making these lists, the leader of each group then considers which topics should be addressed in the beginning stage, which ones should be brought up later, which ones need be only briefly mentioned, and which ones may be unnecessary altogether. This kind of planning definitely helps the leader have a better understanding of what he perceives the group will cover. This big-picture understanding aids the leader during the first few sessions when members clarify how the group can be helpful and which topics may be covered.

For any group, the leader should do big-picture planning. For some groups, this may not be extensive because the topics tend to emerge as the group meets and develops. However, for most groups, considerable time should be spent doing big-picture planning. Talking with colleagues about possible topics, reading books and articles on the subject, and gathering information during the screening process can help with big-picture planning. This process needs to be done before the group begins. It also needs to be an ongoing planning activity because the group is always evolving and the need to cover new and different topics often emerges.

Session Planning

Planning a specific session involves deciding on the topics and group activities as well as delegating an approximate amount of time needed for each. Most groups require a good deal of planning, although only a minimum of planning is necessary for certain kinds of counseling, therapy, growth, and support groups after their initial sessions. Minimal planning is necessary when the members come to understand the purpose of their group and arrive at the sessions eager to discuss concerns important to them and relevant to others. But even in groups where the planning of exercises and topics is minimal, the leader needs to give considerable thought to what kinds of exercises and topics would be helpful. Many leaders make the mistake of coming to the group without thinking about what may be valuable for the members; when the members have little energy, the group falls flat. Groups require planning when the members do not tend to bring issues to the group to discuss, but rather respond to exercises and other activities.

Discussion, education, and task groups are often more effective when thoroughly planned by the leader. The thoughtful leader can organize the session in a way that makes the group both interesting and productive. In the remainder of this chapter, we discuss the considerations that go into planning an effective group session.

Consider the Stage of the Group

One of the first things to consider when planning a session is whether the session is a first, second, middle, or closing session. Planning a first session is very different from planning a middle or closing session. During the first session, there are a number of things that the leader will need to do, such as having members introduce themselves, clarifying the purpose of the group, setting a positive tone for the group, helping members get over any uneasiness, and going over any guidelines or rules for the group. It is important that for most groups, going over the rules should come in the middle of the first session and not at the very beginning. During the closing sessions, the leader should make sure the members are saying and doing the things necessary for ending the group.

Another consideration is for how many more sessions the group will meet. Some groups meet for only one session; planning for that kind of session is obviously different from a group that will meet for 10 weeks. Planning the fifth session when only two sessions are left is different from planning a fifth session when six more sessions remain.

Plan the Format for the Session

When planning a session, the leader will want to consider the format for the session. Some groups work well with the same format each week; for instance, progress reports, an exercise, discussion, then practicing a new behavior, and closing comments; or sharing personal problems the first hour and then discussing some assigned topic that members were given the week before. For other groups, a varied format seems advantageous because it keeps the interest level high. By a varied format, we mean one session might consist of two different exercises and a discussion; the next session might include a written activity, personal sharing, and then some role-playing practice; and another session might consist of a short film. Doing different things keeps members interested and curious. When planning, the leader should always consider whether the format is becoming stale.

A common way to vary format is by using exercises, but the leader will want to be sure not to plan too many and to allot enough time for members to discuss their thoughts, feelings, and reactions to any exercise. As a rule, leaders should plan various types of exercises for a session because some members will respond better than others to certain exercises.

Anticipate Problems When Planning

The leader also needs to anticipate potential problems when planning. For example, if she has asked members to read something for the session, she can anticipate that some members will not have done the reading and can plan ways of processing the material that will not alienate those members. It is sometimes valuable to plan activities with specific members in mind, but it is important to have a backup plan in case those members are absent. In fact, it is always a good idea to have a backup plan in case an activity, exercise, or discussion does not go well.

Planning the Phases of the Session

The leader needs to be aware that each session has three phases: the *warm-up,* or *beginning,* phase; the *middle,* or *working,* phase; and the *closing* phase. During the *warm-up* phase, the leader often has members comment on any thoughts or reactions since the last session. During this phase, the leader also tries to get a sense of the members' energy and interest for the session and any topics or issues they may want to talk about. In the *middle* or *working* phase of the session, members focus on the group's purpose. We call it the middle phase when referring to an education or discussion group and the working phase for other groups. The *closing* phase is devoted to summarizing and ending the session. During this phase, the leader plans summary-type activities that help members integrate what they have learned during the middle or working phase of the group.

There are specific planning guidelines for each phase of any given session. The process of leading members through each of the phases is covered in great detail in later chapters, but here we want to discuss each phase in regard to planning.

The Beginning Phase

A leader should always plan how to begin a session and how long the warm-up phase should be. The first few minutes are sometimes used to review the previous session. The leader needs to decide how much time to devote to reviewing the previous session. Too often, leaders plan a beginning phase that lasts too long. The warm-up phase for most groups is usually less than 10 minutes and should not be more than 15 minutes, except for the first session, where the warm-up phase may need to be longer. With school groups where the sessions are 30 to 40 minutes, counselors will want to plan a brief beginning phase in order to have time for quality interaction during the middle phase.

Some groups require almost no planning of the warming-up time—the members come ready to talk, learn, or work. In other groups, the leader must plan for getting members focused on being in the group. During the beginning phase, the leader plans activities, exercises, or discussions that allow him to assess how members are feeling about being in the group that day. He may plan additional time for warming up if he feels that the group needs more time.

Planning for Introducing a New Member During the Beginning Phase
When planning the beginning phase of a session of an open-membership group, the leader will need to allot time and select a method for introducing new members. The leader may either introduce them or have them introduce themselves. Established members can also introduce themselves by sharing how the group has been valuable to them. Chapter 5 contains several examples of how to introduce new members to the group.

Planning for the Energy Level for the Beginning Phase   The leader should consider the kind of energy level to use during the beginning phase. Some groups benefit from a high-energy opening, whereas others need a calm opening—the need varies with the members and the purpose of the group. Energy can come from the kind of activities used or from the energy in the leader's voice. One elementary school counselor used a high-energy opening by talking

enthusiastically with her attention deficit hyperactive disorder (ADHD) group. She quickly realized this was a mistake; in the next session, she began with a calm voice and a relaxing activity. She found this was much better for these kids. Each group is different, so we cannot say what kind of energy is best for certain groups. We do want to emphasize that the leader should always consider whether the energy level being used is the best one for the group being led.

The Middle or Working Phase

Planning the middle or working phase is very important because it is the time when meaningful interactions and discussions should take place. Planning for the middle phase will vary, depending on the type of group. Careful planning can make a big difference in eliminating negative group dynamics and allowing enough time to deal with the purpose of the group and any diversity issues that may be present. We discuss planning concerns for each kind of group. Also, we present sample session plans later in this chapter that should give you a good idea of how to plan for the bulk of the session.

Discussion and Education Groups   Planning a discussion or education group session requires the leader to first decide what topics or information to cover, then the order of presentation, and then how the topics should be covered. Additionally, the well-prepared leader will estimate as accurately as possible the amount of time needed for each topic or activity.

A leader has many options for covering a topic. She can give a mini–lecture. She can introduce the topic for discussion and have the members discuss it as a group or in pairs. She can invite a guest speaker or show a DVD. (If a speaker is invited, the leader should inform the speaker of the cultural diversity in the group.) She can use one or more exercises.

Task Groups   The planning of a task group depends primarily on its purpose. It is always the leader's responsibility to make each session relevant and productive. Topics and exercises may be useful for some task groups. For example, in a group meeting to improve communications between management and workers, the leader can plan various exercises that help members understand their own communication patterns and style. In a group deciding policies for a new treatment unit, certain exercises might be useful if the group has trouble focusing on the task; the leader can conduct a brainstorming activity or have the group break into two or three smaller discussion groups. *Planning increases the chances that the time will be well spent and the group will be productive.*

Support Groups   In some support groups, members come eager to share their common concerns—whether it be drugs, divorce, weight problems, or their disability; therefore, little planning is needed. In other support groups, the leader may have to provide topics or exercises that encourage members to share. For instance, in a group for veterans with disabilities, the leader might introduce topics such as how members' disabilities affect family relationships, what the hardest times are, or how to handle stress. In a group for spouses of people with Alzheimer's disease, the leader may introduce topics such as accepting the illness, getting some relief time, or dealing with the loss of the partner as a companion. The important thing to remember in planning a support group is to introduce relevant topics that vary from week to week. If the members are constantly bringing up new and relevant topics, very little planning will be necessary.

Growth or Experiential Groups   Because the purpose of growth and experiential groups is to explore some aspect of one's personality, values, or interaction style, it is the leader's responsibility to plan meaningful activities. The leader should plan to focus on either a number of topics or a specific topic and decide whether the group should focus on individuals or on the whole membership. Although the leader will plan each session, either the group or the leader may decide the topics.

The leader needs to consider the various group dynamics and therapeutic forces when planning. For instance, if the trust level is low, it would be inadvisable for the leader to plan activities that deal with in-depth personal sharing. He might rather plan trust-building activities. If the group consists of a couple of members who tend to talk all the time, the leader could plan to use some movement exercises and then have members share what they learned or experienced. Also, the leader has to consider any multicultural issues when planning the middle phase of a growth group, because the group's purpose usually is to explore values and attitudes. For instance, in a group that is exploring relationships between men and women, the leader would need to be aware of the different cultural views among the members and allow extra time for discussion of those differences.

Some growth groups are designed to be intense, whereas others are not; it is very important that the leader understand this. The type of activities planned will most definitely affect the level of intensity. The leader needs to give thought as to how heavy or intense the group should be and how to structure the group so that it is maximally beneficial. School groups are not meant to be too heavy, whereas residential treatment groups may get very intense.

Counseling and Therapy Groups   The planning of counseling and therapy groups varies greatly. Some require almost no planning because the members are ready, willing, and eager to share their concerns. In other groups, members are in pain, but they need exercises and other activities to encourage them to share. In therapy groups that require planning, the leader will want to consider any multicultural issues that need attention and topics that have yet to be covered. The skilled leader sometimes will choose to cover certain topics, hoping to help one or two specific members. For instance, a leader who knows that a few group members are having trouble dealing with anger may plan an exercise that focuses on anger.

The Closing Phase

Planning the closing phase is crucial; a common mistake is to fail to plan adequately for this phase. Some leaders mistakenly let the clock announce the ending; that is, when the designated time to stop comes around, the group ends. One colleague reported to us that her school group for at risk students was missing something, but she could not quite put her finger on the issue that was holding the group back. As we processed her group, we found out that she was allowing the lunch bell ring to signal the end of the group. When the bell sounded, the students immediately headed for the door. This is problematic. The leader should always allow 3 to 10 minutes for summarizing and processing the session. Leaders should give extra thought to planning the ending of the first and last sessions of any group. Having each person comment on what she has learned or what stood out is a good plan for the closing phase. Other closing activities include discussing briefly the topic for the next session, having members discuss in dyads what they learned, or having each member commit out loud about doing something different during the week.

Sample Session Plans

This section contains sample plans for sessions in different kinds of groups. Note that an estimated time is given for each activity to help the leader gauge the flow of the group. This helps greatly during the session because, otherwise, the leader has little idea whether too much time is being spent on a topic. It is important to allot specific amounts of time for exercises and activities but also to realize *the plan can and often will need to change as the session progresses*. The purpose of planning is to help organize a session in a logical sequence.

As you read through the sample plans, you may see unfamiliar terms. Because our purpose here is to give you an idea of how to plan a session, it is not necessary that you completely understand each activity; these activities are explained in later chapters. We tried to include a variety of techniques and activities to show the many different ways to plan a session. After each plan is a discussion of its features.

We also want to make a couple of comments about the times in the margin. We believe that it is a good policy to put the times there as a guide for the leader so she has a sense of how the time is being utilized. Students at first think we are being rigid about putting the times in a plan, but they quickly see that it does help them. When actually leading, the time notations help a leader gauge if he is on schedule. If not on schedule, then he will decide if he wants to try to return to times in the plan. The leader decides this by determining if what is happening in the group is equal to or better than what he had planned. The plan and the times are a guide and should be seen only as that—they are not meant to take away any spontaneity from the group that is valuable and in line with the purpose of the group.

Plan 1

The first session of a parenting group consisting of 10 members:

3 min. (7:00 P.M.)	Introductions—round (name, ages of children, why they came to the group).
5 min.	Discuss the group—format, purpose. (Stress that it is mainly an educational and support group and not a therapy group.) Have members share their needs and any fears or questions about the group. Have them share cultural differences. (Sandwich in the group rules of confidentiality, attendance, no attacking of others.)
2 min.	Sentence completion: The thing I like most about being a parent is _____. The hardest thing about parenting is _____. I get most upset as a parent when _____.
10 min.	Have members share these in large group. (Use their examples in discussion below.)
15 min.	Discuss Adlerian principles of child behavior. (Use charts and handouts.) All behavior is purposeful. Children are not bad—they are discouraged. Four goals of misbehavior.
5 min. (7:35)	Have members share in triads their thoughts about the Adlerian principles.
10 min.	Discuss in large group, then continue overview of principles: Parent's reaction to each of the four goals of misbehavior.
20 min.	Focus on the first goal of misbehavior—attention getting. Use short role-plays to demonstrate. Discuss ways to deal with situations.
5 min.	Dyads—discuss this goal in relation to their children and how parents may handle situations differently.
5 min.	Process dyads.
10 min.	Summarize—what stood out, feelings about the group, one thing they plan to do differently. Hand out reading material. Remind them of next meeting time.

In this plan, the introductory exercise is brief because it is an education group lasting only an hour and a half. Also, the leader knows that the members will be interacting in dyads and triads during the sessions, so they will have those opportunities to get to know each other better. The introductions and discussion about the group are useful because they allow members to share some important information and to mention their fears and expectations regarding the group. The plan also includes looking at cultural differences, because that may be a factor in a parenting group. The purpose of the group and the format are clarified during the first 10 minutes. Group rules are minimal, so no specific time is established to review them; they will probably be mentioned during the first few segments. The sentence completion used early in the session gives members a chance to share their views on parenting. The use of sentence stems helps members get more comfortable and "warms them up." The large-group processing allows the leader and other members to hear each member's concerns. In discussing the Adlerian principles, the leader can use examples from the processing of the sentence-completion exercise and discussion. The leader chooses to use triads to process the discussion of the principles. Using triads instead of the entire group to discuss some topics enables members to talk more; and often in the early sessions, some members are more comfortable sharing in dyads or triads than in the large group.

The leader varies the format to keep members interested. Also, the leader's plan includes some interesting and immediately useful content that is relevant to the group's purpose. Too often, leaders mistakenly plan first sessions that have very little content; thus, some members do not return. Plan 1 has a good balance between content and process. Because it is the first session, more time than usual is allowed for the summary. Ordinarily, the summary would take 3 to 6 minutes. Remember, time periods are approximate but are necessary to give the leader some idea of how long to stay on any activity.

Plan 2

The second session of a growth and support group for fourth- and fifth-graders who don't seem to make friends easily; there is one new member this week:

5 min.	Introduce new member to the group—have members tell their names and what they remember about last week. Comment about the group and its purpose. Also, remind members when they talk to look at others instead of the leader.
2 min.	Have members list things they can do to make friends.
3 min.	Discuss lists in dyads.
15 min.	List ideas on chalkboard. Discuss the ideas. Role-play some of the ideas. Have each member practice.
3 min.	Have each member tell one thing he or she will try this week.
2 min.	Summarize—each member completes "One thing I learned..."

In this plan, the leader uses welcoming a new member as a way to review last week's session. The opening segment is short because the session lasts only 30 minutes. Next, the leader uses a written exercise because this is a good way to get the children focused and involved. For the middle phase of the session, the leader has thought of several interesting ways to focus on making friends. The use of dyads helps achieve one purpose of the session, which is learning how to interact with others. Dyads enable members to practice talking with other children. To close the session, the leader plans a simple but focused ending—having members commit to trying something new and asking them to comment on what they learned in the session.

Plan 3

The third session of a 6-week assertiveness-training group with eight members:

10 min. (4:00 P.M.)	Progress reports, observations from the week, questions.
20 min.	Reenact some "assertiveness" situations from the week (this could last longer if there are a number of situations).
5 min.	Dyads—process thoughts from the reenactments.
15 min. (4:35)	Present the "broken record" technique: Demonstrate. Practice.
5 min.	Reactions, comments, and questions.
15 min.	Round: How guilty do you feel when you are being assertive? (1–10; 10 = very much) Discuss their numbers and how not to feel guilty—teach REBT. Show ABC model. Write on board their irrational self-talk and then rational self-talk.
5 min. (5:10)	Dyads: Discuss the use of REBT when being assertive.
10 min.	Entire group discussion: Things I plan to try this week regarding being assertive.
5 min.	Summary: What stood out for you today? Any wishes for anyone in the group?

Progress reports are helpful both for the member who shares and for the rest of the members who hear how others are using what they learn in the group. Also, progress reports help members see the continuity and flow of the group experience. Plan 3 includes a review, the introduction of new material, and periods of focus on the past, present, and future. The plan uses a varied format that includes a round, dyads, teaching, demonstrating, practicing, interacting, and committing to trying new behaviors during the coming week. The leader also introduces a theory that members can use during the rest of the sessions. In closing, the leader asks the "wishes for anyone" question so that members can say encouraging things to each other and feel the support of other members; this helps build cohesion in the group.

Plan 4

The third session of a weekly therapy group for outpatients of a mental-health center; the group has six members:

5 min. (4:00 P.M.)	Progress reports—ask about Bob's visit with his mother, Ruth's exercise program, Tandy's contract to talk with two people each day.
5 min.	Ask for thoughts, comments, reactions to the week.
10 min.	Review Ellis's ABC model—use examples from their week.
60 min.	Personal work—do yes/no round of who wants to bring something up; if all no's, use backup plan—focus on love relationships: Rate love relationship on a scale of 1 to 10 (10 = great).
	Ask what keeps it from being a 10 (discussion and personal work should come out of this).
20 min. (5:20)	Introduce TA model if it did not come up during the personal work, or continue the personal work.
10 min.	Share (in triads) reactions to TA model.
5 min.	Summarize—"What stood out?" "How will you use REBT and TA?"
5 min.	Write in journals (journals are left for the leader to read).

In this plan, the leader starts by having specific members report on some of the work they have done in group. This fosters continuity; also, when members know they are going to report to the group, they seem to commit a bit more to making changes due to the feeling of having to report back. The leader asks about the week to see whether anyone has something to share. This allows members to share positive or negative things that happened. Personal work could be started here, but the leader wants to spend a few minutes reviewing the REBT model and uses the members' comments about the week to show how REBT can be helpful. The review is brief because the leader wants to allow enough time for individual work. In therapy groups, members often come wanting to talk about some concern. The round (an exercise where everyone comments) helps the leader quickly learn how many members have something to discuss. The leader has allowed for an hour or more for personal work if members are so inclined. The leader is anticipating that many of the members will say yes to having things to work on, but has a back-up plan just in case.

Frequent Mistakes in Planning

We close this chapter outlining some typical mistakes leaders make in planning.

Not Planning

The biggest mistake made in planning is not doing it. Very often, at the end of work-shops that we give, group leaders comment that they now realize that problems with their groups stem mostly from not planning. Unfortunately, some professionals still subscribe to the notion that planning detracts from the group. It is very important to understand this is not true. Good planning is the best way to ensure that the session will be valuable to the group members.

Planning Too Much

The opposite of not planning is planning too many activities for the session. Having too many activities planned often results in superficial coverage of several important topics. It is better to cover a few topics in depth than to skim over several. Our students frequently make this mistake because they are afraid members will not talk, so they plan too many topics for the time period allowed. It is good to have backup plans and additional topics, but it is important for the leader to allow time in his plan to focus on topics long enough that new learning and impact occur.

Irrelevant or Meaningless Content

Too often, leaders choose activities, exercises, or topics that do not interest the members or relate to the purpose of the group. Leaders sometimes use introductory exercises that are irrelevant and, thus, fail to set the appropriate tone, or they conduct activities that are not related to the members' concerns. Leaders also introduce topics that relate to only one or two members; this causes the others to lose interest or become resentful. It is absolutely essential that the leader do everything possible to ensure that the session will be relevant and valuable to most or all of the members. The following are examples of *poor* planning.

- For the first session of a weight-loss group, the leader plans 30 minutes on the topic of organic gardening.
- In a group of eight teenagers, the leader plans to focus on how to select the right college to attend, even though only two members are planning to go to college.
- For a 1-hour session for stepparents, the leader plans a 15-minute mini-lecture on society and the family.
- In a group for couples with marital problems, the leader plans 30 minutes on dealing with children. Only two of the five couples have children.

GROUP COUNSELING SKILLS

In segment 1.1, the leader planned an opening round of asking members to state their favorite color, which would have been meaningless in this group. This segment is an example of planning meaningless activities.

Not Allowing Enough Time for the Group to Have Any Significant Meaning

It is important to realize that the purpose of the group is for members to learn something, gain some personal insights, or accomplish a designated task. Too often, plans do not allow time for the group to go to a deep enough level. A good plan will include exercises and activities that obviously allow members to gain meaningful experiences from the group sessions.

Inappropriate Exercises

Leaders will sometimes plan an exercise for which members are not ready. For example, during a first or second session, members usually are not ready for an exercise that involves sharing about sexual concerns, nor are they ready for certain kinds of feedback exercises.

Too Many Exercises

Another mistake leaders make is to plan too many exercises for a given session. This prevents members from having enough time to process and learn from the exercises, thereby robbing them of much of the value of the exercises. Also, the session will seem like a series of exercises rather than a group where members can share and exchange reactions, feelings, and thoughts. Inexperienced leaders are especially prone to this error, perhaps because they do not fully understand the purpose of the exercise and how to process it, or they fear that members won't have things to say.

Poor Planning of Time

Leaders often plan too much time for activities such as rounds or written exercises. Although the actual exercise usually takes only 1–2 minutes, beginning leaders plan for 5 minutes or more. The processing of these activities may take 10–20 minutes. The flip side of this is also a common mistake—allowing too much time for an activity like a dyad. Some students in sample plans put in a 10- or 15-minute dyad, which is usually far too long. Most dyads are 3–5 minutes. It is important to consider the appropriate time for any activities or exercises. With experience, planning the amount of time for different activities becomes easier.

Poor Planning of the Flow of the Session

A good plan has a reasonable order or flow. Some leaders forget this and plan topics or exercises that are not related to each other. For example, a leader would not want to conduct an exercise that focuses on fun followed by one that focuses on death. Also, leaders sometimes arrange the topics or exercises in a sequence that makes them less beneficial than they could be. For instance, it is a mistake for the leader to plan an exercise where members are providing personal feedback to each other, followed by a discussion of how members see themselves. Rather, the order should be reversed, because it would benefit members more to consider how they see themselves before hearing feedback from others.

Not Planning an Interesting Beginning

Some leaders fail to plan interesting warm-up phases. This is a mistake especially for groups run in institutions—such as prisons or mental hospitals—where members tend to be negative. It can be a mistake to plan a few minutes for opening comments, because members will often offer some complaint about the institution or the program. Leaders will want to plan interesting openings that do not allow negative comments to surface at the beginning. The leader might even establish that the last few minutes of each session will be available for members to air their complaints.

Allowing Too Much Time for Warm-Up

A common mistake is planning warm-up or introductory activities that last too long. These exercises, although important, can drastically reduce time available for more meaningful, productive work in the middle part of the session. It is *imperative* that the leader plan the group so that the most time is spent on the most important issues. Allowing as much as 15 to 20 minutes for warm-up is usually a mistake, because most people want to move on to new material. It is very important to make sure that the opening is productive and not so long as to bore the members.

Not Allowing Enough Time for Warm-Up

When leaders have much to cover in a session, they sometimes forget to plan for the warm-up phase. Members usually need some time to get focused, which is the purpose of the first few minutes of any group. Groups will vary as to how much time is needed for the beginning phase of the session, but it is important that the leader allot whatever time is needed. In the next chapter, we discuss the warm-up phase in detail.

Vague Plans

Many beginning leaders plan their groups too vaguely to be of much help. For instance, the leader might plan to deal with the subject of anger and allow 45 minutes for the topic, but neglect to plan in detail how to introduce the topic and what exercises and activities to use. The leader who plans well plans how she is going to cover the topic and also gives thought to possible spin-off subjects, such as anger at parents, self-talk and anger, and ways to deal with anger.

Lack of Flexibility

Some leaders rigidly follow their plan even when members have raised issues that are more meaningful and appropriate than those planned. Other leaders fail to recognize when their plan is not working. *It is necessary to be flexible and deviate from a plan whenever it becomes clear that members are not benefiting from it.* Imagine the toll in group commitment and interest in the following scenario.

■ EXAMPLE

The leader has planned two activities to improve family communication for a group of teenagers who live together in a detention center. The members tell the leader how angry they are at two of the residents who are not in the group. Their anger is due to a stealing and lying incident. Rather than changing the plan and focusing on their immediate needs, the leader forces the members to try the communication-skills activities. They listlessly role-play their mothers and fathers.

■ ▨ ■

GROUP COUNSELING SKILLS

View again segment 2.1 where the leader was flexible, in that he had planned to do an exercise but shifted to focusing on group dynamics. Being flexible is essential.

Concluding Comments

Planning consists of two parts—pregroup planning and session planning. Pregroup planning deals with such things as the kind of group, when it meets, how long it meets, and who the members should be. Screening is very important and can be accomplished in a number of ways, including personal interview, written forms, or referral from others.

A leader should plan the beginning, middle, and ending phases of any particular session. Planning should include not only the activities and topics, but also the time to be devoted to each. There are many different things to consider when planning each phase of a session. Common mistakes regarding planning are not planning, planning too much, not considering how time is allotted, planning too many exercises, and not being flexible. Remember that, although we emphasize the importance of having a plan, the effective leader is never a slave to that plan. If a valuable new topic emerges during a session, the leader should more than likely alter the plan; conversely, if the plan is not working, the leader should abandon it and use a backup plan. The effective leader is always adjusting the plan during the session.

■ **ACTIVITIES**

1. Write up plans for at least two group sessions using the format of the sample plans. Also write up a brief rationale for why you planned what you did (similar to the paragraphs that followed each of the four sample plans). Leave the plans for a day or two and then review them and see if they need changing. Often they require changes because you see things that don't exactly flow or fit or the designated times are not right.
2. Pick a group that you may lead, plan how many sessions that group will meet, and list all the topics that may be covered during the life of that group.
3. Go back to the plans you wrote and reread the list of common mistakes (p. 81–85) and see if you made any. We feel that reviewing the common mistakes will help you avoid bad planning.
4. With two or three of your classmates or colleagues, decide on a kind of group to plan such as team building for a sports team, a crisis group after a suicide, or a group on dealing with the holidays. Then have each of you write a plan for the session. Then get together with two or three others who planned the same group and compare the plans. This will help you to see that there are many ways to approach a group session and some are better than others. If you do this a few times, you will get much better at planning due to hearing all the different ideas from others.

GROUP COUNSELING SKILLS

1. Review video segments 1.1. and 1.2.
    a. Did the leader have a plan in segment 1.1?
    b. Did the leader have a plan for segment 1.2?
    c. How did the plan help in the overall development of the group?
2. Review video segments 2.1 and 2.2. Note how the leader was flexible with his plan. In other words, he had a plan, but something emerged that said he should alter the plan.
3. If you have watched the entire DVD, think back on some of the obvious segments where the leader was following a plan (7.1—the leader used fuses; 8.6—the leader used sentence completion; 10.1—the leader used Styrofoam cups; 10.3—the leader used common reading; and 13.3—the leader used WDEP).

Chapter 5

Getting Started: The Beginning Stage and Beginning Phase

The First Session

The first and second sessions of any group are often the most important and usually are the most difficult to lead. The first session is difficult because the leader has many different dynamics and logistics to manage: starting the group, introducing the members, introducing the content to the members, and monitoring the members' reactions both to being in the group and to the content. We discuss 19 different concepts to consider in the first session.

1. Beginning the group
2. Helping members get acquainted
3. Setting a positive tone
4. Clarifying the purpose of the group
5. Explaining the leader's role
6. Explaining how the group will be conducted
7. Helping members verbalize expectations
8. Drawing out members
9. Using exercises
10. Checking out the comfort levels of the members
11. Explaining group rules
12. Explaining any special terms that will be used

13. Assessing members' interaction styles
14. Being sensitive to multicultural/diversity issues and any dynamics that may be present
15. Focusing on the content
16. Cutting off members
17. Addressing questions
18. Getting members to look at other members
19. Closing the first session

Beginning the Group

One of the most important considerations for the first session is how to begin the group. How the leader opens the session will have an important bearing on the tone of the group and the comfort level of the members. The leader should convey warmth, trust, helpfulness, understanding, and positive regard. This is the time when members form their impressions of the leader and assess whether or not they think the group is going to be helpful to them.

Unfortunately, members sometimes quit groups that could be helpful because the opening few minutes were boring or intimidating and they tuned out the leader. Others may be put off if the leader inappropriately uses a formal, businesslike manner in the opening moments. For some groups, a formal or firm opening is appropriate, but for most groups, it is less effective. Some leaders make the mistake of opening with a mini-lecture and discussion on issues such as the rules, the meeting time for each session, and the frequency of meetings. When 10 or 15 minutes are spent discussing these issues, many members are bored. Another common mistake is allowing the introduction of members to take too long. Some beginning leaders are afraid to cut off members, so they politely let each member go on for 3 or 4 minutes—this makes for a boring opening for most groups. Remember, the opening few minutes of a first session are very important!

Following are eight possible openings that include an overview of the group and the introduction of members.

Options for Opening the First Session   1. *Start with a brief statement about the group; then conduct an introduction exercise.* This type of opening is perhaps the one most frequently used. The leader gives a brief (1- to 2-minute), well-thought-out opening statement and then has the members participate in an introduction exercise. This prevents members from settling into a "listening" frame of mind; they become active almost immediately and quickly feel that they are participants in a group rather than listeners in a class. This opening is especially useful for groups where the members do not know each other.

■ EXAMPLE

The group is for teenagers whose parents have divorced or separated in the last 4 months.

LEADER: I'm really glad you are here. As you know, this group is for sharing thoughts, feelings, and reactions to your parents' divorce or separation. It is my understanding that each of you has experienced your parents either divorcing or separating within the last 4 months. Through this group, I hope you will realize that you're not the only one feeling the way you do. Having your parents split up causes all kinds of feelings—chances are many of you are having a variety of those feelings. We'll explore them in this group. To get started, I thought we'd do an introductory exercise to learn about each other. I am going to ask each of you to share your name, how long your parents have been divorced or separated, and with whom you are currently living. We'll go around the group. Who wants to start?

TED: I will. I am Ted. My parents are definitely going to divorce or at least I think so. Last week—

LEADER: *(Using a caring voice)* Ted, let me interrupt. For now, just share how long they've been separated and with whom you are living.

TED: Sorry. I am Ted, and I am living with my mom. They separated 4 weeks ago.

MELINDA: I am Melinda . . .

■ ■ ■

2. *Start with a long opening statement about the group and its purpose; then conduct an introduction exercise.* This type of opening is often used for education or task groups, although some leaders use a long opening statement for therapy and growth groups as well. The leader will spend the first 3 to 5 minutes describing the purpose and format of the group in a pleasant, energetic manner, and then he will present an overview of the planned content for another couple of minutes. During this opening, the leader will usually give some background information about himself and his experience in leading groups. A practical reason for using a long opening is to capture the interest of the members who are present when other members have not yet arrived. It is important to understand that a long opening statement must be interesting and informative for the members. If it is boring, the leader can lose the members for the entire session. Leaders should be careful not to bore members with too lengthy an opening. On numerous occasions, we have heard of leaders who talked for 10 to 15 minutes at the beginning—this would be a major mistake.

■ **EXAMPLE**

The group consists of teachers in a large school district. It is the first session in a series of four on teacher burnout.

LEADER: I'd like us to begin. I am Sarah Daniels. I am a counselor at North High School. Over the last several years, I have been studying teacher burnout. As a result of my studies, I have developed what I think is a helpful way of understanding burnout. Over the next 4 weeks, I will be going over the material. Briefly, I'd like to share what each session will be about. Today we will start by . . .
After going over the material for 2 or 3 minutes, the leader concludes the opening statement.

LEADER: I hope you now have an idea of what will take place here and how this group can help. Now, before getting started with definitions of burnout, I'd like to take a couple of minutes and let you introduce yourselves. I'd like each of you to tell us your name, how long you have been teaching, what you teach, and a sentence or two about why you came.

■ ■ ■

3. *Start with a long opening statement; then get right into the content of the group.* This opening can be used in discussion, education, and task groups where the members already know each other or in groups where personal sharing will be minimal. A long opening statement is used when the leader feels the members need an explanation or clarification of the group's content or purpose. The long opening statement would be similar to that in Option 2 above, where the leader outlines the content and shares some information about himself. It differs from Option 2 in that the leader does not plan an introduction of the members because the members know each other or because the group is too large.

■ **EXAMPLE**

The group is for helping 14 unemployed people find jobs. The leader opens the session.

LEADER: I am glad you decided to attend the group. I think you will find the information helpful in getting you back into the workforce. The goal of these group sessions will be to give you information about finding potential jobs, interviewing for jobs, filling out applications, and keeping a positive attitude while looking. Before we get started, I want to tell you a little about myself and about each of the five sessions. . . .
(After going over the proposed content of the five sessions, the leader continues.)

LEADER: Now, let's get started on today's material. We're going to discuss how to find potential jobs. I want each of you to think of three ways that you go about looking for work and then list those on a sheet of paper.

■ ■ ■

4. *Start with a brief statement about the group; then get into the content.* This opening would be used when no introductions are needed (members already know each other) and the purpose of the group is already clear to the members. This is a good opening for many discussion, education, and task groups, especially if they are meeting for a short period, such as an hour.

■ **EXAMPLE**

The group's purpose is to decide on policies for a new treatment unit for adolescents. The leader begins.

LEADER: Let's get started. We have a number of policies to decide on regarding the new unit. The current plan is to meet each Tuesday for an hour and a half at this time for the next 4 weeks or until we feel we are finished. Why don't we begin by listing the kinds of policies we think need to be written? I'll write them as you call them out.

■ ■ ■

5. *Start with a brief statement about the group; then have the members form dyads.* Leaders can use this opening when no introduction exercise is necessary. The leader describes the group briefly and then has members form dyads to discuss either the content of the group or why they have come to the group. This kind of opening is useful when the purpose is already clear to everyone and the members are reasonably comfortable being in the group. It is also useful in certain kinds of task, education, discussion, and support groups.

■ **EXAMPLE**

This is a group for students who are thinking about dropping out of school.

LEADER: I am so glad that you all agreed to come to this group. I am hoping that all of you will benefit from some aspect of our group and hopefully you will find support here for whatever decision you make about school. It is, after all, one of the most important decisions you will make in your life. Let's do this, because you all know each other, I would like for you to pair up with a partner and just share with them what you are currently thinking about in terms of dropping out of school or staying. Share how you are feeling about the thought of dropping out and what your feelings are about staying in school. Also talk about what you would like to gain from attending group.

■ ■ ■

6. *Start with a brief statement about the group; then have members fill out a short sentence-completion form.* When no introductions are needed, using a sentence-completion form is an excellent way to open certain kinds of groups because it

tends to help members focus. This kind of opening is helpful in leading task groups, discussion groups, and some education groups. It can also be used in growth and therapy groups when the members already know one another.

■ EXAMPLE

The group's purpose is to improve staff relations in a hospital unit.

LEADER: As you know, the purpose of this meeting is to improve working relations within the unit. I'd like to start by having you fill out this form, which consists of five incomplete sentences.

■ ■ ■

7. *Start with an introduction exercise.* Starting with an introduction exercise instead of a statement about the group should be done only when the members have a clear idea of the group's purpose. If an appropriate introduction exercise is used, this type of opening can serve a dual purpose: Members can introduce themselves and begin immediately to focus on the content of the group.

■ EXAMPLE

This is a support group for single fathers.

LEADER: Why don't we begin? As a way of starting, I'd like each of you to introduce yourself and tell us the age of your child or children and in two or three sentences how you came to be a single father. Who wants to go first?

■ ■ ■

8. *Start with an unusual opening—one that grabs the members.* There are times when the leader may want to use a creative beginning to get the members' attention, especially if the leader believes that members may not be committed to being in the group. These openings can be interesting and can set a good tone for the session. We have purposely been a little late and harried to start a group on the topic of time management. We have staged a brief, heated verbal exchange before the group began when we were going to teach communications. After the "fight," we get members to talk about what they saw and felt and then introduce the idea of people coming from different ego-states. Then we would do the more formal introduction about the group, rules, names, and so on. The point is that leaders may want to use a creative opening to get members' attention and hook their interest.

These examples illustrate that there are a variety of appropriate ways to open a first session. *Remember, the right kind of opening, combined with enthusiasm on the part of the leader, will have a strong positive effect on how a group starts.*

Helping Members Get Acquainted

In a first session, the leader will want to consider how members will be introduced to one another. If members do not know each other, it is usually beneficial to have them get acquainted soon after the session begins. Members tend to feel more at ease after learning each others' names and spending some time getting to know each other.

The amount of time spent on introductions varies according to the purpose. In groups where personal sharing will take place, more time should be spent helping members get to know one another because members are curious about those with whom they will be discussing personal issues. In most education and discussion groups and in many task groups, only a minimal amount of time needs to be spent on introductions because members either know one another or will not be discussing personal issues. In groups consisting of members from diverse cultural backgrounds, more time will probably be needed for introductions and getting acquainted.

The size of the group can limit the options for the kind of introduction exercise chosen. If the group has more than 10 members, the leader will probably not want to use an introduction exercise involving each member sharing about himself or herself for 1 to 2 minutes because it would take too long. When groups are meeting for a rather short period (an hour or less), the leader will not want to use any introduction exercise that lasts more than 5 minutes. This applies especially to education, discussion, and task groups, and to groups meeting for only one session.

The purpose of the group is probably the most important factor in determining what kind of introduction exercise to use. With groups meeting for educational or discussion purposes, the leader may want to use an exercise that helps people remember names. In growth, task, support, and therapy groups, the leader may choose an exercise that gets members to share relevant information about themselves. The leader may also have members share their reasons for attending the group or their expectations of the session. For instance, it would not be relevant for a leader of a group for cancer patients to have an introduction activity where the members share their names, the names of their family members, where they work, and their favorite hobby. Instead, the leader could have the members state their names, how long they have been receiving treatment, and one fear or feeling about having the disease.

The following are descriptions of several introduction activities.

The Name Round   The name round is probably the most frequently used exercise for learning people's names. In the name round, members simply introduce themselves, sometimes giving names only, but most of the time sharing additional information. Naturally, what is shared will depend on the purpose of the group. For instance, in a parenting group, the leader would have members state the number of children they have and their ages and maybe one concern they want to address in the group; in a changing families group for children, members could tell how long their parents have been divorced, with whom they live, and maybe a word or phrase regarding how they feel about their parents' divorce.

One common mistake of beginning leaders is to have members share irrelevant information. We have heard stories of members being asked to introduce themselves and tell various irrelevant things about themselves. Most members of serious groups are not interested in "cute" openings. A "fun" introduction activity is appropriate for certain kinds of groups (school or church retreats, social groups for the elderly), but it is a mistake to use a light introduction exercise for groups that have a serious purpose—for example, groups dealing with such issues as abuse, addiction, AIDS, anger, or rape. Another mistake is to let members share for too long, thus turning the introduction of members into a 15- to 20-minute activity that tends to get boring.

The Repeat Round   The repeat round is a name exercise where the first member says her name, the next member says the first member's name and then his name, and so on. This exercise is good for helping members remember everyone's name. School kids tend to like this, and it does help with learning the names.

The Introduction Dyad   This activity consists of two members pairing up and telling each other certain things about themselves, usually based on suggestions from the leader. Then all the members come back together in a group, and each one introduces his partner to the group. For example, in a group for children who have trouble making friends, a member might say, "This is Carlos. He likes football and fishing. He has two younger stepbrothers. His favorite subject in school is math." With this exercise, members focus on listening and getting to know one other member better.

The Repeated Dyad   Members pair up with every other member and spend 2 to 5 minutes sharing such things as why they are in the group and what they hope to gain. (This is good for certain kinds of support, growth, and therapy groups.) This exercise should be used only when there are fewer than seven members and the session is at least an hour and a half long; otherwise, it would take too much time to allow each member to form a dyad with every other member.

Milling   For large groups (12 or more members), we sometimes have members mill around and meet each other during the first 4 to 5 minutes of the first group session. The instructions are usually quite simple, such as, "To help you get acquainted, I'd like you to stand up and mill about the room meeting the other group members. Try to learn everyone's name and why he or she is here." A simple activity like this provides an opportunity for members to have contact with one another and speeds up the process of getting acquainted. This is especially good when the leader is waiting for a couple of members to arrive and the others are sitting quietly by themselves.

These are just some of the ways a leader can help members get acquainted. It is important that the leader always consider how introductions are going to be handled. A good introduction exercise is one that is appropriate for the kind of group and the amount of time the group is meeting. *Using large name tags is probably the easiest way to help members remember the names of other members.*

Setting a Positive Tone

Another important task for the leader during the first and second sessions is to establish a positive tone for the group. The tone is the prevailing atmosphere; it stems from several sources, including the leader's enthusiasm and the members' comfort and trust. The leader can establish a positive tone by being enthusiastic and drawing out members, cutting off hostile or negative interactions, holding the focus on interesting topics, and shifting the focus when the topics are irrelevant or only interesting to a couple of members.

It is very important that the leader not let the group focus on negative members or negative issues for a major portion of the first session. A member who is complaining about being in the group or questioning its value can establish a negative tone that may be difficult to alter. Allowing extended hostile or heated interaction between members also contributes to a negative tone. Certainly some time may have to be devoted to these dynamics, but the leader will want to make sure that most of the time is spent sharing and discussing in a positive way. If a negative tone is set during the first two group sessions, members will usually never come to trust one another enough to share personal information about themselves. They may feel that the group is a place to "nail" other members, causing them to either focus on others or fear being attacked by the group.

Setting a good tone for nonvoluntary groups is very important. Leaders of nonvoluntary groups need to be prepared for uncooperative and hostile members who may try to set a negative tone for the group. Also, the leader may need to be rather firm but also show concern and understanding. When leading a nonvoluntary group, the leader will want to have an opening that gets the members' attention and gets them interested immediately. One group leader we know put a garbage can in the center of a group for teenagers who had been caught using alcohol at school and said something like, "I know you don't want to be here, so I want you to get all your complaints out now and then we'll put a lid on them. You have 10 minutes to complain." At the end of that 10 minutes, she stopped them, put the lid on the trash can, and said, "Let's name our group," which ended up being called "The Beach Group"; and they were nowhere near a beach! This got the group off to an interesting start and got members involved and curious. She also made it clear she was in charge.

A good leader gives much thought to the tone he wants to set. Below are some Dos and Don'ts for setting the tone.

Do

> Get everyone to share
>
> Be enthusiastic
>
> Be warm and inviting
>
> Be creative for nonvoluntary groups
>
> Get control early and let people see you are in charge and you know what you are doing

Don't

Let the group focus on negative issues at the beginning of the session

Let one member dominate

Start with boring group rules

Let members attack each other

Come across as authoritarian or demanding

GROUP COUNSELING SKILLS: How to Conduct a First Session

Go to segments on How to Conduct a First Session (5.1, 5.2, 5.3). Watch a discussion and three demonstrations of beginning a group. You will see three different leaders use a variety of techniques for beginning a first session. Pay careful attention to how they set the tone, help members get acquainted, and how they get briefly into the content or purpose of the group. Note in segment 5.2 how the leader covers some leadership skills and confidentiality in the first minute, but does it in a way that is not boring.

Clarifying the Purpose

The leader wants to be sure that the purpose of the group is clarified during the first and second sessions. Clarification is particularly important if there has been no screening interview. Even if the leader has screened the members and has already spent time discussing the group's purpose, it is still a good idea to review the purpose in the group. The purpose of some groups may require more clarification than others. In a group that has been advertised as a smoking-cessation group, the purpose is probably clear to all members; on the other hand, a divorce group could be intended for support or therapy. Therefore, the specific purpose of the group will have to be clarified during the first session.

For any group where the purpose may be confusing, it is a good idea to reiterate the purpose throughout the first two sessions. After the second session, it usually is not necessary to review the purpose unless new members are added to the group or the purpose changes during the life of the group.

GROUP COUNSELING SKILLS: Clarifying the Purpose in First Sessions

Review segments 3.2 and 3.3 to see how the leader clarifies the purpose of the group to the members.

Explaining the Leader's Role

During the first session, the leader should explain what her role will be throughout the sessions: a teaching role, a facilitative role, an active leadership role, a therapeutic role, or some of each. Offering an explanation helps members form a picture of what to expect from the leader.

■ EXAMPLES

EXAMPLE 1 LEADER: Let me take just a minute to explain my role to all of you. As you know, for the next 6 weeks, we will be meeting every Monday evening so that you can share your experience as a single parent. My role in this group will be to facilitate sharing and provide some information. On some occasions, the situation may call for me to become more active and lead the group in counseling a member who is asking the group for some help.

EXAMPLE 2 LEADER: In this group, I mainly will help you share any problems you are having here at school, at home, or with your friends. I will make sure that this is a safe place to share any concerns you have and will help you learn how to problem solve. I will encourage you to share and will ask you to do some different kinds of group exercises that will help you focus on different areas of your life, such as problems with parents, peer pressure, or problems with schoolwork.

EXAMPLE 3 LEADER: In this group, I will introduce you to the dangers of alcohol and drug use. To do this, I will present some information and then get you to share reactions, thoughts, and questions. I will mostly be trying to get you to express your thoughts and concerns and will not be teaching like a teacher does where all you have to do is sit and listen. This is meant to be a group for sharing so I will be asking all of you to participate.

EXAMPLE 4 LEADER: My role in this group is to see to it you make the decisions that need to be made. My participation will be minimal; that is, I will not offer my opinion or ideas because I do not work here and do not know your agency as well as you do. I will encourage you to be open and honest with each other, and I will try to get you to express how you feel about the issues. Also, I will try to structure the time wisely so we can accomplish something each time we meet.

■ ■ ■

Explaining How the Group Will Be Conducted

Closely aligned to explaining the purpose and the leader's role is explaining what will happen during a session. Leaders should clarify during the first session how they plan to conduct the group. The leader will help ease tension and ensure the smooth functioning of the group if she describes the kinds of discussions and activities that will take place in the group. If there is a specific format for the group, the leader would want to explain this.

■ EXAMPLE

LEADER: Each session we will spend the first few minutes sharing comments or any relevant experiences since our last meeting. We'll then focus on anything that one of you wants to talk about. If no one has anything for that day, we'll focus on a new topic. We'll split our time between discussing different concerns you have and topics that we decide we want to cover. We'll always spend the last few minutes sharing what we got out of the session and offering encouragement to each other.

■ ■ ■

In certain kinds of groups, the leader will want to inform members that they will be asked to do certain group exercises and that, at times, the group may get rather intense. Also, he may want to explain how he intends to work with individuals who bring up concerns they want to work on. Hearing this explanation during the first and second sessions will give members a much clearer understanding of what will take place in the group.

A good reason for stating what will happen in the group is that, after hearing a description, some members may decide they do not want to be in the group. If a member decides to leave the group, the leader will want to determine the reason. Depending on the reason, the leader may or may not encourage the member to stay. That is, the leader would not want to urge a member to stay who definitely wanted a different kind of group, but she might try to encourage a member who feared that something bad might happen to him in the group. Usually the discussion with the member wanting to quit is done in private, but sometimes the leader may see the value of discussing it with the entire group.

Included in the discussion of how the group will be conducted should also be a discussion of the potential risks involved in being in a support, growth, counseling, or therapy group because groups can present life-changing experiences. The ASGW *Guidelines for Best Practice* (2008) specifies that leaders are responsible for explaining and discussing the risks of being in a group. Members need to know they may discover uncomfortable things about themselves or their pasts. Also, they need to be informed that they will be challenged to look at how they see themselves, how they cope, and how they interact with others.

Helping Members Verbalize Expectations

One first-session activity that is beneficial for certain kinds of groups is to have members share their expectations of the group. In this way, the leader learns what the members want, and he can further clarify the purpose of the group by commenting. At times, the leader will expand upon some of the expectations voiced if they are in line with the purpose. At other times, the leader will need to point out that certain expectations will not be met by the current group because of its structure and purpose.

■ EXAMPLE

This group is for teenage girls who have had a baby in the last 3 months. The leader has just finished an introduction exercise and decides to use a round to get members to verbalize their expectations. Note also how the leader comments on some of the expectations as they apply to the group.

LEADER: Okay, now that we know a little more about each other, I want to talk about your expectations for the group. I want you each to think of what you are hoping to get from the group. We'll go around and hear from each of you.

ANGELA: I just look forward to talking to kids my own age about having a baby. Talking to grown-ups all the time isn't fun.

LEADER: Certainly one of the main reasons for the group is just that—all of you will get a chance to share with one another, and you do have things in common, that's for sure.

DONNA: I am overwhelmed. Trying to handle the baby, school, my boyfriend, friends! I don't know if I can do it, and I hope to get some ideas.

LEADER: I think all of you will find that the group can really be of help. I think each one of us has some ideas that can help others, and that's the benefit of the six of us meeting.

NELDA: I came because it sounded like something I could learn from.

TANDY: I need help with my baby! I am scared that I will screw up my kid, and I don't want to do that.

LEADER: We will spend some time each week talking about child rearing because I think each of you probably wants to hear about that.

■ ■ ■

Sometimes members attend a first session having expectations that are not in line with the purpose of the group. If this situation arises, the leader will want to reiterate the purpose. If a member remains insistent that the purpose should be different, the leader may have members get into pairs and discuss why they came or some other relevant question while the leader pairs up with the insistent member—this avoids a long discussion or debate in front of the group that may create a negative tone.

■ EXAMPLES

In this first example, the member has an expectation that is not in line with the group's purpose, which is to help first-year college students with study skills. The students are expressing their expectations.

BUD: I want to learn how to prepare for essay exams. My high school was such a breeze, and all my tests were fill-in-the-blank or multiple choice.

AKIRA: I need help with my math problems—I don't understand equations, and the instructor said I should get a tutor, so when I saw the announcement about a study skills group, I thought I would give it a try.

LEADER: Well, Akira, let me clarify something for you and for others. This group is not really for tutoring as much as it is for teaching you how to study. That is, we will not work on any specific course but we will talk about how to study for certain courses, including math. I guess what I am saying is that, if any of you are looking for specific help in a course, then probably a tutor would be better. We are going to talk about how to take notes, how to prepare for exams, and basically how to study. Akira, now that you are here, you may want to stay, or you may really just be looking for math help. If you want a tutor, I'll help you with that after the group today.

■ ■ ■

In this example, one member's expectations are different from the others'. The purpose of the group is for parents to discuss what to do about the many teen pregnancies in the community. Members are discussing their views of the goal of the group.

CARLA: I think it's good that we are meeting. I don't want my daughter to become pregnant, but I don't know the best way to prevent it. So I am hoping that as a group we can come up with some good ideas for educating our kids about sex.

BETSY: That's why I came—to try to come up with something that either the school or community can do.

DOT: I can tell you what we have to do, and that's to stop these kids from having abortions! They gave some statistics about teenage abortions on television that horrified me. I am here to see to it that the school does something about all these abortions!

LEADER: I really don't see this group as focusing on abortions. The purpose of this group is to decide how to prevent so many from getting pregnant.

DOT: I can't buy that. It is our moral duty to stop kids from even considering abortion!

LEADER: *(In a very calm voice)* Let's do this: I want you to pair up with someone you don't know very well and discuss what you think are the different topics that we need to discuss in this group. Dot, I'll be with you.

The leader could tell that Dot was not going to let the issue die, and he did not want the group to focus on a side issue. By using dyads, the leader was able to keep members focused while talking to Dot about the purpose. The leader would want to be careful not to spend the next half hour trying to convince Dot of the purpose. He probably should not spend more than 5 minutes if for no other reason than the other members will likely run out of things to say. This is a situation where the leader might ask Dot to leave if she insists on talking about the abortion issue.

■ ■ ■

A leader can make several mistakes regarding the expectations of the members. Some leaders spend as much as half or three-fourths of a session on the question, "What do you hope to get from this group?" This usually happens when expectations are varied and the leader feels obligated to discuss each one. Probably no more than 8 or 10 minutes should be spent on expectations, and often they can be covered in 5 minutes or less. *A very common mistake leaders make is to ask members for their expectations when they really don't have any.* This can be the case in groups where the members are required to attend or are attending in order to avoid some other activity, such as class or work. The leader may want to ask about expectations but should be prepared for little or no response—or responses that are not in line with the purpose.

■ EXAMPLE

This is a mandatory group at a 30-day juvenile crisis center.

LEADER: I'd like to hear from each of you about why you are in the group and what you hope to gain from it.

DON: Hey, man, I don't want anything—they made me come.

ALTON: There's nothing the matter with me—I hate this group therapy crap!

LEADER: This isn't crap. Hopefully, it will be helpful.

MEL: I want to talk about rock music—the houseparent said we can talk about anything.

LEADER: Come on, be serious. What can you get from this group?

The leader should not have mentioned expectations or should have expected some negative reactions because the members did not volunteer for the group. The leader did not second-guess that there probably would not be many expectations. A better way to handle this would be to mention if anyone had expectations and then quickly move to an interesting exercise rather than pushing the idea of expectations.

■ ■ ■

Drawing Out Members During the First Session

It is advisable that the leader, during the first and second sessions, makes sure that everyone has a chance to contribute. The leader should not force each member to speak; rather, members should feel they may participate if they so desire. If the members believe they haven't had an opportunity to verbalize their thoughts, feelings, or ideas, they may feel left out.

During the first session of a growth, counseling, therapy, or support group, the leader should, if at all possible, get each member to share something because this tends to reduce anxiety about being in the group. It is also important because members are usually curious about each other, and disclosures usually help members feel more comfortable. Be aware, however, that some members will be so uncomfortable or fearful that they will not share very much during the first meeting.

Two of the best ways to get members to share during the first session are the use of written exercises and rounds. Introduction rounds, other rounds, and some written exercises usually will get each member to comment. Written exercises, such as sentence completions or lists, are excellent activities because members usually will feel fairly comfortable when asked to share what they have written. Rounds are good because every member is asked to respond in a word, phrase, or number to some question such as, "On a 1–10 scale, with 10 being very comfortable, how comfortable are you being here in group?"

Use of Exercises During the First Session

During the first session, certain exercises can be used to create comfort, interest, and member involvement. We discuss three exercises below: rounds, dyads, and sentence completions.

1. *Rounds* are the most valuable exercise that we use in the first session because they get everyone to speak, which is important. Earlier in this chapter, we mentioned the *name round*. Other rounds are 1–10 scales on some issue or feeling, such as level of comfort in the group, commitment to being in the group, how it feels to work in a certain occupation, or how much stress members feel in their lives. Rounds can be used during the beginning, middle, and closing phases of the session; the possibilities are endless. We cover rounds in-depth in Chapter 9.

GROUP COUNSELING SKILLS: How to Use Rounds in First Sessions

In each of the three segments showing the beginning of a group (5.1, 5.2 and 5.3) the leaders used rounds in various ways to get members to share information about themselves. You may want to review these segments again and pay attention to how the leader used rounds to facilitate discussion.

2. *Dyads* (pairs) are very valuable in the beginning stage of groups because they give members the opportunity to talk more personally with one other member, creating a more comfortable atmosphere and often energizing them for talking in front of the whole group. Members can be paired with one another to discuss their reactions, feelings, ideas, answers, or some other relevant point. Common mistakes with the use of dyads include letting them last too long or doing too many in one session. Dyads rarely should last more than 5 minutes because long dyads do not allow members to have contact with others, and the leader cannot be sure how members are going to connect because they don't know each other. A member may feel annoyed or intimidated by his or her partner and thus conclude that the group is not helpful.

Any leader deciding to use dyads must first consider whether the members will have something meaningful to say. That is, in nonvoluntary groups, groups where the purpose is confusing, or groups with young children and teenagers, the members may have little to say, so using dyads may be less beneficial.

3. *Sentence-completion exercises* have also proved very helpful in facilitating interaction during the first session. This kind of written exercise gives members a base from which to comment. Also, members are usually very interested in hearing how others responded to the same incomplete sentence. The following are examples of sentence stems that could be used.

In a new group, I feel most comfortable when _____.

In a new group, I am most afraid of _____.

In a new group, I will usually _____.

For a group on stress:

The biggest stress for me at work is _____.

The biggest stress for me at home is _____.

One way I cope with stress is _____.

For a group of elementary school children whose parents are divorced:

The hardest thing about my parents' divorce is _____.

The person I blame the most for the divorce is _____.

When I think of my parents' divorce, I am most angry about _____.

These are just a few examples of exercises that may be helpful during the first session. Certainly other exercises—written, experiential, or verbal—are beneficial. The leader should always keep in mind when selecting exercises for the first session that their purpose is usually to help members get acquainted and feel comfortable or to focus on the content in a meaningful but not too intense way. Some leaders make the mistake of presenting one exercise right after another, which does not leave much time for interaction or for processing the exercises, and it gives the members the impression that the group is about doing exercises rather than interaction and sharing.

GROUP COUNSELING SKILLS: Use of Sentence Completion in a First Session

View again segment 5.3 and watch how the leader uses a sentence completion exercise to get members talking about their lives.

Checking Out the Comfort Level

Feeling apprehensive or uncomfortable during the first session of a support, growth, counseling, or therapy group is quite common. To help reduce this discomfort, the leader might spend a few minutes focused on the topic of comfort level. By inquiring about members' comfort levels, the leader lets members know he is aware that there may be some anxiety and that it is to be expected. In addition, hearing that others are anxious often eases members' anxiety by showing them they are not alone. The leader may want to introduce the topic of comfort during the warm-up phase—that is, within the first half-hour—if members seem extremely uncomfortable. If the leader does not discuss comfort in the beginning, he can introduce it almost any time throughout the session by saying something like, "Let's focus for a few minutes on the topic of comfort in this group," then using any of the following:

- In terms of comfort in the group right now, what is the word or phrase that best describes how you are feeling?

- On a 1–10 scale, with 10 being very uncomfortable and 1 being very comfortable, how would you rate how you are feeling in the group right now?

- On a 1–10 scale, with 10 being very uncomfortable and 1 being very comfortable, how would you rate how you were feeling in the group when we started, and how would you rate how you're feeling now?

- Does anyone want to comment on how he or she is feeling about being in this group?

- I'd like you to pair up with a person whom you would like to get to know better and talk about how you feel about being in the group. Discuss your comfort level and why you feel the way you do. Naturally, some of you are more comfortable than others. You'll have about 3 minutes to do this; then we'll come back to the large group for discussion.

Any of these activities will help members talk about the comfort level in the group. Such discussions often help members feel more comfortable, both through sharing their feelings and hearing that others feel some discomfort. The leader also gains a better idea of the source of discomfort. The leader may choose not to draw out those who rate themselves as very uncomfortable because focusing on them could make them more so. The leader will want to make sure that he does nothing to increase the group's discomfort level at this point.

Explaining Group Rules

There are a number of things to consider regarding rules for the group: what the rules should be, who makes the rules, when to discuss them, and how to discuss them.

What should the rules be?   All groups have rules about attendance; tardiness; being reasonably cooperative and sensitive to others; one person talking at a time; and eating, smoking, and drinking during the session. Most counseling, therapy, support, and growth groups have rules about attacking others, putting others on the spot, and keeping shared personal disclosures confidential.

Who makes the rules?   In most cases the leader makes the rules because the leader understands groups and what rules need to be in place for the group to be successful. Sometimes, the leader uses the deciding of the rules as a group discussion activity. This can be a mistake because certain rules may be deemed unimportant by members. This can also take up valuable time that could be spent on the actual purpose of the group.

When should the rules be discussed?   It is usually preferable to cover group rules as needed rather than opening up with a speech or discussion about them. For some groups, presenting them at the very beginning may be fine (especially for some elementary and middle school groups). However, counselors leading groups with this age need to be sensitive to starting the group with the rules. They run the risk of having group feel like a classroom or the leader being viewed the same as the teachers in the building. It is important if the rules are introduced at the beginning that members not become bored or anxious for something to happen. Also, presenting the rules right at the beginning can set a negative tone if not done in a warm, positive manner.

 GROUP COUNSELING SKILLS

View again segment 5.2 and watch how the leader uses his voice to set a positive tone even while going over a couple of group rules. Also note how he did not spend too much time on the rules and moved on rather quickly to the purpose of the group.

How should the rules be discussed?   Any presentation or discussion of rules for the group should be done in a pleasant, positive manner. Rules regarding such things as no eating, drinking, or smoking during group sessions; attendance; and no attacking of others or putting others on the spot can be briefly discussed because they are rules that the leader has decided upon. Rules about the confidentiality of the information shared among members need more attention because it is very important that everyone understands what it means and that everyone agrees to keep things confidential. The leader will want to get some acknowledgment from each person that he or she agrees to keep material confidential. It should be noted however that confidentiality in groups cannot be guaranteed. The leader should emphasize the importance of confidentiality, and members do need to be aware of this risk.

The following examples show when and how to "sandwich" in the rules and how to focus on confidentiality.

■   E X A M P L E S

It is 30 minutes into the first session of a therapy group.

JAKE: I want to hear what David thinks. He hasn't said anything about his problems.

LEADER: Let me jump in here. I know that some of you may want to hear from other members, but one rule that I have in groups that I lead is that no one will be forced to talk. So, rather than putting David on the spot, you might say that you are curious about what others are thinking. The reason for this rule is that I want people not to have to worry about being attacked or singled out. Any comments on this? *(Lets a few seconds pass)* Let's go back to sharing concerns you are currently working on.

In this example, the leader saw the need to mention a rule and stated it in a natural manner. He also spared David by shifting the focus from him to the rule and then back to the topic. Introducing rules when they are relevant helps members remember them better.

■ ■ ■

This group is in the first half-hour, and the members are discussing fears about being in the group. They are using a sentence-completion form containing a sentence that reads "One thing I am afraid of in groups is _____."

BETH: I wrote that I am afraid of looking foolish.

LEADER: That is a very common feeling. I would imagine that others feel the same way. *(Several heads nod)*

FERN: I wrote that I am afraid of being attacked by other members for something that I say.

LEADER: I want to comment on that. I'd like to establish a rule that no one is allowed to attack another member. We are here to listen and learn from each other, not to attack those who differ from us. How do all of you feel about having that as a rule?

The leader asks the question to hold the focus on "no member will be allowed to attack another member" because she feels it is a very important issue for the group.

■ ■ ■

It is early in the middle phase of the first session, and a member says he has something he would like to bring up. It is obvious that what he is going to say is very personal, and he is the first member actually to say that he wants to talk about a concern. Up to now, members have shared only "safe" things about themselves.

JOHN: I think I want to share something that happened here at the plant that I have never told anyone.

LEADER: John, before you do I want to mention something very important. In the beginning, we discussed briefly that we should keep things confidential. I want to emphasize that rule because John obviously is about to share something important and personal to him. It is imperative that we keep the content of these group meetings confidential if there is to be a feeling of trust. Is this suitable to everyone? *(Looks around the room)* I am going to ask each of you if you agree to keep things confidential. Chico?

CHICO: Yes.

CARLOS: Yes.

ABDUL: Yes.

THOMAS: I agree.

LEADER: Okay, John, let's get back to what you wanted to share.

■ ■ ■

In regard to rules, our point is that the leader should not spend an inordinate amount of time on the rules unless there is some reason to do so. If a member tries to argue about a rule that the leader feels is necessary, the leader should calmly explain why it is important for the smooth running of the group. Sometimes, it is best simply to say what the rules are and why they exist rather than opening them up for discussion. For example, if a leader decides that there will be no smoking or eating during the group, she can tell the group the reason.

LEADER: Because the room is small and some of us are nonsmokers, there will be no smoking during the session. If you feel you have to smoke, you may excuse yourself for a couple of minutes. Also, I'm going to ask you not to eat or drink during the session because it can be distracting.

■ ■ ■

A common mistake made by beginning leaders is to discuss issues like the preceding ones for 10 to 20 minutes. This is usually not necessary and detracts from the purpose of the group. In many kinds of groups, it is appropriate and helpful for the leader to decide the rules and inform the group of what they are.

Explaining Terms

If the leader plans to use special terms, she should explain them to the members. Some terms that might confuse members are *rounds, dyads,* and *exercises.* If the group is a counseling, therapy, support, or growth group, the leader will want to explain the terms she might be using, such as *private logic, REBT, TA, ego states,* or *alter ego.* The leader could explain the terms when she is explaining her role or at any other time that seems appropriate, such as the first time they naturally occur. Explaining terms and procedures in the first or second session reduces the chances of confusion or misunderstanding when they are used in later sessions.

Assessing Members' Interaction Styles

During the first session, the leader will want to note the different ways that members interact in the group. This is extremely helpful for leading the session and planning for future sessions. Every member has a certain style or manner. Some members may be very quiet; others may try to dominate; others may be supportive; and still others may be very critical. By observing these styles, the leader will be able to adjust the plan for the session. Any leader who fails to assess the interaction style of members will make the task of leading much more difficult.

Leaders assess interaction styles through paying attention to what members say, how they say it, and how often they say anything. Too often, a beginning leader will get caught up in the content of the group and fail to observe that not all members are participating or that certain members are dominating.

Being Sensitive to Multicultural/Diversity Issues
and Any Dynamics That May Be Present

Diversity is a double-edged sword. The cultural, ethnic, and gender differences among members mean that there are also potential differences in values, perceptions, and communication styles. These differences can create misunderstandings among group members. For example, in many world cultures, adherence to ethnic or cultural group norms is more highly valued than are individual pursuits and desires. Thus, the simple act of speaking out in disagreement may be a near impossibility for some group members, say from Mexico, China, or Japan. Other major cultural differences that can affect group dynamics include:

- Perceptions and reactions to authority
- The extent to which intimate emotions are revealed
- The manner in which status is afforded
- The manner in which trust is developed
- The importance of time (past, present, or future emphasis)
- Locus of control (internal or external)

On the other hand, these differences, though potentially problematic, are sources of great strength and learning. It is through these very differences that group members may learn to cope in a multicultural world and to transfer new skills that were previously unattainable. Therefore, while sensitivity to differences is important—and clearly the right thing to do—it is important to keep in mind that learning to utilize (for the sake of effective group dynamics) different values and perceptions translates to both personal, group, and, in some cases, organizational effectiveness.

During the first session, the leader should be keenly aware of cultural, gender, ethnic, and sexual orientation differences. She should be tuned into whether any of the differences seem to be causing any kind of dynamics that need to be addressed either during the group or after the group. Comments about the differences can be beneficial for setting a positive tone. For instance, the group leader may say something like:

LEADER: One of the major benefits of groups is that there are a number of different people with different ideas and different views from yours. I think this group has a great mix of people and I think this should make the group rich since everyone can learn from others. Some of you may even be uncomfortable with the differences, but I do believe that in the end you'll find that having people here that are different from you will be very beneficial. Anyone want to comment about how they are feeling regarding the makeup of the group?

Comments like this can open the group up for discussion of differences. During such a discussion, the leader should listen carefully in order to get a sense of the open- or closed-mindedness of the members. If, in the first or second session, the leader hears judgmental or prejudiced comments, she may want to comment on how the group is made up of different people living different lifestyles and that one of the things that she will do as the leader is to make sure there is no "bashing" of anyone's beliefs or lifestyle.

Cutting Off Members During the First Session

It is very important during the first session to not let a member dominate or attack other members. If the leader does not restrain those members, others will feel intimidated or upset because they did not have a chance to contribute. The leader has to be prepared to use cutting-off skills. Sometime during the first session, the leader should explain that he will at times be interrupting members.

LEADER: Something that I may do from time to time is interrupt if I feel you are off on a tangent or others want to speak. Two of my tasks are to keep us focused on the purpose of the group and to give everyone a chance to talk.

Cutting off is an essential skill for group leading and a leader must be prepared to refocus any member who is being very negative or hostile or who is trying to dominate or focus the group on some irrelevant tangent. We devote most of Chapter 8 to how and when to cut off members.

 GROUP COUNSELING SKILLS: How to Conduct a First Session

View again segment 5.2. Watch how the leader explains how he may have to cut off members. Note his very warm, positive tone.

Focusing on the Content

In this book, *content* means the topic being discussed in the group. All groups have a content area. Some groups are very specific—such as assertiveness, coping with divorce, or study skills; other groups are less specific, such as personal problems or personal growth. The leader will want to be sure to focus some of the first session on the content or purpose of the group. Devoting too much time in the first session to explaining rules, making introductions, getting acquainted, and explaining the leadership role will cause members to become bored and lose interest because their needs are not being met. To focus members on the content, the leader can use an introduction exercise that causes them to think about why they came to the group, as in the following example. As the round ends, the leader focuses on content by commenting or asking a question based on something that was said in the round.

■ EXAMPLES

It is the first session of a group of battered women. The leader has briefly discussed the purpose of the group and has had each of the five women introduce herself and tell a little about her situation. The introduction round is on the next-to-last person.

JANE: I'm Jane. I have been married for 4 years. I have two children. My husband has beaten me five times, and each time has been worse than the others. He says it is my fault—I'm confused about whether it is my fault.

DIANE: I'm Diane. My husband verbally and physically abuses me daily. I have been in counseling, but I always seem to let him sweet-talk me into going back with him.

LEADER: Diane, that's a good topic that we will discuss later. I was thinking that for now a good theme to talk about may be the one that Jane and a number of others alluded to about being confused about whose fault it is. I know many women often do think it is their fault that their partner gets so out of control. What thoughts or feelings do any of you have about whether you think it is your fault?

In this example, the leader focuses the group on an important topic that everyone has feelings about. The discussion could last for 10 to 20 minutes and probably would be very helpful because it is a topic that is definitely relevant for all the members.

■ ■ ■

The purpose of this group is to provide help for students who are close to being expelled from school and are concerned about it. The members are discussing their expectations of the group.

BARRY: I hope that people here can help me stay out of trouble. I really want to stay in school—I like being with my friends.

LEADER: I think what Barry is saying applies to all of you—that you want to stay in school. Is that right? *(Sees all the heads nodding)* Let's talk then about what it's going to take to stay out of trouble. What do you need to do to keep yourself out of trouble? Who wants to comment on that?

RICO: I will. I realize that I have got to . . . *(A valuable discussion follows for the next 10 minutes about all the things that can help them stay out of trouble: doing schoolwork, not talking during class, not fighting, hanging out with different friends, and attending the group.)*

LEADER: A while back, we were going over expectations and took off on what Barry said. Does anyone else have an expectation for this group that hasn't been discussed?

MARTHA: I do. I hope that the group can be a place where I can learn to say, "no!" I really need to learn this.

LEADER: That's a good thing to learn, and I think we can talk about that in here. How many of you also have trouble saying "no"? *(Looks around)* Seems like quite a few. We have about 15 minutes left; let's talk about that for a few minutes. I'd like you to think about who is the hardest person for you to say "no" to. We'll go around the group and get each of you to comment. Your friends? Your siblings? Your parents?

■ ■ ■

In each of the preceding examples, the leader has skillfully focused the group on some interesting topics. Another way to move from the process to the content is to introduce an issue or present some information. In a task group, the leader might say, "Why don't we start by discussing the options that are available?" One other way to make the transition from process to content is to use a group exercise.

Addressing Questions

In the first session, members will sometimes have a wide variety of questions that they want answered. Some of their questions will pertain to the purpose of the group, others to the meeting time and place, the leader's credentials, and other details. A common mistake occurs when leaders do not anticipate these possible questions and fail to allot time for members to ask what they consider to be important questions. Answering questions is good, but it is very important that the leader does not allow the first session to become a question-and-answer session. It is also a leadership mistake to take a long time to answer a question that only one member is interested in. If the leader feels too much time is being spent on specific questions that are not relevant to all the members, she can offer to stay and answer additional questions when the session ends.

Getting Members to Look at Other Members

Often, members will speak mainly to the leader unless the leader encourages them to talk to the entire group. Getting members to look at other members is *absolutely essential* because it is helpful in involving members, building group cohesion, and creating an atmosphere of belonging. To get members to look at the entire group or to get them to avoid looking only at you, any or all of the following are appropriate:

- Tell your members you would like them to look at the group rather than exclusively at you when they are talking. You can explain this in the beginning or after someone has spoken directly to you. Ask the person talking and the rest of the members to look at everyone in the group.

- Explain to the members that you are not going to be looking at them all the time when they are speaking because at various times you will be scanning the group. You can also tell them to let your scanning serve as a signal to them to address the entire group.

- Scan the group, because the talking member will tend to seek eye contact with someone; if you are scanning, the speaker will usually look elsewhere.

- Signal the member to talk to everyone by making a sweeping motion with your hand. A sweeping motion consists of bringing your right hand to your left shoulder and then bringing it slowly around until it is more or less pointing to your right.

■ EXAMPLES

Ten minutes into a first session.

LEADER: *(With a kind, gentle voice)* Let me comment on something that just happened and has been happening here during the first few moments of our session. Kim was mainly looking at me during the time she was talking about her problems with her son because I am the leader. Others have also been doing this. What I'd like you to do is to look at others when you talk instead of looking at me, because everyone is interested in what each of you has to say. You will also notice that when you are talking, I may be scanning the group. I will do this for three reasons: to see how others are reacting, to see who seems as if they want to speak, and also to remind you to look at others in the group. Anyone have questions about that?

KIM: I did notice you looking away at times and I was thinking you were being kind of rude. I am glad you clarified that.

LEADER: For some of you, it may take some getting used to, and I may even signal you with my hand to get you to look around.

■ ■ ■

It is the second session, and the leader remembered that the teenage members tended to talk to her only.

LEADER: Let's start. Remember, I will be scanning the room with my eyes. Do you recall what I told you last session about why I am doing this?

WILSON: You want us to look at everyone when we talk and not just you!

LEADER: That's right. Why else?

ROSS: You are not only listening to us when we talk but you are observing others' reactions.

LEADER: Good. So today, try real hard to look at everyone, and if you see me not looking at you when you are talking, take that as a signal to look around. Any comments or thoughts about our first session or observations during this week?

■ ■ ■

It should be mentioned that there will be times when the leader will want a member to address another member specifically. This occurs when a member has a question, concern, or feedback for a specific member. The leader may need to encourage the member to look at the member he is addressing.

Other First-Session Considerations

In many kinds of groups, the opportunity may arise during the first session to focus on one member's ideas, opinions, stories, or concerns. In certain education, discussion, and task groups, it is very appropriate to allow the focus to be held on one issue for an extended period of time. However, in most support, growth, counseling, and therapy groups, it is usually not a good idea to spend more than 10–15 minutes focused on one member. The purpose of the first session is to give members a chance to share their concerns and to get to know one another. Focusing on one member may cause others to feel left out. Another reason to be careful when focusing on a member during the first session is that members may not be ready for in-depth therapy during the first session.

Discussion of certain topics may be inappropriate for the first session. Beginning leaders can err by focusing on any topic that arises or focusing on issues that require more trust and comfort than is present in a first session. For instance, in a group for helping members find employment, the leader would not want to focus on how to present oneself during an interview but rather would probably want to focus the group on skills assessment or how to locate places of potential employment. How to interview is a good topic but should not be discussed until later. Other inappropriate topics for the first session of a growth or therapy group might be sexual issues or death. Usually the leader should wait at least two or three sessions before introducing topics such as these.

Closing the First Session

Closing the first session is similar to closing any other session except that the leader will want to allow more time to hear members' reactions and clear up any questions or other matters that need clarifying. Depending on the kind of group, the leader may want to ask some of the following questions during the closing phase of the first session.

- How was the session for you?
- How was being here different from what you thought was going to happen?
- What stood out to you?
- Was there anything that happened that you didn't understand or didn't like?
- Do you have questions about the group, its purpose, or what is going to happen?
- What did you learn from group today?

During the close of the first session, the leader will probably want to summarize the session and comment again on the purpose of the group and what the possibilities are for the future.

Evaluation of the First Session

After the end of the first session the leader should assess the success of the group. If the first session did not go smoothly, the leader will want to assess why. The following are possible reasons for an unsuccessful first session:

- Members were afraid to talk or share.
- Members were confused about the purpose of the group.
- The group was held at a bad time of day.
- Members came late and disrupted the group.
- Cultural or gender issues inhibited members from fully participating.

- The leader was unclear about the purpose of the group or the members' needs.
- The room was not conducive to groups.
- Members were forced to attend the group.
- Members reacted negatively to the leader.
- The session was not planned well.
- The focus moved from topic to topic too quickly.
- The focus was held on a person or topic too long.
- Too much or too little time was spent on warming up.

Much thought needs to go into planning a second session when the first session did not go well. It may be necessary to ask certain members not to return because they are not appropriate for the group. The leader may need to change the setting, meeting time, or content. Unfortunately, many beginning leaders do not take the time to fully understand why the group did not go well, and they go to the second session with no significant changes from the first session.

The Second Session

The leader continues setting the tone of the group during the second session, being aware that some members may still be uncomfortable. In addition, the leader needs to give thought to the following issues:

- Opening the second session
- Planning for a potential letdown
- Ending the second session

Opening the Second Session

Two important considerations for opening the second session are the introduction of new members and the evaluation of the first session's success.

Introducing New Members   If new members join the group, it is usually a good idea to begin with introductions. Several methods can be used. In the example below, the leader introduces the new member in a manner that gives that person an opportunity to hear what happened in the previous session as well as to get to know the names of other members. This type of introduction also serves as a review for the other members.

LEADER: This is Ralph. He was unable to make our meeting last week. I thought as a way to update Ralph, I'd ask you to share one or two things that stood out to you about what we discussed last week. Be sure to say your name, also.

This method can be combined with one that gives the new members a chance to share their own situations. For instance, at the beginning of a recovery group, the leader could say:

LEADER: As a review, I thought we'd start by having each of you share how your week was; and because Carol is new, you may want to comment on what was most helpful last week in the group. Also share your name.

At the end of this round, the leader could say something like:

LEADER: Carol, if you feel comfortable, you may want to share some of your story, or you may want to wait until later. It's up to you.

Certain kinds of groups will require no planning beyond having new members give their names and a little information about themselves.

■ EXAMPLE

LEADER: *(After asking members to get settled for the beginning of the group)* There are two new members joining us today. I have asked them to tell us their names and some relevant information about themselves.

MELVIN: My name is Melvin Conrad, and I'm glad to be here. I am new in town. My family moved here from New York.

LEADER: Okay, Melvin. *(Looks toward Rhonda)*

RHONDA: My name is Rhonda. I am here because I want to get over my fear of people, and my counselor said this was a good place to do that.

This is perhaps the simplest and briefest method of introducing new members. After the new members give a brief introduction, a round can be used where the other group members tell their names.

Another method of introduction is for the leader to tell the group about the new members. This can be done only if the leader has had the opportunity to meet with the new members before the session has begun. A leader might choose this approach: (1) to minimize the time spent on the introduction, (2) to tell the group something specific about the member that the member might not include in the self-introduction, or (3) to ease in a new member who is very anxious about speaking in front of the group. For example, if a new member is frightened, the leader might say:

LEADER: This is Ted. He's going to be joining the group. Ted told me that he was really apprehensive about coming today, so I told him that he would not have to say anything if he didn't want to. Let's start by talking about any thoughts or reactions to last week's session. What thoughts or feelings did you have about coming back the second time? I'd like each of you to share something and also state your name.

The amount of time spent introducing new members will often depend on the kind of group. In most counseling, therapy, growth, and support groups, an introduction activity of 5 minutes or less is all that is necessary for new members. During this time new members can tell the group their names and a little bit about why they are there, what their interests are, and what they hope to gain from being part of the group. In task, discussion, and education groups, merely having new members give their names may be sufficient.

When new members come to the second session, the leader must decide how much time should be spent informing them of what happened during the previous session. Informing new members of the events of the first session helps them adjust more quickly to the group; however, if there is a lot to explain, the leader should try to do so before the second session to prevent boring returning members with a lengthy recap of the first session.

■ ■ ■

The Success of the First Session　If the first session was reasonably successful and a positive tone was set, the leader will plan a brief warm-up and then move on to the content. On the other hand, if the first session did not go successfully, the leader may choose from three options: (1) restate the purpose of the group and make no attempt to verbalize any of the negative events of the first session; (2) address what went wrong in an effort to explain that future sessions will not be similar to the first one; or (3) elicit from members their reactions to the first session. By addressing what went wrong, the leader acknowledges that the first session was not a good one and can point out ways that the group can be better.

■ EXAMPLES

LEADER:　Okay, let's get started. I'm glad you are back. I thought our first session went fairly well and I truly believe each session will get better as we get to know each other. I'd like to start with this activity to get us all focused on why we are here and how this group can be helpful.

■ ■ ■

LEADER:　Okay, let's get started. I'd like to say something about the first session. When the group ended the other night, I was concerned that some of you may have left feeling discouraged. I realize that not enough people got to share because we focused so much on a couple of you. As we were wrapping up, I sensed that some of you felt a bit frustrated because you asked if every group was going to be like this and whether you would get a chance to talk. Let me assure you that not every group will be like the first one. All of you signed up to be in this group because you felt a need to get support and hear ideas from people who are struggling with the same issues that you are. I know that the group will be most beneficial if you share your thoughts and feelings concerning your common situations. I will make sure that the group does not focus on only one or two members unless the majority of you indicate a desire to do so.

■ ■ ■

Leader: I want to begin this session by getting your reaction to the last one. I feel that our first session was okay, but I do believe these next sessions can be better. Please share honestly any reactions or questions that you had about what we did here last time.

In this example, the leader gives the members a chance to react so that he can comment on their reactions in a positive, clarifying manner.

■ ■ ■

Our point is that the leader needs to consider the success of the first session when planning the second session. The leader will also want to remember that it is usually necessary and helpful to reiterate the purpose of the group during the second session. If the group did not go well, the leader will definitely need to plan to counteract the bad beginning. One leader we know decided to use name tags on the chairs to break up the cliques of eighth-grade girls. She knew she could have a good group, but the first session did not go well because of where the girls were sitting. She assigned seats for the next few sessions and had a very successful group.

It is also helpful, when possible, for the leader to arrive at the second session early and talk informally to members before the group begins. This provides some idea of how members reacted to the first session. It also gives the leader a chance to answer members' questions about the group and to get to know the members a little bit better.

Planning for the Potential Letdown

A skilled leader will anticipate a letdown during the second session. A common mistake of beginning leaders is to think that the excitement exhibited among members during the first session is always present in the second session. He often fails to anticipate that there may be a different energy for the second session. One reason for the change in the members' energy is that much of the first session is spent on members getting acquainted with each other, discussing why they are there, what their expectations are, and the format and rules for the group. Given these topics, first sessions can be filled with a lot of sharing and excitement. In the second session, the focus moves toward personal sharing, and members often experience anxiety about participating. They become hesitant to interact, thus causing a letdown, which can often be disconcerting to a beginning group leader. To help prevent the letdown, the leader can mention at the beginning of the second session that members may not feel as enthusiastic as the first time and may feel a little apprehensive. *The most important thing a leader can do to prevent the letdown is plan a good session based on what she learned from the first session.*

Ending the Second Session

The leader should plan to spend an extra few minutes ending the second session. During the closing phase, the leader will want to hear what the members perceive as being helpful and unhelpful. A round asking the members to describe their positive and negative reactions to the group is a very valuable closing activity.

■ EXAMPLES

LEADER: Let's take a few minutes to wind up the group. We're going to do a round in just a moment. I would like each of you to share what stands out to you the most about being in this group. In addition, if there is anything that you would like to see us do differently, please say so.

■ ■ ■

LEADER: I want to take some time to end the group today so that I can get some idea of how you are feeling about being in this group thus far. Think of how you would rate this group on a 1–10 scale. *(Leader explains the meaning of the scale)* If your rating is not a 10, think what it would take to move the group up to a 10.

■ ■ ■

In both of these examples, the leader would spend time discussing the various responses, clarifying anything that needed clarification, and answering any questions.

The Beginning Phase of Subsequent Sessions

We want to close this chapter by discussing the beginning phase of sessions after the initial two sessions. Every session has a beginning, or warm-up, phase and leaders should always consider how they are going to open each session. The leader has a number of options for beginning a session. Any of the options described below may be used, depending on the group's purpose and the members' need for warming up. As you will note, some of the options get right to the point, whereas others allow for sharing time, comments, or updates. Also, a leader may use more than one option during the warm-up phase of a session.

Education or Discussion Groups
- Before we get started on today's subject, does anyone have any questions or comments about last week or about the handout I gave you?
- Today, we are going to talk about _____. To get you thinking about the subject, I'd like you to do the following. . . .

- I'd like to talk for a few minutes about _____, and then we'll discuss your reactions, feelings, and thoughts.

- We're going to start with a 15-minute film. Afterward, we'll discuss any questions or reactions.

Task Groups

- Let's start with progress reports from each of you. Who wants to go first?

- Let me review briefly where we are and what seems to be the next thing we need to decide.

- Before we start, do any of you have something pertinent you want to share?

Growth or Support Groups

- How has the week been?

- Any reactions to the last session, progress reports, or updates?

- What would you like to talk about tonight—any particular topic or issue you would like to discuss?

- Let's start by thinking about the most significant thing that has happened to you since our last meeting. In a minute, we'll go around and let each of you share this. Who wants to go first? We'll hear from everyone.

Counseling or Therapy Groups

- Let's begin. Last session, a number of you talked about some very important personal issues. I think it would be good if you shared any reactions or thoughts you've had since then. We might do that for a few minutes and then move on to other people and topics.

- I want to start the group a little differently. I want each of you to think about whether you have something you would like to talk about. In a second, we'll go around the room. I'm going to have you simply say yes or no if there is something you would like to address or not. This is just a quick way to find out how many of you have something on your mind. I hope many of you will have something you want to discuss, but it is perfectly okay to say no.

- Why don't we start? First, does anyone have something they'd like to bring up?

- Let's start. What is a word or phrase that describes the week for you? Let's do a round starting with you, Roberta. You look like you're ready.

- Let's start. I was talking with Sammy out in the hall just now, and he said he had something that was really bothering him. I hope we can help. Sammy, you said you wanted to tell the group what happened when you saw your dad.

In the last example, the leader decided to stray from her planned opening because she realized that focusing on Sammy would be a good way to begin the group, plus Sammy had told the leader he wanted her to focus on him. The leader knew what Sammy had to work on was very relevant to the purpose and would take quite a bit of time. In this situation, the leader would want to proceed quickly and then see if others had any pressing concerns to discuss. Sometimes, skipping the warm-up phase can be a mistake (as discussed later in this chapter), but in this last example the leader made a good decision to skip it.

Creative Activities for the Beginning Phase

The leader must always be thinking about the warm-up phase and the best way to start the group. With school groups—especially elementary school groups—time is limited and the kids can be excited and wound up. In one school, this situation was handled in a very interesting and effective way. The group consisted of six very energetic, active sixth-grade girls. The leader had the members sit in a tight circle. She placed a garbage can in the center and had all the members lean in toward the garbage can and talk about what was on their minds, all at the same time. Every member talked feverishly into the trash can about whatever was bothering them. After a couple of minutes, the leader stopped them and "officially" started the group. This seemed to calm the members to start the session.

There are times when the leader may want to use a creative beginning to get the members' attention. Leaders can create a good, creative beginning phase of a session by having members draw something, such as their family on an outing, their earliest memory, or a group drawing where each person contributes. Other creative openings include a dramatic movie clip, a song, or a reading.

Mistakes During the Beginning Phase

Leaders sometimes make one of two mistakes regarding the beginning phase: (1) They let it go on too long by allowing the warm-up to stray from the purpose, or (2) they skip it and don't allow time for members to warm up. A good beginning phase gets members focused on topics or issues that are relevant to the purpose.

■ **EXAMPLES**

The group is meeting to work on anger control. This warm-up phase gets away from the leader.

LEADER: How was the week?

RICK: *(In a slow, storytelling voice)* Mine was very hectic. It started on Tuesday, no, it was Monday. I was walking to school on Jones Avenue and then I went by the site where they are building the new mall. They have the list of stores that are going to be in the mall. There is going to be a Wal-Mart, Sears, and a whole bunch of other neat stores. My mom and I went to the old Wal-Mart and I thought it was big. This one is going to be much bigger, or so my mom says. Anyhow when I turned on Jefferson Street there was a little dog on a leash just like my grandfather's dog. This started me thinking about my grandfather and how much I miss him. So when I got to school, I decided I would go by the office and call him. When I went to the office, I ran into Toni and Sara.

SHERRY: I know Toni and Sara. Sara is actually my second cousin. I spent last Thanksgiving with Sara. I think she is so cool. On Thanksgiving we . . .

ALISHA: I heard this Wal-Mart is going to be the biggest in the state! I like Wal-Mart because . . .

In this group, the warm-up phase could last a very long time, with members getting into stories and topics not relevant to the purpose of the group.

■ ■ ■

Here is the same group, but the leader gets the members back on track.

LEADER: How was the week? Anything come up that you think is relevant to what we have been talking about?

RICK: *(In a slow, storytelling voice)* Mine was very hectic. It started on Tuesday, no, it was Monday. I was walking to school on Jones Avenue and then I went by the site where they are building the new mall. They have the list of stores that are going to be in the mall.

LEADER: *(Knowing that Rick tends to tell long, irrelevant stories)* Rick, briefly what happened that relates to this group?

RICK: Oh, I was just going to tell a funny story about getting my books mixed up with Toni's. That's all.

LEADER: Anyone have something to discuss that fits with what we have been talking about?

HEIDI: I do. . . .

Note the leader's question at the beginning is a little more specific, and he quickly intervenes when it becomes evident that Rick is about to go into an irrelevant story. Often beginning leaders do not pay enough attention to the opening few minutes of a group; thus, the group gets off in the wrong direction and valuable time is wasted.

■ ■ ■

In the following example, the leader skips the warm-up. As we mentioned, it is usually a mistake to fail to allow a minute or so to hear if anyone has something relevant he wants to say.

LEADER: Let's begin.

TRISH: I start working at the cash register on Monday and I'm a little nervous.

DAN: I was nervous when I first had to work the cash register.

SKIP: I got in serious trouble at work this week when I ran the cash register.

LEADER: Trish, say some more about being nervous.

In this example, the leader starts working with Trish before hearing from the others who may have important concerns. The leader should hear more about the trouble Skip got into and from others.

■ ■ ■

Concluding Comments

The first and second sessions set the tone for the other sessions. One very important component of the first session is how the leader opens the session. The leader has many choices. During the first session, the leader needs to pay attention to both content (what the group is about) and process (the interactions, comfort level, attitudes of members, etc.). It is important that the leader not focus too long on one person during the first sessions. The leader wants to set a positive tone and make sure the group is interesting and engaging.

Rules, such as no put-downs or attacking other members, confidentiality, and attendance, need to be covered during the first session. Often, the best way to cover the rules is to let them emerge as the session unfolds. It is usually not necessary to spend much time on the rules.

In planning for the second session, the leader needs to be prepared for a potential letdown. If the first session did not go well, the leader will want to specifically prepare to counteract any negative reactions. Also, the leader often may want to spend extra time closing the first and second sessions to get reactions and answer questions.

The beginning phase of all sessions should be given considerable thought. There are a number of options for opening a session, plus the leader may want to use creative openings at times. The two most common mistakes during the beginning phase are letting the warm-up last too long or skipping the warm-up altogether. Leaders should always be aware of how they are going to start their groups.

■ ACTIVITIES

1. Think of four different groups. Plan the opening few minutes of each of them. Then go back and read the first few pages of this chapter and see if you have the best opening for the given group.
2. Think of at least two groups or classes where a good tone was set. What did the leader/teacher do to create that tone?

3. Think of at least two groups or classes where the tone was bad. What did the leader/teacher do to create that tone?
4. Think of two unique, creative openings of groups that you anticipate leading in your counseling career.

GROUP COUNSELING SKILLS

1. View again segment 5.1.
   a. What kind of tone would have been set if the leader had let the first member talk about her anti-war feelings?
   b. How did the leader help the male member feel comfortable?
2. View again segment 5.2.
   a. What did the leader do to set a very comfortable tone, even though he covered leadership concepts like the use of eyes and cutting off?
   b. How did the leader get members focused on the purpose?
3. View segment 5.3.
   a. How did the rounds help set a positive tone?
   b. Why was the sentence completion helpful?
   c. What were all the things the leader did to set a very positive tone?

Chapter 6

Basic Skills for Group Leaders

Throughout the first five chapters, we have referred to various leadership skills but have not discussed them in great detail. In the next few chapters, we describe specific skills that we feel are essential for good leading. If you have had some training in interviewing or counseling, you will recognize the names of some of these skills because they are basic human relationship skills.

Active listening   Tone setting

Reflection   Modeling and self-disclosure

Clarification and questioning   Use of eyes

Summarizing   Use of voice

Linking   Use of the leader's energy

Mini-lecturing and information giving   Identifying allies

Encouraging and supporting   Multicultural understanding

Active Listening

Active listening entails listening to the content, voice, and body language of the person speaking (Corey, Corey, & Corey, 2009). It also involves communicating to the person speaking that you are really listening. Most of you have probably been trained to listen on a one-to-one basis. Active listening as a group leader is a much more complex task because you listen to many people at one time. The skilled leader actually tries to listen to all the members at the same time and not just to the one who is talking. To the extent this is possible, the leader wants to be aware of what members are feeling and thinking even when they are not speaking. The main technique the leader uses for this is to scan the room for nonverbal gestures, especially facial expressions and body shifts. We hope you can appreciate the complexity of this skill. It is difficult to convey to the member who is speaking that you are really listening while you are, at the same time, listening to other members by picking up on their silent messages. We urge you to practice this skill whenever you are with a group of friends, family, or colleagues. See if you can take in more than just the content of the person who is talking: Try to pick up on what the others are thinking and feeling. Perhaps more than any other, this skill is essential for good group leadership; yet many students try to become skilled leaders without first becoming active listeners.

Reflection

In counseling, to reflect a comment is to restate it, conveying that you understand the content, the feeling behind it, or both. As a group leader, you will find it helpful and necessary to use the skill of reflecting both content and feeling. The purpose of reflecting is twofold: (1) to help the group member who is speaking become more aware of what he is saying, and (2) to communicate to him that you are aware of how he is feeling. As a group leader, you will use reflection at times with individual members, at times to reflect what two or more members may be saying about a topic or issue, and at times to reflect what the entire group is experiencing.

■ EXAMPLES

ALICIA: I'm not sure how I'll do here. I'm a little uncomfortable with all this, but I sure want to start making some changes in my life.

LEADER: Alicia, you seem to be feeling that the group is both an exciting and a scary experience for you at this point.

■ ■ ■

MARTIN: Looking for work is tough on me. I hate going into places and feeling like I've got to beg for anything they can give me.

RANDY: Yeah, that's how I feel about it. Some days I'd rather stay home. I dread the thought of having to face those pompous receptionists.

LEADER: You both seem to be saying that one of the hardest things in looking for work is having to deal with the feeling of being one down.

If the leader is on target with her reflection, it is likely that other members can relate to it. The leader may follow up her reflection with something like this: "I wonder if other people here are having similar feelings as they go out job hunting." In watching for responses, the leader may find that the reflection she has directed to two members has actually encouraged others to become aware of their similar feelings.

■ ■ ■

Anita, a member in a group of abused women, has been talking for 3 minutes about how she dislikes herself for having remained in an abusive situation. The members have been very attentive; and as Anita finishes, it is apparent that others are feeling strong emotions. The leader reflects what she believes to be the feelings of the entire group.

LEADER: From your reactions, I'd guess that most of you are in touch with what Anita is experiencing right now. Some of you may be having similar feelings about yourself.

■ ■ ■

In summary, the use of reflection with a single member, several members, or the entire group clarifies and deepens members' understanding and communicates that the leader is in tune with what is happening. One word of warning comes from Corey, Corey and Corey (2009), who state that "many neophyte group leaders find themselves confining most of their interactions to mere reflections" (p. 21). The warning is a good one, because, in many instances, the use of reflection does not cause members to delve more deeply into the discussion at hand.

Clarification and Questioning

Several authors have discussed clarification and questioning as necessary group leadership skills (Corey, Corey, & Corey, 2009; Posthuma, 2002; Trotzer, 2006). Often, the leader finds it necessary to help members clarify their statements. Clarification may be done for the benefit of the entire group or for the speaker's benefit—that is, to help the member become more aware of what he or she is trying to say. There are several techniques for clarification that you may find useful: questioning, restating, and using other members to clarify.

■ **EXAMPLES**

STAN: I don't think we should accept the proposal. It has too many hidden agendas.

LEADER: Stan, can you tell us a little more about what you mean by that?

Here the leader is attempting to clarify by gathering more information. He is using an open-ended question to encourage the member to clarify his statement.

■ ■ ■

ELLEN: There are times when I think I'm going crazy, and yet I know I'm just off balance because of my divorce. My mom says, "What about the kids?" Carla, my 8-year-old, was crying last night. It's my life, though! I have got to get out. I don't know how my husband will make it.

LEADER: Ellen, you've just said a lot. I'd like to try to clarify how you might be feeling at this point—do tell me if I am off base. There is a part of you that says this divorce is right, and then there is a part of you that says, "Maybe I'm being selfish." Perhaps the rest of you may want to ask yourselves if you have some conflicting views about some current issue of yours.

In this example, rather than questioning further, the leader has taken jumbled information presented by a member and used a statement to reorder it in an attempt to clarify the key issues. This clarification helps Ellen and the others become more aware of what can now be worked on. We cannot emphasize enough the importance of clarification. If a member's thoughts are vague, confusing, or incomplete—as they often are in moments of stress—the rest of the members may have difficulty understanding her. As a result, some members will lose interest, and their minds will start to wander.

■ ■ ■

DANNY: I want a dog, but my mom says no. I know it'd be good for me. She says I wouldn't take care of it—like the rabbit. But I was only 8 then, and I'm 11 now. I know I'd do better in school. I wish my mom wasn't so mean to me.

LEADER: Does anyone think they know how Danny is feeling about his mom and about having a pet?

SALLY: I think I do. Danny is lonely sometimes and feels like having a pet friend would help him. By having a dog, he would have someone to talk to and play with, and that would help him feel better. Then he would do better in school. He says he thinks his mom is mean, but I think he knows she's not—she just doesn't want to take care of the dog. She's probably like my mom and feels that kids are enough to take care of.

LEADER: That sounds right, Sally. Danny, how did it sound to you?

The method of using a member serves the dual purpose of clarifying what the member is saying and also involving other group members, thus generating interest and energy.

■ ■ ■

The leader has the responsibility of trying to maintain clear communication in the group. Confusing messages create frustration and drain group energy if they are not adequately clarified. Clarification is even more important when the group is made up of members from different cultures because the chance of misunderstanding is much greater.

Summarizing

The skill of summarizing is a must for all group leaders. Groups often generate material from a wide range of viewpoints. Because members are busy listening and sharing during the session, they often do not pick up on or remember many of the details. Therefore, thoughtful and concise summaries are very helpful to the members.

A summary is helpful when you have allowed a member to speak uninterrupted for several minutes. Without a summary, members may pick up on small or irrelevant points. The summary tightens the focus and allows the leader to stay with the issue or move on, depending on the needs of the particular member. A concise summary is also useful in making a transition from one topic to another. A summary is especially important if the discussion has been diffuse or has involved overlapping points or ideas. A good summary pulls together the major points and can serve to deepen or sharpen the focus.

LEADER: So far, we've been talking in general terms about changes we would like to make in our lives. Juan and Al both talked about job changes. Betty, you said you wanted to improve your relationship with your husband in some major ways. Someone said she wanted to go back to school. Margaret, I think that was you. A couple of other people wanted to be happier. Now, I would like each of you to take a minute to think about this change you want. *(Pause)*What is one thing you will have to give up to get what you want?

In this example, the summary serves to highlight each member's desire for change and sets the stage for the leader to deepen the focus. A summary can also be used at the opening of a session and is especially helpful if there is unfinished work from the last session or a strong interest on the part of the members to continue the topic. However, the summary should serve to focus the group on the current session rather than to encourage a rehash of the previous session.

LEADER: A lot happened last session. We talked mainly about prenatal care. Betsy talked about smoking and Jane talked about drugs, and they both wanted to quit. Others talked about things they were doing that might not be good. We discussed stress, food, and exercise. We finished with a discussion of what to do during the ninth month. Today, I want us to continue talking about the ninth month, especially the last couple of weeks and the delivery. First, I want to report that I have been talking individually with Jane and Betsy, and they are doing great! *(Group cheers)*

Another good time to use summarizing is at the end of a session. Because many ideas will have been discussed during the session, a skillful summary can be helpful. In our discussion of ending a session in Chapter 15, we address the different ways to summarize and how to use the members to summarize.

Linking

Linking is the process of connecting people together to facilitate bonding. We also call this *tying together*. This is a valuable skill for group leaders, especially in the beginning stage of group, because the leader wants the members to feel connected to each other and to the group. By pointing out commonalities, the leader tends to facilitate the building of cohesion.

LEADER: Renee, I think what you are going through sounds similar to what Sid said earlier about wanting approval from his coach. Sid, would you agree?

SID: Well, I hadn't thought about it until you said that, but you are right. We are doing the same thing. *(To Renee)* What goes through your head when you are cheering?

RENEE: Well, I think it is something like "What if I flub up, will she kick me off the team?"

SID: That's what I do, and it really is nuts because no one gets kicked off anything for a mistake. Can we talk about this together, either here or later?

The leader is always alert to how things one person is saying may apply to another person in the group. The skill of linking should be utilized throughout the group but especially during the first two or three sessions.

Mini-Lecturing and Information Giving

Sometimes the leader needs to provide information to the group. In educational groups, the leader is often the person who is providing the expertise on subjects such as diet, health, birth control methods, or types of post-secondary education. In situations where you are the "expert," you want to do several things when giving a mini-lecture:

- Make it interesting.
- Make it relevant.
- Make sure you have considered cultural and gender differences.
- Make it short (usually no more than 5–8 minutes).
- Make it energizing.
- Make sure you have current, correct, and objective information.

Giving information enables members to learn from the leader and from the discussion that follows. By keeping the comments relatively short, the leader provides good information without turning the group into a class. The key to successful mini-lecturing is to briefly provide new and interesting ideas. Very often, beginning leaders are afraid to give any information or will give boring mini-lectures. A good leader has to have good things to say. In discussion, educational, and task groups, it is important that the leader be well informed about the subject. In growth or counseling groups, the skilled leader needs to have information on all kinds of topics, such as guilt, marital affairs, children, the value of hobbies and pets, and so forth. In almost any group, there are times during a session when a 2- or 3-minute lecture on some subject will help focus the group, deepen the focus, or simply help members understand something about which they are confused. Providing information is helpful in many groups, and the skilled leader not only has beneficial things to say, but knows when and how to say them.

■ **EXAMPLE**

The focus of this group is marital enrichment for young couples who have been married less than 2 years. In the second session, a member asks a question.

SAM: Can marriages go smoothly without working so hard? When does it get easy?

LEADER: That is a great question. Let me comment on that. Most marriages require work, especially during the first couple of years as the partners get to know each other in a different way. Also, differences continue to emerge that have to be discussed. Having to work hard during these first 2 years does not mean it is not a good marriage. Let me tell you three or four ways that each of you can benefit from working on your marriage now. . . . *(Leader talks for a couple more minutes)*

■ ■ ■

Encouraging and Supporting

Because you are interested in the helping professions, you have most likely already learned to provide encouragement and support to others. As a group leader, this ability will be especially important in helping members deal with the anxiety of a new situation and sharing their ideas or personal feelings with others. Members are often concerned with how they will appear to others and sometimes fear they will say something "wrong" or "stupid" in the group. In growth or therapy groups, members sometimes fear they will reveal something about themselves that they will later regret. The skilled leader must take the initiative in providing support and encouragement that will help put members at ease (Gladding, 2008). Acknowledging that some discomfort is normal often eases members' anxiety. For example, a leader might make an encouraging statement, such as, "People in groups may feel a little nervous. That feeling usually goes away as they get to know each other better and learn more of what the group is about."

In addition to the content of what you say, it is important that you communicate your support with warmth in your voice, a pleasant facial expression, and an "open" posture. Your encouragement must be genuine and congruent with your actual feelings. As the level of personal sharing in a group increases, members may require additional encouragement in their struggle to talk about themselves. Often, the primary concern of members is how the other people in the group will react to them if they reveal something very personal. Your encouragement helps members get over their scared feelings and helps them take risks that they otherwise might not take. The following is an example of an encouraging and supportive statement:

LEADER: John, you started to tell us about the problems you have regarding sex. You seem somewhat scared about the prospect of sharing such personal things with us, which is certainly normal. I think you will find that we'll listen without criticism or judgment. We're not here to be critical of you or anybody—we're all trying to be helpful and supportive of each other.

In this example, the leader is supportive and delivers a message to the other members that criticism or judgment would be anti-therapeutic. This is an additional form of protection that the leader provides as part of her role.

Tone Setting

By tone setting, we mean creating the mood for the group. Some beginning counselors are not aware of the tone-setting dimension of group leading; thus, without realizing what they are doing, they set a dull or very serious tone. Other beginners, wanting to be liked, set a very light tone and end up frustrated because no one seems committed to the group. It is important to realize that the leader sets the tone by his actions and words and what is allowed to happen. If the leader is very aggressive, he will create an atmosphere of resistance and tension. A leader who allows members to attack and criticize others permits a fearful tone to emerge. If the leader encourages sharing and caring, a more positive atmosphere is established. The leader is responsible for setting the tone and should consider the following:

- Should the group be serious, light, or somewhere in between?
- Should the tone be confrontive or supportive? (Some groups for addicts, juveniles, and certain kinds of criminals are conducted effectively with somewhat of a confrontive tone.)
- Should the tone be very formal or informal?
- Should the group be task-oriented or more relaxed?

If you ask yourself these questions and then lead according to your answers, you will probably achieve the desired tone for your group. The following examples show how a leader can set different tones for the group.

■ EXAMPLES

Serious Tone

LEADER: Let's begin. Before we start, I'd like you to pull in so that we are not all spread out. Also, I'd like you to put away any food or drinks for now. *(Members do this.)* Okay, let's start by having different members introduce themselves and tell why they are here.

■ ■ ■

Social Tone

LEADER: Let's begin. *(Members remain spread out and continue eating)* I'd like to start by having you tell a little bit about who you are. Tell anything that you think is important or anything you'd like.

■ ■ ■

Confrontive Tone

It is the first session of a group of teenagers who have been caught using drugs. Joe has been talking about how he does not think he has any problem with drugs.

LEADER: Joe, it is clear that you have a serious problem! In this group we can help each other by making sure that people are honest with themselves. *(In a rather confrontive voice)* Does anyone feel that Joe has a problem?

■ ■ ■

Supportive Tone

LEADER: Joe, I hope the group can be of value even though you don't feel that you have a problem. Others of you may feel the same way. Also, I believe some of you do realize that you have a problem. The purpose of the group is to be helpful, and I am hoping that you'll help each other by listening, sharing, and hopefully, caring for one another. For some of you to say that you have a problem will be tough.

■ ■ ■

Formal Tone

LEADER: I am Tom Smith. I'm from the mental health center and I'm here today to serve as the leader of this group. Before we get started, I would like to go over some of the ground rules for this group. The first thing that I would like you to do is to introduce yourself. State your name, where you work, and why you decided to attend the group.

■ ■ ■

"On-Task" Tone

LEADER: I'd like us to get started. We have a lot to cover and only an hour and a half to do it. First. . .

■ ■ ■

In workshops that we conduct, we ask participants to describe the tone of groups they have led or been members of and state whether the group was successful or not successful. Some of the tones reported for the less successful groups are "hostile," "boring," "frustrating," "combative," "slow-moving," and "confusing." For the successful groups, tones such as "warm," "serious and caring," "interesting," and "energizing" were reported.

Another important aspect of tone setting to be aware of is the environment, such as the lighting, seating, and wall decorations—these things can make a difference in the tone that is set. Chairs in a circle without tables set a tone different from chairs around a conference table. Friendly notes in chairs, music, or soft lighting can set a certain tone. Remember, the leader sets the tone, and without the proper tone, groups are less effective than they could potentially be.

Modeling and Self-Disclosure

As a group leader, modeling and self-disclosure are important skills. These skills are also useful for getting members to share thoughts and feelings. Corey, Corey, and Corey (2009) state that "one of the best ways to teach desired behaviors is by modeling those behaviors in the group" (p. 16). Your style of effective communication, your ability to listen, and your encouragement of others will serve as a model for your members to emulate. Your energy and interest in a subject or in the group itself serve as a model for others. If the purpose of the group involves more personal sharing, then your self-disclosure can be used to demonstrate how to disclose and that you are willing to risk and share yourself. Your self-disclosure also indicates that you are human and that you have dealt with many of the same issues in your life that members are presently exploring.

LEADER: Now that you have had a chance to think about the three people who have had the most significant impact on your life in terms of who you are now, let's begin sharing. I'll go first to show how this might work. The most significant person in my life was my mother. She was significant because she supported me and sort of protected me from my father, who was an alcoholic. My brother . . .

Here, the leader demonstrates the depth of sharing that can take place. Self-disclosure can be used to reveal past events, present events, and present feelings about the group or about some members.

■ ■ ■

The following examples show two different kinds of self-disclosure.

LEADER: In my current relationship, my partner and I have some trouble with how we like to socialize. She likes to spend time with lots of people, whereas I really enjoy only one or two people at a time. I think this is one of many concerns that couples deal with. Does anyone have that concern or have other concerns about a relationship?

■ ■ ■

LEADER: I want to share how I am feeling about the group tonight. I feel that people are holding back. I am not sure why. Does anyone else feel that?

■ ■ ■

It is not necessary for the leader to self-disclose on every issue or topic that is discussed in the group. Frequent self-disclosure may, in fact, be distracting and confusing to the members. In addition, self-disclosure by the leader should not be of such intensity that the leader becomes the focus of the group. The preceding excerpts are good examples of how leaders can self-disclose yet make sure that the group does not focus on them.

GROUP COUNSELING SKILLS: Basic Skills

Go to the segment on Basic Skills (6.1) on the *Group Counseling Skills* DVD. Watch a discussion and a demonstration of some of the basic skills mentioned in this chapter, including self-disclosure, linking, and setting the proper tone. Throughout the DVD you will see many of the basic skills being utilized.

Use of Eyes

Knowing how to use your eyes is very important when leading groups. The leader needs to be aware of how his eyes can gather valuable information, encourage members to speak, and possibly deter members from speaking (Harvill, Masson, & Jacobs, 1983). The leader can use his eyes in four ways:

1. Scanning for nonverbal cues
2. Getting members to look at other members
3. Drawing out members
4. Cutting off members

Scanning for Nonverbal Cues

Leaders gather valuable information by scanning the group with their eyes. Although scanning seems easy, most group leaders find it difficult because it is natural to look at people when they are talking. Picture a beginning leader leading a group of 10 members. The member closest to the leader's left starts talking, and the leader naturally turns to look at the speaker. The member talks for 2 minutes about a personal situation. During those 2 minutes, the beginning leader will have made contact only with the speaker and perhaps with the next two members to the speaker's left. For the entire 2 minutes, the leader has made no observation of the remaining seven members. Here are some of the problems and difficulties this leader might encounter:

- Some of the other members may feel excluded because the leader did not make eye contact with them.

- The leader has no idea how most of the members were reacting to what was being said.

- The leader has no idea who may want to speak next.

- Some of the other members may have lost interest because the member talked only to the leader.

If the leader does what is natural, which is to look exclusively at the person speaking, she misses information that is very helpful in facilitating the group. Seeing members' reactions and knowing who wants to add comments makes leading a lot easier. Most beginning leaders can learn rather quickly to scan the group while they are talking. However, *learning to scan when someone else is talking is a skill that takes practice.*

Of course, there are situations when you would want to attend almost exclusively to the talking member, but those situations should be the exception rather than the rule. The rule is to *keep your eyes moving.* Scanning is the best way to pick up the various immediate reactions of the members. Among the most important nonverbal cues to observe are head nods, facial expressions, tears, and body shifts.

Head Nods   It is very helpful to look for head nods indicating both agreement and disagreement when someone is offering an opinion or describing some concern. The leader can facilitate discussion by saying something like, "Biff, you're nodding—what are your thoughts?" or "I notice that some of your heads are nodding in agreement and some in disagreement—let's continue the discussion, realizing that there are differences here." Picking up on head nods can also be useful for drawing out and linking one person with another: "Jodi, you were nodding when Diane mentioned leaving—are you having similar thoughts?"

Facial Expressions   While head nodding implies some degree of agreement or disagreement about an issue, facial expressions may mean that the member has had a similar experience or is in some way relating positively or negatively to the issue. Facial expressions can suggest disapproval, confusion, or some other reaction that the leader may want to clarify.

■ **EXAMPLE**

BARBARA: He really believes that I should be home from work at 5:00 and his dinner should be on the table by 6:00. I am not obligated to make dinner!!

SUE: I agree with you.

JANE: There are no wife's duties!!!

LEADER: *(Picking up on Ann's expression)* Ann, by your expression I'm guessing that you might be having mixed feelings about what Barbara and the others are saying.

ANN: Well, ah, I am. You see, I'm all confused about this. I want to believe what's being said, and yet I sure was raised differently. And, also, there are things I like to do as a wife.

DEE: I feel the same way you do, Ann.

ANN: You do? I thought I was the only one here who was somewhat traditional.

If the leader had not picked up on Ann's reaction, Ann might not have volunteered her thoughts because she was fearful of being different. Some caution is noted here. Facial expressions, including other nonverbal behaviors, may be shaped by one's culture. Thus, while head nodding can safely be regarded as agreement in the United States, it may merely mean acknowledgment in another culture. This is no more evident than for those of us who have had the experience of conducting workshops in other countries. Once, in Asia, one author (RH) was demonstrating group leader techniques while students observed in a "fish bowl" arrangement. The observers consistently nodded and smiled throughout the demonstration. Only later did he discover that they were clueless as to what he was trying to accomplish and why. If you have group members from other countries, be more careful to check their understanding and keep in mind that many countries around the world are "communitarian" oriented; group harmony is more valued than individual pursuits and accomplishments. Therefore, head nodding and smiling can mask confusion, misunderstandings, and disagreements.

GROUP COUNSELING SKILLS: Effective Use of Eyes

Go to segments 6.2 and 6.3 and watch the leader demonstrate ineffective and effective use of eyes. Also, as you view the remaining segments of the DVD, watch how the leader scans the group periodically.

■ ■ ■

Tears   Tears or "tearing up" on the part of a member is an important clue for the leader. While some members may break into tears and sob audibly, often people merely tear up while they are listening to another. The leader needs to be aware of members' tears because they are usually indicative of strong feelings. Whether the leader deals with the tears directly by drawing the member out or chooses to acknowledge them or ignore them depends on the purpose of the group and other factors such as the time remaining, who the member is, and the leader's guess about what is causing the tears. The skilled leader who scans the group will observe members who are expressing their pain silently through tears. Not scanning the group causes the leader to miss this valuable information.

Body Shifts   Members often express themselves through the way they sit and move. Nonverbal body shifts can mean many things, according to the context in which they occur and the cultural perspective of the member. Body shifts during the group frequently indicate confusion, boredom, or irritation. For instance, if two or three members are noticeably confused, the leader may want to use the skills of reflection and clarification, give a mini-lecture that may provide valuable information, initiate a group exercise, or even have the group take a 10-minute break. One body shift that is important to observe is the forward lean, which often indicates the member has something to say. Beginning leaders frequently miss this and other signals from members. As a result, they may ignore those who are ready to speak and resort to calling on members who may have less to say.

Getting Members to Look at Other Members

The leader can use her eyes to signal members to look at others. It is helpful to tell the members you will not always be looking at them when they talk, and your looking at others should serve as a signal to them to look around. When the leader uses the skill of scanning, the talking member will tend to seek eye contact with other group members, which is helpful for group development.

For groups with immigrants and non-U.S. citizens, it is important for the leader to understand that these members may not maintain eye contact in the same manner that native-born Americans do. Rather than being an indicator of low self-esteem or undeveloped social skills, failing to maintain eye contact may be a sign of respect, particularly when the member is unable to maintain eye contact with the leader, an authority figure.

Drawing Out Members

Another way a leader might use his eyes is to make eye contact with those whom he is trying to draw out. By scanning the entire group and contacting particular members, the leader's eyes can serve as an invitation to talk. Beginning leaders sometimes err by maintaining eye contact only with those who are talking and not with those who are silent. The leader's eyes can really encourage members to join in and share. Let's say there is a member who has not spoken much, and it is already the third session. Observation indicates this member is scared and shy. Your kind and encouraging eye contact may help this person venture into the group. Once drawn out, this type of member may speak only to you. You may want to allow this at first and then, as the member becomes more comfortable, ask him to talk to the entire group.

The leader's eyes can also be helpful when a member is revealing something very painful. Encouragement through eye contact and body language may be just what the member needs to fully disclose some previously hidden aspects. This is another example of an appropriate time for the leader to maintain eye contact with only one member for a longer period. Usually this does not result in others feeling ignored, because members are very attentive when someone is doing intense personal work.

Another way for the leader to use his eyes to draw out a member is to make eye contact with that person a number of times while speaking to the group as a whole.

■ EXAMPLE

The group has been in progress for 45 minutes, and the leader is aware that Claire has said very little. The discussion has been about people's different values. The leader decides to shift the focus and try to draw Claire into the group.

LEADER: Okay, now that we've generated a list of different values, let's talk more about you and where your own values come from. *(While scanning the group, the leader intentionally has been holding eye contact with Claire a little longer than previously.)* Think about different people or institutions, such as the church, or scouts, that have had an impact on you. *(The leader, noticing that Claire nodded at the word* church, *decides to say more about religion while looking often at Claire.)* For some, religion may be the major source of your value system. Some of you may be very religious. *(Claire nods, and the leader nods back.)* Sharing that would be helpful in the group. Who would like to share about where values come from? Let's take the influence of religion first. *(The leader ends the comments while looking at Claire.)*

CLAIRE: My family was very religious. In fact, . . .

■ ■ ■

In this example, the leader intentionally ended his comments while looking at Claire, increasing the likelihood that she will speak. Of course, sometimes this will not be effective, and you need to be aware that this technique should be used with care and concern for your members. Unfortunately, some beginners misunderstand the technique and end up using eye contact as a "spotlight," thus creating undue pressure on a member to respond. It is our experience that some members, who are non-U.S. citizens or who have recently immigrated to the United States, are sometimes more difficult to draw out by eye contact. If cultural variance presents this challenge, it may initially be necessary to simply call them out by name. Additionally, you may wish to explain how you are using eye contact to draw out their participation.

Cutting Off

Often, there is one member who tends to speak first on any issue or question. There may be times when the leader wants someone else to comment first, perhaps just for a change or because the talkative member is negative or longwinded. When the leader knows that he is going to pose a question to the group, he can use his eyes to control the talkative member. By looking at the member as the leader starts to ask his question and then slowly shifting his eyes around to other members, he can finish his comments totally *out of eye contact* with the talkative member. This technique subtly invites others to respond and avoids the talkative member's nonverbal overtures to comment. Certainly this does not work all the time, but it can be effective.

■ EXAMPLE

The leader, wishing to get members to share their fears about leaving the hospital, starts by looking at Joe, an overzealous member on the leader's left.

LEADER: All of you probably have some fears about leaving this hospital. I hope that a number of you will share those fears. *(Now scanning the middle of the group)* Who would share some of those fears, no matter how big or small? *(The leader's eyes are now fixed on the members on the right.)*

In this example, the leader is hoping that members in the middle or on the far right side of the group will comment first. By finishing the question with Joe outside his range of vision, the leader increases the chance of someone other than Joe initiating the discussion.

■ ■ ■

Leaders can also use their eyes to help cut off a member who is speaking. If a member has gone on for a while, a very subtle but often helpful cutting-off technique is for the leader to avoid making eye contact with the speaker. Members frequently will "wind down" sooner when the leader is not attending to their comments. (In Chapter 8, we discuss in depth the skills of cutting off and drawing out.)

In concluding this section on the effective use of eyes, we want to reiterate how important it is. By moving your eyes, you are in contact with your members and more aware of the energy of the group. By scanning the group, you will have a better sense of what to do next. All in all, the leader who scans will have much more data than the leader who doesn't. The following examples should help you further understand reasons for scanning the group when you or other members are talking. They are offered as a way of reviewing how the use of your eyes can be of great value to you as a group leader.

■ EXAMPLES

A Support Group for Cancer Patients

Carl is talking about his recent diagnosis of cancer and his family's denial of the whole matter. While scanning the group, the leader notices that Sue's head is nodding vigorously. He asks Sue to share, and she comments on her family's denial and how she dealt with it. Carl listens intently.

■   ■   ■

A Group for Elementary School Children Who Live in Stepfamilies

The leader is talking about how the first few months are hard because of the blending of two families. She notices that Mike, Karen, and Bob are nodding and Jane is looking down. *(The leader knows from Jane's teachers that Jane is having a hard time in her new stepfamily.)* The leader then gets Mike, Karen, and Bob to talk about their hard times while she continues to observe Jane. Toward the end of Bob's comments, the leader notices that Jane seems more relaxed, so she invites Jane to share.

■   ■   ■

A Therapy Group for Alcoholics

Gloria is telling a long story about her history of drinking, one that she has told twice before. By scanning, the leader notices that the members are not paying attention and are starting to drift off. He decides to cut Gloria off by saying in a gentle, caring voice, "Gloria, you seem to be losing us. Are you aware that people aren't listening? My guess is that they are not listening because you have told us this twice before. How can we help you?"

■   ■   ■

A Divorce-Adjustment Group

Mary is talking about how things are better for her now—she and her ex-husband are even talking about possibly dating each other. In scanning, the leader notices some questioning looks and also notices that Betty is starting to tear up. The leader decides to shift to Betty, who reveals that her ex-husband told her yesterday that he was going to get re-married.

■   ■   ■

A Personal Growth Group for Graduate Students

The leader has just introduced an exercise on family of origin, and while scanning, she notices that one member looks confused. She asks the member about his confusion, and he tells the group he was raised in an orphanage.

■   ■   ■

Practice Activities

To conclude this section, try practicing the following two training exercises. They will help you develop more effective use of your eyes in working with groups. Try each several times. The key to these exercises is to make them fun and interesting. See what you can learn.

1. In a group (one you are actually leading or simply a group of as few as three people standing around talking), move your eyes comfortably from face to face. Study expressions and reactions to the speaker. See if you can guess who will speak next. Also, see if you can tell by the data you are gathering from head nods, smiles, and other facial expressions whether the other people are agreeing or disagreeing with the speaker. Try to guess whether the next person will maintain the topic or go off in a new direction.

2. In a group, move your eyes comfortably from face to face. Think about each person's expression. What feeling do you get from it? If you were to make a statement about each person based on his or her expression, what would it be?

Use of Voice

Use of voice is another skill that many leaders overlook. The leader's voice can be used to influence the tone and atmosphere of the group as well as its pace and content. In later chapters, we explain the use of voice to draw out and cut off members.

Use of Voice to Help Set the Tone

A leader conveys how a group will be led both by the content of his words and the tone of his voice. Leaders using a very strong, stern voice may intimidate the members, causing them not to share as much. A nonassertive voice may cause members not to respect or believe in the leader. A warm, encouraging voice often helps the scared, troubled, or withdrawn member.

Listen to your voice pattern, perhaps using some recording device. You will want to develop more than one voice pattern, because, at times, you will need to vary the tone of the group, and your voice can help in that process. Your voice also can communicate a serious or a light tone.

Use of Voice to Energize the Group

The leader's enthusiasm will help to energize the members. Frequently, leaders who complain that their group is "dead" are those who have not learned to use their voice effectively. Discussion, education, and task groups can be ruined if the leader does not demonstrate by his actions and voice that he is interested in the topic and the group. An enthusiastic voice will affect most members in a positive way as long as the leader is sincere. Often, at the beginning of a new group and even at the start of a given session, the leader's voice can be a key factor in generating interest and energy. We recommend that you listen to your own voice when leading and determine whether you are using it to energize the group. If you are not, you can practice using different energy levels in your voice, thus changing your voice patterns and habits. Although this will take some effort, you will find the effort is worthwhile.

Pacing the Group

Closely linked to the tone and energy of the group is its pace, which can also be influenced by the leader's voice. Often, a very slow-talking leader will influence members in such a way as to slow the pace down—perhaps to such a degree that the group moves too slowly. Although there are exceptions, it is best to assume that your voice is having some influence. At times, you will want the group to move faster or slower; by learning to manipulate your rate of speech, you may be able to manipulate the pace of the members. Practice this and evaluate your effectiveness while leading. You will likely be surprised at how much influence your voice can have.

In summary, the leader's voice pattern—which includes tone, pitch, volume, and rate—can be instrumental in leading an effective group.

 GROUP COUNSELING SKILLS

Throughout the DVD series, be sure to note different leaders' use of voice. Sometimes a voice is high energy, sometimes it is slow and thought-provoking, and at other times it is sensitive and caring. The skillful use of your voice is an important skill to master in your development as a leader. Note the different voice pattern in segments 1.1 and 1.2. Also note the more business-task tone in 8.2, and the serious deepening tone in segment 14.3.

Use of the Leader's Energy

Another skill—perhaps we should call it a characteristic—is the leader's energy. Good leaders have enthusiasm for what they are doing. Unfortunately, leaders often hold group sessions at the end of the day when they are very tired. If at all possible, leaders should take a break before a group session. Leaders need to be excited about leading because, if they are not excited, the group members probably will not be. There really is no way to practice increasing your energy level, but it helps to be aware that your energy level affects that of the group.

Identifying Allies

A very useful skill is discovering who your allies are in the group; that is, which members you can count on to be cooperative and helpful. It is important to identify them, for there will be times during a session when you will want someone to start a discussion or an exercise or when you will need someone reliable to play a role or take a risk. Also, when leading therapy groups, you may encounter a situation where one member is working at a very intense level on some issue and another member becomes very emotional and needs immediate attention. A good therapy group leader has to be prepared for such occurrences. One way to handle this so as not to disrupt the work in progress is to ask your ally to be with the member who is very upset. This allows you to feel confident that the member who has become very emotional is getting some support while you are dealing with the "working" member and the rest of the group.

Some members start out being very cooperative and are seemingly allies; but as the group progresses, they desire to take over the group or have the focus be on them. Sometimes your best allies are members who are quiet at first and don't stand out at the very beginning. It usually takes at least a couple of group meetings to identify the members who will be especially helpful and cooperative. In some groups, there really isn't a need to be concerned about allies, but in others it becomes very important to identify them.

Multicultural Understanding

As we have indicated above, awareness of multicultural issues is very important in groups, because most groups are made up of diverse cultural backgrounds. DeLucia-Waack and Doingian (2004) state in their book that multiculturalism is inherent in all group work. The leader not only needs to understand the different cultures of the group members, but also needs to understand how each member's culture affects his participation in the group. Corey (2008) makes some excellent points in his discussion of multicultural issues as they apply to group counseling:

> Each individual must be seen against the backdrop of his or her cultural group, the degree to which he or she has become acculturated, and the level of development of racial identity. . . . Whether practitioners pay attention to culture variations or ignore them, culture will continue to influence both group members' and group leader's behavior, and the group process as well. Group counselors who ignore culture will provide less effective services. (p. 16)

We point out the importance of multicultural understanding here and throughout the book because it is an important issue that is being discussed in all phases of counseling (Sue & Sue, 2003).

Concluding Comments

In this chapter, we describe a number of basic skills for leading groups, such as active listening, reflection, clarification, summarizing, mini-lecturing, encouraging, and modeling. Beginning leaders often fail to realize that these fundamental counseling skills are also useful in group leadership. A skilled leader uses her eyes to draw out members, cut off members, and notice important nonverbal gestures. A good leader knows how to use his voice to influence the tone of the group, the energy of the members, and the pace of the session. Understanding different cultures is essential for the group leader in today's multicultural society.

■ ACTIVITIES

1. In a group or class, observe the leader's ability to use the different skills mentioned in this chapter. Pay close attention to the leader's use of voice, eyes, energy, reflections, clarifications, and summarizations.
2. Practice using different voice patterns (change the pace and the volume) when interacting with groups of people and notice the effect that it has.
3. Look at the list on the first page of this chapter and try to practice the various skills in social settings. That is, practice active listening, linking, self-disclosure, etc. See the impact this has on the social group you are with.

GROUP COUNSELING SKILLS

1. View again segment 6.1.
   a. Did the leader do any linking?
   b. Was the leader aware of multicultural issues? What would you do with the woman who was talking about her child being the only black child?
   c. What would you do with the woman who was talking about being the only Chinese family in the neighborhood?
   d. Did the leader use her eyes effectively? Why did this make a difference?
2. View segments 6.2 and 6.3 again.
   a. How are the group dynamics different in the two segments?
   b. What do you imagine would have happened in segment 6.2 if the leader and member would have continued to just look at each other?

Chapter 7

Focus

In this chapter, we discuss the importance of knowing how to establish, hold, shift, and deepen the focus. We use the term *focus* primarily as a noun to refer to what is happening in the group. At any given moment in a session, the focus is either on a *topic* (love relationships, ways of dealing with parents, trust within the group), an *activity* (guided fantasy, a written exercise, blind trust walk), or a *person* (personal conflicts, fears, concerns, issues, or problems). Throughout a session, the leader establishes the focus on certain topics, activities, or individuals; holds the focus; or shifts the focus. The leader should always be aware of the depth of any discussion or personal work and should, when appropriate, try to deepen the focus. The skilled leader understands that the focus moves from person to person and topic to topic, and it is the leader who is responsible for making sure the focus goes with the purpose of the group. *Knowing how to establish, hold, shift, and deepen the focus is absolutely essential for good leadership.*

Establishing the Focus

There are many different ways to establish focus in a group. The important thing to understand is that the leader is usually the person who establishes the focus. The following sections highlight several ways in which the leader can establish the focus. They are use of comments, use of activities and exercises, and use of rounds and dyads.

Use of Comments to Establish the Focus

Often, the leader can establish the focus by stating to the members what the topic or activity is going to be for the next few minutes.

- Let's focus on the topic of guilt for the next hour.

- Let's focus on Julio for the next 10–15 minutes and try to help him with his dilemma.

- I'd like us to summarize what this last 30 minutes has meant.

- Let's really zero in on one of these topics. It doesn't matter which one, but let's pick one rather than trying to talk about all three.

- The topic for tonight is learning how to budget your time. Who wants to share what they learned from the reading on time management?

Use of Activities and Exercises to Establish the Focus

Using visual aids and having members write or draw something are excellent ways to get members focused. The following are just a few examples of activities that can be used to establish the focus.

1. *Use posters, charts, or diagrams relevant to the topic or task of the group.* Visual aids get the members involved both visually and auditorily.

2. *Use a whiteboard or a large pad to list items or characteristics.* For instance, if the group members are talking about drugs, the leader can go to the board and say, "Let's list the pros and cons of drug use." In a school group, the leader can say, "Let's list the characteristics of a good friend." While looking at the list on the board, members often get more focused by trying to generate new items to add.

3. *Use a whiteboard to draw pictures or visual analogies.* For example, group members could be discussing all the ways they feel they are being held down. The leader could go to the board (or a large flip chart) and sketch a large hot-air balloon with various lead weights hanging off the sides. Each weight would be labeled in terms of pounds (200, 100, 50, 25, 10), and there would be space under each to fill in what that weight represented. This image might prove helpful to members and allow them to focus on what is holding them down and to what degree. Another drawing might be of a road with various roadblocks and choices on it. Having a drawing in front of the members often helps them focus on a topic.

4. *Have members list or write something.* A very helpful focusing technique is to have members write answers on sentence-completion forms. For example, a leader who wants the group to focus on the topic of parents could make up a list of five sentences for members to complete. It might look something like the following:

When I think of my mom, I _____.

When I think of my dad, I _____.

I wish my dad _____.

I wish my mom_____.

The biggest problem I have with my parents is_____.

Another focusing technique that involves writing is to have each member make a list of something. For instance, the leader could have a group of first-year college students list their worries or have elementary school children list their favorite activities.

5. *Have members draw something.* Drawing such things as their favorite scene, the house they grew up in, or their earliest memory helps members focus on topics such as "what I like and value," "what my family was like," and the impact of childhood on present-day living.

6. *Put a large piece of paper on the floor in the center of the group with a stimulus word or phrase on it.* With this phrase in the center of the floor to stare at, members usually stay focused. Some examples of words and phrases that you might put in the middle of the group are Dad, Mom, work, responsibilities, fears I have, changes I can make in my life, and things I enjoy.

7. *Use handouts that contain information you want to cover.* Handouts give members something to look at and relate to. Also, members can take them with when the session is over.

8. *Place an empty chair in the center of the room.* The empty chair can represent different people. If the leader wants to focus on parents, she can have the chair represent one or both parents. If she wants to focus on anger, she can have the chair be someone with whom the members are angry.

9. *Stand on a chair.* The leader can usually focus members on such issues as need for approval or codependency by standing on an empty chair and asking a few questions about the people that the members have "above" them.

10. *Place a small child's chair in the center of the room.* The small chair can represent the free child, the inner child, or the hurt child. By having the chair present, members tend to focus on that part of themselves much more easily than if simply asked to imagine being the child.

GROUP COUNSELING SKILLS: Getting the Focus

Watch 10.2 for a demonstration of using the small chair to focus members.

Other creative techniques include the use of shields, beer bottles, rubber bands, audiotapes, and videotapes. For a complete description of these and other creative techniques, see *Creative Counseling Techniques: An Illustrated Guide* (Jacobs, 1992), a book that encourages counselors to be creative and innovative when counseling individuals and groups.

When used properly, all these techniques can prove very helpful to the leader. There are many direct and creative ways to establish group focus, and it is important to have a number of techniques to choose from. Different situations call for different techniques; through trial and error and experience, you will learn which ones work best in particular situations.

GROUP COUNSELING SKILLS: Getting the Focus

Watch 7.1 for a discussion of focus and a demonstration of using a creative technique to establish focus.

Use of Rounds and Dyads to Establish the Focus

Rounds and dyads are two additional ways to establish the focus. *Rounds* are very useful because they involve everybody and focus members by having them think of what they are going to say. Below are a few examples of how rounds can be used to establish the focus.

- Think of what has been the biggest change since your accident. In a minute, I'm going to have each of you comment briefly on this.
- How much effect do your siblings have on you today—a lot, a little, or none? Think about this, and then we'll do a round.
- In a word or a phrase, what stood out to you the most about tonight?

Dyads help focus members on a topic because members are paired with one another and instructed to discuss various ideas. The following examples illustrate how dyads can be used to get members to focus on certain issues.

- Pair up and talk about ways you can benefit from the group.
- Pair up and talk about your reaction to the reading for the week.

Holding the Focus

Once the leader has the group focused, knowing how to *hold* the focus is essential. The leader is constantly deciding if she should hold the focus or shift it to some other person, topic, or activity. Holding the focus means sticking with what is currently happening. For example, if Mac is discussing the pain he's experiencing over his wife's death and Melvin interrupts and begins discussing his brother's visit, the leader holds the focus by directing the group back to Mac. If members of a group are discussing feelings of insecurity regarding dating and someone asks a question about the five best places to go with a date, the trained leader does not let the topic shift to "places to go" but rather holds the focus on insecurities.

There are three considerations to keep in mind for holding the focus: when to hold it, how long to hold it, and how to hold it.

When to Hold the Focus

Focus on a Topic   The following questions are helpful in determining whether to hold the focus on a topic. (By *topic*, we mean such things as parents, vanity, the value of staying in school, how to budget money, or any other subject the group is discussing.)

- Is the topic relevant to the purpose of the group? If it is not relevant to the purpose, usually the leader will want to shift the focus to a more relevant topic.

- Are the members interested in the topic? If most members are not interested, the leader will probably want to shift the focus, although there are times when the leader may decide to stay with it a little longer.

- Has the focus been on the topic too long? This usually depends on how much the leader planned to cover in the session. If there are five major issues to discuss and the group is still on the first one with only half the session remaining, the focus should probably be shifted.

- Has the group discussed the topic before? Sometimes a group will go over the same issues week after week. If that topic is becoming redundant and there seems to be little energy for that topic, an effective leader will shift the focus.

The answers to these questions will give leaders a sense of whether to hold or shift the focus. When the leader is unsure about whether to stay with a topic, doing a "quick 1–10" will help to decide. The leader can say, "I want to get a quick reading from you on whether we should continue to discuss the issue of __. On a 1–10 scale, with 10 being *very interested* and 1 being *very disinterested,* what number best describes your attitude?" Usually the numbers will indicate whether there is enough interest. If all are low numbers or high numbers, the decision is obvious.

If there is a range, a number of things can be done. The leader may ask those who indicated high interest what they specifically would like to discuss and then focus the group there with a time limit of 5, 10, or 20 minutes. She could split the group and let those with high interest meet for 20 minutes (depending on the time remaining) while the others discuss another topic. Splitting the group is appropriate only in educational or discussion groups where group cohesion is not a major goal. Leaders rarely do this in a growth or therapy group. The leader can also give a break to those who rated their interest as low while the high-interest members continue with the topic. As you can see, the quick 1–10 round can offer information that generates a number of options for the leader.

Focus on a Person   In any group, the focus can easily center on one person. When this happens, it is the leader who decides whether to hold the focus on the person or to shift it to another person or to a topic. The leader must consider a number of things when making this decision.

Does focusing on one person serve the purpose of the group?   Some groups meet for the purpose of doing therapy or personal growth work; in such groups, focusing on one person is appropriate. Other groups meet for discussion, sharing, or accomplishing a task; thus, to focus on one person would be inappropriate.

Is the person benefiting from having the focus?   If the person is benefiting and most of the other members are also, then the leader would want to hold the focus. If the person is benefiting but most of the other members are not, then the decision to hold the focus is more difficult. Rarely will the leader want to hold the focus when only one or two members are involved in what is being said. If the leader cannot engage most of the members in the working member's work, he may decide to meet with the person individually because the issue is not one to which the other members can relate.

Who is talking, and how much "air time" has the speaker had recently?   If the person talking has not spoken in a while or has spoken very little throughout the group's life, it is usually beneficial to hold the focus on that individual. On the other hand, if the person has had the group's attention often in the past, the leader may choose to shift the focus.

How Long to Hold the Focus

One question you may be asking is, How long is the focus held on a person or topic? There is no single answer because it depends on the purpose of the group, which session it is, what happened in the previous sessions, and how much time is left in the current session. Also, different factors must be considered, depending on whether the focus is on a topic or on a person.

Focus on a Topic   How long to hold the focus on a topic depends on a number of things. If the group is an education, discussion, or task group where there are a number of things to be covered, the leader will want to budget the time wisely. Many beginning leaders get so caught up in the content or interaction that they forget that other topics need to be covered. Also, leaders have to be aware when interest in the topic is waning. It is usually best to shift the focus to another topic before the majority of the members get bored and tune out the group.

Focusing on a heavy issue in the early stages of a group is usually not wise. Also, the leader should not focus on topics such as sex or death unless there is ample time to discuss them. A discussion of death can stir up a number of feelings, memories, and fears, so it is probably wise not to hold the focus on death if it comes up during the last 30 minutes of the session. The leader would probably want to say something like, "Let's hold off discussing the topic of death until next week because we really don't have enough time to fully discuss it, and I wouldn't want us to get started on something that might leave some of you hanging."

Focus on a Person   The amount of time to hold the focus on a person depends partly on the kind of group being led. For therapy, growth, and support groups, where holding the focus on one person is appropriate, the upper limit is probably 30 minutes. Naturally, there will be exceptions: Sometimes the leader may stay with one person for an hour or more; however, this should be the exception rather than the rule. In most therapy, growth, and support groups, the usual amount of time is between 5 and 15 minutes. In other kinds of groups (discussion, education, or task), a good rule of thumb would be not to hold the focus longer than 5 minutes on any one person, because you would probably want an exchange of ideas or information from all the members.

Holding the focus for a long period of time also depends on which session it is. Leaders do not want anyone to dominate the first couple of sessions because the goal is to get people to feel comfortable being in the group. If one person dominates, other members tend to sit back and listen rather than think and contribute. Beginning leaders often make the mistake of focusing for too long on one member in early sessions because of their own nervousness or their lack of cutting-off and drawing-out skills.

How to Hold the Focus

When the group is flowing and the focus starts to shift, the leader has access to several skills and methods for holding the focus. The main skill is cutting members off. (See Chapter 8 for a complete discussion.) Whether you are using that skill or one of the methods described next, remember that the most important thing is to *act quickly*. The longer you wait before bringing the group back to the topic or person, the harder it will be, because the members' energy and attention will have become invested in the new person or topic. The most common method for holding the focus is to address the group directly.

- Let's stay with Sandy.
- I want to go back to what Joe was saying. Joe, when did you start feeling that way?
- Can we put that on hold until Karen finishes with her list?
- I believe we may have left Manuel, and I think we need to stay with him a little longer—Manuel, do you want to say more about that situation?
- Let's finish this topic before we start a new one.
- I think if we're not careful, we'll get too many things going at once—let's go back to the topic of _____.

If you decide that you want the group to stay with a certain topic or person for a while, it is sometimes helpful to verbalize this. For example, if your group has been discussing aspects of daily living, you might say, "Let's spend the next 10 minutes talking only about what is difficult for you on a daily basis."

Another way to hold the focus is to conduct a group exercise or use a prop. For instance, if the members were discussing their fears about cancer and the focus shifted to financial concerns, the leader could bring them back to the topic of fears by saying, "I'd like to list the different fears that you are experiencing *(Stands and goes to the board)*. Financial fear is one; what are some others?" Or imagine a task group where eight members are trying to resolve their differences on how the probation office and welfare office can work together. The discussion has turned momentarily to a local judge and how her recent rulings have been inconsistent. Seeing the need to hold the focus on the task, the leader could say to the members, "I'd like to do something a little different. I want each of you to pair up with someone from the other office and come up with a list of suggestions for improving the working relationship of your two offices."

The possible techniques for holding the focus are actually unlimited. With experience, you will develop more techniques. Until then, try to use some of the ideas provided, plus others you will learn later in this book.

GROUP COUNSELING SKILLS: Holding the Focus

Watch 7.2 for a demonstration of the leader holding the focus. You will also see holding the focus demonstrated in many other segments of the DVD.

Shifting the Focus

Although holding the focus and shifting the focus are very much tied together, it is important to conceptualize them as separate skills. Leaders consciously shift the focus when they decide that there is a need for a change in the group. The shift can go in any of the following directions:

- From a topic to a person
- From a topic to another topic
- From a topic to an activity
- From a person to another person
- From a person to a topic
- From a person to an activity
- From an activity to a topic
- From an activity to a person

It is important to notice that "from an activity to another activity" is not listed because this kind of focus shift is usually not appropriate. *One of the biggest mistakes that beginning leaders make is to conduct one activity after another.* Group exercises need to be followed by discussion and not just conducted one after the next. We discuss conducting group exercises in Chapter 11.

When to Shift the Focus

There are two main ways to conceptualize shifting the focus: (1) as a shift *away* from some person, topic, or activity, or (2) as a shift *to* some person, topic, or activity. The leader may shift the focus in any of the following situations:

- The focus has been on one person for too long.
- The focus has been on one topic for too long.
- The focus does not fit the purpose of the group.
- The time left dictates the need for change.
- The leader feels the members need a change to re-energize the group.
- The leader wants to draw another member into the group.
- The leader wants to introduce a new topic or activity.

Shift from a Topic to a Person   Leaders often want to shift the focus from a topic to a person in counseling, therapy, and growth groups, but may do so in all kinds of groups.

■ EXAMPLES

The group has been discussing jealousy, and a number of members have commented on how they handle it. The discussion has been going on for 3 to 4 minutes. The leader decides to focus on one person. Here are two ways the focus can be shifted to a person.

MISSY: I just can't help it—I'm a jealous person. If Frank is talking to some woman at a party, I lose it.

BILL: But why? My wife does that to me, too. I don't like it at all.

TED: I'm a lot more jealous than my wife. In fact, I don't think she gets jealous, and that makes me mad sometimes!

LEADER: Missy, I'm wondering if you would want to explore your jealousy further. You seem to be bothered by it, and I think I detect a desire on your part to get better control of it.

■ ■ ■

Using this same example, the leader merely indicates the desire to shift to a person but does not focus on any one individual.

LEADER: Would anyone like to spend a few minutes talking specifically about his or her concerns with jealousy? It is apparent to me that many of you are concerned about it. Ted, you and Missy and Bill all have talked about how jealousy is interfering in your relationships.

■ ■ ■

The following examples are additional comments that leaders can make to shift to a person:

- I'd like each of you to think about what we have been talking about for the last few minutes. Does anybody want to work on anything regarding this issue?

- Who wants to take this issue deeper? There seem to be several things that you could work on.

- This discussion is good; however, I feel that some of you may have something personal that you want to discuss. Does anyone have something you would like to bring up?

In the last example, the shift would not only be to a person but possibly to a new topic. If the leader doesn't want the topic to shift, a comment like the first example, which is more specific, should be used.

Shift from One Topic to Another   In discussion, task, and education groups, the leader will usually need to shift the focus to cover the necessary material or accomplish the task. To shift the focus, the leader might say any of the following:

- Let's take a minute or two to finish this topic because we need to move on to something else.

- We seem to be about finished with this issue. Who has some other issues or points to bring up?

- We have a lot to cover tonight, so let's go on to something else.

- I would like to change the discussion to focus on what Kay was talking about. She mentioned the effects of the decision. Let's talk about what the rest of you think the effects would be.

In task groups and education groups, there is often specific material to be covered. The leader can help shift the focus by letting the members know the agenda and an estimate of the time needed to cover the topics. For example, the leader could say the following:

- Today, we are going to talk about diet and exercise as they relate to stress. We'll spend approximately 45 minutes on each topic.

- First, we need to decide which proposal we want to accept. Then we need to decide who will do what and discuss the necessary schedule changes that will be required. We have only an hour and a half, so we'll need to watch the time.

In each of these examples, telling the members what the agenda is helps the leader. It is still the leader's responsibility to budget the group's time and to shift the focus when needed, but the clock can be used to do so—that is, by allowing a specified number of minutes for each topic. When the time has run out, the leader can say to the group, "We need to move on because of time." Following are some additional ways that leaders can shift to a new topic:

- We have a lot to cover today, so let's move on to the next chapter.
- Let's turn to another issue that is equally as important as the one we are now discussing.
- There are two more topics that we need to cover today. Let me throw them out to you, and then let's decide which one we want to do next.

Shift from a Topic to an Exercise   Often, when the group is discussing a topic, a group exercise may be useful to further the discussion or involve more members. The leader introduces the exercise by saying something like, "I want us to stay with what we are discussing, but I think an exercise could be helpful now." Or the leader can say, "I want to change the format a little bit. There is a group exercise that fits in with what we are talking about." Leaders often use a round exercise to shift from a topic. For instance, if the group has been discussing a topic for some time, the leader might say, "In a word or phrase, what are you thinking about right now? Let's do a round and hear from everyone." Another round that leaders use after a discussion is, "What are two things that stood out to you? We'll quickly go around the room and hear from each of you." Another easy way to shift from a topic to an activity is to have members form dyads to further discuss the topic that was being explored in the large group.

Shift from One Person to Another Person   If the leader has determined that the focus needs to shift to another person, there are a number of possible things to say. Following are some examples of different situations and different responses:

- Lori, I think it would be good to let you just think about what you have been saying these last 15 minutes; then maybe we'll come back to you later on. What did this bring up for the rest of you? Who wants to explore their reactions or feelings?
- Joe, I'd like to shift to Cindy. *(The leader turns and addresses Cindy.)* You seem to really be relating to this. I noticed a couple of times that you wanted to say something. Do you want to share that now?
- Avid, we'll stay with you for another couple of minutes; then I'm going to give others a chance to share their ideas.

In these examples the leader addresses the person who has the focus and then shifts it. The leader who wants to cut off the member who has the focus will address the group directly. In such situations, the leader might say something like this:

- Does anyone want to comment on what Joe has been saying?
- Let's not focus on Joe, but rather on you. Any thoughts or feelings?
- Cindy, how about you? You seem deep in thought.
- Can anyone relate to what Lori has been saying? *(The leader would look away from Lori and would have some idea of who might want to speak.)*

Shift from a Person to a Topic   There are times when a leader wants to focus on the topic that a person is addressing. This may be because the topic is one that he thinks is relevant for most of the members or because he wants to subtly shift the focus from the member who currently has it. The following examples illustrate this:

- Dean, I want to pick up on what you've been talking about. I think the issue is a good one, and I want to hear how others think and feel about it. What do others of you think about the issue—how do you deal with it and what reactions have you received? (Throwing out so many different questions invites discussion, which in this case is the intention.)

- Carol, you have brought up many concerns that certainly others can relate to. I'd like to spend the rest of the session discussing some of those issues. Let's take the one you mentioned first. (Mentioning Carol by name and using some of the content she has been discussing increases the likelihood that she will not feel cut off.)

- Julio, your thoughts are interesting. However, I am aware that we are running out of time, and we still have one more major item to discuss. Why don't you summarize your position, and then we will move on.

- I want to shift the discussion to the whole group because we really want to hear a number of ideas and views. What do the rest of you think?

Shift from a Person to an Exercise   As mentioned earlier, the leader can use a round as a very good way to shift the focus; that is, ask members to rate on a 1–10 scale or give a word or phrase about some subject. Also, the leader can simply ask the members to pair up and discuss what the member has been talking about, or to talk about any thoughts or feelings they had when the member was speaking. Many other group exercises can be used to shift the focus. The following ways can introduce such exercises:

- I want to take what you are talking about and get the whole group to think about it. Everyone get out a piece of paper and something to write with. I want you to do the following. . . .

- Ruth, your energy and enthusiasm are appreciated. I want to see if I can get everyone as excited and interested as you are. Everyone stand up—I want you to move to this side of the room. Now, here's what I want you to do.

 GROUP COUNSELING SKILLS: Shifting the Focus

Watch 7.3 and 7.4 for demonstrations of a leader shifting focus.

Deepening the Focus

A leader thinks not only of holding or shifting the focus but also whether or not to deepen the focus. *The key to most groups is deepening the focus to a level that is productive and meaningful for the members.* In many groups, members have a tendency to get sidetracked or avoid delving too deeply into their issues. Therefore, it is the leader's responsibility to make sure the group "funnels" to a meaningful depth. Depth is measured differently for various groups—for education and discussion groups, depth is measured by assessing learning and the exchange of ideas. Task-group depth is measured by productivity and how well members are working together. Counseling, therapy, growth, and support groups are measured by new insights about living and belonging and the level of sharing when doing personal work. A leader deepens the focus by using the following techniques:

- Asking very thought-provoking or challenging questions
- Asking members to share at a more personal level
- Working with a member in a more intense manner
- Conducting an intense exercise that gets in touch with some deep, personal issues
- Confronting members about certain dynamics that are interfering with the group

■ EXAMPLES

MOLLY: I think everyone gets angry at their partners.

ED: Sonja and I fight at least once a week.

TONI: I said I didn't want to fight like my parents, but we do.

LEADER: Wait just a minute. I want all of you to really think about what you are saying. Do you really believe you have to fight? I absolutely don't agree with that. Many couples do fight, but they don't have to. I would bet if you look at your fights with your partner, you will see some unhealthy patterns, lots of expectations not in line with reality, and lots of unfinished business from childhood or former relationships.

ED: *(After a minute or so of silence)* I hate to say it but you are right. I want Sonja to be like my first wife was, and she is not. That's what most of our fights are about.

LEADER: Would you like to explore that further?

ED: Yes, I think so.

LEADER: Let's hear from others and then we'll come back to you, Ed.

■ ■ ■

KAREN: I think the government should spend more on research for medical cures than sending all the foreign aid to other countries.

CYNTHIA: I heard that the drug companies are partly the reason why they don't find cures because it would put them out of business.

LEADER: Let's not worry about the politics of finding a cure. Our time can be much better spent sharing personal thoughts and feelings about your disease. What feelings have you had this week?

CONNIE: I sometimes wake up so scared, I can't go back to sleep.

■ ■ ■

LEADER: I want to bring up something I noticed. Many of you have things on your mind because you have shared them in your diaries or in individual meetings with me, but no one shares in the group. There is something holding you back. I know this can be a good experience for most, if not all, of you if we can just figure out what is going on. Think about it. I want us to discuss what keeps you from sharing. Any thoughts?

JUAN: I think I know some of why I hold back.

■ ■ ■

In each example, the leader made a comment or asked a question to deepen the focus. Many less skilled leaders let the group members take the group where they want it to go, which often results in the group not going to a deeper level.

Depth Chart

To discuss the depth of the group in a concrete way, we have devised the *depth chart*. The depth chart is a 10–1 scale, with a 10 representing surface-level talking or sharing, and a 1 representing deep, intense, personal sharing. During the life of a group, the depth of discussion will vary. In the beginning phase, the depth is usually a 10 or 9 because members are telling stories or talking superficially about some topic or issue. As a group moves to the middle phase, the depth should reach below 8 to at least a 7; and for most groups, the leader will want the group

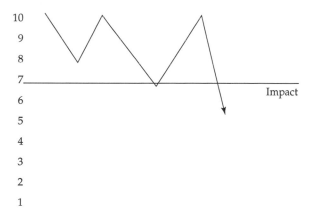

to reach a depth of 6 or below. Too often, groups bounce from topic to topic and never go deep enough to derive any benefit, following a pattern of 10, 9, 8; new topic 10, 9, 8; new topic, 10, 9, 8. In the chart, the interaction of a group is depicted: One topic went to an 8, then a new topic started and went to a 7, and then a third topic was started and went to a 5.

By using a depth chart, a leader can better visualize and understand what is happening in the group. In most groups, the desired depth during the working phase is 6 or deeper, with some groups going to an intense level of 3, 2, or even 1. If the group is staying at the 10, 9, 8 level, the leader needs to intensify the discussion. The leader may want to funnel to a deeper level by using an exercise that encourages members to explore an issue in greater depth. Processing the exercise can lead to discussion or individual work at a level of 6 or lower. In some groups, the leader may draw or explain the depth chart and periodically ask the members how they would chart the discussions and interactions within the group.

When to Deepen the Focus

There are two considerations when thinking of deepening the focus. The first is the phase of the session, because deepening the focus should be done only during the middle phase of a group, not during the warm-up or the ending phases. When there is an opportunity to deepen the focus during the middle phase, the leader should also consider if there is enough time to adequately cover the issue or topic. Beginning leaders often will deepen the focus and then run out of time and leave members hanging—this is not good leadership.

How Deep to Focus

There are a number of considerations regarding how deep to focus a group. The most important consideration is the purpose of the group. Too often in education, discussion, and task groups, leaders mistakenly deepen the focus on individuals. This makes members uncomfortable and can be harmful, because members did not expect or even agree to a therapy group; and, yet, all of a sudden, that is what is happening. *Always consider the purpose of the group before deepening the focus to a very personal, intense level.*

Even if the members are open to going to a deeper level, it is always advisable for a leader to think about the members and the appropriate depth. For most school groups, especially elementary groups, leaders should not want personal sharing to be below a 4. The leader always should consider whether a member can handle sharing personal concerns or receiving feedback in the group. Members differ in the degree to which they are ready and comfortable to share and receive feedback and can be harmed if they are not able to deal with what is being said. Too often, beginning leaders get so involved in the process that they forget to consider if certain members are ready and able to deal with the depth to which the group is heading.

■ EXAMPLE

The leader of this group of elementary kids stops the focus from going deeper, because he sensed that the member was going to get into some serious abuse issues that would not be appropriate for the other members to hear.

ELAINE: My dad isn't mean exactly, but he does make me do things I don't want to do.

MEMBERS: Like what?

ELAINE: *(Head hanging down, in a sad voice)* Not nice things.

MEMBERS: What?

LEADER: You know, Elaine, I think this may be something you and I can talk about privately. Does anyone else want to talk about fights you are having with your parents?

■ ■ ■

There are two other considerations regarding the depth of focus: The first has to do with expertise and the second with multicultural concerns. Sometimes in groups, issues come up that the leader may know little about. It is unethical to push a member into deeper work when the leader does not have the experience, knowledge, and understanding to deal with the problem. Too often, we hear of unqualified leaders dealing with some very intense therapy issues. Regarding multicultural concerns, any leader must consider the cultural background before delving too deeply and too quickly with a group member, because some members may be very uncomfortable. It is very important to get a contract with the member before pushing him into deeper work.

■ EXAMPLE

Here the leader makes sure the member wants to work on the issue she is struggling with. The leader uses another member to help deepen the focus.

DASHA: Ever since coming to this country, I have been confused about my role as a woman. Here, things are very different. I get a point of view from this group that clashes with everything I was taught in my country.

SUSAN: But you live here and are planning to stay here. We will support you. That's what the group is for.

LEADER: *(Interrupts with a kind, warm voice)* Wait a minute here. Dasha, I want you to tell us how we can be of help. Certainly we want to respect what you learned from your country, and at the same time we want to be of help and not confuse you. Do you think the group can be helpful to you right now and if so, how?

DASHA: I do think you can help by helping me get over feeling like I am doing something wrong.

LEADER: *(Deciding to hold the focus on Dasha and try to deepen it)* I think we can do that. Have any of you made changes in your life where you went against your upbringing?

ELIE: My decision to come to this country went against everything I'd been taught. I struggled with the pain I caused my family.

DASHA: How did you get the strength to do what you believed was right for you?

ELIE: I had to trust myself—after much soul-searching, I might add.

DASHA: *(With a thoughtful voice)* I have to learn this. I do have to learn to trust myself. I can see most of you are happy and I am not. I have to come to believe that I have a right to be happy.

LEADER: Would it help to tell us about your culture and what you were taught?

■ ■ ■

 GROUP COUNSELING SKILLS: Deepening the Focus

Watch segments 7.5 and 7.6 for demonstrations of a leader deepening the focus. In 7.5 the focus is deepened on a person. In segment 7.6, watch how the leader deepens the focus on a topic. Also you will see this skill demonstrated in many other segments of the DVD (10.2, 14.1, 14.2, 14.3).

Concluding Comments

A good leader understands that paying attention to the focus is one of the most important skills of group leading. There are many different techniques for establishing, holding, shifting, and deepening the focus. The focus of a group is always either on a person, topic, or activity. To maintain control over what is happening in the group, the leader should be aware of where the focus is and whether it needs to be shifted or held. The leader also must be aware of how deep the session is and may use a depth chart to monitor the development of a session. Before deepening the focus, the leader should consider the purpose of the group, the stage of the group, the phase of the session, the amount of time left, and how deep to focus the group.

In Chapters 2 and 3, we introduced concepts that, along with the focus, serve as maps for understanding the interactions and development of a group. Because these maps are so useful when leading groups, we summarize them here to show how the four go together.

- *Purpose:* Why the group is meeting
- *Stage:* Where the group is in its development (beginning, middle, ending)

- *Phase:* Where the session is (warm-up, working, closing)
- *Focus:* The content of the group (establishing, holding, shifting, and deepening the focus)

■ ACTIVITIES

1. Next time you are in a group, class, or among friends, observe how the focus is either on a topic, person, or activity. Also observe how the focus is either holding or shifting. If appropriate, using comments or questions, consciously shift or hold the focus and, if possible, deepen the focus.
2. Using the depth chart idea, observe the depth of a discussion with a group of people. Try to give numbers, using the 10–1 scale *(10 being surface talk).* If the group is not going below 7, try to deepen the focus by asking a thought-provoking question or by making an insightful statement.
3. Think of a group you might lead. Set a purpose and then a topic that is appropriate. Think of three different ways you could deepen the focus on the topic you have chosen.

 GROUP COUNSELING SKILLS

1. Review video segments 7.1-7.6.
   a. Think about the importance of using the skills of getting, holding, shifting, and deepening the focus.
   b. Imagine how these groups would have gone differently if the leader had not been using the skills of holding, shifting, and deepening the focus.
2. Review the first two segments of the DVD—The Leader Without Skills (1.1) and The Leader With Skills (1.2) – and note the difference in regards to the leader's skills in holding and shifting of the focus.
3. Watch segment 14.3 and observe how the focus is held on a topic (forgiving yourself) and a person (the woman whose father abused her). Also watch the leader briefly hold focus on one member who had voted for herself, since he knew it would only take a few minutes, and then return to the heavier issues.

Chapter 8

Cutting Off and Drawing Out

Cutting Off

To lead an effective group, a leader must be willing and able to cut off members when necessary. Of all the skills we present in this book, cutting off is probably the hardest to use because leaders often fear that they will hurt a member's feelings or that members will become angry. In addition, the skill is difficult because, when growing up, we do not learn to stop others from talking when their remarks are boring, long-winded, or inappropriate. However, a group leader is responsible for ensuring positive group outcomes, and when group members' comments are counterproductive, the leader should intervene.

Cutting off is the term we use to describe a leader's stopping a member from talking (Harvill, Masson, & Jacobs, 1983; Masson & Jacobs, 1980). Other terms used to describe this skill are *blocking* (Day, 2007; Corey, Corey, & Corey, 2009; Trotzer, 2006) and *intervening* (Dyer & Vriend, 1980). Although cutting off may sound as if we are advocating that the leader be rude or authoritarian in the group, we are not. There are simply instances when the leader must interrupt a member to protect other members or to move the group in a better direction.

There are two broad situations when the leader will want to use cutting-off skills: (1) when a member has the floor but is either rambling, storytelling, or avoiding going deeper; (2) when a member is saying something inappropriate. Before discussing these, we want to mention a number of important points regarding cutting off.

Timing

Perhaps the most important thing to understand about cutting off is that it has to be timed properly. The leader should stop members before they ramble too long, argue for an extended period, or offer unhelpful advice. On the other hand, leaders will want to make sure they are not interrupting a legitimate and worthwhile comment; this can anger and frustrate members. Unfortunately, there is no way to spell out exactly when the leader should cut off someone, because each situation is different. Experience and feedback from members will probably be the leader's best teacher.

Use of Voice

Voice tone, pitch, and inflection have a lot to do with how effective a leader is in using cutting-off skills. If the leader seems critical, gruff, or angry, members are likely to react in a negative way. When cutting off, the goal is not to criticize or humiliate but rather to stop something that is not helpful. It is important to remember that members are usually not consciously giving the leader or other members a hard time; rather, they don't understand or have not yet learned how to be productive group members.

Clarifying

It is important in the first session to explain to the members that you will at times cut off certain discussions for various reasons. Often, the leader also explains at the time of cutting off why he is doing it. Explaining is a good practice because confusion and anger can result if someone feels cut off for no apparent reason. Some may think it is because the leader does not like them or that their opinions don't matter. Others may assume that they should not speak unless asked to do so. Of course, there will be many instances when the leader chooses not to offer an immediate explanation for cutting someone off—for example, if the leader feels it is important to move on immediately.

Nonverbal Signals

Sometimes the leader's avoiding eye contact can serve as a signal to let a member know that he wants the member to stop. Some members will wrap up once they notice the leader not looking at them.

Another technique the leader can use is to signal the member with his hand to stop. Just a slight gesture—such as one used by a traffic officer—is sometimes enough to cue the member to wind down.

GROUP COUNSELING SKILLS: Cutting Off

Watch segments 8.1 and 8.2 for a discussion of cutting off and three segments where the leader used cutting off skills.

Cutting Off a Member Who Has the Focus of the Group

In any group, there are times when a group focuses on a member who is rambling, not getting to the point, or avoiding exploring an issue at a deeper level. Some members drone on and on, totally oblivious to the negative effect that their rambling is having on others. If left unchecked, these members often drain the energy and enthusiasm present in other members. Therefore, the leader has to use some kind of cutting-off technique.

The leader has three possible decisions regarding cutting off in a situation where a member has the attention of the group. The leader can *(1) cut and stay with the person, (2) cut and stay with the topic, or (3) cut and leave the person and topic.*

Cut and Stay With the Person   Many times, the leader sees value in interrupting and keeping the focus on a member. There are a number of techniques that can be used.

1. *Ask a question.* The leader, using a kind voice, can cut off a member by asking a focusing type question, such as any of the following:

- How can the group help you with this?
- If we give you 10 more minutes to talk about this, what would be helpful?
- You seem to be rambling and the group wants to help you with this. What is your point? Where are you going with this?
- Do you want to just tell us about this or are you asking the group for some help?

2. *Ask the person clarifying questions.* The leader may interrupt and either ask or have the members ask some questions to break up the monologue of the rambler. The leader will want to be sure that the questions are not ones that encourage more storytelling.

■ EXAMPLES

DANIE: *(Who has been telling stories for a couple of minutes about her alcoholic father and is not expressing her feelings)* And another thing he did was . . .

LEADER: Just a second here. Let us ask you some questions about you and your dad. I want each of you to think of something you can ask Danie that will get her to explore more deeply her feelings about her situation. One question I want to ask is, "How much do you blame yourself for his drinking?"

■ ■ ■

DANIE: And another thing he did was . . .

LEADER: Just a second here. Let us ask you some questions about you and your dad. I want each of you to think of something you can ask Danie that will get her to explore more deeply her feelings about her situation. Who has a question to ask?

MALIK: I do. How can we help you? All you do is come here and tell us stories. Do you really want help?

DANIE: I think I do. But what I was going to say . . .

LEADER: Hold on, Danie. Who else has a question?

LEE: Is there anything we can do to get you to quit denying that your father is an alcoholic?

DANIE: *(Tearing up)* I don't want him to be alcoholic. I really need help.

■ ■ ■

3. *Have the person do some focused activity (perhaps with chairs, drama, or some experiential activity).* Using the example of Danie, the leader could put a chair in front of Danie, ask her to pretend that her father is sitting there, and ask her to have a conversation with him. Or the leader could ask Danie to act out one of the scenes she has been describing, using members of the group to play her father and other family members. (Often reenactment of scenes triggers emotional reactions.) The leader could try many other activities. The point is that the leader has stopped Danie's storytelling, kept the focus on her, and tried to deepen the focus.

4. *Have the person comment to each member (from her seat, or have the person sit in front of each of the members).* At times, having the member who is working repeat statements or questions to other group members can encourage them to go deeper with their thoughts and emotions.

■ EXAMPLE

LEADER: Danie, let me get you to do this. I want you to turn to Lilly and complete the following sentence: "When Dad drinks, I _____."

DANIE: *(Looks at Lilly, who is sitting next to her)* When Dad drinks, I feel that it is my fault.

LEADER: Now look at Amos and start with the same phrase.

DANIE: When Dad drinks, I feel I should do something.

LEADER: Turn to Tomika and start with the same phrase.

DANIE: When Dad drinks, I get scared that someone will get hurt. I feel I have to protect my little sister. *(Begins to cry)*

LEADER: Stay with those feelings.

■ ■ ■

5. *Have the members give the person feedback.* If the member is not benefiting from talking, the leader can interrupt by asking the other members to give some feedback.

■ **EXAMPLES**

LEADER: Danie, I want to stop you for a second, and I am going to ask the group for some feedback. What do you think Danie is trying to say?

HARVEY: I think she is trying to say that she doesn't know what to do, but she thinks she should do something. She is doing what I used to do, which is take responsibility for the family and the drinking because no one else was trying to fix the problem.

■ ■ ■

LEADER: What do you think Danie needs to explore but is avoiding?

SONYA: She seems to feel bad about herself, but she won't talk about it. Danie, you are blaming yourself, and it is not your fault!

DANIE: *(Head down, softly crying)* But why does it feel like it is?

■ ■ ■

6. *Have the members role-play the person.* Allowing group members to role play the working member can provide insight to the member of focus by showing how they are appearing to the group. This can allow for a great deal of insight on the part of the working member.

■ **EXAMPLE**

LEADER: I want you to become Danie. Try with your voice and body to be her. Start with, "I'm Danie, and here's what I am trying to say." Who can do this?

MONICA: I think I can. *(With head hanging and with a weak voice)* My dad came home last night and started in on us.

DANIE: Is that how I really look and sound? No wonder I feel so bad.

■ ■ ■

The leader can even ask the member who is playing Danie a number of deepening questions. If a member can role-play Danie well, this can prove to be very enlightening to her. This activity and the previous one, where feedback was given, can be valuable, because the focus stays on the member, but the member stops talking in order to listen and watch. *Some members actually can benefit more by listening to themselves being discussed than by talking.*

These are just some of the techniques that can be used to cut off and stay with the person. With experience, leaders develop a number of ways to interrupt and stay focused on a member who is rambling or making nonproductive comments.

GROUP COUNSELING SKILLS: Cutting Off—Staying with the Member

View segment 8.3 where the leader cuts off the member but stays with her.

Cut and Stay With the Topic   There will be times when the leader will want to shift the focus away from the member who is talking but stay with the topic. When the leader makes the decision to intervene in this manner, the member often does not feel so cut off. Using the example of Danie, the leader might say:

LEADER: Danie, let me get other members' comments about their relationships with their parents. Can any of you relate to what Danie is saying?

Cut and Leave the Person and the Topic   Inevitably, there will be times when the leader will need to cut off and redirect the group because it is off on a tangent or it is time to start closing the group. In such instances, the leader might say something like:

LEADER: I think we need to move on. I want to shift our attention to an exercise that I think you will find interesting.

The important thing to understand from this discussion is that you have choices when you are thinking about cutting off.

Other Situations Calling for Cutting-Off Skills

There are a number of situations when a leader may want to use the skill of cutting off. We discuss seven of them:

1. When a member's comments conflict with the group's purpose
2. When a member is saying something hurtful
3. When a member is saying something inaccurate
4. When the leader wants to shift the focus
5. When it is near the end of the session
6. When members are arguing
7. When members are rescuing other members

When a Member's Comments Conflict With the Group's Purpose   One of the main uses of cutting off is to ensure that the group's content fits with its purpose. Whenever a member's comments are not in line with the group's purpose or when the group is discussing a nonproductive or unrelated topic, the leader should use cutting off to refocus the group on a more relevant issue.

Too often, when a member talks on an irrelevant topic, the leader lets that person continue indefinitely. Instead, the leader should say something like:

LEADER: Let me interrupt. I think we have gotten away from the purpose of the group. I'd like us to get back to our task, which is . . .

When a Member Is Saying Something Hurtful   Extreme, value-laden comments about certain issues also need to be cut off. Members may attempt to lecture others about such things as the evils of having an affair or an abortion. A member may want to comment at length about how organized religion is a harmful institution and should be banned or about how divorce is the ultimate failure and all marriages can be saved. These types of comments usually represent one particular member's point of view and have the potential of being hurtful. To let that member continue would be a mistake on the part of the leader, especially because other group members could be greatly offended. There are times in support, counseling, and therapy groups when a member begins to make very critical comments to another member. The leader must cut these off.

■ **EXAMPLE**

KIRK: . . . and I just feel that it is important that I share this. I have not been completely honest here. You see, my lover is not a she, but actually is a he—that is, I am gay.

BOB: That's disgusting!! I think . . .

LEADER: Wait a second. Bob, that is your issue. I want to stay with Kirk and his feelings.

The leader should block Bob's comments because the comments were going to be hurtful. Some beginning leaders let a member like Bob continue because they are not comfortable cutting off. This could be harmful to a disclosing member and the group in general.

GROUP COUNSELING SKILLS: Cutting Off Harmful Comments

View segment 8.1 again and think about the harm that would have occurred if the leader had not cut off when she did.

When a Member Is Saying Something Inaccurate   In discussion, education, and task groups, comments can be made that are inaccurate, misleading, or inappropriate. For example, in an education group about birth control, a member might say, "The pill should never be used because it has been proven to cause cancer. I have two friends now who are suffering from its side effects. Let me tell you about them." The leader would want to use cutting-off skills to correct this member's exaggerated statements. Whenever something is being said that is not accurate, the leader should not feel that he has to wait until the person is finished before commenting. In fact, it is best to cut off "speeches" that are not beneficial to the group as soon as the leader identifies them as such.

In counseling, therapy, and growth groups, it is especially important to listen for inappropriate comments or advice because members can say things harmful to others. For instance, a member might say to another, "I think you should divorce her immediately. Any woman who won't go to church with her husband is not a good woman." In this situation, the leader needs to cut off the member for giving inappropriate advice.

A common phenomenon in many groups is the guaranteeing of someone's behavior. That is, a member will say to another, "If you do X, then your wife (son, boss, parents) will do Y." It is important that the leader not let anyone make promises about how another person will think, feel, or behave. Here are some examples of such promises:

- If you get mad a couple of times, she'll change. You just need to let her know who's boss.
- Go home and tell your mom you're sorry for what you did. She'll understand, and all will be fine.

In these examples, members are promising some behavior over which they have no control. The leader should cut off any comments similar to this. One cardinal rule for leaders and members to follow is, *Do not guarantee anyone's behavior other than your own.* Human behavior is highly unpredictable.

■ **EXAMPLE**

The group is composed of stepparents who are sharing feelings and experiences about their particular situations in the hope of discovering new ways of coping.

JIM: My stepson, Jeff, seems to prevent himself from getting emotionally close to me because of his loyalty to his biological father.

EDGAR: *(Dogmatically)* You should spend more time with him, Jim. If you'll limit his time with his father and use it for the two of you, he'll grow to love you more. That's what I did with my stepson, and it's working out okay. I guarantee you that Jeff will respect. . .

LEADER: *(Interrupting)* Edgar, let me stop you here to say a couple of things. First, I appreciate your attempt to help. I'm glad that it is working out well between you and your stepson. I'm not so sure that your particular method will work for Jim and Jeff. What Jeff is experiencing is actually a very common and normal thing. Many stepchildren experience divided loyalty between their absent parent and the new stepparent. Each of you may want to think about this issue as it applies to your children. . . .

In this example, the leader was aware that Edgar was making guarantees to Jim based on his own experience and that his advice was not appropriate.

■   ■   ■

When the Leader Wants to Shift the Focus   Frequently, when a topic has been thoroughly covered or the focus has been held on one member too long, the leader's task is to shift the focus. Sometimes, a natural break occurs in the inter-action, and the shift is easy. At other times, the leader will need to use cutting-off skills to accomplish the shift.

■   EXAMPLES

This is a growth group for high school girls. The topic of discussion is love relationships. While Amy is telling a story about her sister, the leader notices that Sherry seems to want to speak.

AMY: I just don't understand. Tom and Cindy got along so well in the beginning. They were so happy together. They could talk to each other about anything. I thought it was for keeps, but after a couple of months, things were not so rosy. I think they maintained the rela-tionship for several months because they kept hoping they could regain what they once had. Let me give you an example. They were . . . *(The leader notices that Sherry is listening intently and nodding her head in agreement.)*

LEADER: Amy, let me stop you before you really get into the story, unless this applies to something in your own relationship history.
(Amy shakes her head indicating that it is not personal.) It seems that Sherry is reacting to what you are saying, and I want to give her a chance to comment. Sherry, would you like to offer some comments?

SHERRY: Oh, yes. What Amy was saying about the relationship being so good at first and then changing also happened to me. My boyfriend and I ended our relationship a week ago. It just seemed that we suddenly had nothing in common anymore. I . . .

In this example, the leader decides to cut off Amy and shift to Sherry for two reasons. First, although Amy was telling an interesting story, she appeared to have no personal investment in the topic. Second, Sherry appeared interested in the discussion and seemed to relate to it personally.

■   ■   ■

The members have been discussing their families of origin. The discussion has been going on for about 10 minutes, and the members still seem to be on the surface. The leader decides that the *family sculpture* exercise would be a way to get members to really focus on their home environments. The members are currently having a superficial discussion about vacations they had with their parents when they were young.

LEADER: Let me jump in here. I'd like to make this discussion about families more meaningful. An exercise that I have used before and one that is quite helpful in getting you to look at how you were affected by your early family experiences is called "Family Sculpture." This involves having you pick members of the group to represent your family as it was when you were growing up. . . .

In this example, the leader cut off the discussion, moving to a structured activity to funnel the group from merely conversational to insightful reflections.

■ ■ ■

When It Is Near the End of the Session   There are two situations when cutting off is necessary near the end of a session. When leading a group with a designated ending time, the leader sometimes has to cut off members to allow time for summarizing and ending the group promptly. It is very important to have enough time to close the group, and sometimes the only way to do this is by cutting off what is going on.

The second situation is when a member brings up an emotional issue with little time remaining in the session. A skilled leader will quickly cut off the member before he gets too far into his issue. Obviously, this is a difficult situation to handle, but there are times when there is not enough time for dealing with the concern.

■ EXAMPLE

There are approximately 10 minutes left in the first session of a group of adults who were adopted when they were young and who are now trying to find their biological mothers. Tracy starts to talk about her fears and the problems her search has already caused.

TRACY: *(In a distressed voice)* I am so afraid that my search is going to end in nothing. I have so much anxiety and worry. I have three choices now and I . . .

LEADER: *(Using an understanding voice)* Tracy, could I ask you to hold that until we meet next week? What you have to say is so important and I don't think we have enough time now to really deal with your issue, and we need to stop in about 10 minutes. Now, in the few minutes left, I'd like us to summarize tonight and get different reactions to this first session. I think we are off to a good start.

In this example, Tracy's concern is obviously a sensitive and personal one, and the leader is wise to hold off on it until the next session. The leader also does the right thing by cutting her off quickly before the momentum of the group shifts to Tracy's anxiety and worry.

■ ■ ■

When Members Are Arguing   Any time people come together to form a group there is the potential for arguments. Members usually leave it to the leader to stop arguments; if left on their own, some members would spend the entire session arguing. Therefore, the leader has to intervene and come up with better ways of discussing or resolving issues. Ordinarily, it is best to cut off arguments quickly because they are usually not productive and are often detrimental to the group. Arguments do nothing to build cohesion and can erode trust. Arguments can also set a negative tone for the group and use up time that can be spent in a much more productive manner.

In a few situations, a leader might allow an argument to continue for a short period. For example, the leader may want to observe the argument and then focus on process instead of content to help the members learn about their style of interacting and arguing. A good rule to follow is, *Don't let members argue unless it is productive in some way for them or the group.*

When members are arguing, the leader can use the following techniques:

- Cut off and focus on process by discussing what is happening in the group.
- Cut off and focus on content by getting some of the nonvolatile members to discuss the issue.
- Cut off and focus on content by asking the volatile members to continue the discussion but tone down their remarks.
- Cut off and focus on content by discussing the issue calmly herself.
- Cut off and shift the focus to a new issue.

■ EXAMPLE

The group is composed of clients at a mental health center. Members are discussing their different living arrangements; it is the third session.

RITA: I live in a communal-type situation with three men and four women.

SAM: *(Bolts upright)* I think that's disgusting!

RITA: What do you mean by that?

SAM: I mean I think that's wrong—God didn't put us on this earth to live in sin!

RITA: Who says it's a sin?

SAM: God does! In the Bible . . .

LEADER: *(Calmly)* Hold on. Let me say something to everyone. Maybe I haven't touched enough on the subject of attacking one another. Our purpose here is not to judge whether others are right or wrong in their actions or beliefs but rather to listen to the variety of ideas expressed and learn about differences in the way people live. Human relationships require listening without judging. I hope in this group you will learn to get along with people who are different from you. Rita, you were saying . . .

In this example, the leader recognizes that the exchange is not productive. The leader decides to make a brief comment on the purpose of the group, which serves both to cut off the rapidly escalating argument and to inform the members that making moral judgments about the actions of others is inappropriate. By speaking in a calm way, the leader is able to defuse the hostile tone being created.

■ ■ ■

GROUP COUNSELING SKILLS: Cutting Off

View segment 1.1 again and watch what happens when the leader does not cut off. Note the tension that develops. Remember, the purpose of this segment is to demonstrate poor leadership skills.

When Members Are Rescuing Other Members   Some members occasionally present a helpless, "poor me" self-portrait where they present themselves as victims of their environment. When this happens, other members often want to rescue them by saying certain soothing things or by offering all kinds of advice. This usually sounds something like, "It'll be okay; everything is going to work out" or "Don't cry; things will get better." This kind of member behavior is usually not productive because it tends to reinforce the "working" member's belief that he is helpless.

■ EXAMPLE

A group of recently divorced women is meeting for the purpose of support.

ALICE: *(Crying)* I'm just no good to anyone. I'm not pretty and obviously not interesting. The divorce was all my fault. I'm sure no one will ever ask me out.

TERRI: *(Patronizingly)* There, there, Alice. *(Patting her on the arm)* Everything will be okay. There are lots of men out there who are just waiting for someone like you to come along. There's no need to cry. I'll bet your husband . . .

LEADER: Wait a minute, Terri. *(To the entire group)* Helping someone doesn't always involve making them feel better immediately. Alice, I'm not sure if you are asking for help or just telling us your current feelings.

The leader quickly stepped in to prevent Terri from rescuing Alice, because Alice is not making any attempt to improve her situation but, rather, is wallowing in self-pity. In essence, there is no indication from Alice that she really wants to work on her issues. The leader should get such an agreement from her; otherwise, Alice might simply manipulate the group with her "poor me" routine.

■ ■ ■

Certainly it is desirable for members to help each other, but there is a difference between helping and rescuing. Leaders often mistakenly allow rescuing when such behavior should be cut off. A similar mistake is to allow members to hug or touch another who is crying because of a "poor me" attitude. This kind of physical support can serve to reinforce the "I'm weak" position taken by that member. With experience, the leader will come to recognize when it is appropriate to stop rescuing behavior and when it is appropriate to offer support and caring touch.

Practice

In this section, you will have the opportunity to practice what you've learned. Four examples follow, to which you may respond in your own words. Read each one and think about what you would say and why; you may want to write out your responses. Each example is discussed after it is presented.

■ EXAMPLES

The group is composed of prisoners, all of whom have committed violent acts against others. The purpose of the group is to help members overcome their inability to control their anger. The members are talking about events during the past month that have triggered their anger. Don has been talking for the past 90 seconds, and as he ruminates about an event, he becomes angrier and angrier.

DON: And then that @!_#!_ just looked at me and grinned, and I knew I couldn't do a thing about it. If he'd been out on the street, I would have fixed him. The next time that @_#!_ pulls that on me, I'm . . .

Think about what you would say if you were the leader. Your goal would be to stop Don from continuing to speak, because he seems to be escalating his anger. Take some time here to formulate one or two different ways to handle this situation. Here are some possible cutting-off responses:

LEADER: Don, let me break in here if I may. *(Looks at all members)* I want to talk about something I am sensing in the group. I think many of you have short fuses like Don's; when the fuse goes, there is an explosion, and that explosion gets you into trouble—namely, prison. I hope we can lengthen those fuses so that you can stay out of trouble and not hurt anyone unnecessarily. How could Don have stayed calmer in that situation?

LEADER: Don, do you want help with this and if so, how can we be of help?

LEADER: Don, you obviously lost it in this situation. I want you to turn to Bill and tell him one thing you could have done to have avoided becoming so angry.

These are some possible responses. Yours may have been different but equally as effective. The important thing to note in this example is that the member is getting more and more agitated, and Don's comments are not helpful to himself or to other members. This is a definite signal that some form of cutting off is needed.

■ ■ ■

This group is composed of middle school students whose parents are divorced. The leader has been encouraging members to share any feelings they have about their family situation.

SARAH: I've just been hoping that Mom and Dad will get back together. Mom is seeing another guy named Dave, and I just can't stand him. He always kisses me, and it just makes me sick. Sometimes when Dave is there, I sit in my room and cry, wishing that my dad would come back.

MIKE: Your dad was a drunk! Why would you think about him? Anyone would be better than him. I remember when he took us to the zoo. He . . .

What would you say if you were the leader? Stop and think of a couple of responses. Here are some possible responses:

- **LEADER:** Mike, stop. Let's stay with Sarah and her feelings.
- **LEADER:** Mike, let me stop you because I don't think you are tuned into Sarah very well. Sarah, say some more about how you are feeling.
- **LEADER:** Mike, hang on for a second. We need to work with Sarah and then maybe even talk about how everyone in the group can learn to be more sensitive to others. I do want you, Mike, to think about whether you were coming from Sarah's viewpoint or yours. Sarah, let's get back to you.
- **LEADER:** Mike, rather than focus on Sarah's dad, I'd like to work with you on your comments because you often tend to say things that are not sensitive to the member who is sharing. Have others of you noticed that Mike tends to do this? Sarah, we will come back to you, but I do think it is important for Mike to get some feedback.

The leader certainly needs to cut Mike off and then to decide whether to focus on Sarah or Mike. Probably the better person to focus on is Sarah. The leader could also use the incident as a way to talk about being more sensitive to others when commenting. Some leaders might mistakenly get angry at Mike and hold the focus on him and his behavior, thus leaving Sarah, who is in pain. The last response is one where the focus is held on Mike.

■ ■ ■

This is a weekend growth group composed of married couples whose goal is to discuss and eliminate problem areas in their marriages. Couples have been sharing about their hobbies and vacations. One couple, Mary and Tom, are now arguing about problems around taking their vacations.

Tom: Why do we have this insurmountable difference over where to go on vacations? You always demand that we see your parents.

Mary: That's because we only see my parents once a year, but we practically live with yours. Besides, all you want to do on vacation is fish or camp, and you know I hate that! You are so uncaring and unfair! Why don't you care about me?

Tom: Don't start that again. You always do this!

What would you do if you were leading this group? Take a moment and think of two or three different responses. Some leaders might make the mistake of allowing the argument to continue. It is apparent that the couple has fought over this issue a number of times. There are several things the leader could say:

Leader: Let me stop you because I don't think you are hearing each other. *(To the group)* What do some of you think is going on with Tom and Mary? (This holds the focus on Tom and Mary but gets others involved and stops the useless arguing.)

Leader: I want you to stop because it doesn't seem that you are getting anywhere. I want the two of you to listen to others who have probably had similar problems. Have any of you had problems like this? (The leader is second-guessing that other couples have had problems over vacations.)

Leader: I want to ask you something. Why do the two of you get nowhere with this argument? Think about it. What is happening to each of you as you talk? (This holds the focus on them and will probably involve other members, because the focus has shifted to communication patterns.)

Leader: I want to try something here that I think may help you see what you do to each other. I need someone to play Tom and someone to play Mary, and I want you to act out this argument. Tom, you and Mary just watch. I think you'll learn something. Who can play either Tom or Mary? (Cutting off stops the arguing and shifts to a role-play that should generate more involvement for all members. Tom and Mary should especially benefit.)

■ ■ ■

This group is composed of high school seniors. Its purpose is to discuss various situations that young adults face once they leave high school.

LEADER: *(To start the session)* What did you find out about loans and credit? Did any of you ask your parents or friends about this?

LARRY: I did. I found out a lot about loans and interest and how that all works. *(Larry goes on for a couple of minutes.)*

LEADER: How about others of you? What did you find out about the different places to borrow money?

LARRY: Oh, I found out that there were a number of places. They are . . . *(Larry goes on for a couple of minutes.)*

LEADER: *(Notices that members seem to be tuning out)*

It is a good bet that Larry's constant replies are affecting the other members. Any time a leader allows a member to dominate a group, the other members usually share less and feel less involved. This is especially true when the dominant member is not saying particularly interesting things, but rather seems to be talking due to anxiety or a need for attention. How would you respond if you were the leader? Take a minute and think of a couple of responses. Listed below are some of the options available to the leader:

- **LEADER:** Larry, let me cut in and stop you to give other members a chance to speak. Others of you, what reactions do you have?

- **LEADER:** Larry, I want you to hold off on your comments until others have shared.

- **LEADER:** Larry, I notice that you are always ready to speak first. I'm wondering if that has any significance, and I'm also wondering if you'd like some feedback from the group on how they feel about your always commenting. (This shifts the focus to Larry, and the leader would want to do this only if she thought Larry would benefit from feedback. Often, the leader can tell by the members' nonverbal reactions how they are feeling about the talker.)

■ ■ ■

Drawing Out

If cutting off is the most essential skill a leader needs to know, then drawing out is probably the second most important skill. A skilled group leader understands when and how to draw out members. *Drawing out* is the term we use to refer to the skill of eliciting group members' comments. Throughout this section, we discuss various reasons for drawing members out and how to accomplish this effectively.

Reasons for Drawing Members Out

One of the main reasons for drawing out is to get greater involvement from the group members, because one of the benefits of being in a group is to hear different ideas from all the members.

Another major reason for drawing out is to help members who have a difficult time sharing in a group. In most groups, there is usually a member who has trouble talking in front of others. If at all possible, a leader should try to draw out *all* the members during the early stage of the group—ideally, during the first session. Getting members to talk early in the life of the group can ease some of the anxiety about speaking in the group. The longer a shy or silent person waits to make his first contribution, the harder it will be. In addition, involving members during the beginning stage reduces tension in another way—if a member remains quiet for an extended period, the other members usually begin to wonder why. They sometimes imagine that the quiet member doesn't like the group or that he feels superior. By drawing out all members, the leader can often prevent members from making up what others are thinking and feeling.

Getting a member to go deeper is a form of drawing out that is very helpful to members in support, growth, counseling, and therapy groups. Some members will share but not really explore a problem in depth; that is, they stay on the surface. People usually gain more when they explore "uncharted waters."

Reasons for Silent Members

Most leaders consider using drawing-out skills when members are silent. Understanding the reasons for silence is necessary because drawing out is not warranted for all types of silence. A leader often has to decide if drawing out is needed. The following is a list of reasons why members may be silent.

Fear/anxiety	Not prepared
Thinking or processing	Confused
Quiet by nature	Lack of trust or commitment to the group
Not mentally present	Intimidation by a dominant member or leader

Fear/Anxiety   Even when members desperately want to speak, they sometimes do not because they are afraid of what other members might think. They conjure up images of people laughing at them, turning away in disgust, or thinking, "What a stupid fool." Drawing out these individuals is very important because they need to realize they are, in fact, imagining how the group will respond. Drawing out is difficult because the members may feel picked on unless the leader is careful.

■ EXAMPLE

In this example, the leader of an ongoing therapy group knows why Frank is in the group (from the intake interview) and knows that he is afraid to speak.

LEADER: Frank, you have not shared why you are here. My hunch is that you are afraid of what others are going to think of you. All I can say is that we are not here to judge you or anyone else; rather, we are here to help. Would all of you agree? *(Members nod)* Also, Frank, the way you are going to help yourself is by talking about it.

FRANK: It's hard to face anyone. I don't know why I did it.

LEADER: I know you don't, and I hope that by sharing here and in individual counseling, you will come to understand yourself better.

FRANK: *(Looking at the floor)* Well, I'll try. I know that all of you will think this is horrible, but I exposed myself to these teenage girls last month.

LEADER: *(After glancing at the members' faces and seeing that they are concerned for Frank)* Frank, if you will look up you will see that no one here is thinking you are the scum of the earth like you seem to think.

In this example, the leader felt confident about how the members would react because he had been meeting with the group for a number of weeks. Even in a situation like this one, however, the leader cannot absolutely guarantee how the members will react and should be prepared for a negative reaction.

If this leader felt Frank could not handle negative feedback, he would have wanted to avoid drawing him out—or at least have been fully prepared to deal with the various comments.

■ ■ ■

Thinking or Processing A second reason for silence is that members are thinking about or processing the group interaction. Most frequently, this occurs immediately following an exercise or some intense work on the part of a member. Usually the leader can, by scanning the room, pick up on the facial expressions of members who seem to be really thinking or experiencing something. This kind of silence is productive, because the members need time to reflect and think. However, such silences can become prolonged, and sometimes a member who is ready to speak is a little hesitant to do so. Usually, the leader can sense when members are on the verge of speaking and can often elicit their comments through a simple head nod or hand gesture. The leader also has a number of possible drawing-out statements that could be used:

- Go ahead.
- It looks as though you are thinking. Would you like to share your thoughts?
- You seem to be reacting to something. Is there anything you would like to share?
- It seems that you were relating to our discussion on _____.

Quiet by Nature   A third reason for silence is that some members are quiet people. They grew up listening more than speaking and are not in the habit of saying much, even to family and friends. It is important for the leader to assess this and not attempt drawing out if it is going to make the member uncomfortable. However, it is important to realize that, if it is done with caution and forethought, drawing out may help this type of member say more in the group.

■   **EXAMPLE**

In this example the leader decides to try to draw out Lucinda, who has contributed very little during the first three sessions of an education/growth group on improving communications.

LEADER: I'd like to get a number of you to share your reactions to the model, and then we will practice some. Speaking up does seem to be difficult, and knowing these different categories can be helpful. *(In a gentle, caring voice)* Lucinda, I realize that you are a rather quiet person. Did the model give you any additional understanding of yourself?

LUCINDA: It is true that I am rather quiet. I am the quietest in my family.

LEADER: Do you know why you were quiet?

LUCINDA: Because it wasn't safe to talk and my sisters were mean and no one seemed to want to hear what I had to say.

LEADER: I think it is safe here in group and we do want to hear what you have to say *(Members' heads nod)*.

LUCINDA: I guess it is a habit. I'd like to not be so quiet.

LEADER: And we'd like to hear from you.

In cases where the leader understands that a certain member is quiet by nature, it would be important that the group be made aware of this so they don't harbor negative feelings toward the quiet member.

■ ■ ■

Not Mentally Present   Some members are silent because they are not mentally present. Their thoughts are on things outside the group, such as their term papers, financial worries, or children. Allowing these members a couple of minutes to talk about what is on their minds can help them focus on the group.

■   **EXAMPLE**

The leader has noticed that Phil has been silent for the first 20 minutes of the group and decides to draw him out.

LEADER: Phil, you have been quiet. Is there something on your mind?

PHIL: Well, yes, I guess I am not with it today. My father is at the doctor's right now because he has a spot on his lung, and they are supposed to tell him what it is.

LEADER: Even though this is not really in line with our purpose, if you would like to take 5 minutes or so to talk about that, we could. Obviously, it is a major concern.

PHIL: But this group is about career planning and job interviewing.

LEADER: I realize that, and I think we can spare 5 minutes. Also, if we allow you some time, then you may be able to focus a little more on what we are talking about here.

■ ■ ■

Not Prepared   In certain groups, members may not be prepared; thus, they will be silent. In discussion, education, and task groups in particular, there are often out-of-group assignments to complete before the next session. A member who has not completed the assignment will probably not be as involved. Drawing out these members in an effort to combat their silence will be largely unsuccessful. What is needed instead is a way to motivate the members to do the assigned work.

Confusion   Members may also be silent because they are confused. Rather than speaking up or asking for clarification when they are unsure about what is going on in the group, some members will remain silent. It is good for the leader to be aware of this kind of silence because, when members are confused, they often withdraw or get annoyed with the leader. If the leader thinks the members are being silent for this reason, the following might be an appropriate comment:

LEADER: I have noticed that some of you have been quieter than usual. I was wondering—is it because you might be confused because things have kind of jumped around?

Lack of Trust or Commitment to the Group   Members are often silent if they don't want to be in the group and have no commitment to what is happening. This lack of commitment is common in nonvolunteer groups, such as groups for drunk drivers, prisoners, or adolescents in group homes. Another reason for silence is that members don't trust the leader or some of the other members in the group. When there is little trust, members will tend to be relatively silent.

Intimidation by a Dominant Member or Leader   A final reason for members' silence is because the leader or one of the members tends to dominate, causing others to sit back and listen rather than contribute. Also, in situations where one person dominates, members may have found that, when they have tried to speak, they were interrupted by the dominating person, and the leader did nothing.

There will be some instances in which a member is silent and the leader has no idea why. In these situations, the leader may choose to ask the member directly, put himself in a dyad with the silent member and then ask, or wait until the end of the session to ask.

Direct Method for Drawing Out Members

The most direct method of drawing out members is to ask them if they would like to comment or if they have any reactions to what is taking place.

■ EXAMPLES

This group is composed of high school teachers who are discussing the current guidelines for handling behavior problems in the classroom. Ron, who is usually very verbal, has not spoken.

LEADER: Ron, we've discussed many new procedures, and several ideas have been offered. Is there anything that you would like to offer at this time?

RON: Well, yes, I have one idea that I think could work. It deals with . . .

■ ■ ■

This group is composed of members who have AIDS. One member has died recently; John, his close friend, has been very quiet.

LEADER: *(Very calmly and supportively)* John, you have been very quiet this session. I can only guess that it may have to do with Ted's death. Is there any way we can help?

JOHN: Well, yeah, I really do think about Ted a lot—especially on group night. I . . .

■ ■ ■

Drawing Out Delicately

Sometimes, drawing out is a real art. The skilled leader is able to get a member to talk, share, or express herself without feeling forced or pressured. The challenge is to be able to invite members to share but to give them a number of ways to decline at the same time. The idea is to give members *permission* to speak—possibly even gently encouraging them to do so—without alienating them. Beginning leaders often make the mistake of putting people on the spot when they are trying to get them to speak. For example, such a leader might say, "Marvin, what do you think?" or "Cheryl, you have been quiet—why don't you share your ideas?" In certain situations, this type of probe would be totally acceptable, but if Marvin and Cheryl were not ready to speak, they would certainly feel on the spot.

The art of drawing out is evident when one is able to allow "outs" for the members while getting most of them to join in and share. One way to provide an out is to call on two or three members instead of just one. Then the leader can use her eyes to see if one of those members seems willing to speak. Focusing one's eyes for too long on a member can make him feel as though he were under a spotlight, so the leader will not want to gaze at just one member for any length of time. By looking at the member for a brief moment, the leader can invite the member to speak with her eyes. By shifting her eyes, the leader gives the member an out and relieves him of any pressure beyond that caused by having his name mentioned. (This slight pressure would be intentional because the leader would be trying to draw the member out.)

Two other components of drawing out are the leader's voice and attitude. At no time should the leader use a tone of voice that could be interpreted as condescending. The leader should never ridicule or embarrass a member for not being an active participant but rather should try to understand that member and then, if it seems appropriate, try to draw him out.

Two examples follow. The first one illustrates how *not* to draw out; the leader puts a member on the spot and does not give her an easy way out. The second example illustrates a more effective way to use the skill.

■ EXAMPLES

The group is composed of high school seniors who are about to graduate. They have been discussing plans for after graduation. It is near the end of the session, and one of the members, Jackie, has not spoken.

LEADER: *(In a demanding tone)* Jackie, why haven't you said anything? Would you like to tell us about your plans? *(The leader maintains eye contact with Jackie. All members of the group have their eyes on her.)*

■ ■ ■

This is the same group and situation as in the preceding example.

LEADER: *(Tentatively)* Jackie, I've noticed that you have been silent this session. I am not sure if you would like to comment or not. Certainly we'd like to hear from you if you feel comfortable. *(Shifts his eyes to scan the group)* Who would like to comment on anything that they are thinking about? *(The leader watches to see whether Jackie seems to want to talk.)*

In the first example, the leader comes on too strong. Also, the leader puts Jackie on the spot by maintaining eye contact and directing the group's attention to her. If Jackie is quiet because of discomfort, the leader's behavior can only increase that discomfort. Another error lies in not giving Jackie a choice whether or not to participate.

In the second example, the leader is tentative in his approach and does not focus the group on Jackie. In fact, the leader acknowledges that Jackie has not spoken, invites her to do so if she wishes, and then moves on. Because of this, Jackie feels no unnecessary pressure to speak. Assume that Jackie is pregnant and is considering whether to share this in the group—the leader in the second example has a much better chance of drawing her out than the leader in the first example.

■   ■   ■

GROUP COUNSELING SKILLS: Drawing Out

Go to the segment on drawing out (8.4, 8.5) and hear a discussion regarding drawing out. Watch a demonstration of the right and wrong way to draw out.

Use of Dyads for Drawing Out Members

Dyads can be used when members seem to be rather quiet and take a long time to warm up. When members are paired and given directions to discuss something of interest, the inevitable result is that the two individuals will talk to each other. The energy generated is often sufficient to stimulate comments in the large group from members who might otherwise have been silent. When the dyad is completed, the leader may use any of the following responses to draw out members:

- Who would like to comment on what you discussed?
- What are your reactions to discussing _____?
- What did you learn by discussing _____ with your partner?
- Please comment on any thoughts or feelings you may be having.
- Joe, what did the two of you discuss?
- Chandra, what did you learn in your dyad?

These questions are usually nonthreatening, because the members are warmed up as a result of the dyads. Also, the members will usually have something to say, because they were just discussing the issue.

Another way the dyad can be used to draw out a member is for the leader to pair up with the member he wants to draw out. By talking with this member, the leader can often encourage him to share in the larger group, or at the least, the leader can find out why the member has been silent. It is appropriate for the leader to ask a member why he does not talk much. However, it is usually best to do so privately.

Use of Rounds for Drawing Out Members

Rounds are another very useful technique for getting silent members to say something, because in a round, the leader is asking everyone to comment without singling out any one member. Most members are willing to share a word, phrase, number, or brief comment.

Another way to draw out a member through a round is to end the round on the person to be drawn out. In this way, the leader can more easily ask the member questions because he is the last to comment in the round, and the focus must shift from the round because it is complete.

■ **EXAMPLE**

The group is composed of women who are single parents. All group members have been actively involved in the discussion except Beth. Interest in the current topic is beginning to wane, so the leader decides to shift the focus to a new topic that may add energy and get Beth involved.

LEADER: Okay, if we're finished with this issue, I'd like to shift the focus. In a word or a phrase, what is the hardest thing about being a single parent? Think about that for a moment; then I'm going to get everyone to comment. *(After about 10 seconds)* Jamie, in a word or a short phrase, what is toughest for you? *(Jamie is seated next to Beth who has been quiet and the leader wants to draw out. Starting the round next to Beth and going the opposite direction means that the round will end on Beth.)*

JAMIE: It's finding time for myself.

SALLY: *(Also seated next to Jamie)* Being both parents!

JANE: Money—making ends meet.

MOLLY: Dating and not feeling guilty.

BETH: Not feeling appreciated by anyone.

LEADER: What exactly do you mean by not being appreciated?

BETH: My teenage daughter doesn't appreciate any of my sacrifices or efforts. She blames me for the divorce.

LEADER: I believe others here struggle with that. Could you say a little more about your feelings and your daughter's feelings?

BETH: Well, my daughter . . .

In this example, the leader chooses to focus on Beth and purposely has the round end on her. The leader then draws her out by asking some follow up questions.

■ ■ ■

Use of Written Exercises for Drawing Out Members

Another method of drawing out is to have members complete a writing task. Writing tasks can be making lists, answering some questions, or completing sentences. Drawing out in this manner is non-threatening because the leader merely asks members what they wrote. With the answers in front of them, members usually do not mind being asked to share their responses. Also, when the leader calls on members, it does not seem as if the spotlight is on them but simply that the leader wants them to share their written answers. If you have a number of quiet members, we strongly recommend the use of written exercises. When members can read what they have written they often get over their fears of speaking in a group.

GROUP COUNSELING SKILLS: Drawing Out Using Sentence Completion

Go to segment 8.6 to see a demonstration of the use of writing to draw out a member.

Use of Eyes to Draw Out

Another component of drawing out that we have alluded to in the earlier examples is the use of the leader's eyes. It is often possible to elicit comments from members by establishing eye contact with them and holding that contact for a few seconds. The leader's eyes are especially useful in drawing out members who are waiting to talk. By acknowledging people with his eyes and possibly a slight nod, the leader can often get them to comment. Or, if someone else is talking, the leader can cue others with his eyes and a slight nod indicating that they will be next to speak. One way to draw out a member while giving her an out is by maintaining a lot of eye contact with that member while speaking to the entire group.

■ E X A M P L E

LEADER: *(Looking mainly at Carol)* Is there anyone else who wants to comment on his or her relationship? *(Scans the group, then looks again to Carol. When Carol does not seem to be ready to respond, the leader shifts his eyes to other group members.)*

If this is done skillfully, Carol would feel gentle pressure to speak, but the leader's broad request for comments allows Carol to refrain if she chooses. The leader has to believe in Carol's right not to speak. That is, if the leader is really trying to force Carol to talk, staring at her will cause her to feel singled out, and she will not hear the leader's words but rather the intent, which would sound to her like, "Carol, SPEAK!"

■ ■ ■

Use of Movement to Draw Out

Another way to draw out members is to use movement exercises. The reason for this is that often times quiet members will participate and the leader can draw them out by asking them why they positioned themselves where they did or why they took the pose that they did. We discuss movement exercises in greater detail in Chapter 10.

GROUP COUNSELING SKILLS: Drawing Out Using Movement

Go to segment 8.7 to see a demonstration of the use of movement to draw out a member.

Additional Comments Regarding Drawing Out

It is important to assess how much a particular individual needs to talk. Sometimes leaders mistakenly believe that it is important for all members to speak up equally. Some members find it comfortable and beneficial to participate verbally at only a minimal level, yet they learn a great deal. The rule is, *Don't draw out unless it seems needed.* Also, before drawing out a reluctant member, it is important to consider the kind of response the member will get from other members.

If the tone of the group is such that the leader feels a negative response is possible, drawing out has to be done carefully or not at all because the member may be too uncomfortable.

There are some members you may not want to draw out. Beginning leaders think they should always draw out uncommitted members, and this often is not the best option. When drawn out, uncommitted members will frequently resist the efforts of the leader and the other members and try to create a negative tone. We suggest that leaders be careful with uncommitted members and members who do not seem focused at the beginning of the session. You may choose to run the group as planned, choosing *not* to draw out members who don't seem focused. Frequently, the interaction and comments of the other members will help get those members aboard, which means that no drawing out is necessary.

Practice

As in the previous section on cutting off, you now have an opportunity to practice. Think of various drawing-out responses to the following three examples. You may want to write down your responses and then compare them to ours, which follow each example.

■ EXAMPLES

The group is composed of seven women who are patients in the mental health unit of a community hospital. The group meets daily. All the members have been there for at least a week except for Ambuja, who has been in the hospital only 3 days. Ambuja has commented only when asked, and each time she has said very little. She is in the hospital because she attempted suicide. How would you try to draw her out if you were the leader? Take a minute and think of some different ways to draw out and then check our suggestions below. Jot down a couple of responses.

LEADER: Ambuja, you have not said too much yet in the group. I think you would probably find it helpful to share some of your thoughts, feelings, and reactions to being here in the hospital. I do think we can be of help to you if you will just open up to us.

In this method, the leader asks Ambuja directly if she wants to share. It is important to note that the leader keeps commenting after initially urging Ambuja to talk. These additional comments let the leader observe Ambuja's re-action; if she seems resistant or afraid, the leader may move on by saying something like, "Well, Ambuja, it seems like that would be too uncomfortable. We'll move on and hopefully you'll share later."

A second way to draw Ambuja out is to use a round that ends on her. The leader could ask the members to comment in a word or phrase on how they are feeling now about whatever it was that brought them to the hospital.

MARY: I'm doing better. My family was here yesterday.

DOT: I understand why I am so depressed. Being here has really helped.

AMBUJA: I am doing okay.

LEADER: What do you mean when you say you are doing okay?

AMBUJA: Things don't seem as bad as they did.

LEADER: Maybe you can tell us a little about how it was.

AMBUJA: I think I would like to. The reason I am here is because . . .

Still another way the leader might get Ambuja to participate would be to focus on the topic of suicide, because Ambuja has attempted suicide.

LEADER: A number of you have mentioned that you were depressed or lonely. I'd like to talk about how you have chosen to handle those feelings. I know for some of you, suicide may have been considered or even attempted.

MARY: I have never thought of suicide, but I sometimes feel that life really stinks. I didn't know how to deal with my feelings, but things are getting better.

LEADER: Ambuja, what about you? I know a little about your history although I do not know many of the details.

AMBUJA: Well, uh, I tried suicide because I have been so lonely since my husband left me. The feelings are . . .

■ ■ ■

This group is composed of six ministers who are on a weekend retreat to discuss the stresses and strains of being a minister. During a discussion about the effects that being a minister has on families, both Mike and Jake have been exceptionally quiet and look troubled. How would you, as the leader, try to draw these people out? Take a minute to think of at least two different ways to draw them out.

In this situation, the leader may guess that the ministers who are quiet are having problems at home. The leader must decide whether to draw both out at the same time or just one of them. To draw both out, the leader could say something like:

LEADER: Mike, I can't help but notice that both you and Jake have been quiet since we started the discussion about families. *(Looking at both of them)* Would either of you like to comment?

If the leader wanted to draw out only one of them, he could address that person directly:

LEADER: Jake, you seem to be thinking about what we are saying. My guess is you are thinking about your family situation.

The leader would choose to draw out only one member if it appeared that one was in greater need or if the other did not seem ready to share. By focusing on the one member, the leader could later draw out the other when he seemed more open to sharing. The leader could also use an exercise that would get at the ministers' feelings about their families.

LEADER: On a 1–10 scale, with 10 being *very stressful* and 1 being *not stressful,* how would each of you rate the stress that the ministry has caused your family?

■ ■ ■

This group is composed of five college women who are discussing values as part of Mental Health Week. The discussion is about premarital sex. Helen has been quiet the entire session. Carolyn has shared with the group that she is not a virgin and now has her head down as April talks about how she plans to save herself for her husband because it is God's way. Susan and Janice have shared some of their thoughts but have not commented personally on their feelings about premarital sex. They seem to be uncomfortable as they listen to April. How would you continue the discussion if you were the leader? Take a moment and think of a couple ways to draw out the other members.

The leader probably would want to stop April from talking, because other members seem to be reacting to what she is saying. The leader would then need to decide whether or not to draw out Carolyn, who is obviously feeling bad. If the leader decides to do so, she could say something like this:

LEADER: Carolyn, it is important for you to realize that what April is saying is her opinion. Other members feel differently. When she was talking, I could not help but notice your reaction. What were you thinking or feeling?

The leader could also choose to draw out Janice and Susan, because their opinions might differ from April's. Drawing them out first could make it easier to later draw out Helen and Carolyn. If the leader senses that Carolyn is feeling quite bad, she would probably shift the focus to Carolyn. Because the leader could see that the other members differed with April, he could use a brief exercise to elicit comments from others. This would also serve as a way to cut off April.

LEADER: I want each of you to complete this sentence: "For me, sex is _____."
This exercise enables the leader to hear from Helen, Janice, Susan, and Carolyn and makes it easier to draw out those members because the leader can simply ask them about their responses.

■ ■ ■

Concluding Comments

Cutting off and drawing out are absolutely essential skills for good group leading. Knowing how and when to draw out and cut off members improves the quality of the group because the leader is able to get more involvement from the members. Cutting off allows the leader to make sure that the content of the group fits with the purpose. Cutting-off skills are needed to hold, shift, and deepen the focus. It is important to understand when cutting off a member, the leader can choose to cut and stay with the member, cut and stay with the topic but not the member, or cut and leave the topic and the member. Many situations require that the leader use cutting-off skills, including when a member's comments are hurtful, off track, or inaccurate; when the focus needs to shift; when members are arguing or rescuing other members; or when the group is near the end and the leader does not want to start a new topic.

Members are silent for a number of reasons including being fearful, not mentally present, not prepared, confused, bored, not committed, or intimidated. By understanding why members are silent, the leader can better choose how and when to draw out certain members. Rounds, dyads, and written responses are three excellent ways to draw out members.

■ ACTIVITIES

1. In groups or classes, observe the cutting-off skills of the teacher or leader. Observe if the teacher/leader waited too long to cut off. What skills from this chapter would you have used to handle the different situations if you were the teacher/leader?

2. In classes or groups, observe the drawing-out skills of the teacher or leader. Observe if the teacher/leader waited too long to draw out or if she let a few people dominate the discussion. What skills from this chapter would you have used to handle the different situations if you were the teacher/leader?

GROUP COUNSELING SKILLS

1. View segments 3.2, 3.3, and 5.1 and watch how the leader had to use cutting off skills.
    a. What would have happened if the leader had let the discussion continue in each of the segments?
    b. Think about how clarity of purpose and cutting off go together in the three segments.
    c. Note how in segment 5.1 the session could have turned into a debate about whether the war was the right thing to be doing.
2. View segment 6.3 again.
    a. How did the leader draw out other members? Was that helpful?
3. View segments 8.4 and 8.5 again.
    a. Note the differences in the two approaches.
    b. What did the leader do to get the male member talking?
    c. What are your thoughts about the delicate timing and art of drawing out?

Chapter 9

Rounds and Dyads

Rounds

A round is an activity where every member is asked to respond to some stimulus posed by the leader. In all groups, rounds are extremely helpful in gathering information and involving members. Rounds also help in controlling overly verbal members. *The value of rounds cannot be overemphasized—no skill, technique, or exercise mentioned in this book is more valuable than a round.*

There are three kinds of rounds: (1) the designated word, phrase, or number round; (2) the word or phrase round; and (3) the comment round.

Designated Word or Phrase Round   These rounds can be completed quickly because the members respond with either a designated word or phrase. By designated word or phrase, we mean that the leader asks the members to use one, two, or three possible choices when responding to a question or issue, such as "yes or no" or "very helpful," "helpful," or "not helpful."

■ **EXAMPLE**

LEADER: I want you to think about the film you just saw and give your reaction using one of three descriptions: "very valuable," "valuable," or "not valuable." *(The leader gives members a moment to decide and then goes around the group, hearing from everyone.)*

The round helps keep one member from commenting for a long period of time before the others have had a chance to give some reaction. Also, by hearing the members' reactions, the leader can lead a better discussion.

■ ■ ■

Another designated phrase round is here/getting here/not here. This round is usually done at the beginning of a session as a way of assessing if the members' attention is on the group or something else. This round serves two purposes: It helps the leader know who is mentally present, and it serves as a signal to the members to turn their attention to the group.

■ EXAMPLES

LEADER: Let's start with a round of here/getting here/not here—that is, are you focused on what we are trying to do and what you can contribute and learn from the group, or are your thoughts somewhere else? If you are focused on the group, say "here"; if your thoughts are somewhere else, say "not here." And don't be afraid to say "not here." If you feel you are getting here, you can say that.

RUDY: Here.

JULIE: Here.

ALICE: Getting here.

MERV: Not here.

KELLY: Here.

MEL: Not here.

LEADER: Is there anything we can do to get you more here?

MERV: I'm getting here—I've got a job interview at 4:00 today, and I am nervous.

MEL: I'm tired. Also, I didn't eat lunch. I'll get here.

LEADER: Okay, then we'll begin. Merv, would you want to take 5 minutes to discuss your job interview before we get into the topics for today, which are what to do when you slip from your diet and how to handle holiday feasts?

■ ■ ■

GROUP COUNSELING SKILLS: Use of Rounds

Watch segment 9.1 (Here–Not Here Round) for a discussion of the value of rounds and demonstration of the here–not here round.

LEADER: *(Near the beginning of the session)* Who has something they would like to talk about tonight? We'll do a simple yes-or-no round. If you have something you'd like to discuss, just say yes; if not, say no. *(Pause)* Frank, we'll start with you.

FRANK: No.

ERIC: No.

FRED: Yes.

ABA: Yes.

TRACY: Maybe, not sure. If we have time, check back.

MARTIN: Yes.

HERO: Yes.

LEADER: Because there are a number of *yeses*, briefly, what is your *yes* about?

FRED: Mine is about fighting with Mom about playing football.

ABA: I want some help on how to handle it when I see my dad for the first time since he left 3 years ago. It is going to happen in 3 weeks.

MARTIN: I want to talk some more about getting along with my stepdad.

In this round, the leader quickly found out that there were a number of people wanting to work on some issue. The follow-up for the *yeses* was helpful to determine who was in need now and who could wait if need be. This kind of round is especially helpful in support, counseling, and therapy groups, because the leader has no way of knowing who has concerns they want to bring up.

■ ■ ■

GROUP COUNSELING SKILLS: Use of Rounds

Watch segment 9.2 for a demonstration of the yes/no round.

Designated Number Round   The 1–10 round can serve many purposes. For example, it can encourage members to think more specifically about the topic. A 1–10 round usually generates interest because members are curious about how their rating compares to that of other members. Here are some examples:

- On a 1–10 scale, with 10 being *very comfortable,* how comfortable are you being in the group?

- On a 1–10 scale, with 10 being *very much,* how much did you like the article you read for this week?

- On a 1–10 scale, with 10 being *very valuable,* how would you rate tonight's group?

- On a 1–10 scale, with 10 being *a lot,* how would you rate the amount of fighting, arguing, and tension in your early home environment?
- On a 1–10 scale, with 10 being *great,* how would you rate your current love relationship?

GROUP COUNSELING SKILLS: 1-10 Round to Shift the Focus

View segment 7.3 again. Watch how the leader used the round to shift the focus in order to concentrate the members on a new topic, and to gather information about their struggle with the topic.

Word or Phrase Round   For this round, the members are asked to respond with only a word or a short phrase, because the leader wants members to keep their comments brief. Here are some examples of word or phrase rounds:

- In a word or phrase, how are you feeling about being in this group?
- In a word or phrase, how would you describe your feelings about school?
- In a word or phrase, how would you describe our task as you see it?
- I'd like to hear from everyone, so I want you to think of a word or phrase that describes your reaction to the proposal.
- How would you describe your feeling about exercising? In just a word or phrase.

GROUP COUNSELING SKILLS: Opening Round—Word or Phrase

Watch segment 9.3 for a demonstration of a word or phrase round.

Comment Rounds   The comment round is used when the leader wants members to say more than just a few words, either because the leader thinks they will benefit from hearing comments or because the question does not lend itself to a word or phrase answer.

- Let's do a brief round of progress reports—how has the week been? What have you tried?
- I'd like to get a brief reaction from each of you regarding how you think we should approach the task.
- What stood out to you about the group today? We'll do a round and hear a brief comment from everyone.
- When you think of remarriage, what feelings or thoughts do you have? Take a moment and think about this, and then we will get a brief comment from everyone.

- When you think of parenting, what is hardest for you? Let's hear from each of you briefly.

By using a round instead of just asking the question, everyone will get a chance to speak, instead of just one or two eager members.

Uses of Rounds

In this section, we discuss eight uses of rounds.

1. Build comfort, trust, and cohesion
2. Get members focused
3. Gather information and locate energy
4. Shift the focus to involve all members
5. Draw out quiet members
6. Deepen the intensity
7. Process exercises
8. Summarize

Use of Rounds to Build Comfort, Trust, and Cohesion   Rounds provide an easy way for members to talk and thus often help members feel more comfortable. Simple and specific information rounds during the first and second sessions, when members are still getting to know each other, can be useful in building comfort and trust. Members are curious about each other, and rounds can satisfy some of that curiosity. The skilled leader is always thinking of possible rounds that will ease members' discomfort and help them get to know more about one another. Also, information rounds help members feel linked to each other when they hear that their situations are similar.

Use of Rounds to Get Members Focused   The round gets members to focus on an issue or topic in two ways: First, members have to think of what they are going to say; and second, members listen to others as they comment on the subject at hand. Any of the three kinds of rounds can be used to focus the group.

■ EXAMPLES

The group is made up of first-year college students who are having difficulty adjusting to college. To get the group focused, the leader might say one of the following:

LEADER: On a 1–10 scale, with 10 being *very well,* how well did the week go for you?

LEADER: In a word or phrase, how would you describe your week?

LEADER: Let's do a quick round. I want you to think of the best and worst things that happened to you this week. I'd like to hear from everyone.

■ ■ ■

The group is a task group in a human resources agency. They are discussing a new program. The members are having difficulty focusing on one issue. The leader might say the following:

LEADER: I want us to talk just about the staffing of the program. Think of how many staff members we'll need. In a minute, we'll go around and I'll get each of you to state the number you think we need. Then we'll discuss your rationale and so forth.

■ ■ ■

Use of Rounds to Gather Information and Locate Energy   At various times, a leader wants to know how members are thinking and feeling about some issue, topic, or assignment. The round is an excellent way to get this information in a quick, controlled manner. The following two examples further illustrate the value of rounds with respect to focusing, gathering information, building interest, and locating the energy in members.

■ EXAMPLES

This group consists of four students who are doing a placement at the mental health center. The leader decides to start with a round to find out how much the students know about medications.

LEADER: I want to get some idea of what you know about therapeutic drugs. On a 1–10 scale, with 10 being *quite a bit* and 1 being *very little,* how would you rate your current knowledge?

JAN: Uh, about a 2.

DEEPA: 1.

EDDIE: 4.

ART: 8 or 9.

LEADER: Art, why an 8 or 9?

ART: I did a 3-hour independent-study course on medications and wrote a 25-page paper on the subject. I'm glad to be here, though—I want to learn more.

LEADER: Good, and certainly feel free to comment. Let's do another round; then we'll get started. How do you feel about using drugs as a form of therapy? Respond with "believe in them," "don't believe in them," or "not sure."

JAN: Not sure.

DEEPA: Believe in them.

EDDIE: Don't believe in them. My brother has had all kinds of medications, and he is still not any better after 3 years.

ART: I started out a nonbeliever, but after doing the paper and talking to different therapists, I see some value in medications in certain situations.

■ ■ ■

This group is a discussion and education group for parents. The members have been assigned a reading in a parenting book that the leader plans to discuss.

LEADER: Let's do a word or phrase round on your reaction to the chapters on mealtimes and fighting. Sandy, let's start with you.

SANDY: I liked them very much.

PAT: Helpful, but hard.

MELINA: I don't know if I agree with the idea of letting kids settle their own fights. My kids differ in age by 4 years, and—

LEADER: Can you hold that?

MELINA: Oh, sure.

LEADER: Bill, what about you?

BILL: Mealtimes still have been bad—I've got some questions.

DANIA: I tried to get my husband to read it so he'd understand, but he wouldn't. *(She starts to tear up a little.)*

LEADER: *(To the whole group)* Not getting cooperation from a partner can be very frustrating. Dania, let's talk after the group about your situation, okay? *(The leader purposely chooses not to go into Dania's pain.)*

DANIA: Yeah, I do need to talk to someone.

LEADER: *(Decides to do a second round to focus the group)* What is hardest for you at mealtimes? I'd like each of you to briefly comment on mealtime problems.

PAT: Getting them to eat what I fix!

BILL: Getting them to the table, to not fight at the table—you name it!

LEADER: Sandy, what about you?

SANDY: Dealing with the baby while trying to give my 3-year-old some attention.

LEADER: Looks like tonight should be interesting and helpful. We'll start with mealtimes. Your comments and questions are helpful to me in knowing where to start. Let's begin by...

Note in all the preceding and following examples how the leader is using the round to get members focused and talking. This is why we say the round is a very valuable exercise.

■ ■ ■

Use of Rounds to Shift the Focus to Involve All Members Rounds can be used to shift the focus from a person to a topic. If one person has been talking for a while, the leader may use a round to get other members involved. Members who have been drifting away during the session often get re-involved when asked to participate in a round.

■ EXAMPLE

It is the second meeting of a support and therapy group for teenage boys. Andre has been talking for a couple of minutes about how bad his home life is.

ANDRE: … and it really is unbelievable how strict it is.

LEADER: Andre, I want to get everyone in on this. Each of you think for a minute of a word or phrase that describes your home life; then we'll do a round where each of you will comment. *(Leader waits a few seconds and scans the room to see when the members seem ready.)* Okay, let's start here on my left, with Gary.

GARY: Well, you see they are divorced and, uh, it all started…

LEADER: Gary, let's do this for now: Tell with whom you live—like mom, brother, sister—and then add the word or phrase that best describes your home life. *(The leader changes the round a little, realizing that the group would benefit by hearing each person's living situation.)*

GARY: Okay, my mom, my grandmother, and my two older sisters. As for a description—lousy—everyone is always bossing me around.

TIM: My mom, my stepdad, and my little sister who is 2. My other brother lives with my dad on the farm. As for how it is at home—bad. My stepdad and I hate each other! Just last week

LEADER: Hang on, Tim. Let's get everyone to comment; then we'll come back to you and others.

ASID: I live with my mom and dad. They are real old, though—in their fifties. They just don't understand how things have changed.

RICK: I live with my grandparents—my mom can't handle me with her three other kids. My real dad—well, I don't know where he is; I think he's in Georgia—he left when I was 2. As for things with my grandparents, well, they are okay, I guess. Boring, but my grandparents let me do what I want. *(The leader lets Rick speak a little longer than the others because up until now he has not said very much in the group.)*

JOE: I live with my uncle—my dad was killed in a car accident, and my mom is in the, uh, well, the hospital. Nerves and stuff. It's bad—my uncle really doesn't want me there. *(Joe is the last person.)*

LEADER: Let's talk about how your home life affects your behavior; that is, how the environment you live in may be contributing to some of your problems in school and on the street.

After this round, the leader has much more information and a much clearer idea of the kinds of home conditions members are experiencing. The round opens up options and aids the leader in deciding where to focus. Also, the members are now more involved in the topic.

■ ■ ■

In the preceding example, the leader, wanting to focus the entire group on the topic of home environment, spun off from what Andre was saying. There will be other instances when the leader will want to involve all the members because the member talking needs to be cut off. For example, in the following group, business executives are discussing how to bring more enjoyment to their lives. One member has been talking on and on about his summer vacation plans, and the leader interrupts him:

LEADER: Jamil, let me jump in and pick up on what you were saying about summer plans not being fun-oriented. Think about your summer; I want to get each of you to briefly say what your plans are and if they are fun-oriented. I'll give you a few seconds and then we'll do a round.

In this example, the leader used a round to stay with the topic and expand it to include the entire group.

■ ■ ■

Use of Rounds to Draw Out Quiet Members   By definition, a round gets everyone to respond, thus giving the leader greater opportunity to encourage members to share or draw out any member who has remained silent for a long time. If a leader wishes to encourage a certain member to share more, she can end the round with that member. When the round ends, the leader can naturally focus on the last person who talked—the one the leader wants to draw out.

Use of Rounds to Deepen the Focus   In support, growth, counseling, and therapy groups, rounds can be used to get members to delve deeper into their thoughts and feelings.

LEADER: I want each of you to think for a minute—what do you believe affects your feelings of personal worth the most? Now really think about this—think of a person or situation in your daily life that would describe this. It may be "Mom," "work," "my weight," or something else. What would it be? We'll go around and get each of you to comment.

In the next example, the leader uses a comment round to deepen the focus for members in a group for widows.

LEADER: Now that we have shared how each of you came to be a widow, let's go a step further and talk about your feelings and fears. In a couple of sentences, how would you describe what you have been feeling since your husband's death?

■ ■ ■

Use of Rounds to Process Exercises   After a group exercise, the leader may want to get a sense of what all the members are feeling and thinking. A good way to do this is by using a round. Sometimes a quick word or phrase round will provide a lot of information.

■ EXAMPLE

The group has been discussing their fears about being in the group for about 10 minutes.

LEADER: Now that you've talked about your list of fears, how do you feel? In a word or phrase, how would you describe your feelings now?

WAYNE: Better!

AKIRA: A little more comfortable, but still scared.

SARAH: Much better.

TOM: I still have my fear of being laughed at.

TANDY: It was helpful to hear that others were afraid. I still am hesitant to share a couple of things. I guess I want someone else to go first as far as sharing "heavy" stuff.

■ ■ ■

Another benefit of processing an exercise with a round is that it keeps the dominating member from taking over, because the leader is calling for only a word or a phrase. Very often beginning leaders let the first person who speaks continue for a long time without hearing from the others. Frequently, the first person to speak is not the one who really wants or needs to work on something. By using a round, the leader has a much easier time cutting off the talkative member.

Use of Rounds to Summarize   At times the leader may want to use some kind of round as a way to summarize reactions to the session. A round gives the leader a chance to hear the important things that members experienced. The leader can then close the group, addressing the important comments heard during the round.

Additional Comments About Rounds

In this section, we discuss six additional aspects of rounds.

1. How to set up a round
2. Where to start a round

3. Stopping in the middle of a round
4. Handling members who are hesitant to talk
5. How to process a round
6. Overusing rounds

How to Set Up a Round   Rounds, like any other group activity, have to be set up properly. The leader has to think about when a round would be useful and then introduce it in such a way that the members understand what is being asked of them. The leader also needs to allow enough time for members to formulate their answers and not let an eager member start before the others are ready. Further, the leader needs to specify the kind of round: a word or phrase round, a 1–10 scale only, a scale with comments to follow, or a comment round. Leaders who lead groups with elementary aged children should be aware of the possibility that the round produces all the same responses from the members. The leader of elementary groups will want to be creative in using rounds by possibly having the members to write out their responses.

Where to Start a Round   The leader chooses where to start a round. It is a good practice to vary the starting point so that different members get to speak first and last. It is important to think about where you start and end your rounds. In some groups there will be members who always tend to be negative. By arranging the round so that the negative members are neither the first nor last to speak, the leader gains some control over the tone.

Avoid beginning with members who are long-winded or always confused about what the group is trying to do. If a member tends to ramble, it is easier to cut her off if she is not the first or last person in the round. As we have mentioned earlier, on occasion the leader will want to end a round with a certain member in order to draw out that member.

Stopping in the Middle of a Round   Normally it is best to finish any round, especially a serious round where members have had to give much thought to their answers. If the leader does not complete the round, the members could feel stranded. But the leader must be flexible; if she is conducting an information round that is not of a personal nature, stopping in the middle of the round can be fine. During an information round, a good topic may be raised, and the leader can spin off from it into a group exercise or mini-lecture that is more beneficial than completing the round. If the leader does stop a round in the middle, it is best for her to acknowledge that she is aware of doing so. The leader can quickly scan the group to see if any member seems upset at stopping.

When doing a serious, personal round, there will be times when a member might begin to cry or indicate the need for immediate attention. The leader then has to decide whether to continue the round or work with the member. The leader has several options from which to choose:

■   The leader can work with the member, stating that she will try to get back to the round.

- The leader can explain to the member that she will come back to him but that it is important to let everyone share.
- The leader can ask the members how they feel about stopping the round so that the group can help the troubled member.
- The leader can ask a member in whom she has confidence to step out with the troubled member while everyone finishes the round. This is appropriate only if the round will take considerable time.

Handling Members Who Are Hesitant to Talk   When doing rounds, there will be times when a member either refuses to comment or can't comment because of fear, confusion, or lack of anything to say. If the refusal is based on fear, skipping that member is usually the best policy. Some beginning leaders make the mistake of focusing on that member, which often makes the individual feel even more uncomfortable. If the refusal is based on a negative attitude, the best policy again is to move on to the next person, making a mental note about the problem with that member. Although the purpose of rounds is to hear from everyone, the leader should rarely push someone into commenting. If a member is not ready to comment when her turn comes, simply tell her you will come back to her at the end. Be sure to do so!

How to Process a Round   Most rounds need to be *processed*. Processing involves discussing the responses in a focused, conscious manner. If a leader conducts a 1–10 round or a word or phrase round, he has many options for following up:

- The leader can ask different members questions about their words or ratings—for example, why they were low or high.
- The leader can pair up the members according to their answers or ratings and have them discuss the topic further.
- The leader can focus on one member specifically.
- The leader can do a follow-up round for further information.

■ EXAMPLES

The leader has just completed a round asking, "Is there someone in your life right now with whom you are angry?" Everyone has responded "yes." The leader then does a follow-up round:

LEADER: We'll do a second round. I want you to state who this person is; that is, mom, friend, boss, or whoever—then in a sentence or two, state what your anger is about.

Doing both of these rounds gives the leader a lot of information to work with and gets the members focused on the topic.

■ ■ ■

The leader has just done a round asking how each member of a group of women sees her present love relationship. The round has just ended and the leader processes the round by focusing on one member.

LEADER: I want to go back to what Melba said. Melba, what exactly did you mean by distant? Did you mean you feel distant or that the relationship is distant?

■ ■ ■

The leader has just completed a word or phrase round on the members' reactions to three chapters in a book and decides to focus on a topic.

LEADER: It seems like many of you got something out of the three chapters. Let's start with the first chapter—some of you said this was the best reading for you so far. Nelly, you mentioned that the chapter made you think about how change *is* possible. Let's talk about change.

■ ■ ■

Overusing Rounds   *Even though rounds are very valuable, beware of overusing them.* Some beginning leaders conduct one round right after the other. Overusing rounds can cause members to become bored, confused, or resentful of what they may view as a gimmick. Use the rounds to get members focused and thinking, not just to fill time.

Dyads

A dyad is an activity where pairs of members discuss issues or complete a task. Dyads are immensely valuable because they can be used for so many different reasons. Group leaders need to know when to use dyads, how to pair up the members, and the length of time dyads should last.

Uses of Dyads

In this section, we discuss eight uses of dyads:

1. Developing comfort
2. Warming up members and building energy
3. Processing information and group exercises
4. Finishing a topic
5. Getting certain members together
6. Providing leader/member interaction
7. Changing the format
8. Providing time for the leader to think

Developing Comfort   In the first or second session of a group, members are often uncomfortable at the prospect of talking in front of other people. By placing members in dyads, they can talk to just one person. Dyads also provide better contact between members; members experience each other as individuals rather than as faces in the group. For these reasons, a leader should consider using dyads during the first session. It is important to always consider whether the members are ready and willing to talk in dyads. For instance, if members are forced to attend, then dyads probably are not a good idea, because the members will more than likely not have much to say. The following examples of dyads could occur at almost any time during the first session.

LEADER: So you can get a little more comfortable with some of the other members, I would like each of you to pair up with someone whom you don't know very well and share why you decided to be in this group.

LEADER: We are going to do something a little different now. I am going to ask you to get into pairs and talk for a few minutes, and then we'll come back to the group and share your various thoughts. This way you'll get to know one other member a little better and you'll get a chance to share your ideas. I'd like you to share your ideas about _____.

LEADER: I would like you to get into pairs and discuss how you are feeling about being in this group. Discuss your hopes, excitement, and fears.

■ ■ ■

Warming Up and Building Energy   Warming up and creating energy are often needed when beginning a group and introducing a new topic. One option is to begin a session by having the members get into dyads: The leader asks the members to pair up and talk about such things as their week, the assignment, their hopes for the session, or their progress on a project.

■ EXAMPLES

This career-awareness group for 11th-graders is beginning its third session.

LEADER: Let's get started. *(Pauses until members become quiet.)* To get warmed up, I am going to pair you up and have you discuss some of the things you have thought about as a result of our last meeting. As you recall, we spent a lot of time talking about the pros and cons of college and technical school. What have you thought about? We'll take just a couple of minutes to do this. Get into pairs.

■ ■ ■

In the following example, dyads are used to warm up a group of parents regarding their feelings about having a child who is mentally and physically challenged.

LEADER: During the next few minutes you are going to get a chance to share your feelings about your child. To start with, I'm going to ask you to pair up with a person next to you and for about 3 minutes share two or three of the hardest things you have dealt with as a parent; then we'll come back to the large group and continue that sharing.

■ ■ ■

Topics such as sex, marital problems, or fears often can be shared more easily in a dyad than in a large group. By starting the topic with a dyad, the leader can get members focused and ready to share their thoughts and feelings.

LEADER: We've agreed that sex is an important issue to discuss. Let's begin by pairing up and talking about some of the things you'd like to explore. Talk about any topics you think would be good to bring up and any concerns you have about discussing sex.

■ ■ ■

Processing Information and Group Exercises   Members can also benefit from dyads when they have just learned some new material or have just completed a group exercise. The dyad provides each member with the opportunity to give reactions, share ideas, or raise questions. If the leader processed the exercise or information in the large group, more time would be needed and also considerable time would elapse before the last few members got to speak. The dyad allows everyone to share immediately.

■ **EXAMPLE**

The group is an assertiveness-training group and the leader has just presented information about the differences between being assertive, nonassertive, and aggressive.

LEADER: To give you a chance to process what I have been saying, I want you to pair up with someone you have never been paired with before and discuss what we have just been talking about. Try to relate the information to yourself; that is, how you are assertive, nonassertive, or aggressive. We'll do this for about 5 minutes.

■ ■ ■

Finishing a Topic   Dyads can be helpful in ending a discussion about a topic because they are a good way to give everyone a chance to talk when the leader needs to save time.

■ EXAMPLE

The group members have been discussing ways of improving their relationships with their parents; the leader feels that the topic is winding down and that the group needs a break.

LEADER: I think this discussion has given each of you food for thought. Before taking a break, I'd like you to get into pairs and talk about what the last 30 minutes have stirred up in you and what you are going to do differently, if anything. We'll go for about 5 minutes and then take a short break. Be sure to focus on your relationship with your parents.

■ ■ ■

Getting Certain Members Together In some group situations the leader may want to get certain members talking to each other. This may be because they have something in common, such as both being single parents or both recently experiencing the death of a parent; or it may be because they don't feel comfortable with each other and the leader thinks that if they had a few minutes together some of the discomfort might dissipate. Another reason to pair certain members is because they have differing views on an issue. As the leader gets to know the members and as issues come up in the group, the leader may see the usefulness of dividing the group into pairs to give certain members a chance to interact with one another.

Providing Leader/Member Interaction Whenever a leader needs to spend more time with a member—helping to finish something, providing encouragement, or helping to clarify something—the leader can put the members into dyads and pair herself up with that member. The leader can also use the leader/member dyad to get to know the members better.

Changing the Format Dyads also can be used to provide a refreshing change from sitting in the group and are useful whenever the leader senses that members are restless. Members often value the opportunity to talk to just one member.

Providing Time for the Leader to Think Because groups are so unpredictable, there may be times when the leader needs some time just to think. By placing members in dyads, the leader obtains a timeout period without the group actually taking a break. The leader gives the members something relevant to talk about in their dyads while she plans what to do next.

Pairing Members for Dyads

In the examples given so far, we have, for the most part, implied that members choose each other without any specific instructions from the leader. Often this system works fine. However, on many occasions, the leader will choose to facilitate the pairing, either to make the process go smoothly or because the leader has a particular goal in mind.

Members Choose   One approach to pairing is allowing members to choose whomever they wish to be with in a dyad. The leader can say, "Pair up with someone" or "Choose a partner." The members then make a choice. Friends may choose each other or a member may identify with another member based on something that was said in the group. If there is an age spread in the group, older members may pair with each other, as may members of a similar racial background or members who are married or divorced or who have children. Usually members pair in the most comfortable way possible. For this reason, allowing members to make their own independent choices usually is a less-threatening experience. A word of caution here: Although this method usually goes smoothly, the leader should be on the lookout for any negative reactions. There may be some who feel uncomfortable with this method, such as those who find it reminiscent of feeling left out when not chosen for a team. In groups where there is great diversity, letting the members choose may work well or may be a mistake, depending on the members and their backgrounds. The leader also needs to pay attention to make sure everyone is in a dyad.

A disadvantage of allowing members to choose on their own is that they often continue to choose the same people and, therefore, do not get acquainted with other members of the group. Because the purpose of the dyad may be for members to have contact with those they don't know, the leader might say any of the following:

LEADER: Pair up with someone you would like to know better.

LEADER: Pair up with someone who seems to be different from you.

LEADER: Pair up with someone with whom you don't feel comfortable.

■ ■ ■

A variation on having members choose at random is for the leader to choose a member who in turn picks a partner.

LEADER: Tim, pick a partner to be with.

   TIM: James.

LEADER: Okay, Carol, you pick someone.

  CAROL: Ralph.

■ ■ ■

Leaders Choose

By seating   One of the easiest ways to assign dyad partners is by seating arrangement. While pointing at two members sitting next to each other and then moving to the next pair, the leader says, "The two of you pair up; the two of you, and the two of you." Even in this situation, the leader may want to exercise some control over who pairs up with whom. This can be done by starting the pairs at any point in the circle. Suppose a group of six is sitting in a circle in this order: Joe, Bill, Bob, Sam, Roy, and Ed. If the leader starts the pairing with Joe and Bill, the other two pairs would be Bob with Sam and Roy with Ed. But if the leader wanted to split up Bob and Sam, he could start pairing with Bill and Bob, thus leaving Sam with Roy and Ed with Joe.

One common mistake that beginning leaders make is to say to the group, "Turn to the person on your left and talk about...." This seems as if it would work; however, if everyone tried to talk to the person on her left, no one would, in fact, talk to anyone!

By leader's discretion Sometimes the leader will think that some member would benefit by being in a dyad with some other member. In this case, the leader can assign the dyads by saying, "We are going to spend the next few minutes processing what has happened here. Tom, you and Carl pair up; Jana, you and Phil; Isao, you and Sharon."

The leader may pair people on the basis of similarities or differences. For example, the leader may decide to pair those who feel religion is very important in their lives with those who either feel similarly or with those who feel differently. The pairing would depend on the leader's purpose. In addition, the leader may want to avoid pairing certain people, such as those who do not like each other or those who have a strong relationship outside the group.

Another point to consider is that the leader can choose whether or not to be in a dyad. At times the leader will want to talk with one member in particular; when setting up the dyads, the leader pairs up with that person. If there are two members the leader wants to be with, the two of them can be put together and the leader joins them. Be careful about not always paring yourself with the same member. Although there may be times when you want or need to pair yourself with one particular member, it is not typically a good idea to always pair yourself with that member.

Additional Thoughts About Dyads

How Much Time to Allow Dyads can last anywhere from 2 to 10 minutes, depending on their purpose. If the time is too short, members may get frustrated. On the other hand, if it is too long, they may get bored and wander from the topic. For instance, in a group to help clients at a rehabilitation center learning how to get a job, dyads to discuss techniques for greeting a receptionist may need only a couple of minutes. By contrast, dyads to discuss feelings about going out and applying for a job could take 5 to 7 minutes.

When leaders are using dyads to build energy, they should end the dyads before the discussion has peaked, so that the members bring some energy back to the group. However, if the members are working on a task, the leader needs to give them ample time to finish. Keep in mind that some pairs may move at a very slow pace, so the leader should not wait until the very last pair finishes, because the others' focus and/or energy will be lost.

Leaders should always tell the members in advance the approximate amount of time that the dyad will last. Sometimes the leader can see that either more or less time is needed once the members have been talking for a while. In that case, asking the members how much more time they need is a good way to judge the amount to allow. It is also helpful to give members some warning before bringing the dyad to a close. For example, the leader might loudly say one of the following:

LEADER: We'll go for another 2 minutes.

LEADER: Please wind down in the next 30 seconds or so and then come back to the large group.

Time warnings are very helpful when there are a number of subjects the leader wants the members to cover in dyads, such as the answers to five questions or feelings about school, work, and friends. Often people get stuck on one topic or one person; the time warnings help keep them moving. Also, time warnings and the proper allotment of time bring dyads to a smooth end. Abrupt endings can cause members to become frustrated and angry with the leader.

Giving Clear, Simple Instructions   Make sure the instructions are easy to understand and that everyone does understand them. Usually the directions are given before the members pair up. However, if the instructions are somewhat complex, it is often better to have members get into pairs first and then tell them what to do. If the leader gives lengthy or confusing instructions for the dyad, members may misunderstand and fail to do what is asked.

Making Sure Members Stay on Task   Often members may be slow getting to the task or may stray from the intended purpose of the dyad. The leader may want to remind members of the purpose about 30 seconds or a minute after the dyad has started. To ensure that the dyads are on target, the leader should listen in on each of them for 10 to 20 seconds to hear if they are in fact doing what was asked. If not, the leader can urge the members back to the topic. The leader can also get some ideas for discussion in the large group by listening in.

The Leader's Role During Dyads   The leader has many options during the time that members are in dyads. It is up to the leader to decide whether or not to participate. In any case, the leader should first make sure that everyone understands the dyad's purpose. If the leader decides not to be involved in the dyads, the time can be used to plan the remainder of the group. A leader who is participating may pair up with a member, float from dyad to dyad, or join one dyad for the entire time. It is important to remember that while participating in a dyad, the leader still needs to be aware of the time, give time warnings, and end the dyad at an appropriate point.

The Physical Arrangement for Dyads   Usually the dyads take place in the area where the group is meeting. However, at times the leader may want them to meet in other parts of the room or even in other parts of the building. This would be appropriate when the dyads are going to last for a relatively long time (8 to 10 minutes) or the leader feels that the members can benefit from being in a more private, less noisy situation.

Using Triads Instead of Dyads   Although this section is about the use of dyads, there are times when grouping members in threes instead of twos can be valuable. With three people, more ideas or points of view are presented. For this reason, triads are often used in education, discussion, and task groups. Another advantage is that even if one person is not involved, the other two people can interact. A disadvantage is that quiet members may be able to "hide" more easily while the other two members carry the conversation. Also, more time is usually needed for a triad than for a dyad because all members need time to express themselves.

Concluding Comments

Learning to use rounds and dyads effectively is important for any group leader because they can be used in so many different ways and situations. There are three kinds of rounds: a designated word, number, or phrase round; a word or phrase round; and a comment round. Rounds are useful because they allow the leader to gather information quickly and they help with drawing out and cutting off members. Rounds also can be used for deepening the focus, shifting the focus, and processing an exercise or discussion. A leader should consider where to start and end a round and how to handle a hesitant member. *A mistake of beginning leaders is to overuse rounds.*

Dyads are important for developing comfort, warming up members, processing exercises, and providing time for the leader to think. The leader has many choices as to when and how to use dyads. Members can be paired up by where they sit, by choosing a partner, or by the leader choosing the partners. It is important to pay attention to the selection process.

■ **ACTIVITIES**

1. Think of a group that you may lead and then think of at least five possible rounds that you could use over a series of group sessions.
2. Think of three major topics; then think of rounds that would help members focus or delve deeper into those topics.
3. Think of a group you may lead and then think of three dyad situations that would be helpful.

GROUP COUNSELING SKILLS

1. View segments 5.1, 5.2 and 5.3 and watch how the leader used rounds in the opening of the group.
   a. What do you see as an advantage of using rounds during the first few minutes of a group?
   b. How does the leader benefit from using rounds?
2. View segment 14.3 and observe the value of the round regarding unfinished business.
   a. How did the leader benefit from the round?
   b. How did members benefit from the round?

Chapter 10

Exercises

The term *exercise* is used among group leaders to refer to an activity that the group does for a specific purpose. An exercise can be as simple as having members get into dyads to discuss a topic or as involved as the "blind trust walk," which entails one member leading around a blindfolded member. Other examples of exercises include reading and discussing a poem, completing sentence stems, and drawing pictures of situations or feelings. In other words, *when the leader directs the behaviors, discussion, or attention of the group members by using a specific activity, it is an exercise.* In this chapter, we discuss the reasons for using exercises and the kinds of exercises available for use in groups. In Chapter 11, we discuss introducing, conducting, and processing exercises of all types.

According to Yalom (2005), structured exercises were first described for group work in the T-groups of the 1950s. Since then, the use of exercises in groups has been described in great detail by a number of authors. In fact, a number of books that contain nothing but group exercises have been written. With just a little effort, one can find books of group exercises on almost any subject for almost any population by searching the Internet or a source such as Amazon.com. Most experts now agree that group exercises can play an important role in making a group meaningful and interesting (Corey, 2008; Gladding, 2008; Yalom, 2005). Exercises that are well thought out and used properly can be of great benefit in almost all groups.

The exercises described in this and the following chapter come from a variety of sources. Some appeared initially in the excellent resource volumes of Pfeiffer and Jones (1972–1980). Others originated in Stevens's (1972) and Simon, Howe, and Kirschenbaum's (1978) work. Many of these exercises have been modified over time and passed along through workshops or by word of mouth. *It is important for the beginning leader to adapt exercises both to the needs of the group and to the age level, cultural background, and sophistication of the members.*

GROUP COUNSELING SKILLS: How to Conduct Exercises Effectively

Go to segment 10.1 and watch an introduction to exercises and a segment where the leader uses a creative exercise.

Reasons for Using Exercises

There are at least seven reasons for using exercises in a group:

1. To increase the comfort level
2. To provide the leader with useful information
3. To generate discussion and focus the group
4. To shift the focus
5. To deepen the focus
6. To provide an opportunity for experiential learning
7. To provide fun and relaxation

Exercises Help Increase the Comfort Level

Exercises may be used to increase the comfort level of the members. Many members experience some degree of anxiety during the first couple of group sessions. Getting-acquainted exercises often increase comfort among members. The use of dyads can be helpful in increasing comfort during the early sessions and when preparing to discuss a very personal topic. Written exercises help with comfort because members often feel more comfortable reading what they wrote; that is they know they have something to say.

Exercises Provide the Leader With Useful Information

Exercises may be used to get information from the members. Rounds are often used in this way. For instance, the leader might ask members to use a single word to describe their home environment when they were growing up. In describing their home environment, members might use words such as playful, warm, hostile, cold, competitive, abusive, or healthy. By hearing how each member describes her early environment, the leader obtains information that can help her to focus the group. Another way to gather information about the home environment is to have members draw a family scene. An exercise where members talk about what kind of animal they would like to be can be very informative for the leader. Throughout this chapter, we discuss many more exercises that are useful in gaining information about the members.

Exercises Help Generate Discussion and Focus the Group

Using group exercises increases member participation by providing a common experience. Also, exercises serve as a way to stimulate members' interest and

energy. Some exercises can be helpful when dealing with members from different cultures because exercises can make concepts more visual and concrete. An
exercise can be used to get members focused on a common issue or topic. For
example, if the leader wanted to focus the group on the benefits of good study
skills, he could say:

LEADER: On a piece of paper, I'd like each of you to list three benefits of
planning your study time.

Or if the leader wanted to focus the group on the topic of anger, she could
use different lengths of cord to represent one's "anger fuse" and could say:

LEADER: I want you to think about your anger and the length of your fuse. *(Points
to all different sizes of cord from 1 to 12 inches)* Pick from the different fuses
the fuse that best represents you—a short, medium, or long fuse.

GROUP COUNSELING SKILLS: How to Conduct Exercises Effectively

View again segment 7.1 where the leader uses fuses as an exercise.

Exercises Can Shift the Focus

A leader may want to use an exercise to shift the focus when he feels a new topic
is needed. For example, if the leader wanted to shift from discussing anger at
parents to feelings about themselves, he could say:

LEADER: It seems like each of you has a wide variety of feelings of anger toward
your parents. I hope our discussion here has given you some new ways
to look at your relationship with them. Now I would like us to shift
to a different topic—how you feel about yourself. I want you to think
of three things that you like about yourself and three things you don't
like about yourself.

Exercises Can Deepen the Focus

Exercises can be quite powerful and cause members to gain insights into themselves. Certain exercises can cause members to get more in touch with who they
are and how they interact. Many feedback, trust, creative, fantasy, and movement exercises are designed to deepen the focus because members are asked to
share or experience something at a more intense level.

GROUP COUNSELING SKILLS: How to Conduct Exercises Effectively

Go to segment 10.2 and watch an exercise where the leader uses a small chair to
deepen the focus.

Exercises Provide an Opportunity for Experiential Learning

Exercises can also be used to provide an alternative approach to exploring issues other than through discussion. Sometimes it is helpful to get members to act out themes rather than just talk about them. For instance, let's say the group discussion centers around not being accepted by peers. To focus on this theme in a way other than through verbal sharing, the leader could have all members except one stand and gather in a tight circle with arms interlocked. The member outside the circle would then be instructed to attempt to break into the circle by whatever means possible while the members try to prevent the individual from entering. This exercise usually gets at feelings of loneliness and members' methods of attempting to gain the acceptance of others. Another experiential exercise is to have members pair up and experience the "pulls" on them as they try to reach their goals:

LEADER: This is an exercise about trying to reach your goals and feeling what keeps you from getting there. I want each of you to think about the goals that you hope to achieve in the next 2 to 5 years. (*Pause*) Now, I want you to pair up and then number off either 1 or 2. (*Members get into pairs and determine who is 1 and 2.*) Number 1, you will go first— face away from your partner, and extend your right arm back. Number 2, you take your partner's arm by the wrist with both your hands. On the count of three, Number 1, while thinking about your goals, you try to make progress; and Number 2, you offer some resistance (*Leader demonstrates this with a member.*). The resistance may help you to get in touch with what is holding you back.

Exercises Provide Fun and Relaxation

Certain exercises can loosen up the group through laughter or relaxation. Using these kinds of exercises may be quite helpful when the group seems to need a change of pace and it is the kind of group where it would be appropriate. One fun exercise is called "pass the mask," where one member makes some kind of face at the next member and that member tries to make the same face back; then, the second member turns to the next member and makes a new face. The third member copies the mask and then creates a new one for the fourth member. This takes place rapidly and usually results in fun and laughter.

There are a number of relaxation exercises. A popular one calls for the leader to take a few minutes and go through a series of relaxation steps. The leader asks members to close their eyes and, starting with their heads, try to relax their muscles. They proceed to the neck, shoulders, and so on, until the entire body is relaxed. Another relaxation exercise is a group massage. In this exercise, one person lies on the floor and is massaged gently by all the other members. For some members this is a new experience because they have experienced little or no touching. In our later discussion on touching exercises, we discuss the value of this exercise and offer caution about using such an exercise.

One common mistake of school counselors is that they spend too much time making the group fun and relaxing and not enough time making the experience meaningful. As one elementary counselor said, "I realize I have too much fluff in my groups." In summary, exercises may be used to increase interest and energy, generate a focus for the group, gather information, reduce anxiety, and have fun. In addition to these general uses, there are particular instances during any group where the leader may wish to use an exercise to accomplish a goal that is specific to what is happening in the group at the moment.

When to Use Exercises

An opening name-and-information round is often helpful when beginning a new group. Exercises may also be used when opening any of the subsequent group sessions. During the first several minutes of a group session, members often are not focused on the task at hand. They may be nervous and unsure of what will take place, or they may be thinking about something that happened just before coming to the group or something that concerns them at work or at home. *Using an exercise to structure the first several minutes often helps members get focused on being in the group.*

As the leader develops a plan for a particular group session, it is helpful if she considers what exercises might be useful. For example, if she plans to focus on members' relationships with their parents, she could consider using a checklist of parent–child relationships, a sentence-completion exercise, a 1–10 round, or word or phrase round to begin the discussion. Then she would want to consider other exercises, such as having members role-play communication problems with parents or exercises that involve Transactional Analysis (TA), because it is an excellent theory for understanding interpersonal relationships. *It is important to remember that exercises are usually not in and of themselves helpful; rather, it is the time spent personalizing and processing the exercise that is the helpful component.* Many beginning leaders mistakenly conduct one exercise after another and do not spend enough time discussing the material that comes up as a result of the exercise.

Kinds of Exercises

There are many kinds of exercises. We discuss 14 types in this chapter. Certain kinds of exercises will be more useful and relevant than others, depending on the kind of group you are leading; the issues to be dealt with; and the age, cultural background, and needs of the members. In some instances, these exercises are interchangeable in terms of their purpose and utility, but there are times when a certain kind of exercise is better than another. We discuss each kind in some detail:

1. Written exercises
2. Movement exercises
3. Dyads and triads
4. Rounds
5. Creative props
6. Arts and crafts exercises
7. Fantasy exercises
8. Common reading exercises
9. Feedback exercises
10. Trust exercises
11. Experiential exercises
12. Moral dilemma exercises
13. Group-decision exercises
14. Touching exercises

Written Exercises

Written exercises are among the most versatile and useful of all the exercise types. Written exercises are structured activities where members write lists, answer questions, fill in sentence-completion items, write down their reactions, or mark checklists relating to an issue or topic. The major advantages of written exercises are that members become focused while completing the writing task and members have their ideas or responses in front of them when they are finished. Drawing out members tends to be easier when they have answers or reactions readily available. Writing out responses eliminates the pressure of having to create responses on the spot.

Sentence-Completion Exercises   One of the most useful types of written exercises is the sentence completion. A sentence completion is a written statement with a portion left blank for the member to fill in. Sentence completions generate interest and energy among members because members are usually curious about how other members have responded to the same sentence stems. Sentence completions can be devised for any topic or issue. For example, if the topic of discussion is divorce, the following sentence-completion exercise could be developed to help generate discussion:

Being divorced means _____.

The hardest thing about being divorced is _____.

When I think of future relationships, I _____.

The thing I would most like help with from the group is _____.

There are only four sentence stems here, but a leader can develop as many as he likes. The length and kind of sentence completion should depend on the kind of group, the purpose of the group, and the depth of answers desired. Usually a leader does not want more than 5 or 6 sentence stems, although there may be times when as many as 10 are used. Also, a leader may use only one sentence stem to generate discussion for an entire session.

The following are three additional examples of helpful sentence-completion questionnaires. The first example is an excellent one to use in the beginning of many kinds of counseling, therapy, growth, and support groups. It could be used right after any introduction exercise or later in the first session. The questions give members a chance to share many thoughts and feelings about being in the group and about themselves. Also, the questions are worded so that the leader can use the responses to comment on how the group will be conducted and what will happen in the group.

When I enter a new group, I feel _____.

When people first meet me, they _____.

When I am in a new group, I feel most comfortable when _____.

When people remain silent, I feel _____.

I feel annoyed when the leader _____.

In a group, I am most afraid of _____.

The following sentence-completion form is intended to generate discussion about how individuals view themselves.

My greatest asset is _____.

I need to improve _____.

I regret _____.

My best accomplishment is _____.

Compared to others, I think I am _____.

I want most out of life to_____.

My biggest fear is _____.

I am _____.

This sentence-completion exercise can be used to focus discussion on members' thoughts and feelings about sex.

I think sex is _____.

Many of my feelings about sex come from _____   .

Discussing sex in this group is _____.

I would like to have sex _____ times a week.

The sexual topic I would most like us to discuss would be _____.

Devising sentence completions that are consistent is very important. If you are devising your own sentence-completion forms, be sure that the sentences focus the members in the areas that you desire. For instance, in the third example above, the leader wants to focus on issues pertaining to sexual activity. An inappropriate sentence stem is "I enjoy being the sex I am because _____." It is inappropriate because it would generate discussion about gender and sex roles rather than sex and sexual behavior.

Listing Exercises   Having members make a list is another very useful written exercise. Lists can be done quickly and can easily be geared to the level and needs of the group members. Some examples of lists include: characteristics of friendship; hobbies, and other recreational activities; important people; positive personal qualities; traits desired in a love partner; or characteristics inherent in the ideal job. Making a list is useful to members because it allows them to summarize their thoughts in a succinct fashion; it also helps them to focus. Once the list is complete, it can be used in a variety of ways. The leader can ask members to share a portion or the entire list, or have members share lists in dyads or triads. For example, in an education/growth group about stress, the leader may ask members to list things that are stressful to them. Once the members have done so, the leader could ask them to get into triads and discuss their lists, starting first with work stressors, then home stressors, and then other stressors.

Written-Response Exercises   The third type of written exercise is called a *re-sponse* exercise, because the leader asks members to respond in various ways to problems or questions posed by the leader. The following are examples:

- Members write their own epitaph or obituary.

- Members write short responses to questions such as, What is the role of a school counselor? or How does having children change one's life?

- Members complete multiple-choice questions, state preferences, or give one-word answers to different questions.

- Members write reaction papers after viewing movies or TV shows or reading books or poems.

For example, knowing that a certain movie will be on TV, the leader might ask the members to watch it and write a personal reaction reflecting what the movie meant to them. The members then bring their reactions to the group. In each case, members have their reactions or answers in front of them when the leader asks them to share their responses.

Diaries   A fourth type of written exercise uses diaries either during the session or at home. Within a session, members write personal reactions to what has taken place in that session. Often this is done at the end of the session; the leader allots the last 5 or 10 minutes for members to write.

LEADER: We're now finished except for writing in your diary. As I explained last week, this is time for you to write any thoughts, feelings, or reactions that you have had during the session. Take as much time as you'd like to write. Also, remember that your diary will be a good summary of the group and may be something you will want to read years from now.

The diaries are usually left for the leader to read; this gives her both immediate feedback about the session and the opportunity to write comments in the diaries. The leader gets an idea of what the members are gaining from the group and what might need to be addressed in future sessions. We have found that some members write things that they would not say in the group. Also, leaving the diaries enables the leader to write back to the members. (The members usually read their diaries at the beginning of the next session.) Written comments can be encouraging statements, clarifying comments, or suggestions regarding how the member may use the group experience. Riordan and White (1996) found that 9 out of 10 members report feeling favorable toward the practice of writing in a diary.

If the leader feels that members will not respond honestly or deeply because they know he will read the diaries, he may choose not to have members turn them in. The obvious disadvantage to this is that the leader does not get to read what the members are saying about the group experience.

Diaries can also be used at home. Members take their diaries home and write their reactions to the group or to anything that happens to them during the week that is relevant. These journals or diaries would periodically be given to the leader. Reading the diaries helps the leader know what is helpful in the group and also how members are reacting to and feeling about things that happen to them during the week. An advantage of jotting down thoughts or events throughout the week is that members focus on themselves at different times during the week and not just during the hour or two each week that the group meets. Writing also helps members remember what happened to them so they can report these happenings to the group. With the member's permission, comments from a diary may also be shared with other members if the leader feels something has been mentioned that would be helpful to the whole group.

Movement Exercises

Movement exercises require members to do something of a physical nature; that is, the members move around. The movements can be as simple as standing up and moving about in order to stretch or as complex as "breaking in," an exercise in which members, standing and holding hands, try to keep a member who is circling the group from breaking in. Many examples of movement exercises are described next.

Changing Seats This exercise involves members standing and then finding a different seat in which to sit. The purpose is to allow members to stretch and move around and also to sit next to and face different members by virtue of changing location. The leader might introduce this exercise by saying:

LEADER: I'd like you to stand up and take a minute to stretch; then find a seat other than the one you had. Try to seat yourselves by members you have not sat next to.

Milling Around This exercise involves having the members walk around. There are a number of activities that the members may do while milling, such as experiencing or avoiding eye contact or touching another member gently on the shoulder or elbow. The specifics of what to do while milling depend on the purpose of the exercise. The milling would last for no more than 3 minutes. To begin, the leader might say the following:

LEADER: I want you to stand up. *(Members stand.)* We are going to do a nonverbal milling exercise. The first thing I want you to do is to move about the room with your head down, avoiding eye contact with anyone. *(Members do this for about 1 minute.)* Now I want you to mill around, but this time make eye contact for as long you desire.

This exercise gets members in touch with their comfort level with others. It can be used in groups that are exploring their feelings about interacting with others.

Values Continuum With this exercise, members position themselves according to how they think and feel about an issue. The leader designates certain locations in the room as symbolic of a viewpoint. One side of the room represents one point of view, and the other side the opposite point of view. The members are asked to stand in the middle of the room and then move to the position on the continuum between the two designated spots.

LEADER: I want everyone to stand up and line up here in the middle of the room behind Jim. *(Allows members to do this.)* Okay, now on the count of 3, I am going to ask you to position yourself where you feel you are on the continuum that I am about to describe. The continuum is from the wall on your right, which will be "high risk taker," to the wall on your left, which will be "play it very safe." *(Pause)* Everyone understand? Okay—on 3, position yourselves. Ready? 1, 2, 3.

The benefit of having members walk to a designated area is that all the members have to declare their position at the same time and everyone can visually see how others feel about a given issue. It also offers a change in the format; instead of stating their position, this exercise gives members the opportunity to move and to view others' positions. Also, everyone is communicating, they are just doing it nonverbally with their feet. Possible continuums include the following:

saver _____ spender

winner _____ loser

happy _____ unhappy

interesting person _____ boring person

life is hard _____ life is easy

easy to trust _____ hard to trust

like school _____ hate school

GROUP COUNSELING SKILLS: Movement Exercises

Review segment 8.7 for a demonstration in which the leader uses a value continuum to focus on the issue of liking school.

Goals Walk   In this exercise, the members line up across from each other. Each member will take a turn walking through the area between the members. The members act as obstacles in the walker's path toward his or her goals, which are at the other end.

LEADER: I want everyone to stand up and make two lines with three on one side and four on the other. Stand a few feet apart, making sort of a path. What we are going to do is have each of you walk down the path. Let me have a volunteer. *(Hilda volunteers and steps to the front of the group, where the leader is standing.)* Hilda, in a minute, you're going to walk through the group. I'd like you to look down the path and envision reaching your goals and life being fairly smooth as being at the other end. Okay, now I want you to think of your goals and then tell us how difficult you perceive it will be to reach those goals. If you see it as hard at first, then, Jane, you and Sandy will want to sort of block her and make it hard because you are in front here. If it is going to be hard in the middle, then Kevin and Karen will make it hard. I know some of you have some pretty tough things ahead of you. What we want to do is give each person a chance to experience physically some of the bumps in the path toward his or her goals. You'll make it hard by blocking, holding, or whatever, but it is important to not make it impossible and also not to laugh because that will take away from the person's experience. Okay, Hilda, tell us how you see the path ahead.

If done right, this exercise can be very thought-provoking. If members know each other well, certain members in the line can play certain characters in the person's life, such as drinking buddies, old lover, ex-spouse, mother, or the "bottle." The leader has to pay close attention to make sure it does not get too physical or turn into a joking kind of activity. We have used this in many different ways and found it to have great impact.

How Far Have You Come?   In this exercise, the leader has the members stand side by side and think about how far they have come during the group in terms of reaching their goals.

LEADER: I think this exercise can be of help in getting you to see where you are in the group. Everyone stand up and line up next to each other. *(The leader stands about 8 feet away.)* If the imaginary line that I'm drawing represents your reaching the goals that we talked about in our first session, how far have you come toward reaching them? Some of you have come pretty far; others, not so far, but I want each of you to position yourself in terms of your progress. On 3—*(Pause)* 1, 2, 3.

After people position themselves, there can be much discussion. The leader can also have them put one foot forward, symbolizing a step toward their goal, and have each person talk about what the next step could be.

Sculpt Your Feeling About the Group   This is an exercise where the leader has the members stand in a circle and "sculpt" how they feel about the group, using their body and hands.

LEADER: I want everyone to stand and make a large circle. In a minute, I am going to ask you to indicate how you are feeling about this group by using your body language and position. If you are really into the group and open for it, you would come to the center and have your arms open. If you are against the group, you would turn your back to the group and have your arms closed around you. You can use your body, your arms, your hands, anything to express exactly how you are feeling about the group. Everyone understand? *(Pause)* Okay, on 3—1, 2, 3.

This is an excellent exercise if the group is not going well and the leader believes it has some potential. The exercise should lead to a discussion about the group.

 GROUP COUNSELING SKILLS: Movement Exercises

Go to segment 10.4 for a demonstration in which the leader uses this sculpturing exercise.

Family Sculpture   Similar to having members sculpt how they feel about the group, in this exercise, the leader has members sculpt their families as they see them now or when they were growing up. This exercise is usually very revealing. Members find it interesting to sculpt their own family and to see how other members sculpt theirs. The exercise is used to generate discussion about past and present family relationships.

■ **EXAMPLE**

The group is composed of male teenagers.

LEADER: Today we are going to focus on our families. To do this, we are going to do an exercise called *family sculpture*. What this entails is that each of you will sculpt your family by picking other members to play your parents or the adults you live with, your siblings, and any other significant person in your family and positioning them to show how they relate to one another. For example, the parents may be holding hands or they may be far apart with their fists raised. The kids may be close together or very far apart. Some may be close to Dad but not Mom, or they may even have their backs to their parents. Who will volunteer to go first? I'll explain more as you go along.

TONY: I will. What do I do?

LEADER: Stand here in the center. Who lives at home with you?

TONY: My mom, my dad, and my little sister.

LEADER: Pick a member to be each one of these, and pick someone to be you.

TONY: Bob, you be my dad. Sam, you be me. Don, I guess you will have to be my mom, and Bill, you be my sister.

LEADER: Now position these people as you see them. Are your mom and dad close?

TONY: No, they hardly speak. They would be at the opposite ends of the room. Can I put them there?

LEADER: Sure. Where would you put you and your sister?

TONY: My sister is real close to my mom, so I would put her over there with her. I am not close to anyone, so I would be way over in the other corner away from everyone. Gee, this is heavy!

The leader usually spends 2 or 3 minutes discussing the sculpture as each member designs it. When everyone has had a turn, a long discussion usually takes place on family issues.

Group Sculpture   Similar to family sculpture, group sculpture is an exercise that has the members sculpt how they see the group. This is different from the sculpture where members sculpt themselves. In this exercise, a member sculpts everyone; that is, members position people in the group in accordance to how they see the different relationships and roles of the members. This can be a good exercise for groups where members know each other well, such as in a residential group or a long-term counseling or therapy group. It serves as a feedback exercise because members show how they see the different members of the group.

Home Spot   In this exercise, members stand in a circle holding hands. Each one picks a spot in the room to try to maneuver the group toward. Because most members have a different spot and all are holding hands, many different dynamics occur.

LEADER: Let's try something different. We've been discussing how many of you do not always go after what you want and need. There is an exercise that I think you'll find interesting. I want you to stand up and move your chairs all the way against the wall. *(Members do this.)* Now come to the center and form a circle, holding hands. Not too tight of a circle. Now I'd like each of you to look around and pick a spot in the room. In a minute, I am going to ask you, while still holding hands, to try to move to that spot. This is to be done without any talking or laughter. Your main goal is to get to your spot, without letting go of the other members' hands. Get ready. Okay, try to move to your spot.

Members will pull, push, give up, kneel on the floor, and so on. The leader will stop the exercise after a minute or so and then process the various reactions. The purpose of the exercise is to focus members on how hard they try to get what they want.

Personal Space   This exercise consists of members standing in a circle not too close to each other—almost at arm's length. The leader then instructs them to close their eyes and to feel the space around them, exploring around their head and in front, to the sides, and in back of them. The leader then instructs them to venture out of "their space" by using their arms, which usually results in members touching each other. Discussion often centers on the comfort level of their space and feelings about venturing out. Eventually, the leader will want the discussion to move toward members' feelings about their space as they live their daily lives.

Become a Statue This exercise requires members to stand at some distance from each other; on the count of three they all become statues to show how they see themselves, either in the group or in their lives outside the group (depending on the purpose of the exercise). This exercise is good for giving members the chance to visually represent themselves.

Trust There are a number of trust exercises that involve movement. These are discussed later in this chapter in the section titled "Trust Exercises."

Reasons for Using Movement Exercises There are at least five good reasons for using movement exercises.

1. Movement exercises give group members a chance to *experience* something rather than discuss it.

2. The drama of movement exercises may cause members to remember what took place in the group more readily in the days or weeks following than might otherwise occur if only discussion is used.

3. Movement exercises usually involve all the members. That is, all members are up and doing something, whereas in discussion exercises some members may not be involved.

4. Movement exercises give members a chance to stretch and move around. This can be good for young people and for members who have been sitting for a long while. It is important to remember that members can become bored and fatigued if seated too long or if the format remains unchanged for extended periods.

5. Most movement exercises usually get the members to "talk" with their feet, such as when they position themselves on a continuum. Therefore, leaders can draw members out by having them do some kind of movement and then asking them to comment on why they positioned themselves as they did.

Cautions When Using Movement Exercises Various situations and client populations may not be conducive to using movement activities. Leaders should not attempt strenuous movement activities with the elderly or people with significant health problems. Any time the exercise calls for vigorous movement, make sure objects such as chairs, desks, or tables are well out of the way. Also make sure that members remove eyeglasses or any other items that may be damaged or that may injure others. Some movement exercises involve touching, and some members do not want to be touched by other members.

Dyads and Triads

Dyads give members a chance to (1) interact with one other individual, (2) practice some skill, or (3) do an activity that calls for two people to interact in some prescribed manner. We discussed the use of dyads extensively in Chapter 9, but we did not discuss the use of dyads as a specific exercise, as in the following.

One exercise is called "I Have To—I Choose To." In this exercise, members pair up and take turns saying aloud their list of things that they feel they "have" to do. Then they go back and change the recitation from "I have to" to "I choose to." A variation of this is to start with the phrase "I need," which changes to "I want." These kinds of exercises give members a chance to hear how they can change some of their demands or needs. Saying statements out loud to another person makes more of an impact than saying them only to oneself.

Another dyad exercise is one in which a member says to the partner, "I should ..." and the partner firmly responds, "No, you shouldn't!" Each partner goes through his list of "shoulds" and experiences being told no. This exercise helps members think through what really are "shoulds" in their lives.

Another dyad or triad exercise that can prove to be very enlightening is to have members pair up and have each assume the role of one of her parents. Then the "parents" talk about their son or daughter. This exercise can help members experience how they perceive their parents' opinions of them and is a valuable exercise for all age groups. Stevens (1972) calls this exercise "parents' chat."

Rounds

As we said in Chapter 9, rounds are probably the most valuable exercises available to a leader. One kind of round not mentioned in Chapter 9 is the forced-choice round. This consists of the leader reading a statement and the members stating how they feel about the statement. The members would usually respond with *strongly agree, agree, disagree,* or *strongly disagree.* The following are some examples of statements that could be used:

- Blacks and whites should never marry each other.
- Extramarital affairs are always harmful
- Divorce means failure.
- A person's personal worth is always changing.
- Physical attractiveness is very important.
- One should love one's parents no matter what.
- Having children is essential for happiness.

As you can see, responses to these kinds of sentences have the potential to generate a lot of discussion. The leader's skill comes in choosing appropriate statements. Forced-choice sentences can serve as an effective way to stimulate interaction in a group.

Exercises Using Creative Props

Impact Therapy (Jacobs, 1994) emphasizes making counseling multisensory and concrete. The use of different counseling props is a way to make group counseling more multisensory, interesting, and engaging. Items such as rubber bands, Styrofoam cups, a small child's chair, and an empty beer bottle all can be used in groups. The following group exercises show how leaders can use props effectively.

Rubber Bands

■ EXAMPLES

LEADER: I want each of you to take one of these thick rubber bands *(One that stretches over a foot.)* and stretch it until you feel the tension. Hold your hands out and experience the stress. Because this group is on stress management, I thought that rubber bands may help you to see how you are doing dealing with your own stress. Since our meeting last week, has your stress increased or decreased? I want you to either increase the tension or loosen it. Also, think about ways you can reduce your stress and note that for the tension on the rubber band to decrease, you have to do something! Think about this for a minute, and then I'll ask you to share your feelings and thoughts.

■ ■ ■

LEADER: This is now the third meeting of our couples' group, so I thought we would take a look at the tension you have in your relationship. I want each of you to get with your partner and take a rubber band. *(Some playfully act as though they are going to "pop" their partners.)* I see some of you already are kind of acting out parts of your marriage. I want you to think about how you can use the rubber band in various ways to symbolize your relationship and interactions. I'll give you about 2 minutes to work with your partner and the rubber band. *(Members work together for a few minutes.)*

JANE: We pulled until it nearly broke and then we sort of looked at each other. Neither one of us gave in, though, so here we sit with the tension at its maximum.

ETO: Ours was very different. We played with it, and then we each popped each other sort of hard.

■ ■ ■

Styrofoam Cups

■ EXAMPLES

LEADER: I want each of you to take a cup and a pencil. I want you to think of the cup as representing your personal worth, and then I want you to punch holes in the cup as you think about the things that cause you not to like yourself. A hole may represent your appearance, not having friends, your parents' reactions to you, your intelligence, or anything else you can think of. When you are done, each of you will get a chance to share your cup. Some of you may have some holes that you don't want to share yet with the group and you can just say something like, "There are two more big ones that I am not ready to share yet." The point of the holes is to help you see what you may want to work on in the group.

GROUP COUNSELING SKILLS: Creative Exercises

View segment 10.1 again for a demonstration in which the leader uses Styrofoam cups. See how the leader uses the holes in the cup to get members to share more deeply about themselves.

■ ■ ■

LEADER: I want everyone to look at this cup I am holding and think of it as your own self-worth. *(The leader now stands on a chair.)* As I stand and start to squeeze the cup, I want you to decide to whom you give your worth —the person you have on the chair that you allow to hurt or squeeze you. *(Everyone looks up and seems to be in deep thought.)* Any comments or reactions?

■ ■ ■

Small Chair

■ EXAMPLE

LEADER: We have been talking about having fun, so I want you to focus on the idea of having fun. To help you, I want you to look at this small chair and think about the fun little boy or girl inside you. I want you to think about what happened to him or her as you have grown up. Because many of you said you don't have fun, we need to hear from the child part of you. *(All stare intensely at the chair. A couple of members start to cry.)*

CATHY: This is very powerful for me. I stopped having fun when I was 14 because of something that happened. *(Cries)*

MATT: I used to have fun, but when my mom died, I felt that I had to help out, and I have been doing that ever since.

LEADER: What about others of you? Our goal is to get you to have fun—to listen to that part of you that wants to enjoy life.

■ ■ ■

GROUP COUNSELING SKILLS: Creative Exercises

View segment 10.2 again for a demonstration in which the leader uses the small chair to focus on when members feel like a little girl or boy. Note the power of having the small chair present.

Beer Bottle

■ **EXAMPLE**

LEADER: I want each of you to look at this beer bottle and this string. I want you to let the string represent either your life, your ability to control your mood, or your tolerance for not getting angry. Now watch what happens to the long string as I put it into the bottle. What do you see?

CARLOS: It gets shorter.

DOTTIE: It gets gobbled up. Disappears.

LEADER: Now, what do you take this to mean for you? *(The leader places the bottle in the center of the group. Everyone stares at it.)*

■ ■ ■

These are just some of the props a leader can use to focus the group on a topic. Some other useful props are shields, playing cards, and furnace filters (Jacobs, 1992).

Arts and Crafts Exercises

Arts and crafts exercises require that members draw, cut, paste, paint, or create something with a variety of materials. These exercises can generate interest, focus the group, create energy, and trigger discussion. Arts and crafts exercises allow members to express themselves in a different way; that is, members can put their thoughts and feelings into a project before they share verbally with others. This activity is especially helpful for members who have difficulty identifying or expressing feelings directly. For this reason, arts and crafts exercises are useful with younger children, but they are also useful for all ages. Having members draw their dream house or their imaginary coat of arms can stimulate very interesting discussions.

One example of an arts and crafts exercise involves the use of paper bags, magazines, scissors, and tape or glue. All these materials are passed out to each member. Members are then told to look through their magazines and cut out any word, phrase, or picture that describes them right now. Those aspects they are willing to share with the group are to be pasted on the outside of the bag. Those they are not willing to share are placed inside the bag. When it comes time for discussion, members hold up their bags and tell the group about themselves. This exercise is particularly useful in helping members become acquainted with each other, and it makes sharing easier. The leader can also choose to focus on what is in the bag by discussing why people tend not to want to share parts of themselves.

A second reason for using arts and crafts exercises is they can serve as projective devices for the members' thoughts, feelings, and experiences. That is, current problems may be represented in a creative project. For example, the leader might ask members to draw a picture of themselves and their family engaging in a typical interaction. Often, much is revealed by such drawings.

A third benefit of arts and crafts exercises is that members seem to enjoy seeing what other members have drawn, painted, or built. Thus, sharing oneself and listening to others becomes more interesting when members can see what is being talked about.

Another reason for using arts and crafts exercises is that they are nonverbal and may be helpful in groups where language is a problem. We encourage leaders who have members from many different cultures to consider these kinds of exercises if they are finding it difficult to get members involved in other kinds of exercises. One note of cautions for school counselors; school groups are often very limited in the amount of time that is available. Therefore, school counselors who choose to use arts and crafts exercises should pay particular attention to the time requirements of such exercises and sometimes allow for additional sessions for processing arts and crafts exercises.

Fantasy Exercises

Fantasy exercises are most often used in growth and therapy groups. Fantasies help members become more aware of their feelings, wishes, doubts, and fears. An example of a fantasy exercise is the "common object," in which the leader directs the members to imagine themselves as an object that is in the room (a book, wastebasket, cup, purse, window, pencil, chair, and so forth). The leader guides the members through the fantasy by asking what it feels like to be the object, what life is like being that object, their role in life, and so forth.

■ EXAMPLES

LEADER: *(Very slowly and softly)* I want you to look at this briefcase, and I want you to become this briefcase. Think about what your life is like as a briefcase. How does it feel? *(Pause)* What happens to you as a briefcase? *(Pause)* What is it like being a briefcase? *(Pause)* In a few seconds, I am going to ask you to share your experience of being a briefcase. I would like you to start by saying, "I am a briefcase, and as a briefcase,...."

■ ■ ■

LEADER: I want each of you to close your eyes and get comfortable. *(Pause)* *(Using a soothing voice with a slow pace)* Now I want you to imagine that you are a tree. *(Pause)* What kind of tree are you? *(Pause)* What are your surroundings? *(Pause)* What is life like as a tree? *(Pause)* How does it feel being the tree that you are? *(Pause)* Okay, who wants to go first and share what he or she experienced?

■ ■ ■

Other examples of fantasy exercises include a movie fantasy (members imagine that they are watching a movie of their lives and they think of the title, producer and director, main characters, and audience reactions); the hot-air balloon fantasy (members imagine they are in a hot-air balloon trying to lift off but are weighted down by various weights in their lives); the "wise man" fantasy (members imagine taking a trip up a mountain to visit an old wise man to get an answer to an important question); and the funeral fantasy (members imagine their own funeral and the reactions of people attending it).

When members discuss their fantasies, the leader encourages them to determine if the feelings attributed to the object or fantasy do, in fact, apply to their daily lives. Because certain kinds of fantasy exercises may cause members to explore thoughts and feelings that have been denied to their conscious awareness, leaders who use fantasy exercises should be prepared for members to get in touch with some painful material.

Common Reading Exercises

In common reading exercises members read a short passage, poem, or story. Such readings often serve the purpose of triggering ideas and thoughts and of deepening the focus on some topic or issue. For example, in growth groups, the "Gestalt prayer" (Perls, 1969) may serve as a stimulating common reading:

> I do my thing, and you do your thing.
>
> I am not in this world to live up to your expectations
>
> And you are not in this world to live up to mine.
>
> You are you and I am I,
>
> And if by chance we find each other, it's beautiful.
>
> If not, it can't be helped.

Although members have a variety of reactions to this passage, it usually triggers discussion about demands and expectations placed on others as well as the need for approval and acceptance. Other passages and poems that have proven effective have come from *The Prophet* by Kahlil Gibran or poems by T. S. Eliot. The following example comes from Robert Frost's poem "The Road Not Taken."

> Two roads diverged in a wood, and I—
>
> I took the one less traveled by,
>
> And that has made all the difference.

This is a very inspiring passage and often gives members permission to be different and not follow the crowd. As members read the passage, they are reminded of incidents in their own lives concerning choices they have made. Some may have taken the less-traveled road, while others did not. Usually a good discussion follows the reading of this passage.

The key factor to keep in mind when using common reading exercises is the purpose of the group. Make sure that the material will trigger thoughts related to the purpose. Also, consider the intellectual capabilities of the members when asking them to read and react to a poem or written verse. Obviously, the preceding examples would not be appropriate for elementary school children. There are interesting materials written for all educational levels.

GROUP COUNSELING SKILLS: Creative Exercises

Go to segment 10.3 for a demonstration in which the leader uses a common reading.

Feedback Exercises

One potential benefit of being in groups is the opportunity to hear what others think of you. Listed here are a number of feedback exercises that may be valuable to members. Feedback exercises allow the members and the leader to share their feelings and thoughts about each other. Leaders should not conduct a feedback exercise unless they feel the members have enough goodwill to try to be helpful rather than cruel or insensitive. It is best to avoid conducting a feedback exercise with members who have no desire to be helpful or to listen to feedback from others.

First Impressions   This is an exercise where members share their first impressions of other members. This can be done in the first session or can be used in later sessions when the members have had a chance to revise their first impressions. If used in a later session, members get a chance to hear how they are perceived now and how they were perceived when others first met them.

Adjective Checklist   Members take turns being the focus of the group. Members are given a written list of 15 to 20 adjectives that describe people, and members pick 3 to 5 adjectives that describe the member who is receiving feedback. Using the adjectives gives members a structured way to describe each other.

Talk About the Members   There will be times when the leader will decide to focus on a member for the purpose of giving her feedback. The leader would have members talk about the member, focusing on whatever the leader thinks would be helpful, such as how she presents herself, issues she is avoiding, or positive qualities. When doing this, the leader may have the member being discussed sit quietly and close her eyes, or turn around so she is not facing the group. This depends on the member receiving feedback, the members giving the feedback, and the kind of feedback that is about to be given. If the leader feels the members will speak more openly if the member who is receiving feedback is not watching, the leader may have that member turn around. Also, many people have said they can listen better when they are not looking at others while they are being talked about. The leader should use caution when conducting this type of exercise and should do this only when it is helpful for the member receiving the feedback.

Strength Bombardment   This exercise is similar to the preceding one because the members talk about each other; but in this exercise, the feedback is done in a more organized fashion. That is, the leader directs the group to describe the strengths of the designated member. The leader appoints one member to keep a list of all the strengths so that the member can have the list when the exercise is over. A variation is to also list weaknesses or areas needing improvement.

Wishes   A nonthreatening way to give feedback is by using wishes. The leader sets this exercise up by asking members to verbalize any wishes that they have for a given member.

LEADER: What I would like you to do is think of wishes that you have for
                  various members. We'll focus on one person at a time, and anyone
                  who has a wish for that person will say, "My wish for you is ...."

This is a good exercise for members who are concerned for each other and who have various things to say to each other. It is a good exercise for support groups and for some growth, counseling, and therapy groups.

GROUP COUNSELING SKILLS: My Wish for You

Go to segment 15.2 for a demonstration in which the leader uses a "my wish for you" exercise in her closing of the group.

Metaphorical Feedback   The leader asks members to think of an animal, a character in the movies or on TV, or an inanimate object, such as a sunset or a babbling brook, that reminds them of a designated member. Each member gets to hear how others see him, but the feedback comes in metaphorical fashion.

Written Feedback   In this exercise, members are asked to write out feedback for each member of the group. This is usually done between sessions because it can take quite a bit of time. The value of this kind of feedback is that members experience reading about themselves from the point of view of a number of other people. Most people have not received written feedback from six or eight people at one time. This kind of feedback activity should be used only with members who are basically stable and members who have been meeting for quite a while. The leader would provide members with instructions on what kind of feedback to write.

Most/Least Feedback   This kind of feedback involves members sharing how they feel about other members by using a "most" and "least" designation. For example, the leader may ask members to designate the following:

- To whom they feel most similar and least similar
- With whom they feel most comfortable and least comfortable
- Whom they trust most and whom they trust least
- Who they feel is working hardest in the group and who they feel is working the least

This kind of exercise can create much interaction and must be used with care. The leader can ask for just one category, such as "most comfortable," instead of both categories. Members not only give feedback, but receive feedback by being named by others. After the initial round of members offering their views, members should be allowed to ask questions about why they were named by another member.

These are just some of the feedback exercises that are possible. Different kinds of feedback exercises elicit different kinds of responses. The important things to remember when deciding to focus the group on feedback are the level of trust and goodwill of the members and the purpose of the group.

Trust Exercises

Because groups involve sharing, *the amount of trust that members have in each other is a group dynamic the leader must assess.* If the leader finds that members do not trust one another or that more trust seems to be needed in the group, he may choose to have the members participate in trust exercises. Each of the following exercises is intended to focus members on the issue of trust.

Rounds   Listed are some examples of rounds that can be used to initiate a discussion of trust:

- On a 1–10 scale, with 10 being *a person who can trust others easily* and 1 being *someone for whom it is difficult to trust,* how would you rate yourself?

- In this group, do you feel that there is a lot of trust, moderate trust, or little trust? I want you to think how you would respond to that question, and we will go around the group and hear from each of you.

- When you were growing up, would you say your environment was very trusting, moderately trusting, or not trusting at all?

In each of these rounds, the issue of trust is the focus. The first two could relate directly to the group, whereas the last one would reflect what members learned about trusting at an early age. Certainly some of what they learned is probably affecting them in the group.

Trust Lift   In this exercise, members stand in a tight circle with one person in the center. The members gently move that person around by the shoulders for about a minute. During this time, the member's eyes are closed, his feet are stationary if possible, and everyone is silent. Then, the members gently take the person by the feet, waist, shoulders, and head and gradually lift him over their heads. Then they slowly rock the person while bringing him gently to the floor. A member willing to do this would be trusting the group not to drop him. The leader should focus discussion both on being lifted and on being responsible for lifting.

The obvious caution for this exercise is that the members must be capable of lifting the person. Also, the leader should be prepared for one or two members to choose not to participate because of their fear of being dropped or perhaps even of being touched. During this exercise, the leader must make sure that someone holds the person's head and neck to ensure comfort.

Trust Fall   The trust fall exercise is done in pairs or threes. It consists of one person standing, with one or two members right behind her. The person in front falls backward, and the others catch her at a safe distance above the floor. The cautions mentioned in the trust lift also apply to this exercise. This exercise should not be done on hard surfaces, such as tile or concrete.

Blind Trust Walk   This exercise is done in pairs, with one person blindfolded and the other serving as a guide. During the exercise, there should be no talking except for directions, such as "step down." The purpose of the exercise is for members to experience trusting another person to lead them. When doing this exercise, the leader would want to be in a setting that would accommodate members walking around without interference. It will probably not work in an agency or school unless there is a very large room or it is after hours. Each member should be led around for about 5 minutes to get the effect; ideally, the walk should be such that the blindfolded member experiences more than walking around in a circle. That is, it is good to have members maneuver around doors, chairs, steps, tables, and so on. In addition, during the processing of this exercise, most of the time should be spent discussing trust, although some time will be spent on discussing the experience of the walk.

Experiential Exercises

Several group exercises can be classified as experiential because the members are involved in some kind of individual or group experience that is active and often challenging. Some experiential exercises can also be used to build trust. Probably the most well-known set of experiential exercises is the "Ropes Course," which is "a blend of activities designed to take individuals and groups beyond their own expectations, or perceived willingness to try" (Rohnke & Tait, 2007). The activities are done outdoors on a carefully designed course made up of ropes. Some of the activities are very challenging and seem dangerous, which force individuals to come face to face with themselves (Rohnke & Tait, 2007). Other activities on the ropes course depend on members cooperating with each other; thus, it is good for team building. Some group leaders use the ropes course as one part of their group, whereas other leaders just lead groups through the ropes course or some other kind of experiential activity.

When thinking about experiential exercises, it is important to make sure that the exercise fits the purpose. There are many outdoor activities that are fun and interesting, but they may not be appropriate for the group you are leading. If an experiential component fits with your purpose, it is a good idea to consider using experiential activities because they are interesting and give your members a very different experience.

Moral Dilemma Exercises

Several group exercises can be considered "moral dilemmas"; that is, a story is read or passed out to the members and each member has to decide how she would handle the situation. Some of these stories involve stealing food to sustain life, deciding who is allowed to stay in a lifeboat, or deciding whether to tell the authorities about a crime. Simon, Howe, and Kirschenbaum (1978) describe one involving a fallout shelter and who is let in. Probably the most popular moral dilemma exercise is called "Alligator River." It is a story about a woman needing to cross a river to obtain a lifesaving medicine. She must decide whether to give in to the demands of the riverboat captain in order to get across. You may wish to use these exercises or invent your own. Moral dilemma exercises have been found to be very helpful in facilitating discussion among adolescents.

■   E X A M P L E

LEADER: You are on a ship when it wrecks. Seven people want to get into the life raft, and it holds only five. The people are you, a 12-year-old hoodlum-type kid, a 52-year-old retired teacher, a 30-year-old star baseball player, a 22-year-old auto mechanic, a 62-year-old preacher, and a pregnant, 39-year-old homemaker. Who would you think should *not* be allowed on the life raft?

■   ■   ■

These exercises usually generate a discussion about values, justice, and fairness. They can be used at the beginning of a session and become the focus of the entire session, or they can be used as an exercise that takes about 30 minutes to discuss and process.

Group-Decision Exercises

These activities involve members working together to solve some sort of problem, such as being lost on the moon with certain supplies. The group would be asked to determine the best way to use the supplies. Depending on the size of the group, the entire group may work together as one unit or be divided into two or three groups of four members each. Another activity calls for sharing resources such as rulers, scissors, tape, paper, string, and pencils to complete a project. This one would usually be done nonverbally. Members would be given different resources and a task to complete; they would be told that they can share or do anything they like except talk in order to complete the task. It would either be stated or would quickly become apparent that they do not have all the resources themselves and that other members of the group have different resources than they do. This kind of activity is interesting and, depending on how it is used, can generate discussion about competition, sharing, and cooperation.

Johnson and Johnson (2009) describe a number of different kinds of group-decision activities. Two examples are (1) having members try to figure out the right supplies to take ("Winter Survival") and (2) having members try to complete a complicated puzzle through cooperation ("Hollow Squares exercise").

Touching Exercises

A number of exercises can involve touching. Some are done with the entire group, such as a group massage or milling and touching; others are done in pairs, such as members lightly touching each other's hands or faces. Touching can be a very comforting and supportive activity if done properly. Many trust exercises involve touching in some manner. Also, some people are "touch deprived," and therefore, being touched can be a very helpful and freeing experience.

We cover touching exercises as a separate category because there are some cautions to consider when doing them. *Any leader using any exercise where touching is going to be involved must consider the appropriateness for and comfort of the members.* First, be aware that some members may not be comfortable with physical contact. If an exercise involves any form of touching, be sure everyone understands what will happen and then allow members to opt out of the exercise. Second, in almost all situations, it is best to avoid touching exercises that may have a sexual connotation. Some massage exercises, for example, may be interpreted as sexual unless properly conducted. With this exercise or any other that may be misinterpreted, the leader would want to be *very* careful to explain the exercise and its purpose and to allow members to choose not to participate. Exercises that tend to arouse sexual feelings usually serve no useful purpose, may frighten members, and may inappropriately arouse feelings between two members.

■ EXAMPLE

LEADER: Because each of you is not used to positive comments or positive touch, I want to do an exercise that involves positive feedback as well as some nurturing touching on the shoulders. One at a time, each person is going to sit in this chair, and members are going to come up and gently touch your shoulders and say one or two positive comments about you. For many of you, hearing the positive comments will be uncomfortable as will be the touching. Some of you may find that touching the other person is uncomfortable. Let me demonstrate what would happen. John, come sit here. *(Leader gently rubs John's shoulders and says something positive.)* I want to encourage you to try this if at all possible, and then we can talk about what this was like to receive and give feedback. Does anyone have any questions or comments about how they are feeling about doing this? *(Pause)* If you want to go toward the last, let me know and that is fine. If you are not comfortable doing this, please let me know that as well. *(Pause)* Who is willing to be first in the chair?

■ ■ ■

Concluding Comments

Using exercises can be very beneficial, especially when the proper experiences are chosen. There are at least seven reasons for leaders to use exercises, including generating interest and energy, shifting the focus, deepening the focus, providing valuable information, providing an opportunity for experiential learning, increasing comfort, and providing fun and relaxation. A skilled leader understands why and when to use exercises. We discuss 14 kinds of group exercises: written, movement, dyads and triads, rounds, creative props, arts and crafts, fantasy, common readings, feedback, trust, experiential, moral dilemmas, group decision, and touching. There are many good books on exercises for all kinds of groups. You will want to explore various sources that pertain to the population with which you are working.

■ ACTIVITIES

1. Think of a group and its purpose. Then list at least two creative, two movement, and two other exercises you could do with that group.
2. Think of three topics (such as anger, guilt, or divorce); then develop two written exercises that could be used to initiate discussion on each of the topics and two exercises that could be used to deepen the focus on each of the topics.

GROUP COUNSELING SKILLS

1. View again segments 5.5 and 8.6, in which the leader uses sentence completion exercises.
   a. How did the exercise help the leaders?
   b. How did the exercise help the members?
   c. How did the leader process the exercise? That is, how did the leader use the sentence completion in a way that it was interesting?

Throughout the DVD you will see many exercises conducted and processed. Always watch the way the exercise is introduced, conducted, and processed, which is the subject of the next chapter.

Chapter 11

Introducing, Conducting, and Processing Exercises

For exercises to be productive and useful, they must be introduced properly, conducted properly, and processed in a way that is helpful for the members. In this chapter, we address each of these important skills.

Introducing an Exercise

Proper introduction of an exercise means giving clear instructions to members on how to carry out the exercise. This is as important as the exercise itself. Leaders often give ample thought to the exercise, but if their instructions are not clearly presented and if certain cautions are not expressed, the likely result will be confusion, and the exercise will be almost meaningless.

During the introduction of an exercise, it is important to set the right tone. To accomplish this, the leader should pay careful attention to the use of his voice. If the exercise is to be a serious or thought-provoking one, the leader will want to slow down his delivery, using pauses and a quieter voice. If it is to be an energizing, fun exercise, the leader would want to speed up the delivery, using a very enthusiastic voice. Too often, leaders fail to use their voices effectively, and the exercise does not produce the desired kinds of responses.

When introducing an exercise, it is also important to gain the cooperation of the members. Therefore, members should not be made to feel the leader is doing something to them or that they are being forced to participate. *It should be made clear that members have the right not to participate if they so desire.* There is greater likelihood that the exercise will be beneficial if the members are participating of their own free will.

General Considerations

Inform Members of the Purpose and Procedure   When introducing most exercises, the leader will want to inform the members of the purpose and how the exercise will be conducted. A straightforward introduction allows members to have more understanding of the exercise and increases cooperation.

■ EXAMPLES

Effective Introduction

LEADER: Today I am going to show you some pictures I cut out of a magazine. I am going to ask you to make up a story about one scene. One purpose of this exercise is to help you realize that each of us has our own way of seeing things. There are no right or wrong answers, and I think you will find this really interesting.

In this example, the leader tells the members what the purpose is and that there are no right or wrong answers in the hope of relieving any uncomfortable feelings that members might have about sharing their stories. In the following example, the leader is less effective because she does not tell the members why they are being asked to make up stories about the various pictures.

■ ■ ■

Ineffective Introduction

LEADER: I want you to look at the picture and tell me what you see. Who wants to go first?

■ ■ ■

In some exercises it is not desirable to inform the members fully of the purpose, because telling them could interfere with the effect. When introducing such exercises, it is a good idea to tell the members that the purpose will be explained following the exercise. Again, the leader's attitude as reflected in tone of voice, gestures, and related cues will be a major factor in ensuring cooperation.

Avoid Confusing Directions   When introducing an exercise, the leader must clearly present what the members are to do. If the instructions on how to complete the exercise are not clearly presented, members become confused and do not fully participate. If the group consists of members from different cultures, the leader must make sure all members understand the directions. The directions should be as simple as possible. If the exercise is a complex one where members are going to be asked to do a number of things, we suggest that leaders practice giving the directions to colleagues or friends before doing so in the group. In the following ineffective example, the leader would have seen that the directions were too vague had he practiced them with someone first.

■ EXAMPLES

Ineffective Introduction

LEADER: Each of you will receive an envelope that has a task described in it and some materials. You are to try to complete the task without talking to others. The tasks are different. The goal is to try to finish before anyone else.

The exercise involves members cooperating with each other; they may actually share materials and work together to complete the task, but the leader fails to point this out. By failing to tell them that they may share, this leader causes some members to become frustrated and think that materials were omitted from their envelopes or that others were given more items and that the exercise is unfair.

■ ■ ■

Effective Introduction

LEADER: Each of you will receive an envelope that has a number of things in it, such as tape, a pencil, or a ruler. Also included is the description of a task to complete. The task will be something such as "Make a 3-inch by 6-inch red rectangle and tape it to a white circle." In order to complete the task, you will need to share with others because your envelope will not include all the materials necessary for completing the task. You can negotiate with other members, but you can do this only nonverbally—that is, no talking. The goal is to try to finish before anyone else.

■ ■ ■

When giving directions for an exercise, the leader should be watching members' reactions. Nonverbal cues will often tell her if the members understand the directions. If the directions are not clarified at the beginning, members will interpret how to do the exercise in many different ways, causing the leader to have a difficult time processing it effectively. Also, members find it very frustrating when they do not understand directions.

Another mistake occurs when the leader comments on how the exercise will help the members focus on some topic when, in fact, it does not do so. Members focus in one direction; then, when the leader gives the actual directions, they are confused.

■ EXAMPLES

Ineffective Introduction

LEADER: Today we are going to focus on how you have fun in your life. I think more thought needs to be given to this topic of fun. I want you to pair up and, with your partner, discuss how you and your family spent weekends, vacations, and summers when you were young.

Here the leader makes two mistakes: The leader implies that the discussion about fun will relate to the present but then focuses the members on the past. Second, the leader assumes that fun takes place only on weekends and vacations. This may be the leader's frame of reference, but she overlooks the fact that people can have fun completing a difficult task, playing with children, cooking dinner, and so forth.

■ ■ ■

Effective Introduction

LEADER: ... I want you to pair up with your partner and discuss the different ways you have fun by yourself and with others. Think about during the week and weekends and vacations, all the different ways you have fun.

■ ■ ■

Ineffective Introduction

LEADER: In a minute, I'm going to ask you to do an exercise that should get you in touch with your thoughts about the difficulties of having a deaf child. There are many difficulties, and I think this exercise will help you get in touch with them. Get out a sheet of paper and a pencil. *(Pause)* I want you to write down the first things that come to mind when I say these key words: *anger, guilt, failure.*

Again, the leader is operating from his own frame of reference. Of the many difficulties that parents of a deaf child may encounter, feelings of guilt or anger may be one, but others have to do with educational issues, financial problems, babysitting and day care, obtaining public services for their child, handling their own fatigue, and so on. By saying that this exercise will get members in touch with their feelings and then doing an exercise that does not necessarily tap into their feelings, the leader's introduction is confusing to the members.

■ ■ ■

Ineffective Introduction

LEADER: Today we are going to talk about your family of origin and what life was like in your home. I want you to think of the different feelings you had growing up: how you felt about your mom, dad, and any siblings. Maybe there were other significant people in your life such as a grandparent, neighbor, or teacher. On the paper in front of you, I'd like you to draw a rough sketch of the house you grew up in. You can fill in the area around the house—really, anything you want.

As you can see, the leader switched the focus from feelings about family members to a visualization of the house in which members grew up. The two may be related, but they also may be totally unrelated.

■ ■ ■

In each of these examples, the leader gets the members thinking one way and then does an exercise that is only slightly related or not related at all. Beginning leaders frequently do this, causing members to be quite confused. New leaders make this mistake primarily because they have not thought through the issue sufficiently. For instance, in the third example, the leader apparently jumped to the conclusion that focusing on the houses members grew up in would stimulate them to think of their families. After considering this more thoroughly, the leader would realize that the drawing exercise would probably get members in touch with feelings about themselves or events that occurred, rather than with feelings about family members. Obviously, there is a major difference in these two topics. A leader should make sure that the introduction fits the exercise *and* that the exercise is relevant to the topic being discussed.

Avoid Lengthy Directions   A common mistake group leaders make when introducing exercises is giving directions that are too long or complex. If the instructions are long or complicated, it may be best to give them in stages. For example, if the leader wants members to form triads and each member to play a certain role for the exercise, he should have them form triads and determine who is playing which role before proceeding to the next stage of the instructions.

■ EXAMPLES

Ineffective Introduction

LEADER: I want you to get into threes; one of you will be the mother, one will be the child, and one will be the father who is returning the child from a weekend visit with him. Each of you should be upset about something—the mom can be upset about how the dad is always late in bringing the child back. The child is upset about a number of things—he wanted to stay with the dad longer and wanted to go with his dad next weekend, but the dad had to say no. The dad is upset about not being able to keep his son longer and because he could not have his son next weekend for a special occasion.

■ ■ ■

Effective Introduction

LEADER: I want you to get into threes. *(Pause while they do this)* Now I want you to decide who will be the mother, the dad, and the child. *(Pause—leader checks to make sure everyone is doing this.)* Okay, now all those who are playing Mom, here's the role I want you to play.... All those playing Dad, here's the role I want you to play.... And all those playing the child, here's the role....

By presenting the instructions in stages, this leader minimizes the confusion.

■ ■ ■

Other Common Errors   Leaders sometimes assume that the members are prepared to discuss some magazine article, movie, or task assigned from the last session. Instead, the leader should first ask the members if they have completed the assignment. At times, the leader may want to go ahead with the exercise even if one or two members are not prepared, telling them to observe or participate as best they can. An alternative plan is always needed, however, in case the majority is unprepared.

Failure to tell members how long an exercise will last is another mistake of beginning leaders. Without guidelines concerning time, members may either rush to finish or procrastinate and be halfway through when it is time to stop. Something direct, like "We'll spend 5 minutes on this exercise," is sufficient.

GROUP COUNSELING SKILLS: Introducing an Exercise

Go to segments 10.1, 10.2, 10.3, and 10.4 and pay particular attention to how the leader introduces the exercise in each of these segments. You can watch the entire segment or just the introduction of each exercise and how it was conducted. Later you will be encouraged to watch how the exercise was processed.

Exercise-Specific Considerations

Written Exercises   When introducing a written exercise, the leader should distribute or ask members to get the necessary materials (usually paper and pencil), let members get settled back into the group, and then give the instructions. If the leader fails to do this and the members have to search for materials, one or more members will forget the instructions.

A leader should always be prepared to provide the necessary writing materials such as pens, pencils, and paper. Even if the leader is certain that members will bring materials with them, it is a good idea to have extra materials on hand in case pencil leads break or ink runs out. When passing out any forms that are going to be completed, it is best to turn them facedown and ask members not to look at them until the instructions have been given completely. Also, the leader should check to see if every member can read and write.

Movement Exercises   When introducing movement exercises, it is often best to have members stand and move to the designated starting position before giving the instructions. It is also important that the leader not give the instructions while the members are moving around, because they will not be paying attention.

■   **EXAMPLES**

Ineffective Introduction

LEADER: We are going to do a movement exercise involving milling. Each of you is to start out in a spot in the room that is far from the center. I am going to ask you to walk around, moving to different parts of the room with your eyes looking downward; then I am going to have you mill around while glancing at each other. Then you will make steady eye contact. Okay, move to a spot that is away from the center. *(Members move to various spots; a couple have to find new spots because another member is there already.)*

JAMES: Now what do we do first? I forgot. Do we glance at each other?

■ ■ ■

Effective Introduction

LEADER: We are going to do a movement exercise involving milling. First, I want each of you to find a spot in the room that is far from the center. *(Pauses while members do this)* I want you to look down. *(Checks to see that this is happening)* In a minute, I am going to ask you to mill around while looking down; then I will have you do some additional things. Okay, please start milling around, but continue to keep your heads down.

■ ■ ■

Arts and Crafts Exercises   Introducing arts and crafts exercises is very similar to introducing written exercises, because materials should be in front of the members before directions are given. Of course, arts and crafts exercises may require many more materials, such as paste, scissors, paint, crayons, and rulers. It is important to provide the space necessary for members to participate in the exercise in a comfortable manner.

Common Reading Exercises   When introducing common readings, the leader may choose to give the instructions before handing out the reading, or he might want to hand out the reading first, facedown. Usually it is a good idea to tell members to mark the sentences or paragraphs that stand out to them as they read—this helps when processing the exercise, because the leader can ask which sentences or paragraphs they marked. Also, the leader may wish to briefly introduce the reading to help the members get a sense of what they will be reading.

Fantasy Exercises   When introducing a fantasy exercise, leaders should speak slowly to evoke the feelings and images necessary. It is also important to suggest that members close their eyes during the exercise, but also give them the option to leave their eyes open. Giving members such a choice can help them feel more comfortable with the fantasy exercise. Some leaders make the mistake of closing their eyes. It is important for leaders to keep their eyes open and observe the reactions of the members. Observing the members helps the leader pace the exercise. Also, some members may not be able to get into the fantasy; if the leader observes this, she can anticipate different reactions from those members than from the others.

Feedback Exercises   When introducing a feedback exercise, the leader should allow members enough time to think about what they are going to say before they give feedback to other members. The leader will also want to take a minute or two to explain the value of giving helpful feedback. She may want to give examples of what would and would not be helpful. If a leader is not careful in the instructions, the members may give only superficial and meaningless feedback.

Conducting an Exercise

When conducting an exercise, there are at least six considerations of which the leader needs to be aware:

1.   Ensuring that members follow instructions
2.   Allowing members to not share
3.   Handling emotional reactions
4.   Changing or stopping the exercise
5.   Informing members of the time
6.   Deciding whether the leader will participate

Ensuring Members Follow Instructions

Once members begin the exercise, the leader should observe whether they are following through as expected. For example, when members are talking in pairs, they may discuss an issue unrelated to the purpose of the exercise. If the leader observes this, she may move quietly to those members and clarify what they should be doing. If the leader sees that members are laughing or talking when they were instructed not to, the leader will want to intervene, especially when the exercise is meant to be a serious, thought-provoking experience. If a number of members seem confused, the leader may want to go through the instructions again.

Allowing Members to Not Share

In many exercises, such as in rounds or sentence completions, members are asked to respond with a number, a word, or a short answer. The leader needs to be prepared for a member wanting to pass, either because the member feels uncomfortable sharing or because she has not formed a response. When this situation arises, the leader should avoid causing the member discomfort by holding the focus on her. When everyone has commented, the leader may or may not want to bring the focus back to that member. This will depend on how uncomfortable the member seems and the purpose of the group and exercise. Some leaders make the mistake of waiting for a member to respond; this usually causes that member to become more uncomfortable.

■ EXAMPLES

The leader is conducting a round where members describe their early home environment in a word or phrase.

MIKE: Loving, but strict.

MARTY: Good, steady.

ROSA: Can you skip me? I just don't want to say.

LEADER: That's fine. Bill, how about you?

BILL: Happy.

SAM: Good with my mom, hell when Dad was home.

LEADER: Rosa, is it hard to share because it hurts too much?

ROSA: Yes, and I would rather not discuss it right now. Maybe later.

LEADER: Sure. Let's come back to what all of you said. I want you to think about how your upbringing affects you today.

■ ■ ■

In the last example, the leader allows the member to not participate in the dyad with another member, but he ends up in a dyad with the reluctant member. Often members will share with a leader but not other members. In this example, the leader has asked members to get into pairs to discuss their feelings about their marriages. The dyads have been in progress for about 45 seconds when one member gets up and walks toward the leader.

PEGGY: I don't feel like talking about this; can I be excused?

LEADER: *(To Peggy's partner)* Dan, why don't you join Jim and Gloria? Peggy, let's you and I talk for a minute so that I know what is going on.

■ ■ ■

If a member chooses not to participate at all in an exercise, the leader will want to do everything he can to make that member and the others as comfortable as possible with that decision. Depending on the exercise, the member may sit and observe or leave the room temporarily. If possible, the leader will want to determine why the member does not want to participate and, if appropriate, let the other members know why. In most instances, the leader would not want to take too much time determining the reason if it was going to detract from the exercise. As a general rule, unless a member is experiencing a major psychological crisis, it is best not to let one member's needs stop an exercise.

Handling Emotional Reactions

When doing an exercise that focuses members on personal issues, the leader must be prepared for one or more members to react emotionally. Fantasy exercises, feedback exercises, and some movement exercises tend to do this more than others, but any exercise can stir up intense feelings. If the leader sees that a member is experiencing a strong emotional reaction, she has several options. The option she chooses will depend on the intensity of the situation, the kind of exercise, and the purpose of the group. The leader can stop the exercise and focus on the member; form dyads, pairing up with the member to discuss his or her reaction; or acknowledge the member's discomfort and continue the exercise, allowing the member to listen and learn from the discussion among the other members. If the leader feels the member's reaction is too intense to be handled then, the leader might choose to have the member take a break until the exercise is over or to have another member take a break with that member.

■ EXAMPLES

The group has completed giving feedback to two of five members in the group.

LEADER: Okay, let's move to Kathy next. Look over the list of 25 adjectives and think of those that best describe Kathy.

JOE: Quiet, reserved, caring.

MIGUEL: Quiet, warm, sensitive.

BETTY: Caring, quiet, nice.

LEADER: *(Noticing that Kathy is starting to tear up)* Kathy, would you like to talk about what you are feeling?

KATHY: I don't like it that I am quiet. I wanted so much for someone to say intelligent or strong. All I have ever been seen as is *quiet!* I hate it!

LEADER: Would you like to discuss this some more? *(Kathy nods.)* Okay. Let's talk about how you can change that. Before we start, because our time is limited, I'd like to ask Joe and Yoshe if we can postpone their feedback until next week. *(They nod.)* Kathy, tell us how you would like to be different.

■ ■ ■

The group is discussing a sentence-completion form. The questions pertain to attitudes about sex. The sentence they are discussing is "I feel _____ about my early sexual experiences."

LEADER: This question is one that may get you in touch with some guilt or pain. I hope you will be willing to share what you wrote, and perhaps more.

DIANE: I said mostly okay.

DON: Guilty about one thing—good about the rest.

LEADER: Sharon, what did you answer?

SHARON: *(Starting to cry)* I don't want to talk about this right now.

LEADER: Okay, we'll skip you. *(Looking around the group as he talks)* I do want to say that no matter what any of you did, you do not have to feel guilty about it. Hopefully we can focus on how to let go of guilt. Sharon, if it gets too uncomfortable, let me know; otherwise, I hope that you will listen and maybe later join in. Carol, what did you answer?

CAROL: I said that I feel I learned a lot from those early sexual experiences.

■ ■ ■

Changing or Stopping the Exercise

When doing an exercise, the leader sometimes decides to change it or to stop. He might do this either because he feels that it is not producing the kinds of responses he had anticipated or because a good topic for discussion has emerged.

■ EXAMPLE

The members of a growth group were asked to list three significant people in their lives. Two of the five members have already shared their lists.

BOBBI: My dad is the most significant person in my life. Last week he went into the hospital with cancer.

JUDE: *(Abruptly)* My mom has cancer, too. I didn't put her down as one of my most significant people, but I'm really scared she might die.

LEADER: What we might do for a few minutes, if Bobbi and Jude would find it helpful, is to talk about this.

BOBBI: I think it would help me.

JUDE: It would definitely help me.

LEADER: Okay, let's focus on Bobbi and Jude now, and then we may come back to your lists a little later.

In this example, it seems appropriate to stop the exercise and focus on Bobbi and Jude, who both have immediate needs in common. Illnesses and worry are topics to which most members can relate.

■ ■ ■

Informing Members of the Time

Leaders should keep members informed about how much time is left to complete the exercise. A statement such as, "Take about 2 more minutes to complete the exercise" is usually a sufficient cue to let members know the amount of time left. Informing members of the time remaining gives them some idea of how to pace themselves to complete the exercise or wind down discussion.

Members are then better prepared to return to the large group to process or discuss material from the exercise. Also, by observing members' reactions to an exercise, the leader may want to lengthen or shorten the amount of time that was originally allotted to it. For instance, if the leader sees that members are actively sharing in their dyads, he may choose to let them continue for a couple of minutes longer than originally planned.

Deciding Whether the Leader Will Participate

Leaders have the option of participating or not participating in an exercise. When deciding whether or not to participate, leaders should consider the following:

1. *As a nonparticipant, the leader can closely monitor group members' activities.* For example, if members are talking in dyads and their discussion is not on task, the leader can intervene and help them focus by reiterating the purpose.

2. *By listening and watching rather than joining in, the leader can hear what members are saying and see what they are doing.* During the processing of the exercise, a leader may even use what she heard by saying something like, "I was listening to John and Eileen, and Eileen brought up a very important point about...." When doing this, be sure you are not revealing to the group something that the member was intending to share only with her dyad partner.

3. *The leader may not want to participate because the members may focus too much on the leader's opinions or comments.* In most rounds or sentence-completion exercises, the leader usually should choose not to participate to avoid emphasis on his answers unless the answers can be very useful for the members; in other words, the leader should participate only when his participation can be of value to the members.

4. *By not participating, the leader can more easily get a sense of when the energy for the exercise is waning or when members have neared completion of the task.* In certain kinds of exercises, the participating leader can get so involved that

she loses track of time, forgets to pay attention to the energy of the group, or both.

5. *A leader should not do personal work in a group he is leading.* As a rule, the leader should not participate in an exercise that could cause him to focus on his own thoughts, feelings, or "unfinished business." However, it is a good idea for him to have previously done or given considerable thought to any exercise that he uses in a group.

Leaders' participation in the activity also has its benefits.

1. *Leader participation can help members get to know the leader.* Members are usually very interested in the leader's opinions, ideas, reactions, and feedback. If members view the leader as distant and nondisclosing, they may be less likely to share personally relevant material in the group.

2. *The leader may wish to participate to create a certain effect.* For example, in certain kinds of groups, the leader may want to play devil's advocate to get the members to see both sides of some dilemma.

3. *Participation may also be helpful in a dyad exercise if the leader sees the need to give feedback or to help out a particular member.*

4. *The leader may participate in an exercise when there is an odd number of participants and an even number is needed.*

Processing an Exercise

Exercises merely act as catalysts for initiating discussion by triggering thoughts and feelings. *Understanding the processing of exercises is essential because the processing of the exercise is by far the most important phase of any exercise.* By *processing,* we mean spending time discussing thoughts, feelings, and ideas that result from doing the exercise. Many books on exercises tell the potential leader what materials to use and how to conduct the exercise but spend very little time discussing how to process the exercise. In this section, we address not only how to process an exercise, but also a number of considerations regarding the processing of exercises.

Although some exercises do not need processing because they are used for warm-up or for fun, most exercises are of little value unless they are processed. For many exercises, the processing and the conducting of the exercise overlap because the discussion is part of the exercise. This is true for some feedback, sentence-completion, and experiential exercises where the leader asks processing questions while conducting the exercise. For other exercises, such as a trust walk or completing the ropes courses, the processing occurs when the exercise is completed.

The leader will want to consider several questions regarding the processing:

1. What is the goal of the processing?
2. How much time is needed for adequate processing?

3. What processing methods should be used?
4. What kinds of processing questions should be used?
5. How much time should be spent discussing the actual exercise?
6. Should the focus be on the entire group or on one individual?
7. When should the focus be held, and when should it be shifted?
8. Is the exercise present-centered or past-centered? Do I want to focus on the past or present?

Goals of Processing

There are three possible goals when processing an exercise, each having a slightly different focus.

1. *To stimulate sharing and discussion about topics or issues.* This is the goal of most exercises. Sentence completions and other written exercises are used to get members talking about different subjects. Often movement, experiential, common reading, and moral dilemma exercises lead to beneficial discussions.

■ **EXAMPLE**

LEADER: As you were listening to others' responses, what was triggered for you?

MORRIE: I did not realize that others felt the same fears I did. Especially Roger, you and I seem so similar. I have all kinds of thoughts going through my head.

LEADER: We'll come back to you in a minute. Anyone else want to share his or her reactions?

ROGER: I do have all kinds of fears. I've never talked about them before this group.

■ ■ ■

2. *To stimulate members to delve deeper into thoughts and feelings.* Leaders often use fantasy exercises, certain common readings, creative exercises, and many other kinds of exercises to get members in touch with their feelings. The goal is to help members share at a deep, personal level.

■ **EXAMPLE**

LEADER: What did this reading get you to think about regarding how you are living? Are you living life as if it is a dress rehearsal?

BRENDA: Sure made me stop and think. I know I am not happy in my relationship and haven't been for months. Certain phrases really hit home for me.

FRANK: Many phrases hit me. I am just going through the motions of living and not working hard on my marriage. Like it says, life is not a dress rehearsal!

■ ■ ■

3. *To stimulate sharing and discussion related to the group dynamics and group process.* For example, a trust walk exercise can lead to a discussion about trust and then specifically about trust within the group. An exercise where members rate how they feel about the group will usually lead to a discussion about the group dynamics and group process. Group-decision exercises and experiential exercises often lead to processing that focuses on what is happening within the group.

■ EXAMPLE

LEADER: I want you to think about the meaning of this exercise. All of you sculpted how you felt about this group and not one person put themselves as open or toward the center of the group. What do you think this means?

ALEXIS: We don't trust each other or something. I know I worry about being judged.

CARLETTA: I want this to be a good experience. The last group I was in was great. No one shares much here. I would, but no one else seems to want to.

NINA: *(To the leader)* Do you think something is wrong with the group?

LEADER: Let me say it this way—so much more could happen in the group.

■ ■ ■

GROUP COUNSELING SKILLS: Processing an Exercise

Now go back to segments 10.1, 10.2, 10.3, and 10.4 and pay particular attention to how the leader processes the exercise to get members to go deeper into themselves.

Time Needed for Adequate Processing

A leader should always make sure there is enough time to process the exercise to the depth desired. Many exercises are designed to take members to a very deep, personal level. Unfortunately, a number of group leaders fail to allow enough time for processing. They either begin the exercise when there is not adequate time to discuss members' reactions or they move on to another activity too soon. Both of these mistakes can lead to frustration, confusion, and a shallow, meaningless experience.

■ EXAMPLES

Ineffective Processing

LEADER: I want you to think of an animal that you would like to be if you could be any animal in the world. What would it be? *(Pause)* Who wants to go first?

FRANK: A cat.

DANNIE: A tiger.

MEL: A big black bear.

SHARON: A bird.

LEADER: Any comments?

SHARON: Dave reminds me of an alligator.

DANNIE: I agree, he does. He sort of sits and waits.

LEADER: Any other comments? *(Pause)* Now I'd like you to think of where you would like to live if you could live anywhere you wanted.

In this example, the leader does not spend time discussing the members' choices before going on to a second exercise. Therefore, very little, if anything, is gained from the exercise. The skilled leader has a purpose for doing the animal fantasy exercise. The leader would spend a few minutes having members share why they chose their particular animal and how that may relate to their own lives. This exercise can lead to discussion that can last an entire session if the leader understands its purpose.

■ ■ ■

Effective Processing—allowing enough time for deeper exploration

LEADER: I want you to think of an animal that you would like to be if you could be any animal in the world. What would it be and why? *(Pause)* Who wants to go first?

FRANK: A cat.

LEADER: Why?

FRANK: They are independent, take care of themselves, but they are also taken care of by their owner.

DANNIE: A tiger because they are feared, fast, and pretty.

SHARON: A bird because they are free, can soar, and are not confined.

LEADER: How does the animal you pick either remind you of yourself or get you in touch with something you desire?

SHARON: I don't feel free right now in my life, and I feel very confined by my boyfriend.

LEADER: We'll come back to you. Let me hear others' insights.

FRANK: Wow! I thought this was sort of dumb at first, but I'm blown away. I really want someone to take care of me and my girlfriend expects me to take complete care of her. No wonder I resent her! I do need to talk about this some more.

Another mistake leaders make regarding time is letting the exercise take up too much time, leaving only a few minutes for processing. For example, the elementary school counselor could mistakenly give members 15 minutes to draw their families and then have only 5–7 minutes to talk about the drawings. *In most cases, the majority of time allotted to an exercise should be for processing the exercise and not for conducting it.*

■ ■ ■

Ways of Processing

When an exercise has been conducted and completed, it can be processed in several ways:

1. Rounds
2. Dyads or triads
3. Writing
4. In the entire group
5. In any combination of the preceding four ways

The round is a good way to start the processing. The leader can say something like, "In a sentence or two, what stood out to you about the exercise?" or "Let's go around the group and hear from each of you as to what you thought of the reading."

A leader may want to use dyads or triads when there seems to be a lot of energy and members can benefit from sharing their thoughts and feelings. Using dyads or triads gives everyone a chance to talk. Writing can be used after exercises where members have many thoughts and feelings they might want to express but not share with anyone else. Exercises that are very thought-provoking and emotional, such as family sculpture or certain fantasy exercises, may lend themselves to this kind of processing, along with other kinds of processing.

Even if the first three ways are used, the majority of the processing will occur among the entire group. The first three ways listed often serve as a way to start the processing. Once the group is warmed up, the leader can use questions to stimulate the discussion, such as, "Does anyone want to share thoughts or feelings?" or "What was triggered for you?" or "Let's talk about your reactions." The leader can also use these questions at the beginning of the processing if she feels that no warm-up is necessary.

■ **EXAMPLES**

Members have just completed an exercise where they drew egograms (a transactional analysis diagram) of themselves at home, at work, and with their family of origin.

LEADER: This activity usually stirs up a lot of thoughts and feelings. First, I am going to get you to pair up and share your egograms and any thoughts that you have. Let's see, the two of you pair up, and the two of you, and the two of you.... *(Allows 5 minutes for sharing)* Let's come back to the large group. What have you learned from doing this exercise? Do you see some changes that you want to make?

In this example, the leader uses dyads and then the whole group for processing the exercise. In the next example, the leader uses a round and then opens the discussion to the entire group with questions that will deepen the focus.

■ ■ ■

LEADER: *(After viewing a 20-minute movie)* Let's do a quick round on your reactions to the movie on a 1–10 scale, with 10 being *has you really thinking* and 1 being *the movie had no impact.* Who wants to start?

RAMOS: 10.

CLYDE: 8.

MARLENE: 9.

PAULETTE: 8.

TRAY: 8.

LEADER: So everyone is really thinking. We should be able to have a very interesting session. What hit you? What are you thinking about?

■ ■ ■

LEADER: *(After conducting an exercise where everyone explores his or her own personal space)* What did you experience in doing this exercise?

MONICA: I felt comfortable until you asked me to go outside of my space. That did not feel good. I worried about invading others.

ANNETTE: Me too. I worried about touching someone.

ANITA: I didn't mind and I kind of liked it. I felt sort of confined in my space.

LEADER: That's interesting and something we can explore. Some of you felt comfortable outside of your space and others did not. Let's talk about how your experience just now relates to your life and not just to the exercise.

■ ■ ■

Kinds of Processing Questions

The skilled leader will always consider the kinds of processing questions to ask, because her questions direct the focus of the processing (Kees & Jacobs, 1990). The questions can cause members to focus on the exercise, the group, issues or topics, or on individuals. Questions such as "What happened?" "What did you draw?" and "What part of the reading stood out?" are the kinds of questions that get the members to talk about the exercise. These questions are often used at the beginning of the processing phase, but some leaders make the mistake of using only these questions, which can lead to a superficial group.

If the leader wants the members to go deeper, she should also use other kinds of questions, such as the following:

- What insights did you get from doing this?
- What feelings were stirred up for you?
- How can you use this exercise to help you in your life?

Leaders will always want to make sure that their questions are congruent with the goal of the exercise. The biggest mistake leaders make is asking questions that do not foster any in-depth exploration—questions that generate discussion at the 10 or 9 level instead of at the deeper 8, 7, or 6 levels. The processing questions should help funnel the group to a deeper level. Glass and Benshoff (1999) discuss a model for processing certain kinds of exercises. Their article emphasizes the importance of asking the right questions at the different stages of processing. In the appendix to their article, they list specific questions for the nine different stages they outline as important in processing an exercise.

Time Spent Discussing the Actual Exercise

Often, the leader has to decide how long to discuss the actual exercise. For instance, if the group has just engaged in a fantasy exercise, the leader would want to let members tell their fantasy, but the main purpose of processing is to get them to talk about what feelings they encounter. The same is true of a movement exercise where people struggled to reach their goals. The processing is initially on what it felt like when they had to struggle, but the leader would want to rather quickly center the discussion on the struggles they are having in their lives, not the struggle in the exercise. It is very easy to allow members to share at a superficial level about the exercise itself and thus not maximize the benefit of the exercise. Many leaders make the mistake of having members merely talk about the exercise and do not try to take the discussion to a deeper, more meaningful level. Leaders can eliminate this mistake by asking good, thought-provoking questions that tap into the emotions and feelings of the members.

■ EXAMPLES

The leader has just completed a movement exercise where the members were told to form a circle and hold hands. Then the leader asked members to silently pick a spot in the room toward which they were to try to pull the rest of the group. The purpose of this exercise is to see how determined and persistent members are and to see how they attempt to get what they want.

> **LEADER:** What was that like? What happened?
>
> **JOSÉ:** Boy, that was tough. I really got into that exercise. Sandy, you should have seen the look on your face as you tried to pull away from the group!
>
> **SANDY:** Yeah, I was surprised at how strong you were, José. All I could think to do was to free myself from your grip.
>
> **DONALD:** I had no idea that you girls could pull as strongly as you did....

It is evident here that the discussion is conversational. No real learning is taking place, because the members are merely discussing their actions during the exercise itself. This is fine for the first couple of minutes, but to effectively process the exercise so that the members learn from it and apply this learning to their lives, the leader needs to ask some additional questions such as, "Think for just a moment about what this exercise meant to you. What did you learn that you can apply to your current life situations?" The leader could also say, "Did this exercise have any meaning for you in terms of your lives outside this group?" Group discussion following such leader prompts might sound something like the following:

> **ANGIE:** Yes, I think I learned something. The thing that stood out to me about this exercise is that I tend to fear competition. I've always shunned opportunities to compete and, as a result, I think I've been missing out on some potentially rewarding experiences.
>
> **DONALD:** That's interesting, Angie. I feel almost the opposite, in that I always compete and have a difficult time just enjoying life without always comparing myself to others. I often come up short when I play the comparing game.

In this dialogue, the group members are applying their reactions to their lives, and the exercise acts to trigger thoughts. Keep in mind that the exercise usually only stimulates members' reactions. It is the leader's guiding statements that often cause members to personalize the experience.

■ ■ ■

This group has just completed a fantasy exercise that involved having the members visualize themselves on a journey to see an old wise person.

Ineffective Processing

> **LEADER:** What was it like seeing the wise man?
>
> **JERRY:** My wise man had a long, gray beard.
>
> **TED:** Mine was dressed in a long, white robe and carried a cane.
>
> **CRISTINA:** When we met each other, I gave him a hug.
>
> **JANET:** "He" was a "she" and she never said a word to me, but I know that she was glad to see me because she smiled.
>
> **LEADER:** What else happened when you saw the wise man or woman?
>
> **JOEY:** I was frightened. I thought he had too much on his mind to see me.
>
> **TAMMY:** It felt good. He was glad to see me and I wanted to stay longer.
>
> **LEADER:** Did the wise man or woman give any of you an answer to your question?
>
> **TED:** Yes.
>
> **JANET:** She just smiled when I asked her my question.
>
> **LEADER:** What about when you left? How did you feel?

The discussion could continue like this for the entire session, with members recounting what they thought and imagined during the exercise. The discussion would remain on a surface level, with no significant learning taking place. The members are not applying the exercise to their lives.

■ ■ ■

Effective Processing

> **LEADER:** Did any of the thoughts, feelings, and images you had as you went to see the wise person relate, in any way, to your own personal life?
>
> **CRISTINA:** It did for me. Seeing the wise man was just like going to see my grandfather. I'm always glad to see him and we always hug.
>
> **JOEY:** I was really scared as I walked up that mountain, I was afraid that he wouldn't be glad to see me or wouldn't have time for me. I sometimes feel that way when I'm at home. I have four brothers and sisters, and sometimes I feel like Mom and Dad don't have time for me.
>
> **LEADER:** Maybe that's something we can talk about in a minute. It seems important.
>
> **TED:** It felt like the wise man was telling me not to worry about school and home so much. I worry a lot about those things sometimes, and it makes me sad.
>
> **LEADER:** I never thought of you as worrying about your home life. Would you like to talk about that?
>
> **TED:** Yes, I think I would.

LEADER: Okay, we'll do that sometime before the session is over. I want to get a few more comments about the experience of seeing the wise person. Janet?

JANET: When I asked the wise woman my question, she just smiled. Then I realized that I have the answer inside me, and I don't always have to rely on other people to make decisions for me.

LEADER: Any significance or importance that you changed the person to be a woman?

In this processing, the members are relating in a personal manner. The exercise opens avenues for discussion and allows members to share their thoughts and feelings as well as to hear the reactions of others. Because processing the exercise has caused members to share personal information, several concerns have emerged. The leader may now choose to focus more intensely on Ted's or Joey's concerns.

■ ■ ■

Focusing on One Member or on the Entire Group

When processing exercises for personal growth, support, and therapy groups, the leader sometimes has to decide whether to focus on one person or on the group. *It is usually best at the beginning of the processing phase to hear from all the members who feel like sharing in order to get a sense of what is going on with the members.* This can be done by using rounds or by just asking for some brief comments about members' reactions to an exercise. If there are members who would like to work on something, the leader has to decide whether focusing on one person is better than continuing the discussion with the entire group. The last scenario is a good example of the leader deciding whether to go with a group discussion or an individual focus on either Ted or Joey.

It is difficult to give specific guidelines about when the leader should focus on individuals. In a growth group, you may not want to hold the focus too long on one individual. If the group is a support or therapy group, it is often very beneficial to let the focus be on one person for 10 to 20 minutes, especially if that person is willing to work at a deep personal level (6 or below on the depth chart).

■ EXAMPLES

In this example, the leader focuses on one person for a while.

LEADER: As you were listening to others' responses, what got triggered for you?

MORRIE: I did not realize that others felt the same fears I did. Especially Roger, you and I seem so similar. I have all kinds of thoughts going through my head.

LEADER: We'll come back to you in a minute. Anyone else want to share his or her reactions?

OTHERS: ...

LEADER: Morrie, do you want to work on getting rid of those fears?

MORRIE: Most definitely. My fears keep me from doing all kinds of things. Probably my biggest one is ...

■ ■ ■

Using the same example, the leader chooses to focus on a topic rather than one person.

LEADER: Let's take the topic of fears. How does fear affect your life?

MORRIE: My fears keep me from doing all kinds of things. Probably my biggest one is fear of mistakes at work. Just the other day, I had a situation that ...

LEADER: *(With a caring voice)* Morrie, let me interrupt you. I'd like us first to discuss in general our fears and how they affect us, and then we'll go into specific situations that have occurred recently. Anyone else want to comment about their fears?

ROGER: My fear is more related to women and what they will think. I don't worry about men's approval.

STEPHANIE: That's so interesting. I don't think my fears have to do with others but more myself. I fear failing at new things so I don't try many new things.

■ ■ ■

Holding and Shifting the Focus

An error commonly made by inexperienced group leaders when processing an exercise is to focus the group for too long on the first person who talks. It is usually best for the leader to give all or most of the members a chance to talk before holding the focus on any one person or issue. Exercises should create energy and interest among all the members. Focusing prematurely on one member may result in losing the interest and attention of others who have not had a chance to react to the exercise. Also, be aware that the first person who speaks may be speaking out of anxiety, a need for attention, or a desire to please the leader. This member's response may therefore be a function of those needs rather than a reflection of genuine feelings about the issue.

■ EXAMPLES

Ineffective Processing

LEADER: *(Following a sentence-completion exercise)* Who would like to share an answer with the group?

TOD: *(Appearing eager to respond)* I would. On that question concerning my thoughts on divorce, I thought about what different reactions people have. My one uncle was depressed for months and hardly left his house except to go to work. My other uncle, however, seemed to be happier as a result and went on about his life as though nothing had happened. What do you suppose was the difference?

LEADER: I don't know. What do you think the difference could have been?

TOD: *(In a storytelling voice)* Well, one difference could have been the length of time that they were married or the fact that one uncle had been divorced once before. He told me ...

In this example, Tod is the first to speak, and his response is not relevant to the group. His voice indicates he is not speaking introspectively but rather with a storytelling intent. The leader makes an error in continuing to focus on him instead of tapping into the energy generated from completing the sentences.

■ ■ ■

Effective Processing

LEADER: Who would like to share an answer with the group?

TOD: *(Appearing eager to respond)* I would. On that question concerning my thoughts on divorce, I thought about what different reactions people have. My one uncle was depressed for months and hardly left his house except to go to work. My other uncle, however, seemed to be happier as a result and went on about his life as though nothing had happened. What do you suppose was the difference?

LEADER: I'm not too sure in their particular cases, Tod. If you are interested in exploring this, you and I can do it after the group adjourns. Right now, however, I would like others to share their specific answers with the group.

TIM: For number 1, I said divorce does not always mean failure.

LEADER: What did others answer for number 1?

DORIS: *(Crying)* I do feel like a failure. I never wanted to put my kids through a divorce and a broken home. *(Sobbing)* I just don't know why this had to happen and what I did wrong.

LEADER: Doris, I know you blame yourself, but from what you have told us, your husband had a serious drug problem. I want us to focus on Doris but I do want all of you to think about this failure issue. *(With a kind voice)* Doris, I want you to look at us and tell us truthfully what you think you could have done to save this marriage, given your husband's drug problem.

In this example, the leader chooses not to focus on Tod, even though there seems to be some energy. Many novice leaders are so relieved that someone is speaking that they will focus on the first person to speak rather than give others a chance to comment briefly. Also, the leader realizes that it would be a mistake to hold the focus on Tod, because the purpose of the exercise is to get members talking more personally about divorce. By shifting the focus from Tod, the leader allows Doris to share her deep-seated feelings.

■ ■ ■

Present-Centered or Past-Centered Exercises

Although most exercises focus on the present, many are designed to get members to reflect on their pasts. Members may be asked to draw the houses they lived in when they were young or to describe how they felt when they were 10 years old. A potentially powerful exercise that focuses on the past is to have members bring in pictures from childhood.

There is no right or wrong about where exercises should focus. We do feel that, in most cases, focusing in the present about the past is usually more productive than just focusing on the past. The reason for this is that group members cannot change their past, but they can change how they are affected by it. It is good to focus on the past to get at various hidden and possibly painful issues, but then it is usually important to bring the discussion to the present. The following questions can help to do this:

- How do you think your past affects you today?
- What can you learn from looking at those past relationships?
- It is important to take a look at how our past experiences affect us today. What did you learn?
- Does this stir up some unfinished business that you may want to work on?
- What feelings from your childhood do you need to sort out?

The leader should almost always be considering how to help members in the present even when conducting a past-centered exercise. We stress this point about past-centered exercises because we have seen too many group leaders focus on the past and not have members consider what they need to do in the present to change their feelings or thoughts. Too often, leaders process a past-centered exercise by just having the members describe past experiences. This gets members to reflect or tell old childhood stories but doesn't help members address any issues that are currently bothering them about their past.

■ EXAMPLES

Ineffective Processing

LEADER: Now that you have drawn the house you grew up in, what did that bring up for you?

KIM: It made me think about all the times my dad got drunk and yelled and screamed at me for no reason.

CINDI: I felt sad that my parents sold that house two years ago. I loved that house and had such good memories. I liked the neighborhood—lots of friends to play with.

SONNY: I always wanted a bigger house. Four of us had to sleep in one room. I still resent it! I do have some good memories of the times my grandpa visited. He was a great guy—he loved music so he always had us playing music.

LEADER: What kind of music did you play?

SONNY: All kinds. One time he …

■ ■ ■

Effective Processing

LEADER: Now that you have drawn the house you grew up in, what did that bring up for you?

KIM: It made me think about all the times my dad got drunk and yelled and screamed at me for no reason.

CINDI: I felt sad that my parents sold that house two years ago. I loved that house and had such good memories. I liked the neighborhood—lots of friends to play with.

SONNY: I always wanted a bigger house. Four of us had to sleep in one room. I still resent it! I do have some good memories of the times my grandpa visited. He was a great guy—he loved music so he always had us playing music.

LEADER: Let me get you to come to the present and think about what you just said or felt and let's talk about any feelings you may have as a result of your childhood

KIM: Like what?

LEADER: For instance, Kim, what effect does your dad's screaming then have on you now? Or with Cindi—any feelings about your parents selling the house?

CINDI: You know, I realize that I am very mad at them. I think that I didn't have a good Christmas because I am still mad at them.

LEADER: Let's hear from others and then we'll come back to you and talk some more about that *(Cindi nods).*

KIM: I'll tell you what his screaming did—it causes me to cringe when anyone even raises his or her voice at me. I know my husband sometimes gets loud and I freak out. We have actually fought about this on numerous occasions.

■ ■ ■

Concluding Comments

This concludes our discussion of exercises. We hope this chapter combined with Chapter 10, "Exercises," gives you a better understanding of the kinds of exercises, when to use them, how to introduce them, and how to conduct and process them. Throughout this chapter, we have pointed out a number of common mistakes made by leaders when using exercises. The following is a review of some of the main points to consider when using an exercise in your group:

- Choose the kind of exercise that is best for what you are trying to accomplish.
- Make sure the exercise is relevant to members' needs and the group's purpose.
- Make sure directions are clearly stated.
- Try to clear up any confusion before the exercise actually begins.
- Keep directions short and simple.
- Make sure all necessary materials are in members' hands before introducing the exercise.
- Place handouts or sentence completions facedown before starting, to avoid distraction.
- Generally, have members stand up and get situated before giving directions for movement exercises.
- Give directions that include enough information for completing the exercise successfully.
- Allow members to not participate.
- Explain the purpose of an exercise before beginning it.
- Announce how long the exercise will last.
- Remember that exercises are means, not ends. Learning comes through processing.
- Open processing discussions with thought-provoking, open-ended questions.
- When processing an exercise, make it relevant to group members' lives.
- Do not use exercises one after another without processing sufficiently in between.

■ ACTIVITIES

1. Think of three exercises that you have never conducted before. Write down how you would introduce, conduct, and process the exercises.
2. Think of groups or classes where exercises were used to facilitate discussion. Think about the leader's effectiveness at introducing, conducting, and processing the exercises. This activity is especially helpful when you pick leaders who did not do a good job in introducing, conducting, and processing.

GROUP COUNSELING SKILLS

1. View segment 5.3 and watch how the leader introduced, conducted, and processed the rounds and sentence completion exercises.
2. View segment 7.1 and watch how the leader introduced, conducted, and processed the exercise on anger using fuses.
3. View segment 8.7 and watch how the leader introduced, conducted, and processed the exercise using movement to get quiet members talking. Why was this movement exercise valuable given that the leader had three quiet, hesitant members?
4. View segment 14.3 and watch how the leader introduced, conducted, and processed the simple round exercise regarding unfinished business?
    a. What skills did the leader use during the processing phase?
    b. What did the leader do to get members to go deeper?

Chapter 12

Leading the Middle Stage
of a Group

The most important stage of a group is the middle or working stage, because this is when the members should be working, learning, and deriving maximum benefit from being in a group. In the middle stage, members discuss, share, and work on problems or tasks. The emphasis in this chapter will be on groups that meet for a number of sessions; however, the information will also be useful for groups that meet only once or twice, because they will also have a middle stage.

In this chapter, we discuss the planning and assessment tasks that leaders face during the working stage as well as some essential leadership techniques and activities that can help. We also offer outlines for covering common topics, discuss the mistakes that leaders often make during the middle sessions, and present strategies useful to certain types of groups. In the next two chapters, we continue the discussion of leading middle sessions, focusing on the use of counseling theories and conducting counseling and therapy in groups.

Planning and Assessment

During the middle stage, the leader must decide how much planning is needed based on the purpose of the group, the personalities and needs of the members, and the levels of trust, interest, and commitment. Some leaders plan the entire series of sessions before the group begins and fail to modify those plans according to the evolution of the group. *It is important to realize that session plans conceived well in advance or plans from a group that worked for you last month may not work for the current situation.*

Assessing the Benefits

Periodically during the middle stage, the leader will want to assess the group's value to its members and make adjustments if the group is not beneficial. To assess the benefits of the group, the leader can use any of the following activities:

- Conduct a 1–10 round on how valuable the group has been. The leader would follow up with a discussion of the ratings.

- Conduct a comment round in which the leader asks each member to comment on the value of the group.

- Initiate a discussion of the value of the group by saying something like, "For the next half hour or so, I'd like people to comment on how this group is being helpful." This differs from a round in that not everyone necessarily comments, and the discussion will be more extensive.

- Have members review each topic discussed. Getting members to comment on what has stood out to them can help the leader evaluate the effectiveness of the group experience. If the members fail to recall the main points or if they have little to say, there is a good chance the group is not as beneficial as it could be.

- Ask members to write for 5 to 10 minutes on what they have gained from the group up to this point. Good stimulus questions include the following:

    How is this group helping you?

    What activities are most beneficial to you?

    How do you feel about the group?

    What things do you dislike about the group?

    What would make the group better for you?

- Leaders can have members write at the end of the session and leave what they write, or leaders can assign out-of-group projects to be brought in at the next meeting or mailed in.

By engaging in one of the preceding activities, the leader should have a better understanding of how the members feel the group is benefiting them, which in turn will help improve future sessions. Although it is the leader's responsibility to try to make the group a meaningful experience for everyone, it is important to remember that this is not always possible. Some individuals may lack the personal resources, such as attention span or communication skills, to benefit from certain kinds of groups. Likewise, the leader should not be overwhelmed or feel defensive if members have various criticisms. It is important that leaders remember that not everyone will always like everything that takes place in the group.

Assessing Members' Interest and Commitment

During the middle stage, leaders should also assess members' interest and commitment levels. To assess the interest and commitment of the members, the leader observes the frequency of absences and late arrivals, which is often one indication. Also, the leader observes the energy throughout the session. The leader looks for patterns of disinterest over a period of two or three sessions rather than in a single session, because outside stresses and concerns can easily affect a member's level of commitment for any given session.

When the members' interest seems to be declining, the leader may first want to assess whether the loss of interest applies to everyone or just a few of the members. When only a few members have lost interest, the leader will want to try to understand why. It may be that members' interest levels were low from the beginning because they were forced to be in the group. Members may also not be committed to the group because they don't find the content interesting, don't feel their needs are being met, and aren't ready to make changes in their lives. No matter what the reason, the leader will want to try to remedy the situation, possibly by using one of the following options.

If most members have lost interest, the leader can:

- Decide that the group has served its purpose and end the group
- Change the format of the group to generate new interest and commitment
- Bring up the issue for discussion in the group

If a few members have lost interest, the leader can:

- *Bring up the issue with the entire group,* keeping in mind that there will be differences of opinion. The discussion may prove helpful in clarifying the purpose of the group and in revealing why certain members are not interested. Depending on what is said, the leader may or may not be able to make changes that will increase some members' interest.

- *Meet with those whose interest seems low* and talk to them about how they could be more involved. If they are no longer committed to the group, the leader may choose to ask them not to return. This option should not be used often, but it should be considered, because no group can go well when a number of members lack commitment to its purpose.

- *Give members permission to drop out of the group.* This can be done in two ways: (1) mention that some may want to drop out and this would be a good time to do so; or (2) have a closing session for the current group, letting members know they have the option of requesting to be in a second group that is starting immediately.

Assessing Each Member's Participation

During the middle sessions of any group, the leader will want to consider each member's frequency and style of participation. Although there is no "correct" way to participate in the group, active, verbal participation is usually better for most members than merely observing or occasionally commenting. As a rule, it is desirable to try to get quiet members to share their thoughts and feelings, in the hope that they will become more comfortable sharing in the group. There will be times when getting members to share more is either not possible or not desirable.

A related member-participation problem arises when the leader feels that members are making only superficial comments. To change the level of participation, the leader can use a variety of skills and techniques:

- He can change his voice so that it reflects a quiet, deliberate tone and indicates a more serious mood, to which members will tend to respond more seriously.

- She can mention her observation of what is happening and suggest that the level of participation change. She can use the depth chart as a visual tool, showing that the group is not going below 7 with any discussion.

- He can shift to an exercise or activity that has the potential for generating more serious discussion.

- She can shift to a topic that will generate more personal discussion.

Assessing Members' Trust Level and Group Cohesion

During the working stage, the leader needs to be aware of the level of trust that the members are feeling. When the leader does not pay enough attention to the continued development of trust, it may deteriorate and lead to members feeling uncomfortable in the group. If a leader finds herself in a situation in which the group's trust level is low, she will want to focus on the issue of trust, either by bringing it up for discussion or by using one of the several trust exercises, such as the trust walk.

Assessing How Much to Focus on Content and How Much
to Focus on Process

During the working stage, the leader should pay attention to both group content and group process and should constantly decide what the proper balance should be between the two. It is important to mention this because no matter what the purpose, there will be times when focusing on process is very important and necessary. A common mistake made by leaders is to ignore the process and just focus on content. Not focusing on process can lead to a very superficial group in which dynamics exist such as members dominating the group; members not trusting each other; or members feeling attacked, judged, or inferior. If the leader wants the group to be maximally beneficial, he has to monitor group dynamics, especially if they are negative.

Screening Out Members

There will be times when a leader will have to make the difficult choice of asking a member to leave the group. This should be done only after numerous attempts have been made to help the difficult member become a cooperative group member. We know of many situations where a group has been "sacrificed" because the leader was afraid to ask a member to leave the group.

Some leaders want the group members to decide whether another member should be asked to leave, and in some situations, this may be a good idea. However, most of the time the leader should make the decision because the leader is in the best position to decide whether the member is interfering with the development of the group. *Always keep in mind that it is your responsibility to try to make sure that a group has the proper membership composition so that it can be maximally beneficial.*

Dealing With Breach of Confidentiality

There will be times when a breach of confidentiality by one or more members in the group occurs. This obviously is a situation that must be given much thought. Before anything is done, the leader should talk to the member who breached confidentiality to get some idea as to what happened and why. If the leader finds out that the occurrence was accidental and innocent, then the leader may consider letting the member remain in the group. Before deciding, the leader definitely must get a sense of how the other members feel about having the member involved in future sessions. This can be done at the start of the next session with either the member present or not present. Having the member stay depends on the situation, the other members, and the member who breached confidentiality. If the member stays, he could be attacked by some or all of the other members (especially in groups of teenagers) and not be able to handle it, or he may benefit greatly from the feedback and comments of the other members. The leader has to gauge what she thinks is the best approach for helping the group and the member. There are no set answers for this type of situation except to give it much thought and, if possible, consult with colleagues to get their input and suggestions.

If the breach of confidentiality occurred out of anger, revenge, or idle gossip, then the leader may feel the member should not be allowed to remain in the group. In this case, the leader would need to tell the member he cannot return to the group and then process with him any feelings he has. If at all possible, the leader would want to turn the situation into a learning experience for the member and for the group when it meets the next time.

One of the most difficult situations that can occur around breach of confidentiality is when the leader, due to agency policy, does not have the option to ask a member to leave the group. The leader must then decide the best way to minimize the effects of having the member remain in the group. Needless to say, this is not a good situation, but it does occur in certain settings.

Leadership Skills and Techniques for the Middle Sessions

Several skills and techniques are especially appropriate for the middle sessions. To make the group a valuable and worthwhile experience, the most important skills to remember are cutting off; drawing out; and holding, shifting, and deepening the focus; all of which have been discussed in earlier chapters. In this section, we elaborate on some additional skills that are valuable when leading middle sessions. Because we have already mentioned these in previous chapters, our descriptions are brief.

1. Using progress reports
2. Introducing topics for discussion
3. Stimulating members' thoughts
4. Varying the format
5. Changing leadership style, if warranted
6. Changing the structure of the group, if warranted
7. Using voice to get members to think
8. Using outside materials and assignments
9. Meeting with members individually
10. Informing members in advance when the group is ending

Using Progress Reports

In many groups, members often share aspects of their lives that need to be followed up on during the next session. An excellent way to do this is by starting each session with progress reports from various members. Not only is this helpful to the members who share their progress, but this kind of sharing also helps build cohesion in the group. Some leaders make the mistake of letting progress reports take up too much time, when 5 to 10 minutes should be sufficient.

LEADER: Why don't we start? I think it would be good to get updates on what has happened since last session. I recall that a number of you said you were working on some significant issues. How was the week? Let's spend 5 minutes or so catching up with what happened.

Introducing Topics for Discussion

To keep interest high, the leader must continually be listening for new slants or themes as members discuss various subjects. When the leader sees that the energy is starting to wane, he will want to introduce new topics for discussion. The leader can accomplish this by spinning off from what has been said—that is, by shifting the focus to a topic that has emerged from the ongoing discussion.

■ EXAMPLES

The members have been discussing communication with their spouses and how to handle trouble areas, such as children, in-laws, and money.

JANE: We do okay in most of these areas. Money problems we now seem to have under control. We still have problems over sex and religion. We cannot discuss those at all. I really do feel at a loss. Last Easter was really a bad scene. He refused to go to church! But I guess all couples have some areas of conflict. I know my parents fought about many different things.

LEADER: Let's take a look at communication with regard to religion. For some couples, this is a major source of friction. Anyone want to comment?

In this example, the leader took a topic that one of the members mentioned and introduced it to the group by making a brief comment.

■ ■ ■

The leader can always choose to introduce a new topic as the need arises.

LEADER: Another topic that's important to talk about in regard to communication with your spouse is sex. Let's spend some time discussing how you and your partner communicate about sex. How good is your communication with your partner about your sex life?

■ ■ ■

Stimulating Members' Thoughts

Leaders must be prepared to stimulate discussion because members may not always be ready to share their ideas. To stimulate the group, leaders may use exercises and various activities. The leader may also use some general questions or comments that encourage and facilitate sharing and discussion. Sometimes all the leader needs to do is ask a general question. At other times, the leader will want to make a brief statement and then ask a question. Many leaders use questions only and do not realize the value of sometimes prefacing their questions with a brief comment. Below are a few examples of ways to stimulate thought:

- Many of you seem to be deep in thought. What are the one or two points that stood out to you?

- The feelings that Zeda is sharing are quite common, and often people don't express these feelings. I appreciate Zeda's honesty. We'll come back to her in a minute, but first, let me ask, does anyone else have similar feelings?

- I think some of you would disagree with what has been said and it is important that you share your thoughts. Would anyone like to react or comment?

- In listening to the comments, I felt that many of you were holding back your true feelings. For this group to be truly helpful, I urge you to share how you really feel. *(Pause)* Any comments on what I just said?

Varying the Format

The leader should always consider the format of the group and whether it needs to change. In some groups, members seem to prefer and benefit from the same format. The leader will want to vary the format only when she sees that the group members are bored with the same agenda. If the leader senses that changing the format would be beneficial, she can decide or have the group decide on how to spend time so that the sessions are more interesting and helpful.

LEADER: It seems to me that we may want to change how we have been doing group. There are many excellent topics that we could cover, but we mostly spend time with different people's issues. It does seem that members are getting help, but my question to you is, do you want to devote the whole time to members' issues that sometimes seem to be repetitious, or do you want me to think of some group exercises that would trigger other issues?

DAX: I like it the way it is.

MILLIE: I think the group could use some new things. I am kind of bored.

TRAY: Can we do both? I would like to know that I can come here and talk about my problems, but group exercises sound good to me.

 GROUP COUNSELING SKILLS: Varying the Format

View again segment 8.7. In this segment, the leader decides to vary the format and conduct a movement exercise.

Changing Leadership Style, If Warranted

Sometimes during the middle stage of the group, the leader may feel there is a need to change the style of leadership. Often, this takes the form of doing less leading and encouraging the members to take more responsibility. The leader has members do most of the cutting off, drawing out, and generating topics for discussion. Other situations may dictate that the leader take a more active role, especially if the group has evolved into a therapy group.

Changing the Structure of the Group, If Warranted

There may be times during the middle stage of the group that the leader will see the need for a change in structure. Changes may take the form of adding new members, meeting less often, or having an extended meeting, perhaps over a weekend. Before deciding on any of these changes, the leader would want to introduce the idea for discussion.

In certain kinds of groups, some members want one purpose for the group, whereas others will want the group to serve an entirely different purpose. When members want two or more different structures or purposes, a difficult situation exists. Each situation is unique, so the solution is not always the same. The following are options for dealing with such a situation.

- The leader can divide the group into two subgroups. (This is often not possible because of size, time considerations, and so on, but it is an option to be considered.)

- The leader can divide the time in half—that is, half the time the group will do one thing, and half the time it will do another. (This will work only if the members can be cooperative when the group is doing the half in which they are not as interested.)

- The leader can let the members decide how to handle their differences of opinion about what the group should be doing.

- The leader can inform the group that there are no options, because the group has a specific purpose to which they must adhere.

If you find yourself in this situation and you take some action, it is important to realize that some members may be upset with you or with the group, creating a dynamic that will need to be monitored.

Using Voice to Get Members to Think

As mentioned in Chapter 6 on Basic Skills for Group Leaders, the leader's voice can often serve to both energize and change the "tone" of the group. Leaders should always be aware of the effectiveness of their voice in accomplishing the goals of the group. In particular, in certain kinds of groups, they may use their voice to get members to think more complexly about an issue. This can sometimes be accomplished by slowing their speech, deepening their tone, and pausing before encouraging a response to give members time to reflect. This process can take the members to a deeper level.

GROUP COUNSELING SKILLS: Using Voice

Go to segment 14.3 and listen carefully to how the leader uses his voice to get members to go more deeply into themselves.

Using Outside Materials and Assignments

Some groups lend themselves to homework assignments. Homework can be in the form of reading assignments, writing assignments, or *doing* assignments. By *doing*, we mean such things as calling someone, talking to a certain number of people, signing up for some kind of lessons, varying the morning routine, and so forth. For many groups, assigned outside reading, TV shows, and other forms of homework can serve as a way of keeping members involved in the group between sessions. Also, homework can serve as a stimulus for discussion for the next group meeting.

One useful assignment is to have each member write an encouraging letter to herself that she brings to the group with a self-addressed, stamped envelope. The members leave their letters and the leader mails them in between sessions so each member gets a letter from him- or herself during the period between sessions if the group meets only twice a month. The leader may choose to read the letters and make some additional comments or just mail the letters, depending on what seems more beneficial.

Meeting With Members Individually

In certain kinds of groups, during the middle stage, the leader may want to meet with some or all the members individually to discuss feelings about the group. Such a meeting gives the member a chance to share his opinions and reactions to the group with the leader. It also gives the leader a chance to discuss various issues with the member without the time constraints and dynamics that exist during a group session. Some experts advocate that meetings of this nature can detract from the group. We have found the opposite to be true, because some members may need the opportunity for some private time. Often these individual meetings help the member to share more in the group. Simply stated, counselors are in the business to be helpful, and we encourage leaders to do whatever they can, within ethical guidelines, to be as helpful as possible.

Informing Members in Advance When the Group Is Ending

Leaders may want to inform members at least 3 to 5 weeks in advance when the group is going to end. Leaders usually determine the ending of a group during the beginning stage, although there will be occasions when no ending time is set. Even when the ending time is set, it is a good idea for the leader to remind the members that the group will be ending in a few weeks.

Middle-Session Topic Outlines

Too often an important topic is brought up in the group but is not handled very well because the leader was not prepared to discuss the topic. *One of the most important things a leader can do during the middle stage of a group is to think through the different issues that are relevant so that she is prepared to focus on the issues in a meaningful way when they arise.*

We thought it would be helpful to outline the key issues, introductory exercises, and other exercises of topics common to many kinds of groups. We outline four topics: the need for approval, self-esteem, religion, and sex. These were selected from a list of common topics that emerge as focal points during the life of a group. We could have chosen several other topics, such as worry, anger, love relationships, divorce, death, or parents—all are major topics. The purpose of these outlines is to give you some idea of how to think through a given topic. Here we offer ways to focus on each topic and deepen the focus so that the discussion is meaningful. We suggest you use this structure for any major topic that may arise in groups that you are leading. It is important to realize that much thought must be given to the appropriateness of any of the exercises described in these outlines.

Topic 1: The Need for Approval

Key Issues
1. Sources of approval: parents, lover, boss, children, and friends
2. Where the need for approval comes from
3. How people seek approval
4. How strong is the need for approval
5. Positive and negative ways that people seek approval
6. Trusting oneself
7. Dependence/independence
8. Difference between needing and wanting approval
9. How to reduce approval-seeking behavior
10. Use of REBT, TA, and attachment theory to understand need for approval

Possible Introductory Exercises
- Round: How important to you is the approval of others? (1 to 10)
- Dyads: Discuss early experiences in your family. Did you feel you were approved of? How does that affect your current functioning?
- Rounds or dyads: Whose approval do you seek and how do you seek it?
- Written exercise: List people whose approval is important to you. Arrange them in order of importance. Then discuss in dyads, triads, or in the group.
- Sentence completion or rounds:

  If my parents did not approve of me, I would _____.

  If my supervisor/teacher did not approve of me, I would _____.

  If my spouse/lover did not approve of me, I would _____.

  If I sense disapproval, I _____.

Deepening Rounds, Dyads, and Exercises
- Round: The need for approval is a desire, a necessity, or a burden. (Choose one.)
- Written exercise: Make a list of gains and losses resulting from your approval-seeking behavior.
- Dyads: Discuss ways you attempt to gain approval from others and classify each as effective or ineffective.
- Round or movement exercise: Respond with strongly agree, agree, neutral, disagree, or strongly disagree to the following statement: Approval from others is more important to me than self-approval.
- Set up some role-play where members experience disapproval.

- Give feedback to each other (make sure it isn't all positive). Discuss reactions.

- Have members pair up. One stands while shaking a finger, looking very disgustedly at the other, who sits in small chair. Discuss the different reactions, memories, and so on.

- Set up approval situations; then get members to discuss how using REBT and TA can help.

Topic 2: Self-Esteem

Key Issues

1. Definition of self-esteem
2. Sources of self-esteem
3. Raising self-esteem
4. Possibility of changing feelings of self-esteem
5. Parents' role
6. Siblings' and friends' role
7. Spouse's or lover's role
8. School, grades, intelligence, and self-esteem
9. Appearance and self-esteem
10. Sports and self-esteem
11. Work and self-esteem
12. TA and the child ego state
13. REBT, self-talk, and self-esteem
14. Defining winners and losers
15. Guilt, shame, and self-esteem

It is important for anyone leading a group on self-esteem to have a theoretical understanding of self-esteem. We mentioned TA and REBT, but certainly there are other theories that are useful when working with self-esteem. We have had very good results with school-age children using these theories.

Introductory Exercises

- Round: If 10 is *liking yourself a whole lot* and 1 is *hating yourself,* what rating would you give yourself?

- Round: What one or two things affect your self-esteem—that is, affect how you feel about yourself?

- Written: Using a 1–10 scale, with 10 being *very good,* list how you feel about yourself on the following: appearance, intelligence, and personality.

- Written: In a sentence or two, define self-esteem. Then write down your ideas regarding it: Can I change, and if so, how? If not, why not?

- Dyads: Pair up and discuss how you feel about yourself and why.
- Sentence completion: I feel better about myself when _____.
- Sentence completion: I feel bad about myself when _____.

Deepening Rounds, Dyads, and Other Exercises

- Round: What is one thing you need to do to improve how you feel about yourself?
- Round: What negative sentences do you tell yourself that cause you to feel "less than" others?
- Dyads: Pair up and talk about what you were told about yourself by significant others when you were growing up.
- Creative-prop exercise: I want each of you to take a Styrofoam cup and think of it as your self-esteem or self-worth cup. Now I want you to take a pencil and punch holes in the cup, with the holes representing the holes you have in your self-esteem. Many of you have big holes from childhood, parents, school, and various other relationships and incidents. Take a minute or so to think, and then punch your holes.
- Movement: I want everyone to stand and line up side by side, facing me (about 8 feet away). I am going to draw an imaginary line here in front of me that represents your feeling really good about yourself. In a minute, I am going to have you move toward the line to represent where you see yourself. Where you are standing now is feeling very "not okay" about yourself. . . . On 3, move—ready, 1, 2, 3. *(Everyone moves.)* What can you do today to help you move closer to this line?

Topic 3: Religion

Key Issues

1. Early messages/parental messages
2. Religious history of members
3. Benefits in your life
4. Restrictions in your life
5. Religion as a personal choice versus a "should"
6. Effects of religion on

   a. guilt
   b. sexual issues
   c. marriage and divorce
   d. abortion/birth control

7. Determinism versus free will
8. Life after death

9. Importance of religion in your life

10. Belief in God

With any discussion of religion, the leader needs to be aware the discussion can become very emotional and heated, which, in most instances, would not be the purpose. Rather, the usual purpose of a discussion about religion is to help members feel comfortable with their beliefs and behavior and to be tolerant of others.

Possible Introductory Rounds and Dyads

- Round: What issues regarding religion would you like to discuss?
- Round: Briefly tell your religious background and where you currently stand with regard to organized religion. (Church member? Nonmember? Nonbeliever?)
- Round: How much influence does religion have in your life? (1 to 10)
- Round: Does religion cause any problems in your life? (yes/no)
- Dyads: Are you bothered by any current issues concerning religion? If not, what were some past issues that bothered you?
- Dyads: Do you profess a particular religion? How do you practice your religion?

These introductory rounds and dyads would be useful to the leader in gathering information about how the members feel about religion. The introductory activities would also get members focused on the topic. The following exercises would be used only when appropriate and usually would not be used as beginning rounds to introduce the topic of religion.

Deepening Rounds, Dyads, and Other Exercises

- Round: If you are currently in a relationship, do you and your partner agree or disagree about religion?
- Dyads or triads: Discuss briefly what is the most disturbing aspect of religion in your life.
- Dyads or round: What do you find the most helpful and the most difficult about your religious beliefs?
- Triads or round: Regarding religious training, what would you do differently with your children than your parents did with you?
- Written exercise: List early messages about religion.
- Set up some relevant role-play situations where religion in some way is causing a problem.
- Respond to the following statements with strongly agree, agree, neutral, disagree, or strongly disagree:

    Religion is the opiate of the masses.

    We all have free will.

    There is life after death.

Topic 4: Sex

Key Issues
1. How you learned about sex
2. Satisfaction with sex life
3. Guilt
4. Early experiences
5. Difficulties and inhibitions regarding sex
6. Preferences, frequency
7. Sex without love
8. Sex and religious beliefs and early messages about sex
9. Communication with partner
10. Orgasm
11. Masturbation, fantasy
12. Extramarital sex
13. Homosexuality

It is important for any leader discussing sex to be clear about the many different issues, because the members probably won't be. Any leader choosing to discuss this topic should not be judgmental and should be tolerant of various sexual attitudes, beliefs, and behaviors. The leader also must be prepared to deal with members' negative reactions to such issues as homosexuality, affairs, or unorthodox sexual practices.

Introductory Exercises
- Round: If 10 is *very comfortable,* how comfortable are you with discussing sex in this group? (1 to 10)
- Round: If 10 is *very important,* how much importance do you place on sex in your love relationship? (1 to 10)
- Dyads: What are some issues related to sex that might be discussed in the group? (Have pairs report back to the entire group some topics they discussed.)
- Round: Complete the following sentences:

    I think sex is _____.
    Discussing sex in this group is _____.
    Many of my current feelings about sex come from _____.

- Round: In a word or phrase, how would you describe your present sex life?

Deepening Rounds, Dyads, and Other Exercises
- Reaction sentences: Have members give their reaction in writing, in a round, or by indicating where their opinion would lie along a continuum from strongly agree to strongly disagree to any of the following sentences.

Masturbation is a bad thing.

It is my obligation to make sure my partner has a satisfying experience.

If either partner fails to have an orgasm, the encounter is a failure.

Everyone should have sex before marriage.

To have a good sexual relationship, you must be in love.

Sex is fun.

- Round: I would like to have sex _____ times a week.
- Triads: What is your greatest concern or fear regarding sex?
- Round: Do you have any leftover or current guilt regarding sex? (yes/no). (If there are *yeses* the leader could ask if the members want to work on their guilt. Or the leader could introduce a helpful discussion about sex and guilt.)
- Round: In a word or phrase, how would you describe your comfort communicating with a partner when having sex?
- Written exercise: List your expectations in a sexual relationship.
- Round: If my partner had an affair, I would _____.
- Written exercise: Write on a 3-inch by 5-inch card anything pertaining to sex that you would like to talk about. (The exercise is anonymous so that members can write such things as having been sexually abused, having an affair, or having certain sexual fantasies.) The leader would then collect the cards and lead a discussion about the various written comments. (This can be a very powerful and helpful exercise if conducted properly.)

As we said in the beginning of this section, the preceding examples are just some of the key issues and possible exercises for the chosen topics. There are many more exercises that could be outlined. Our intent is to encourage you to think through a topic thoroughly before you lead a group on it. The processing of any of these exercises can take a group to a deeper level.

Middle-Session Leadership Tactics for Specific Groups

Besides the skills and techniques already discussed, specific kinds of groups call for particular leadership tactics. In this section, we briefly discuss some additional techniques for education and task groups. In the next chapter, we discuss skills that are useful for the working stage of growth, support, counseling, and therapy groups.

The Education Group

In the middle stage of an education group, the leader must pay much attention to shifting from giving information, to facilitating discussion, and back to giving more information again. This sequencing keeps the group flowing and increases the chances of helping members learn and apply their new knowledge to their lives. The key is to provide enough information and enough sharing and discussion time. Often, beginning leaders lose sight of the experience of being a group and focus too much on providing information, or spend too much time on sharing and don't cover enough information. A true education group will have a good balance of information and interaction.

The Task Group

The task group leader's role during the middle stage is to help members generate options and help them move toward a decision or resolution. Because the task group involves a group goal rather than individual goals, members may take strong stands on issues. The leader will always want to consider how the members feel about each other and about the task on which they are working. The leader needs to be aware of who the more influential members of the group are and what type of pressure they exert on other members. Also, the leader should be aware of any hidden agendas of the members. In other words, when leading a task group, the leader must watch for many different group dynamics and must be willing to focus on the dynamics if they are interfering with the progress of the group.

Helping Members Generate Ideas and Options   The discussion of various options during a task group is sometimes difficult because members become emotionally identified with their own ideas and find it hard to discuss others. Leaders must be able to get members to discuss and exchange ideas in a productive manner. The leader's choice of any of the following strategies depends on the number of members in the group, the kind of goals the group is working toward, the level of agreement among members, and their attitude of cooperation. Brainstorming, the fishbowl, working in small groups, and guided fantasy often prove to be valuable tools for generating options and moving the group to some resolution.

Brainstorming   In brainstorming, leaders have members generate as many ideas as possible without regard to practical limitations. The theory behind brainstorming is that people often impose unnecessary limitations on their creativity by assuming constraints that may not exist or that may be possible to change. Once ideas are out in the open, members may come up with creative changes that eliminate the constraints. The basic rule for brainstorming is that no idea is too wild or crazy to be introduced. Because ideas are not evaluated or censored during brainstorming, the members' feelings of defensiveness are reduced. Brainstorming may be done in the entire group or in small groups of three or four. A time limit helps the group stay focused.

Once ideas are brainstormed, overlapping ideas should be eliminated or consolidated. Then the remaining ideas are listed, discussed, and ranked. The leader can then examine several of the better ideas in greater detail with the group and elaborate on them as needed. If the leader uses the brainstorming technique effectively, every member should feel he has had the opportunity to provide some input.

The fishbowl   The fishbowl is a technique that a leader can use with a variety of groups; it works especially well with larger groups. The group is divided, with half the members forming an inner circle and the other half, an outer circle. While the inner group discusses an issue or idea, the outer group listens. (People often can listen better when they know they are not going to speak.)

After a given time period, the members switch places, with the new inner group sharing its reactions to the previous discussion. The new inner group may provide constructive criticism or build on the ideas already generated.

Small-group variations   Small-group interaction (3 or 4 members to a group) can almost always be useful, in that members have the opportunity to discuss ideas in greater detail and more people get to talk because the group is smaller. Members in small groups may all work on the same task or on different phases of the task. The results of the small-group discussions are then shared in the larger group.

Guided fantasy   In a task group, the guided fantasy provides a chance for members to picture, think about, or get a feeling for the outcome of various solutions generated by the group. Also, members may imagine the outcome and then construct what must happen for that outcome to be realized, thus generating various solutions. The following is an example of how a guided fantasy could be used.

■ EXAMPLE

A school counselor is leading a task group of parents. The task is to develop a valuable summer program for school kids in the community. The leader introduces a guided fantasy by saying:

LEADER: *(Using a quiet voice)* At this point, let's think about the outcome of the program you might envision. You might want to close your eyes to try this. Picture an ideal summer day when the program is in place. What are some of the things that are happening? What different things do you see happening and where are they happening? *(Pause)* How many different programs do you see going on? *(Pause)* When you are ready with your ideas, write them down.

This technique helps establish goals, which assists the leader in developing and maintaining the focus.

■ ■ ■

Helping Members Move Toward Resolution   One of the primary functions of the task group leader is to make sure the group accomplishes its goals. Groups can easily over-discuss an issue but not resolve anything. The skilled leader is always thinking about when and how to help the group accomplish its purpose. If the group is not progressing, one good strategy is to focus the members on the process so that they can become aware of what they are doing.

LEADER: I want to stop you and have you focus on what is happening in the group—not the content but the process. What is going on here that is keeping us from getting more accomplished? Think about what you are doing and what others are doing. I think some of you may even have some strong feelings about what is happening.

Common Mistakes Made During the Middle Sessions

There are numerous mistakes that leaders can make during the middle stage of a group. We discuss the following ones:

- Underleading or overleading the group
- Letting the warm-up phase last too long
- Letting the focus shift too often
- Focusing too long on a member
- Focusing on only one or two members
- Planning only one or two exercises or activities
- Failing to allow time to process an activity
- Choosing uninteresting speakers

Underleading or Overleading the Group

The skilled leader leads to the degree that members gain from his guidance; beginners often mistakenly lead too much or too little. It is possible to overlead—that is, not letting the members have enough input in the group. This is especially detrimental if the leader is focusing on boring, uninteresting, or irrelevant material. On the other hand, it is possible to underlead by turning the group over to the members when they do not understand how to make the group valuable.

Letting the Warm-Up Phase Last Too Long

Workshop participants have shared that too often in the beginning of a session they have let members ramble or focus on irrelevant subjects. The purpose of the warm-up phase is to get the members focused on being in the group. The skilled leader pays close attention and makes sure that the opening does not drift along or head in a direction that is not useful or productive. *Remember, the majority of the time during middle sessions should be spent in the working phase and not the warm-up phase.*

Letting the Focus Shift Too Often

Inexperienced leaders often make the mistake of not holding the focus long enough so that there is impact. In any group situation, it is easy for the focus to move from topic to topic unless the leader holds and deepens the focus. The leader should always be aware of the focus and the depth of the focus. During the working stage, the leader should try to deepen the focus to a level that is meaningful for all or most members.

Focusing Too Long on a Member

It is a mistake to focus too long on a member who does not understand the content of the group. Beginning leaders often cater their group to the confused or slow member, which results in only a marginally valuable group for other members. Here are some of the options available if a member does not seem to understand the content:

- Take time to explain, if it can be done in a relatively short time.
- Have members try to explain or clarify the issue.
- Tell the member you will explain after the session or at a break.
- Tell the member you will meet with him at another time to go over the material.
- Arrange for another member to meet with that member to go over the material.
- Ask another member to go to another part of the room with that member and explain the material. You would not want to do this often because the helpful member would be missing the group.

If a member repeatedly has difficulty understanding material in the group, the leader may ask that person not to remain in the group.

Focusing on Only One or Two Members

If a group has a member who is very talkative or very "needy," some beginning leaders devote week after week focusing on the same member. This practice is easy to fall into because the member seems to need help and the other members all want to be helpful. Leaders also tend to focus on the resistant member. Too often, beginning leaders devote a considerable amount of time trying to help this member while the member rigidly resists. This is often ineffective and wastes much valuable time.

One way to avoid focusing on just one or two members is to use a member assessment technique. The leader can answer the following questions about each member.

- How does "X" feel about coming to the group?
- What does "X" need to learn from group?
- What does "X" need to talk about but is afraid to bring up?
- How much "air time" has "X" had in the last few weeks?

By answering these questions for each member, the leader should be able to get some sense of what each member wants or needs from the group. The answers help a great deal in planning the session and also enable the leader to go into a session with a number of possible options and topics.

Planning Only One or Two Exercises or Activities

Another mistake is to plan only one exercise or activity. It is always wise to have backup plans, because there are times when your initial plan does not generate much energy.

Failing to Allow Time to Process an Activity

It is important to allow enough time to discuss and process any film, guest lecture, or group exercise. Usually the majority of the time should be for sharing and processing rather than for viewing the film, listening to the speaker, or doing the exercise.

Choosing Uninteresting Speakers

For educational groups, when using a guest speaker, the leader should make every effort to ensure that the presentation is interesting and stimulating. It is helpful to meet with the speaker in advance to get a preview of the presentation and to make sure the speaker is clear on the purpose of the group and her presentation.

Concluding Comments

In this chapter, we have outlined skills, techniques, and roles that the leader can use during the middle sessions. When planning the group, the leader should assess what will benefit the group and the members' interest, commitment, and trust levels. When leading the middle sessions, the leader should stimulate thought; introduce new topics; use her voice effectively; and vary the format when necessary. The leader is always thinking about the leadership styles and the structure of the group and should change either of them if necessary. The leader should also keep in mind the kind of group she is leading, because different strategies are needed for the various kinds of groups. Planning for different topics is very important during the middle sessions. By outlining the key issues, introductory exercises and activities, and deepening exercises, leaders will be prepared to lead groups on various topics that are planned or that come up during the session.

Leaders make a number of mistakes during the working stage: underleading or overleading, letting the focus shift too often, focusing too long on a member, focusing on only one or two members, planning only one or two activities, failing to allow time to process an activity, and choosing uninteresting speakers.

■ ACTIVITIES

1. Pick two topics that you think you will cover in a group sometime in your career and then make a list of possible issues, introductory exercises, and deepening activities that cover the topic. Use the middle session topic outlines presented earlier in this chapter as your format.
2. Review the common mistakes. Reflect on a group experience where some mistakes were made. What were those mistakes and what could the leader have done differently?

GROUP COUNSELING SKILLS

1. View again segment 10.2 and watch how the leader uses a small chair in a middle session. The leader would know the members enough to assess that the exercise will generate deeper self-exploration.
2. Watch segments 9.2 and 9.3. In each of these, the leader uses an opening round to get a read on the members. Why are these opening rounds helpful during the middle stage a group?

Chapter 13

Using Counseling Theories
in Groups

The importance of understanding theories of human behavior cannot be over-emphasized when leading any group that focuses on support, personal growth, life decision-making, counseling, or therapy. Leaders of counseling and therapy groups should have a strong basic knowledge of theory as applied to individual counseling before taking on the challenge of group therapy. Groups on anger, stress, anxiety, and depression will be effective only if the leader can use theory to help members understand their thoughts, feelings, and behaviors. To a lesser extent, it is helpful to have some understanding of one or more theories when leading psychoeducational groups and certain discussion groups.

Often during a support or counseling group, the focus is on one member's concern for a few minutes. When working with one member, the leader directs the personal work by using theories and techniques to help the member gain insight and understanding about his problem. *No leader should lead counseling groups without an in-depth knowledge of counseling theories.* Unfortunately, many people who lead therapy groups have neither experience in individual counseling nor a background in counseling theories. These group leaders think all they need to know is information about group process and group dynamics, and then the members will be the agents of change. This is not true. For instance, in groups for sexual abuse victims, agoraphobics, suicidal patients, sex offenders, drug abusers, children of alcoholics, and codependents, members need a leader who has a complex understanding of their pain because the members have no theoretical understanding of their problems. We encourage leaders not only to use theories during the sessions, but also to teach group members the basic tenets of one of the major counseling theories. We usually teach Rational Emotive Behavior Therapy (REBT) and Transactional Analysis (TA) because these theories are very valuable in understanding human behavior and can be learned rather quickly by members regardless of their age.

Very often in therapy groups, the focus is held on one member for 10 to 20 minutes (sometimes longer). During the time when the group is focusing on a member, the leader has two basic choices: to have the members try to help the working member by using one or more theories that have been taught, or to conduct a few minutes of individual counseling while engaging the other members in some way, if at all possible. To conduct individual counseling, the leader needs to have the theoretical knowledge and skills to take the session deep enough so that the members are very involved even though they may be simply watching and offering comments elicited by the leader. For leaders who do not yet have the ability to conduct interesting and engaging counseling, we suggest using the members' personal experiences and/ or expertise and the leader's knowledge of theories. Rarely is it a good idea to conduct slow-moving individual counseling while members watch and listen, although unfortunately, this is done quite often and the members become bored.

The purpose of this chapter is to briefly summarize several contemporary theories that we believe have particular relevance for group work and then focus on examples of how each of these theories may be applied in group situations. We decided to briefly discuss the theories and then offer examples of the theories being used in groups because it is our assumption that most readers will have already studied counseling theories and only need a review. We also realize that there is much more that a leader can do with each theory, but we mainly wanted to give you some initial ideas about how to use each theory in groups. As you use the theories, you will develop many of your own ways to implement them. Also you may want to seek out specific books and articles on how the different theories are used in group counseling. As we have said numerous times, we strongly believe that *knowing counseling theory is essential for leading counseling and therapy groups.*

Cognitive Behavioral Therapy

Cognitive Behavioral Therapy (CBT) is based on the principle that one's thoughts cause one's feelings. There are several approaches to cognitive behavioral therapy, including Rational Emotive Behavior Therapy, Rational Behavior Therapy, Rational Living Therapy, Cognitive Therapy, and Dialectic Behavior Therapy. Two of the biggest names associated with CBT are Ellis (REBT) and Beck (Cognitive Therapy). In this chapter we focus on REBT. Other cognitive therapies would be conducted in similar fashion in that the principles, terms, and techniques would be taught and the members would be asked to look at how their thoughts cause their feelings.

Rational Emotive Behavior Therapy

One of the leading theories in the field of counseling is Rational Emotive Behavior Therapy (REBT), founded by Albert Ellis. It is an excellent theory for use in groups because it can easily be taught to the members, who can quickly learn how to apply it to themselves and to other members. The theory is based on the premise that *thoughts cause feelings,* and in groups, the leader helps members to focus on changing their feelings by looking at what they are telling themselves. Thoughts such as "I should always be the best, and if I'm not, I'm a failure" or "It is terrible when life doesn't always go my way" are examples of the kinds of things that might come up in different groups. REBT is quite helpful for children, adolescents, and adults because it helps them to feel more control by knowing that their feelings are caused by their thoughts.

The Model

Ellis developed an ABC model of understanding feelings and behaviors. The letter A represents the *activating event* to be evaluated. The letter C represents the *consequences* or the emotional reaction experienced. B represents the *beliefs* used in evaluating the activating event (A) and ties A and C together. It is not the occurrence of an event that causes feelings, but rather the person's interpretation of that event. Most people have never examined the negative, exaggerated, self-defeating self-talk in which they engage. Most people believe that A causes C, but in fact it is B: What they are telling themselves is what causes C. Once the members learn the theory, they often are the ones to help other members challenge, dispute, and replace the negative self-talk. For example, if Horace is talking about feeling very shy at a dance and not asking anyone to dance, using the model, the leader could lay out the problem on a whiteboard like this:

(event)   A = being at a dance
(self-talk)   B = I'm ugly; no one would ever want to dance with me.
               It would be awful if someone turned me down if
               I asked her to dance!
(feeling)   C = shy; fearful, bad (behavior = stand in corner)

Teaching REBT to the Members

In group counseling where the leader plans to use REBT, the first thing that needs to be done is to teach the theory to the members. We suggest two ways to introduce and teach REBT to the members. The first is to take a problem that a member has brought up in the session, such as the one above with Horace, and write it out and teach all the members the ABC model and the theory behind the model. In other words, use a real problem from one of the members but take considerable time to teach the idea that thoughts cause feelings.

A second way to get members to focus on this theory is to start by asking them, "Where do feelings come from?" Many will say from "others," "the heart," "the past," or "situations." This leads to presenting the idea that *thoughts cause feelings.* We suggest using a whiteboard and handouts that lay out the ABC model. Then discuss some examples of how the model works with such feelings as anger, guilt, or worry. By showing the members how, for example, it's not traffic that causes anger but what they tell themselves about traffic that causes them to feel angry, members begin to see how thoughts cause feelings. The key is to get members to understand the ABC model and to start seeing that their thoughts cause their feelings or to at least consider the notion that it is not their love partner or boss or parent who makes them mad, but rather they make themselves mad by what they tell themselves.

To introduce REBT and to show group members that it is not the event that causes feelings but rather the self-talk, one example that can be used is to divide the group in half and tell one half to pretend that they are excellent students in school—make all A's—and the other half to pretend they are D students; then have them assume that they all make a C+ on a test. Then ask them how they feel. The A students will say "bad" and the D students will say "good." The leader can then ask the members, "If events cause feelings and you all experienced the same event (got a C+), shouldn't you all feel the same?" This often generates discussion about the effects of our thoughts on our feelings, which is the basis of REBT. Also the leader can comment on how people often tell themselves all kinds of "shoulds," "oughts," and "musts" and also engage in exaggerated self-talk that creates feelings that lead to negative or destructive behaviors.

 GROUP COUNSELING SKILLS: Theories—REBT

Go to segment 13.1 and watch an introduction to the use of theories in groups and a segment where the leader uses REBT.

By using the whiteboard and other creative techniques, such as two chairs (one marked rational self-talk and one irrational self-talk) or two cassette tapes (one old and used tape and one still in its wrapping), a leader can help members to visualize the basic principle of REBT that people have a choice as to what they tell themselves. Also by using a handout with some basic REBT information on it, members usually can understand the basic premise of REBT. To help them further grasp the notion, we sometimes use Ellis's list of irrational ideas that people tell themselves. We ask members to read the list and circle the irrational ideas they currently tell themselves. This leads to further discussion about the importance of our self-talk when it comes to understanding our feelings and behavior. Granted many, at first, don't buy the idea that their thoughts cause their feelings, because most people believe that people and events upset them. They have never really considered that they may be causing and sustaining the majority of their negative emotions. Here is the list of Ellis's main irrational sentences. We also provide a list for kids based on the original list of 15 irrational ideas.

Ellis's 15 Irrational Ideas

1. It is a dire necessity for an adult human being to be loved or approved by virtually every other person in one's life.
2. One should be thoroughly competent, adequate, and achieving in all possible respects if one is to consider oneself worthwhile.
3. Certain people are bad, wicked, and villainous and they should be severely blamed or punished for their villainy.
4. It is awful and catastrophic when things are not the way one would very much like them to be.
5. Human unhappiness is externally caused and people have little or no ability to control their sorrows and disturbances.
6. If something is or may be dangerous or fearsome, one should be terribly concerned about it and should keep dwelling on the possibility of its occurring.
7. It is easier to avoid than face certain life difficulties and self-responsibilities.
8. One should be dependent on others and needs someone stronger than oneself on whom to rely.
9. One's past history is an all-important determiner of one's present behavior, and because something once strongly affected one's life, it should indefinitely have an effect.
10. There is invariably a right, precise, and perfect solution to human problems and it is catastrophic if this perfect solution is not found.
11. One should become quite upset over other people's problems and disturbances.
12. The world should be fair and just and if it is not, it is awful and I can't stand it.
13. One should be comfortable and without pain at all times.
14. One may be going crazy because one is experiencing some anxious feelings.
15. One can achieve maximum human happiness by inertia and inaction or by passively and uncommittedly enjoying oneself.

Common Irrational Beliefs of Kids

1. I must be liked by everyone, and if I am not it is awful and I can't stand it.
2. If someone calls me names, it must be true and I can't stand it.
3. I should be the best at everything I do and if I am not, I am worthless.
4. Some people are bad and I have to dwell on how to get back at them.
5. It is awful when things are not the way I would very much like them to be.

6. My unhappiness is caused by others and I have no ability to control my unhappiness and have no ability to make myself happy.

7. It is easier for me to avoid certain troubling situations than to face them.

8. I cannot depend on myself—I have to depend on others for my strength.

9. My past causes me to be the way I am and there is nothing I can do about it.

10. There is a perfect solution to every problem and it is terrible if I cannot figure out the perfect solution.

11. I must become upset and stay upset over other people's problems.

12. Things should be fair and if they are not, it is awful and I can't stand it.

13. I should never be uncomfortable or inconvenienced and when I am it is awful and I can't stand it.

14. I can achieve and be successful even if I do nothing and have no plan of action.

15. It is my fault if my parents fight (drink, are getting divorced).

16. Because I am adopted (in foster care, have less money), I am less than other kids.

17. Because he/she did that to me (physical, sexual, emotional abuse), there is something wrong with me and I don't deserve to be happy.

18. If I love my stepdad (stepmom), it means I don't love my dad (mom).

These lists can be used to generate good discussion about members' irrational beliefs. The discussion of the different sentences can lead to personal work by one or more of the members if the purpose of the group is problem solving or therapy.

Using REBT in Groups

Clarifying the event, person, or situation (A)   Whenever an issue is brought up, it is usually helpful to clarify the specifics of the situation that are troubling the member. For example, if a member, Anna, is talking about how much her in-laws upset her, the leader may ask Anna if it is mostly the mom, the dad, or both, and how often she is upset. The leader may have the members ask questions to help Anna clarify what she means. The leader could say to the group, "Using the ABC model, what do you hear as the activating event?" By using this process, it involves the members and it keeps them thinking about how this theory can be used with most situations. As a result of this focusing process, Anna may say something like, "It's really just my mother-in-law and it's mostly about my parenting of my daughter."

Clarifying the feelings and/or behavior (C)   Once it is clear what the situation is, usually the next step is to clarify the feelings or behaviors associated with the event. The leader may ask questions or the members may ask questions to help the working member specify her feelings. In the example of Anna, after hearing her describe her feelings, the leader might say, "Anna, what would you say is the main feeling?" She might say, "I feel hurt" or "I feel very angry" or both. The leader could say to the group, "What do you hear as the main feeling that we should help Anna with? What is the C in the ABC model that you think Anna may need to work on first?"

Clarifying the negative self-talk (B)   Once A and C are clarified, the leader concentrates on identifying the self-defeating, not true, irrational self-talk that the member is telling herself. In this example, the leader would focus the group on helping Anna figure out her self-talk, especially if Anna can't seem to figure it out herself. The leader could say something like, "What do you think Anna is telling herself that is causing her to feel the way she does?" Members may offer suggestions such as, "I must have my mother-in-law's approval and if I don't it means that I'm a bad parent," or "She should not treat me the way she does. She has no right to criticize me."

Changing the feelings by changing the self-talk   The most important part of REBT is to get members to see that what they are telling themselves is not true. In our example, the leader would facilitate work with Anna by trying to get her to tell herself something different—something that is rational and true. The leader would seek input from the other members about what it would mean if her mother-in-law did not approve and what alternatives Anna could tell herself about her mother-in-law's behavior that would result in her not feeling so angry. The benefit of using REBT in groups is that members can get involved in helping the working member because they would be familiar with the model that the leader is using. We believe one of the most important advantages of using REBT is that members can use it to help other members and also the members may apply it to themselves while trying to help another member.

■ EXAMPLE 1

The school counselor is leading a personal exploration group of sixth graders. The group members know REBT. The group is focused on Joey, who has just learned he has been cut from the school's soccer team.

LEADER: *(Standing at the whiteboard and writing)* So you got cut from the team. We'll write that here, at A. And how are you feeling?

JOEY: Sad. And mad. It wasn't fair that I got cut. There were two guys that made it and they were worse than me. The coach doesn't like me.

LEADER: *(Writes "sad" and "mad" at C. Then the leader looks around the group, ready to write at B.)* Does it make sense that Joey feels both mad and sad?

BRUCE: Yeah. But life isn't always fair; at least that's what we talked about last week from that list.

LEADER: *(The leader writes: "It isn't fair that I got cut" at B.)* What do we need to help Joey with?

DAMITA: We have to help him dispute his self-talk.

LEADER: Okay, let's stay at B. What else is Joey thinking or telling himself? Joey, I'm going to get the group's ideas and then get you to clarify if what we write up here is what you are telling yourself.

JOSH: Maybe that because he got cut, he's not athletic. And that would be terrible.

LEADER: Good. Let's do one or two more.

PACO: He could be telling himself that because he got cut he'll never be successful at anything. Also, he said he thinks the coach doesn't like him.

LEADER: *(Writing at B)* Joey, look at our list at B. Is this sort of what you're thinking?

JOEY: Yeah. All of that.

LEADER: Are you willing to work with us to see if these are true? And if they are not true, will you work to stop telling yourself these thoughts?

JOEY: Yeah.

LEADER: As you look at the list, which one is the toughest to tackle?

JOEY: I think that Mr. Franks doesn't like me. I know I'm not that good at soccer. But I like Mr. Franks a lot. I don't want him to think I'm a jerk.

LEADER: *(Draws a line under "The coach does not like me." Also adds, "He thinks I'm a jerk!" Looks around the group.)* Anyone want to start disputing this?

PACO: Just because the coach cuts you from the team, it just means he can carry only a certain number of players, not that he doesn't like you.

LEADER: *(Using a Not True/True grid, he writes Paco's statement next to "The coach does not like me. He thinks I'm a jerk.")*

Not True	True
It isn't fair that I got cut	He could only pick so many players.
The coach does not like me.	It has nothing to do with him liking me.
He thinks I'm a jerk!	His not picking me does not mean he thinks I'm a jerk—just not one of the best soccer players.
Mad, Very Bad	Better

In divorce, anxiety, anger, and all kinds of other groups, the same general format as this one can be used for members to help each other. The leader focuses on getting members to help other members dispute irrational sentences that are causing problems in their lives.

■ ■ ■

■ EXAMPLE 2

The group is made up of 10 members in an inpatient facility where the membership changes on a daily basis due to new admissions. This group is one of three groups that the members will be in that day. It is important that the leader have some activity that can be of benefit to most members. Using the list of irrational sentences given previously can usually create a productive group.

LEADER: I'd like to start by having you look at this list of sentences and pick out any that you think are true or pick out ones that you want to discuss for one reason or another. If you have trouble reading them, I'll help, or maybe your neighbor can help you. *(Waits a minute or so until most appear to have finished the list.)* Anyone have one?

KATE: I do. Number 9—One's past history is an all-important determiner of one's present behavior and because something once strongly affected one's life, it should indefinitely have an effect. I think what happened to me when I was young will always cause me to hate men.

LEADER: Did anyone else pick that one?

DICK: I did. My mom's murder causes me to be depressed every day.

JUNE: I picked that one. I would not be here if it weren't for my husband. He ran off with my cousin and now they are living in Canada. I'll never get over that.

LEADER: I think we'll work with this one sentence today and then focus on others tomorrow when we meet. Many of you believe that your past has determined your current life and I'm going to present a whole other way to look at your past. The truth is that it is not your past or certain events that make you feel bad but rather it is what you are currently telling yourself about the events that are causing you to feel bad.

KATE: Like what? If those men would not have abused me, I would not think all men are scum.

LEADER: Let's look at that, and I want all of you to help out with this. *(To the group)* Do you think that Kate is right about all men are scum or that those men were scum?

MARIO: I'd say it was those men. I'm a man and I never treat women badly. In fact, they always say I'm too nice.

LEADER: Mario, maybe later we can focus on your being too nice but for now, I think you made a good point. I say this to you, Kate, and really to all of you. The key to healthy living is to challenge and dispute self-talk in your head that makes you feel bad. Many of you have been telling yourselves things for years and I hope today's group gets you started in disputing the self-talk in your head that is not true. Kate, do you want us to help you with this?

KATE: I don't like feeling the way I do.

LEADER: *(To the group)* What do you think Kate is telling herself about her past and what can she tell herself?

The leader would focus on Kate and other members' irrational, self-defeating self-talk about their past and try to get the other members to dispute the thoughts of a member who brings up different ideas. The leader would try to get the members, such as Kate, June, and Dick, to realize that what happened to them was very unfortunate, but they are not less of a person and they can have an enjoyable and fulfilling life.

Suggestions for More Reading

There obviously is much more to REBT than what we covered in these few pages. Our goal was to briefly review the theory and show how it can be used in groups. For more information about REBT, we suggest reading *A Practitioner's Guide to Rational-Emotive Therapy* (Walen, DiGiuseppe, & Dryden, 1992). An excellent book for school counselors is *Rational Counseling with School-Aged Populations: A Practical Guide*, by Wilde (1992).

Reality Therapy

Reality therapy, based on the work of William Glasser, proposes that human beings are responsible for making choices about behavior and that such choices are intended to meet five basic human needs: survival, love and belonging, power (achievement), freedom (to make life decisions), and fun (Wubbolding, 2000). Glasser's original work in reality therapy has evolved into what he terms *choice theory*, with the focus on the importance of interpersonal relationships in the satisfaction of human needs (Glasser, 2000). Of particular interest to the group leader is Glasser's belief that many "symptoms," such as nonclinical depression and anger, are behaviors intended to control others and the environment. Therefore, his theory considers conduct such as "angering" and "depressing" as active choices, which can be altered in favor of more constructive behaviors.

Choice theory focuses little on the past and relies on the group leader to play an active role in helping members to make better choices and to develop more positive plans of action. When using reality therapy, the leader's ultimate goal is for members to accept responsibility for their behavior and to make better choices. In order to facilitate change, the member must understand her inseparable, but distinct, components of behavior: *acting, feeling,* and *thinking*, along with basic *physiology*. Reality therapy contends that *physiology* and *feeling* are more difficult to modify than *acting*. Reality therapists believe that most of the time we can choose how to act, regardless of how we feel emotionally. To a lesser extent, we can also choose what we *think*.

Using Reality Therapy in Groups

Wubbolding (2000) identified an acronym to assist the reality therapy group leader in helping members work toward changing their behaviors in a more positive direction. The acronym, WDEP, stands for *want, doing, evaluation,* and *planning.* The first few times the leader uses this in the group she may want to outline it on the whiteboard, putting up the letters and filling them in as the member works through the process.

Identifying *wants (W)* is an important starting place. When a member brings up an issue or problem with which she wishes help, the leader who is using reality therapy will ask in various ways: "What do you want?" If the response is general or unclear, the leader will press forward by asking, "What do you *really* want?" In a group setting, in particular when members have bonded with one another, the leader may have one or more members ask the working member questions to clarify what she really wants.

Once a member becomes clearer regarding what she wants and that "want" is something that the member has control to change or achieve, the leader and members ask questions to get the working member to state specifically what she is currently *doing (D).* The next step in the WDEP strategy is *self-evaluation (E).* This stage requires that the member examine the effects of specific behaviors that she is currently doing. The leader or members ask "Is what you are doing getting you what you want?"

The final and most important stage is *planning (P).* Here, again with the help of the group, the member sets up both short- and long-term goals that incorporate her new behaviors. It is essential that plans be simple and specific in detail, realistic, involve action (as opposed to avoidance behavior), not be dependent on another person or event to be carried out, and have a start time along with criteria to determine success. Group members help with the development and refinement of a plan and assessing its success. The presumption is that no plan is magic, that a member who is committed to change will be willing to accept partial success and continue to revise her plan to move closer to the successful fulfillment of her needs.

As we have mentioned, behavior change does not occur through magic but requires a continuous process of refining needs, taking action, evaluating, planning, and reevaluating outcomes. As members establish their goals and formulate plans, the group setting provides an excellent venue in which members receive feedback from one another and the leader in order to better meet their needs. The atmosphere is noncritical, is non-blaming, and focuses on what changes will help meet a need or goal rather than on why success was not achieved. Effectively applied, reality therapy both identifies and tracks a member's behavior to enhance the chances of success. Reality therapy also stresses the importance of accepting responsibility for the consequences of one's behavior.

GROUP COUNSELING SKILLS: Theories—Reality Therapy

Go to segment 13.3 and watch a segment where the leader uses Reality Therapy and WDEP.

■ EXAMPLE 1

In a rehabilitation counseling group, Joe verbalizes a desire to return to work. He points out, however, that he won't be allowed to return to work until he completes 3 weeks of physical therapy, which he says he is unable to attend because he lacks transportation. After several members make suggestions regarding transportation that Joe dismisses as unrealistic, the leader decides to help Joe clarify what he *really* wants.

LEADER: Joe, everyone in our group talks about the same goal of returning to work. It's like, that's what we're supposed to say. *(The leader uses a soft, slow voice, expressing care in his tone.)* If we were to ask you what you *really* want, deep down inside, what would you tell us?

JOE: *(Tearing up)* I would like to spend more time with my kids. *(Pause)* And I don't want to get hurt again on the job.

LEADER: *(Recognizing that Joe is actually meeting his needs by staying home, the leader wishes to help him determine whether his choices are realistic. Again, using a kind, supportive, and nonjudgmental tone)* Can you afford to stay at home just now?

JOE: *(Shakes his head no)* Agnes is working two jobs. It's not fair to her. She's not getting any time with the kids at all.

LEADER: Let me ask you this question again. What do you really want?

JOE: I'd like to work at a job where I'm not so tired when I get home and where there is less chance of getting injured.

LEADER: Is avoiding the physical therapy helping you in that direction?

JOE: *(Shaking his head)* No.

LEADER: As you become more physically fit, we can talk about options for work. *(Turning to the other members)* Joe had the courage to say what he really wants just now. How are others of you feeling about where you are in your rehabilitation process?

TOM: I realize that I'm not being honest with what I want.

COOPER: I know what I want. I realize that what I'm doing is never going to get me what I want, which is a better job.

LEADER: When we finish with Joe, we'll work on both of those things.

■ ■ ■

■ EXAMPLE 2

In this example, we see a group of five women who have been mandated by the court to attend a counseling and parent education group for eight sessions to work on improving their parenting skills. This is the third session. The leader has explained the WDEP model. One member, Roxie, has said she wishes to be more patient.

LEADER: Roxie, we've taken care of the "W," your wish to be more patient. And we know that a lot of what you've been doing with your kids is yelling, being short with them, and being very verbally abusive. And you've said you know this will not get you what you want. Can we help you develop a plan to get your patience under control?

ROXIE: That would be great.

DARLA: Has there ever been a time when you were patient with anyone?

ROXIE: *(Thinking)* I guess when my grandmother was sick in the hospital, I would go there when I could. She couldn't feed herself and I sat with her.

LEADER: You sat with your grandmother. What else were you doing?

ROXIE: Putting small pieces of food in her mouth, waiting for her to chew.

DONNA: When you were waiting, were you thinking, "Come on Grandma, chew it up so I can get out of here?"

ROXIE: *(Laughing)* No, no. I was very calm. I was thinking, this is my grandmother, I love her, and she needs me now.

LEADER: *(Looking around the room)* Is this a good start for Roxie?

SUSAN: Yeah. She knows what being patient is, how it feels.

YOLANDA: She's in touch with her love part. She knows she can show love and be patient.

LEADER: Right. Two behaviors you were doing, Roxie, might be helpful with your kids. You were sitting down. And you were waiting for your grandmother rather than trying to make her do something. How might those two behaviors be helpful?

ROXIE: I don't take time to sit with my kids. And, you're right, I'm always wanting them to do something instead of listening to them when they want to tell me something.

LEADER: If you were doing those two things, sitting and listening, would you be showing more patience?

ROXIE: Yes.

LEADER: Now let's make a plan. Let's think about each of your children. What specifically will you do? And when will you begin? *(To the members)* While we try to help Roxie with a specific plan, I want each of you to think about some specific things you want to do differently with your kids.

YOLANDA: I can think of some things I need to do.

LEADER: Good, let's first work with Roxie then we'll work with you.

■ ■ ■

■ EXAMPLE 3

This is the fifth session of a group of four teenage boys in a detention center.

LEADER: Today we're going to talk about basic needs that all of us have. This famous doctor came up with these and I think we can have a good discussion. I want you to look at this list of basic needs and I want you to think if these needs are currently being met here at the center and at the place you were living before being sent here. Here's the list.

Freedom and Independence
Love and Belonging
Sense of Power and Achievement
Fun
Survival

HECTOR: I'm not sure what all these mean.

LEADER: That's fine. Let's take one and I'll tell you what it means and then we can talk about it. Let's start with love and belonging. Everyone needs to feel this and when you don't, you often will fight, seek out a gang, or become a bully. Does any of this sound familiar?

HECTOR: I've never felt love from anyone. My mom was busy doing men all the time so she never had time for me. I'm used to not being loved.

GEORGE: I'm like Hector. I've already been in three foster homes. My last foster parents tried to love me, but they were too into religion for me. That's not me.

ALEX: I feel like people here care about me more than I've ever had. All this group stuff gets us close. I've said things in group that I've never said before, and when I found out my brother was killed, it felt good that people just sat with me. I've never had anyone do that.

JOHN: I joined the gang because my family didn't care about me. I don't know if I should go back to it when I get out.

LEADER: These are all good points. I think we'll spend this session just talking about the love and belonging need and then discuss the others tomorrow or the next day. What is the best way to find love and belonging? Also, who in your life can provide this for you in a positive way? John, I agree that it probably is not a good idea to go back to the gang for a sense of belonging. I'm hoping you can develop a better plan. What are your thoughts on all this?

The leader then holds the focus on this topic and uses the WDEP model to help each of the members.

■ ■ ■

Suggestions for More Reading

Glasser, W. (2000). *Counseling with choice theory: The new reality therapy.* New York: Harper Collins.

Wubbolding, R. E. (2000). *Reality therapy for the 21st century.* Philadelphia, PA: Brunner-Routledge (Taylor & Francis).

Adlerian Therapy

Alfred Adler, rather than believing human behavior to be controlled by instincts, as did Sigmund Freud and others of his time, suggested that much of who we are is the result of family and social interactions throughout early childhood. Adler is known for his belief that a person's birth order has a major influence on development of personality. Adlerian psychology, also referred to as *individual psychology,* emphasizes the notion that *all behavior is purposeful.* Behavior is intended to overcome a sense of perceived inferiority (feeling *less than*) resulting from the inability to be "perfect" or as good as others during childhood.

As children strive to compete with older siblings, friends, and adults in performing certain tasks, they often lack the developmental skills necessary for success and develop a feeling of inferiority. Also during the development years (0–10 years), children attempt to find their place or role in the family. Many factors influence this process, including birth order, intelligence, attractiveness, athletic ability, parental and grandparental preferences, and gender. As a result of this striving and the level of a child's perceived success, the child will draw conclusions as to what is valued in the family. For example, a child may conclude that to be loved she must always please others, or accumulate great wealth and power, or play a traditional gender role, such as rearing children. A group leader using Adlerian theory will focus members on their "private logic," which includes mistaken goals and guiding fictions about themselves, the world, and others. Adlerians believe that if people can understand the purposefulness of their behavior, they have a much better chance of changing behaviors that are not useful or helpful.

GROUP COUNSELING SKILLS: Theories—Adlerian

Go to segment 13.2 and watch a segment where the leader uses Adlerian Therapy.

Using Adlerian Therapy in Groups

We present a number of examples to further explain the theory and show how it may be used in groups.

■ EXAMPLE 1

This is the fourth session of a group of eight high school students who have an alcoholic parent. The leader decides to focus for a few minutes on some of the Adlerian concepts about birth order.

LEADER: *(After the warm-up period)* I thought today we would take a break from talking directly about your parents and the effects of their drinking, and we'd focus on you and your siblings. I do think you will find this interesting and helpful. We are going to talk about your birth order and how it affects your thinking and behavior in your family. Raise your hand if you are a firstborn child. *(Leader waits and looks around the group.)* What effect does it have on you? *(Leader gets a couple of comments.)* How about a second born? *(Checks hands and gets a couple of comments.)* Who was a middle child? *(Again looks around and sees members doing likewise. The leader continues through the youngest and the only child.)* There is a theory that believes that your birth order has a major affect on how you see things. First, I'm going to have you get in pairs or threes and talk about how you think your birth order is having an impact on you and then we'll get back and discuss your thoughts and your reactions. It's important to realize that you act the way you do in part due to your birth order.

The leader has now stirred interest, gotten the members involved in the process quickly and, perhaps most important, has members aware of similarities and differences among themselves regarding birth order. Next, the leader may ask members to share what it is like to be a firstborn, and so forth. Depending on the makeup of the group, certain characteristics will be described. As this exchange continues, the leader will elaborate on typical characteristics of the different birth order positions.

The firstborn child is often independent, identifies with parents, and may take on responsibility similar to adults, especially in caring for younger siblings. A second child may compete with an older sibling or go off and develop her own "place" in the family. For example, if the firstborn does well at academics, the second child may attempt to achieve at athletics or in some other area, depending on the opportunities available. Should a third child come along, the second child becomes the middle child and may feel "squeezed," competing with an older sibling and striving for the attention that is now going to the new arrival. Middle children sometimes develop the role of "negotiators," that is, arbitrating between the older and younger siblings or between siblings and parents. The youngest in a family is generally attended to by older siblings, parents, and grandparents and may remain the "baby" of the family. An only child may have characteristics similar to a first child: independence, identification with adults, responsibility, and high achievement.

There will be many exceptions to the general rules of birth order, and the role of the leader using Adlerian theory is to help the members consider the extent to which these characteristics work for or against them in their present lives.

It is important for the leader to remember that birth order characteristics are never rigid and may vary greatly, depending on age gaps between siblings, children's physical health, demands on parents, divorce and remarriage, and so forth.

Dialogue following the discussion may look something like this.

LEADER: Any thoughts or comments about all this discussion?

RUDY: I never have thought about any of this. I always feel like the peace-maker when Dad drinks, but now I see that being the middle child may have something to do with this. Very interesting. I'm going to really think about this.

TOM: I've always feel the burden of being the good kid because my brother is getting in all that trouble. It never occurred to me that I might be the way I am because of the way he is. I feel Mom can't take much more so I have always tried to be good.

GLORIA: I always knew I resented my stepsister but now I have a better idea why—she took my place as the firstborn! I want to talk more about that.

LEADER: That's good, Gloria. The key for all of you is to realize that each of you behave in certain ways due to your birth order. What we want to do here is to examine your private logic, guiding fictions, and mistaken goals. It's obvious that many of you have things you want to talk about.

The leader would then focus on members' birth order and how their siblings influence who they are and how they think about themselves.

■ ■ ■

■ EXAMPLE 2

This is a group for women who suffer from social anxiety. It is midway through the third session.

LEADER: I think what would be helpful would be a discussion about how each of you found your place in your family and tie that in to your current fears and anxiety. This famous psychologist thought this was a very important thing to understand. *(Pause)* So how would you answer this question: When you were 6 or 8 years old, how would you say you found your place? For example, you might say "being the peace-maker," or "being good."

CAROL: There was so much fighting; I tried to be invisible and just blend into the woodwork. I was one of eight kids.

LEADER: We'll come back to that. Others, how did you find your place?

HILARY: Mom made sure that we were quiet all the time because we didn't want to ever wake Dad up. I was the quiet, good kid, but my brother was always messing up and getting in trouble with Mom or Dad.

CHAR: I always felt inferior to my sisters. I had an older sister who was a superstar and great looking and a twin who was better at everything. When I went with them, they talked and I just listened and hoped someone would talk to me.

ASRA: In my culture, women were considered less than men, especially at social gatherings or at the mosque, so I learned to be quiet and stay out of the way.

LEADER: What are all of you thinking as you reflect on what's being said or what you said?

CHAR: That we each found our place in different ways because of our home situation or siblings.

LEADER: Exactly. I think it would be useful to help each of you examine the development of your private logic regarding how you found your place when you were young. As a kid, it may have made sense to be quiet and afraid, but now that you are grown and live in a different environment, it no longer makes sense. The purpose of this group is to help you explore the purposefulness of your behavior so that you won't be afraid of social situations. Who wants to share their thoughts?

ASRA: I will. I'm always afraid. Everyone says I'm very shy.

LEADER: I want you to think for a moment what your life might be like if you chose not to find your place by being shy. In fact, I would like to ask you to try something. *(The leader pauses for emphasis.)* I would like you to visualize yourself as the opposite of shy. How would you be?

ASRA: An assertive, confident person.

LEADER: Could you act like that in here? What is something an assertive, confident Asra would do or say?

ASRA: *(Thinks, looks around the room and then looks directly at two of the members.)* You two are buddies and I know you usually go out after the group. I'd like to go with you sometime.

CONNIE: Sure. How about this evening?

LEADER: Let's talk about how this feels to you, Asra.

ASRA: It feels good. I wish I could do this out in the world. It is safe here.

LEADER: What you are saying applies to everyone here. Your shyness or fear made sense growing up, but what I want all of you to see is that it does not make sense now that you are grown women. You do not have to find your place now like you did when you were growing up.

CHAR: This makes so much sense. I just thought I was born this way. I never knew I could be any different.

The leader would focus on helping members see their private logic regarding people and social situations and try to help them see that circumstances are now very different.

■ ■ ■

■ EXAMPLE 3

This is the second session of a group of seventh graders focusing on improving self-esteem. It is 10 minutes into the session.

LEADER: I want to talk about an important guiding thought process that influences self-esteem. It is called *guiding fictions.* I'm going to explain it and then have you think about any guiding fictions that you have.
A guiding fiction is a false belief learned as a child that is currently directing your life. Guiding fictions may include beliefs such as, *I must be perfect to succeed or be loved. Because my parent never talks to me, there must be something wrong with me. There is no way I can ever amount to anything.* Most of you are unaware of some of your guiding fictions, and we are going to try today to help you get in touch with some of them. Take a minute and try to think of any thoughts like the ones I mentioned that may be guiding you.

KEVIN: I don't know if this is one, but I always think I'm a loser because I'm not as good in sports as my brother.

LEADER: That would be one. Others of you?

VICKI: Mine doesn't have anything to do with sports. Mine is with grades. I'm dumb because I can't make all A's and my mom and dad go bananas over my two brothers' grades.

ED: My mom tells me I'm lazy and worthless all the time, especially when she's stressed out about work or some boyfriend.

LEADER: Ed, what would you say your guiding fiction is about what your mom says?

ED: I always feel bad because Mom's always cutting me down.

LEADER: What do you think about yourself?

ED: Something's wrong with me because I can never please Mom.

LEADER: Do others of you tell yourself something is wrong with you?

VIARA: I always feel something is wrong with me. I'm never good enough and never will be—that's what I believe about myself.

LEADER: Let's focus on these ideas. Do you see how they cause you to feel bad about yourself?

VICKI: I can see it in others but not me. I am dumb. I am terrible in math.

LEADER: Vicki, that's a guiding fiction that you can challenge because it is not true. For one thing, I know you are not terrible in math. I believe you make C's and B's in math. Let me say again, a guiding fiction is something that guides you but is not true. I want each of you to either comment on your guiding fiction or on one of the other members'.

ED: Vicki, because you aren't as smart as your brothers or not good in math sure doesn't make you dumb. I know you are a great reader and you've helped me in science.

LEADER: What do you think about what Ed is saying? Can you see how this mistaken thought guides you and causes you to feel bad?

VICKI: *(With a sad voice)* But Ed's not my mom or dad.

LEADER: Vicki, we're looking at whether your thought about being dumb is fiction. Is it true or not that you are dumb? How many of you would say it is not true? *(Everyone raises his or her hand.)*

In this example, the leader would continue to explore the different guiding fictions and try to get members to see the fictional part of their guiding beliefs. The leader would continuously challenge the members to look at thoughts that are guiding them.

■ ■ ■

■ EXAMPLE 4

This is the third session of a group of college freshmen.

LEADER: I want to talk about something that may shed some insight into why you might be anxious. When growing up, most people form some mistaken goals that often stay with them for life. Mistaken goals are goals that you have based upon some faulty logic or thinking. A mistaken goal might be *I must get good grades to prove to the world that I'm not a dummy.* Or *I must do better than my sibling so that I'll remain my parent's favorite.* Another may be *I must become a doctor or lawyer or teacher or whatever in order for my parents to love me.* What I'm saying is that you may be driven by some mistaken goal that formed during your childhood that you are unaware of. Does this trigger anything for anyone?

WAYMAN: I know I want to do well because all my life I heard I was the lazy one just like my dad. I don't want to be like him—he's a homeless alcoholic. Everyone thinks I'll fail. I worry about it all the time. That's why I joined this group, because I'm a nervous wreck.

LEADER: *(To the group)* So what would be Wayman's mistaken goal?

GAIL: To quit worrying?

LEADER: That's what he wants to do but his mistaken goal would be what?

KAHIL: Isn't it that he has to succeed to show people he's okay? I thought last time we talked about how we are all okay and need to accept ourselves.

LEADER: That's right. The mistaken goal would be *I must do well to prove that I'm okay and that I won't be like my alcoholic dad.* Wayman, it's good that you want to succeed but hopefully it will be for you and not to simply prove these people wrong. You can make the decision to not be like your dad and that has nothing to do with making it here at college. This is a good example of a mistaken goal. We'll come back to this in a few minutes, Wayman. You think about it. I just want to hear from others and then we'll discuss different people's mistaken goals. How about others of you?

VANN: I have to become a doctor because my sister is a dentist and I could never live with myself if she made more money than me. Also at family reunions I know people would favor her over me. Now they make a big deal over her being a dentist and I want them to make a big deal over me.

IAN: Do you want to be a doctor?

VANN: What do you mean? I don't feel I have a choice.

LEADER: What do you think Vann's mistaken goal is?

The leader would focus the group on helping members identify and challenge their mistaken goals and then help members see how life can be a series of choices rather than striving to reach some mistaken goals that are based on early messages.

■ ■ ■

■ EXAMPLE 5

It is 15 minutes into the fourth session of a divorce-recovery group for people who have been divorced for 6 months or more.

HILDA: I just feel so off balance. I don't do anything and I don't go anywhere. My life is awful.

LEADER: Let me pick up on that and talk about ways to make all of your lives better. *(To the entire group)* I want to get away from talking just about your marriage and divorce. This psychiatrist named Alfred Adler describes three important life tasks that appear to be universal and must be dealt with. They are social relationships—family and friends; love relationships; and work. No doubt one of these life tasks is out of whack for all of you—love relationship—but let's look at the other two. My concern is that you are not putting any effort into the other two tasks, and with your love task being at a low point, it is no wonder you feel bad and off balance. What are you doing in the other two tasks?

ROGER: What do you mean about work? I go to work but it's not the same. I hardly talk to anyone and I don't enjoy it like I used to.

LEADER: Enjoying work is what this refers to. Ideally, a person enjoys the work he or she does and I know all of you have jobs that you can enjoy.

MARQUITA: Since the divorce, I just go through the motions of teaching, and it's really not fair to those first-graders.

BARB: I used to love going to work at the bank. I loved talking to the customers and the other tellers. Now, I just go and put in the time.

LEADER: This is exactly why I brought the topic up. You can't do anything about the divorce but for sure you can do something about your attitude at work and that can help you feel more positive about life. Just because your love life is not going well does not mean you can't enjoy work. In fact, it is much better if you do try to enjoy work, even if you have to fake it some. That is, fake it 'til you make it (*Members laugh*). I want us to focus on work and how to enjoy it more and then we'll look at the other life task of family and friends.

DARLA: That'll be good. Friends are begging me to do things but I tell them I'm not ready.

BARB: I've completely shut out my family. (*Others nod their heads.*)

LEADER: We'll come back to family and friends, and I can see that most of you are neglecting that life task as well. Let's focus right now on work. What can you do to make your work more enjoyable?

The leader would focus this session on these two life tasks because they are important to a balanced life and then would follow up each week on how people are doing in these areas. Using the Adlerian concept of life tasks often can be helpful in many different kinds of groups.

■ ■ ■

Suggestions for More Reading

Sonstegard and Bitter's (2004) book is solely about using Adlerian theory in group counseling and therapy situations. It is excellent. The book is titled *Adlerian Group Counseling and Therapy.*

Transactional Analysis

Transactional Analysis (TA) is a comprehensive theory of human behavior developed by California psychiatrist Eric Berne. TA theory has many important and valuable concepts, such as scripts, strokes, and games that can be useful in groups. In this section we focus primarily on the TA concept of ego states and scripts because they can be easily taught to group members.

According to TA theory, everyone has three ego states: the Parent, Adult, and Child. These ego states are developed as a result of childhood "messages." Messages such as, "You are a bad child" or "Only stupid children make mistakes" or "Don't trust anyone," may come through direct comments from parents or other caretakers or through early life experience. There are two parts to the Parent Ego State: the Critical Parent and the Nurturing Parent. The Child Ego State also has two parts: the Natural, Free, or OK Child and the Adapted or Not OK Child.

Which ego states are dominant within a person depends on a person's experiences. For example, Julie is a person who was raised by a very critical mother. Regardless of how Julie tried to please, her mother found fault. As Julie grew into her preteen and teenage years, she incorporated many of the negative comments her mother made to her about everything from her appearance to her friendships. As a young adult, Julie used her mother's judgments as if they were her own beliefs. Julie *internalized* her mother's critical comments and developed her own Critical Parent Ego State. Now Julie criticizes herself for making common mistakes and often gets very angry at these errors. She also is critical of others and at life in general when things don't go well for her. Because Julie's mother did not deliver many nurturing messages, Julie has difficulty nurturing herself or others.

As a very young child, Julie felt the pressure to conform to her mother's demands. Therefore, while Julie was developing her Critical Parent, she was also developing an Adapted Child Ego State, seeking approval of others, fearing disapproval, and conforming or adapting to situations to avoid criticism. Now Julie is living her life using her Critical Parent Ego State and her Adapted Child Ego State, with perhaps less Natural Child and Nurturing Parent. Most importantly, however, is the fact that Julie does not use her Adult Ego State, especially in interpersonal decisions, and seeks out relationships that are ultimately critical and abusive. In a group, the leader who uses this theory would try to help Julie become aware of her different ego states and how each ego state influences her decisions and interactions.

Teaching TA to Group Members

TA can be taught by the group leader in mini-lecture format, but we feel that a better way to introduce TA is by using a member's problem or situation. The following example shows one way to introduce and teach TA to the members. It is the second session.

LEADER: Many of you have mentioned fighting or arguing with different people in your lives. I think this is a good time to introduce some tools that can help you understand that better. Tonight we're going to discuss Transactional Analysis, or TA. Many people have found these ideas very helpful and I think you will too. Julie, if it is okay with you I thought we might use your example with your boyfriend.

JULIE: That's fine with me. I want to stop fighting with him.

LEADER: Give us an example of a typical fight.

JULIE: I like some attention on holidays and birthdays. He often waits until the last minute or even forgets. Like last week, it was our 1-year anniversary of dating and he didn't get me anything. We got in a big fight. I yelled at him and he yelled back and then I started crying.

LEADER: That's a good example. *(Leader goes to whiteboard and draws as he talks.)* In each of us are three parts or ego states: the Parent, Adult, and the

Child. *(Draws three circles.)* So Julie, you have these three parts and your boyfriend has these three parts. What is his name?

JULIE: Holden.

LEADER: *(Draws three circles under Holden's name. Glances at members and sees them all looking at the whiteboard.)*

Julie   Holden

LEADER: The Parent part is the part of you that is either nurturing or critical or the part that has all the *shoulds* for yourself and for others. In your case, would you say you are more critical or nurturing in the relationship?

JULIE: Critical, most definitely. I'm critical of him, of me, of everything. I'm not as bad as my mom, but I'm afraid I'll get like her as I get older.

LEADER: All of you, once you understand this model, you will have a much better understanding of yourself and of others, and you can make a choice as to what ego state you want to be in. Let's now go to the Child part. That ego state actually has two parts—the Fun Child and the Hurt, Angry, or Pleasing Child.

ZENA: I get my feelings hurt all the time—is that the Child part?

ROSE: Me too, and then I get real mad.

LEADER: You're right. You would be in the Child ego state. Julie, how about you?

JULIE: I'm all over the place. Often I'm hurt and then I get real mad and throw a fit, which he hates because I break things and then there are times when I go all out to please him. I'm a mess.

LEADER: I think understanding your ego states will make a great difference. I want to teach about the Adult and then we'll spend the rest of the session talking about how each of you can apply this to your lives. The Adult is the thinking part—the rational part. Like right now, I think most of you are in your Adult part listening to me and thinking about your own situations. I hope none of you are in your critical part, beating up on yourself as I describe the ego states.

CORRIE: Gosh, that's exactly what I was starting to do because I realize I'm so critical of my boyfriend because of the way I was raised. He's always said it was my fault that we fight and now I see maybe he was right.

LEADER: Corrie, I hope you can use your Nurturing Parent and Adult part today because beating up on yourself certainly will not change things, but learning this will.

CORRIE: I knew I was messing up but I didn't know how. I think this might help me.

LEADER: Let me say a little more about the Adult. If you stay in the Adult part, you'll find you will rarely if ever fight with someone because you are thinking and understanding the situation and you are not raising your voice or feeling hurt or trying to win. You are thinking. Most fighting happens when people are in either their Child or Critical Parent or both or are switching back and forth between the two, but they are not in their Adult.

JULIE: That's me most of the time—hurt and critical and not thinking. My boyfriend even says to me, Julie, stop and think for a minute.

LEADER: We'll work on that in a few minutes. Let me get some general reactions to this. Let's talk about anything you are thinking about as you look at yourself through this model. This applies to just yourself or your interactions with others like boyfriends, friends, bosses, or family members.

The leader would then have a discussion about the different ego states. He would try to get members to focus on some of their specific concerns using this theory. Once he felt the members understood the ego states, he would try to get members to see how the Adult functions differently from the Child in situations, such as the ones Julie or Corrie were describing. The key in TA is to help members get an Adult perspective on situations that tend to be negative or volatile. Often the leader or the members use the whiteboard to draw the specific interactions that are being described. If you are not familiar with this theory, we encourage you to seek out additional reading that shows the different ways to present TA.

Using TA in Groups

Once the leader teaches TA, she can use the Parent, Adult, Child concepts in numerous ways when working with one member or with the entire group. One reason TA is an excellent theory to use in groups is that it can be used in a variety of visual and experiential ways. The leader can:

1. Draw PAC circles in various sizes with arrows going from the different ego states on a whiteboard to represent interactions being described by the working member.
2. Draw PAC circles in various sizes on a whiteboard to represent the working member.
3. Use chairs (small child's chair or stand-in chair) to represent either the Child or Parent ego state.
4. Act out the scene and then have members play the different ego states.

■ **EXAMPLE 1:** **Drawings of Interaction**

This continues the example of Julie from above.

LEADER: Julie, I want to focus on the transactions that you and your boyfriend have. It sounds to me like you interact during the fights from either the Critical Parent or Hurt/Angry Child. What ego state does he come from?

JULIE: He stays calm for a while and then he blows up and starts putting me down and then we end up yelling at each other.

LEADER: Let me draw this for you. I also think others of you can benefit from seeing this.

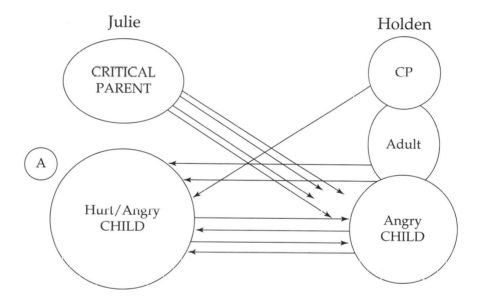

The leader would explain the drawing and get Julie and other members' reactions about how they often fight from their Critical Parent and Angry Child and how they may have a small Adult sitting on the sidelines. Often the drawing helps members better see what they are doing that fuels the fighting in their relationships.

■ ■ ■

■ **EXAMPLE 2:** **Drawing of Different Size Ego States**

It is the second session of a parenting group. The leader taught the members TA in the first session. It is 10 minutes into the session, and members are sharing about how they tried some of the things discussed in the first session. Four have shared, and Maxine and Paula are left to share.

MAXINE: When you said last week that you thought the TA model was one of the best tools you've ever learned for helping parents and how it absolutely can change the way we parent, I thought you were exaggerating, but you were right. I've been paying attention to which ego state I'm in and stopping myself from going to the Critical Parent. I'm amazed at how much I was in my Critical Parent. No wonder there was so much yelling and fighting between me and the kids.

PAULA: I did good the first couple of days but then Wilson made me yell at him. He knows I have to leave for work by 7:30 and he was watching TV at 7:15 and was not dressed. He knows better—that's what gets me. And then my little one, who is 4—that's a whole other story. At the doctor's office we had to wait for over 45 minutes and he would not sit still. It was embarrassing that he made me yell at him in the waiting room.

LEADER: Paula, would you like to understand what happened in those two situations?

PAULA: I'm here because I don't want to be like my mom. I don't yell all the time like she did but I can't stop myself sometimes.

LEADER: *(In a kind, caring voice)* We can be of help and I do want to say this to all of you—no one makes you yell at him or her. That is your choice. You choose to yell, and the TA model can help you with this.

ROBERTA: *(To Paula)* I did something I've never done before. I stopped myself almost in mid-sentence. I went into my daughter's room and started to yell at her about the room and for some reason I thought about the PAC model we talked about and I stopped after just a couple of words and then used the nurturing part. Oh, what a difference! We didn't fight. We actually spent the next 20 minutes talking while we together picked up her room. It was great.

LEADER: Paula, let me show you something that may help. From what you described, your Critical Parent is much larger than your Adult part. *(Draws circles—everyone looks at the drawing.)*

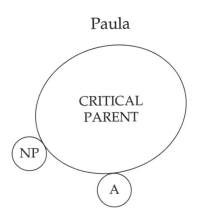

Paula

CRITICAL PARENT

NP

A

PAULA: That's right. My mom was worse. Can I ever get my Adult and Nurturing Parent to be larger than my Critical Parent?

ROBERTA: Let me jump in here again if I may. I just realized that I was able to have my Adult and Nurturing Parent be in charge with my daughter this week, but boy, I'm just like the drawing when it comes to my husband. I lost it with him.

LEADER: For all of you, it is possible to get your Adult and Nurturing Parent to be in charge, but that's why we are meeting for eight weeks. It takes practice, awareness, hard work, and determination to change. Paula, you can do this if you pay attention and not do what is automatic, because automatic to you is yelling, given what you've told us about your mom.

PAULA: I don't know how my Adult is supposed to think.

LEADER: *(To group)* Any ideas?

MAXINE: What about realizing that your kids are kids? No 4-year-old can sit still for 45 minutes. I can't tell you how many times I thought about that Adult phrase we learned last week: "Get your expectations in line with reality." That's helped me so much. Paula, do you have your expectations in line with reality regarding Wilson and your little one?

PAULA: Not really. I just expect them to do what I want them to do.

MARLA: I just realized I don't either. I want my kids to act like I did, which was to always be good. But I was scared to death not to be. My kids aren't afraid of me so they are going to act differently. That's the Adult perspective, right?

LEADER: Most definitely. In this group we are going to try to strengthen the Adult part by giving you information and letting you share thoughts and ideas. The goal is to gain an Adult perspective on a situation and hopefully shrink the Critical Parent. One of the best things you can do is to get rid of most of the SHOULDS you have for your children and get an Adult perspective on how they are. Paula, let's take Wilson in the morning. What does he do and how can you better understand him?

PAULA: But he should get dressed before he watches TV or whatever!

ROBERTA: That's the Critical Parent part, right?

LEADER: Right. Getting your expectations in line with reality will create a much calmer morning than having "shoulds" for Wilson.

PAULA: That's the problem. I think I'm getting it. I've got to understand better how Wilson is in the morning and help him get himself ready instead of yelling at him.

LEADER: Say some more. That's coming right from your Adult.

■　■　■

■ **EXAMPLE 3:** Use of Chairs

This is a group for getting along with ex-spouses. The members were taught TA last week and are now discussing issues that came up during the current week.

LEADER: All of you can complain or you can do something about it.

IVAN: I am afraid she'll not let me see the kids if I say something to her. Last time I did, we had a huge fight.

LEADER: *(Pulling out three chairs to the center of the group—one chair is a small child's chair.)* Which chair were you in the last time you fought—was it from the Critical Parent *(Leader stands on one of the chairs)*, was it from the Angry Child *(Leader sits in the child's chair)*, or was it from the Adult *(Leader puts a sign that says THINK in the chair representing the Adult)*?

IVAN: Well, uh, it was not from the Adult chair.

LEADER: All of you look at the three chairs. Which seat are you in when you interact with your ex? From what you said last week, no doubt some of you have difficult ex-spouses, but what we can do here is get you to look at what ego state you come from when you interact with them.

PHYLLIS: I start in my Adult and then I end up in the Critical Parent chair. *(She stands on the chair.)* I blasted him before we got divorced and I still do. It makes no sense.

LEADER: I'd like to teach all of you how to stay in the Adult. Are you ready to learn how to stay in the Adult chair? *(Everyone is staring at the chairs in the center.)*

The leader then leads a discussion using the chairs, having members sit or stand in the various ones as they describe their interactions with their ex.

GROUP COUNSELING SKILLS: Theories—TA

Review segment 10.2 and watch how the leader uses the small chair and the Adult chair.

■ ■ ■

■ **EXAMPLE 4:** Acting Out the Ego States

It is a changing families group for eighth-graders. It's the third session and the members have learned TA.

LEADER: Because many of you have said you fight with your parent or step-parent, let's act out a couple of situations. Tommy, what about the one you were describing with your stepdad about homework? Are you willing to have us act that out?

TOMMY: Okay. I'd like to see how to get him off my back!

LEADER: He comes into your room and offers to help you with your math or science, right?

TOMMY: *(Angrily)* Yeah, what business is it of his how I do? I'm not his kid.

LEADER: *(To group)* Listen carefully because I'm going to ask one of you to play Tommy and someone to play his stepdad. Are you saying that he enters in an upbeat, helpful mood and you bite his head off? What does he end up doing?

TOMMY: Yeah, he's in a decent mood and leaves pissed off, slams the door.

LEADER: Who wants to play Tommy and who wants to play his stepdad? *(Two volunteer.)* I want you to be studying and I want you to come into his space and ask if you can help. Toby, act like you are reading or something.

CLIFF: *(Acting as the stepdad, using a kind voice)* Tommy, need any help? I've got some time.

TOBY: *(Acting as Tommy with a gruff voice)* No!! I told you I would ask you if I needed any!! Quit bothering me.

CLIFF: Look, I'm just trying to be helpful. I know you can go to college if you put a little effort into your studies.

TOBY: It's none of your business whether I go to college!!

LEADER: *(Stopping the role-play)* Tommy, is this close to how it goes?

TOMMY: Yeah. You guys are good.

LEADER: They did do a good job because you have done a good job describing the scene. What do you see in this role-play? What ego state is he in?

CLIFF: He just jumped down his stepdad's throat. He's in his Angry, Hurt Child, I would think.

LEADER: Do others agree? *(Heads nod.)*

TOMMY: How do I get out of my Child? What should I do?

LEADER: We can show you in a minute, but first can you tell us why your Child reacts to him like you do?

TOMMY: Well, uh, *(Tearing up)* he's not my dad. I miss my dad and when Mom married my stepdad that pretty much meant that my mom and dad weren't going to get back together.

LEADER: So you take it out on him?

TOMMY: Yeah, I guess that's right.

LONNY: I'd like to say something. Watching this was real helpful. I am completely in my Child with my stepmom.

TOBY: Playing the Child part sure helped me to see what I do sometimes. Are you going to help us stop acting the way we do?

LEADER: I'm going to try to make this group a place where you can help yourselves like you are doing now.

CLIFF: I like this TA stuff and this role-play stuff.

■   ■   ■

Other Aspects of TA

In this chapter we just touch on some of the many theoretical aspects of TA. Group leaders who use TA often discuss members' life scripts, egograms, stroke economy, or games that they play with significant others. For those interested in more information about TA in groups, an excellent place to start is the Web page: ta-tutor.com. This Web page has 400 handouts you can download. Also, *TA Today* by Stewart and Joines (1987) is a good introductory book on Transactional Analysis.

Gestalt Therapy

Fritz and Laura Perls developed Gestalt therapy in the 1940s, with emphasis on the importance of healing through the recognition of "blocks" to fully experiencing the "here and now" (Corey, 2004). Gestalt therapy, an existential approach, focuses on creating a therapeutic environment in which the client gets "in touch" with unfinished issues by "presentizing," re-experiencing, and integrating such experiences into current awareness. Regardless of past experiences, what is important is the client's interpretation of those events in the here and now. Gestalt theory recognizes that clients tend to compartmentalize their lives, "hiding" disowned or unacceptable parts from the conscious self. The ultimate goal of therapy is the integration of these parts and movement toward independence, maturity, and self-actualization. While many approaches to therapy had relied heavily upon the therapist's interpretation, the Perls promoted the concept that only the client can effectively interpret his awareness (Strumpfel & Goldman, 2002).

Fritz Perls introduced the concept of the "hot seat," a voluntary experience where the therapeutic focus is on a single member while other members watch. He also adopted the "empty-chair" technique, whereby a chair is used as a prop. For example, the client may be asked to imagine an absent person in the chair and speak to that person and then switch chairs and play that person in response. Many therapists use Gestalt techniques in conjunction with other theoretical models. In group settings, exercises and activities, such as guided fantasies, are used to generate awareness and create a here-and-now experience. Using Gestalt techniques requires a thorough knowledge of each technique and the skill to apply it. Because awareness occurs in the present moment, considerable psychological pain may result as members delve into feelings and recount difficult, perhaps traumatic, experiences from the past. Therefore, leaders must not only have the knowledge and skill, but also be prepared to deal with the intense emotions that may be generated.

Using Gestalt Therapy

In this section, we offer a number of examples showing how Gestalt techniques can be used in various group situations to heighten members' awareness.

■ **EXAMPLE 1**: Putting Someone in the Empty Chair

Betty is a young woman whose parents died several years earlier in an auto crash while on a driving vacation. Betty has brought this up before and has started once again to talk about her parents.

BETTY: *(Crying)* I don't think I can make it without them.

LEADER: Betty, do you want to try to finish this unfinished business?

BETTY: I don't know how.

LEADER: Are you willing to try? I've got some ideas. Do you want us to try to help you with this?

BETTY: I have to do something. I don't want to feel this way forever.

LEADER: Okay, let's do some work. *(The leader sets up two chairs in the center of the group facing the member, one to represent her mother, one her father.)* Which parent do you wish to address first?

BETTY: My mother.

LEADER: *(The member is looking at the leader. The leader, using her hand to direct the member's attention to the "mother chair," speaks in a gentle voice.)* What would you like to say to her?

BETTY: *(The member shifts, stares at the seat of the empty chair and tears up.)* I miss you so. Why did you leave me? You know I need you. Did you have to go on that trip with Dad? I know you really didn't want to go. *(The member's voice rises in pitch toward the end of her comments, suggesting feelings of anger.)*

LEADER: How are you feeling?

BETTY: Sad.

LEADER: What else? *(The member gazes at the leader, as if not quite ready to identify her feeling. The leader's voice, while kind, is more intense.)* I noticed your tone changed, as if perhaps you are feeling some anger toward your mother for leaving you, for going on this trip she didn't want to go on and not coming back?

BETTY: *(Sobbing)* How can I be angry at her? She's dead. *(In Gestalt theory, the member has compartmentalized her feelings of anger and denied them.)*

LEADER: *(Soft, reassuring voice)* It's okay to be angry at someone we love. If you sit on your anger, it will be difficult to put this behind you. *(The leader again uses a gesture to direct the member's attention to the empty chair.)*

BETTY: *(Sobbing, in a loud, angry voice)* Why did you go? Why did you die
and leave me all alone? You know how hard it is to live without your
help!

LEADER: *(The leader scans the group briefly, observing that the members appear very
involved.)* What do you need from your mother in order to let
her go?

BETTY: I want to know that she loves me and that she didn't mean to leave me
alone.

LEADER: *(Gesturing to the empty chair)* I'm going to ask you to sit over there, in
that chair. *(The member moves to the chair representing her mother.)* I'd like
you to be your mother. What do you have to say to Betty?

BETTY: *(Having changed seats, she speaks as her mother.)* I do love you and I didn't
mean to leave you. It was an accident, something we couldn't avoid. It
wasn't something I did on purpose. I would not have left you on
purpose.

The leader directs the "dialogue" between Betty and her mother for several
minutes, having the member switch seats until she is able to realize that her mom
did not "do this to her" and that her anger is unfounded. In this example, the
group leader uses the empty chair to help the member *presentize* her feelings toward her mother, state and release those feelings in an acceptable way, and integrate this new awareness. When Betty seems finished, the leader turns to the
group.

LEADER: What did Betty's work mean to you?

DEION: This blew me away. Betty, I was right with you. I've been mad at my
dad for his drinking and this helped me to realize that he's not doing
this to me. This was very powerful. Can I talk about this?

LEADER: Sure. Let's hear from others and then, Deion, you can do whatever
work you need to.

ERIC: I just kept picturing my grandfather in the chair and thinking of all
kinds of things I want to say to him.

Many who are not familiar with Gestalt Therapy often comment on how
difficult they believe it will be to ask a member to talk to an empty chair and
even move into that chair to play another person or another part. As you read
through the various examples, we hope it is apparent that the working member
is so involved in the experience, she follows the leader's directives. There are
occasions when a working member may have trouble getting into the idea of
talking to an empty chair because the member is experiencing some discomfort
for one reason or another. The following dialogue, using the same situation as
before, shows how the leader would handle such a situation.

LEADER: *(After carefully setting the stage with Betty)* What would you like to say to
your mother?

BETTY: I don't know.

LEADER: *(Looking at the empty chair, rather than at the member)* You said you had some feelings toward your mother. What can you say to her about those feelings?

BETTY: I don't know what to say.

LEADER: *(Still focusing on the empty chair)* Mom, I have some feelings that I just can't get out. *(Turning to the member)* Try that.

BETTY: Mom, I have some feelings I just can't get out.

LEADER: *(Again, speaking to "Mom" in the empty chair)* "One feeling is . . ." Go ahead.

BETTY: One feeling is . . . anger. *(She sobs.)*

Here the leader knew she had set up the therapeutic situation correctly and could see that the member was not bringing her mom into the present. By pushing the member gently and playing the member and using the sentence completion, she helped the member to get into the experience. If the member had continued to not be able to "put her mom in the chair," the leader could drop the use of the chairs, pair the members up, pairing herself with the working member, and discuss one-on-one what the member was experiencing. The value of the empty chair is that it is so powerful that even when only one member is in the "hot seat," most members are thinking about someone they would have in the hot seat.

■ ■ ■

■ EXAMPLE 2: Inner Dialogue

In the fifth session of a counseling group, members are discussing love relationships and marriage. One member has been unable to make a decision about her marriage. In this example, the leader uses an empty chair to facilitate an *inner dialogue*.

LEADER: This has been a struggle for you, Sally, trying to decide whether you want to leave your husband or not.

SALLY: There is a part of me that does, and a part that doesn't.

LEADER: So it seems as if there are two parts with opposing views.

SALLY: Yes. And depending on which one is running things, that's how I feel. I try to make a decision, but just when I think I've made it, the other part takes over.

LEADER: What would you think about having the two parts talk it out? Would you like to try a dialogue? *(In anticipation, the leader pulls up an empty chair.)* You could start in one part and say what you'd like to the other part in that chair.

SALLY: Where do I begin?

LEADER: You choose. Start as either the part that wants to leave or the part that wants to stay.

SALLY: I'll do the part that wants to leave first. I just don't want to be married to him any more. He is abusive and I know he's had affairs and is probably having one now. I don't love or respect him and I'm not happy. We just go through the motions. It doesn't make sense.

LEADER: Now switch chairs. Sit in the opposite chair and take the other side.

SALLY: *(Switches chairs; the leader observes the change in the member's posture. She now slumps and looks down as she speaks.)* But in his own way, he loves me and he's a good provider. Besides, I've grown to love his family.

LEADER: Now switch chairs. Tell the part that wants to stay why you need to leave.

SALLY: *(Switches to the first chair: Again, her posture is more upright, her voice firmer.)* It's over. There is no reason to stay.

LEADER: Ask her what she is afraid of.

SALLY: What are you afraid of? *(Switches seats)*

SALLY: *(The member tears up, speaks in a little girl's voice.)* I'll be alone. He takes care of me. I don't know what I'll do if I'm on my own. I haven't worked in 14 years.

LEADER: Switch back to this chair and again be the part who wants to leave. *(She does.)*

SALLY: *(Pointing to the other chair)* She's hanging on. She is really afraid of being alone. And I think she is stronger. I'd like to strengthen this part so I can free myself up to make this decision.

■ ■ ■

■ EXAMPLE 3 : Empty Chair—Role Reversal

This is the fourth session of five high school students meeting to discuss conflicts with adults, particularly parents and teachers. Bill has been discussing problems with his father.

LEADER: So, Bill, can you tell us more about your dad?

BILL: He's a royal pain. He's gone all the time. When he comes home, all he does is bitch and complain. I'm tired of it.

LEADER: He complains about you, about the family? What exactly?

BILL: Everything.

LEADER: Can you be your dad? I mean, can you be that complaining old man we've heard you talk about so that we have a better idea of what you have to put up with?

BILL: *(Sneers and shuffles his feet.)* Sure. What, right here? Just be him?

LEADER: Tell you what. Here is a fresh chair. *(The leader moves a chair into the circle next to the member.)* Move into that chair and be your dad. And I'll interview you, kind of probe you to get you to tell us more about yourself. *(The leader is purposefully structuring the role reversal to tap into the information he wishes to draw out of the working member.)*

BILL: *(Body language communicates reluctance as he moves to the next chair. He sits with his legs and arms crossed.)* Okay, shoot. What do you want to ask me?

LEADER: Mr. Adams, Bill tells me you're gone a lot and when you come home, all you do is complain.

BILL: *(As the dad)* That little pipsqueak! He would talk about me behind my back. Like he ever contributes anything to the house. I'm out busting my ass, and all I get is lack of respect. You think I like working two jobs? I'm tired when I get home. Then I got to do half the things he was supposed to do.

LEADER: *(The leader sees that Bill has quickly gotten into the role of his dad.)* So you feel you have a right to complain.

BILL: *(As Dad)* Damn right. He goofs off in school while I'm out there trying to make ends meet. You think I don't want to be home more?

LEADER: Are you saying you are concerned about your family?

BILL: *(As Dad, hesitantly)* Yeah. Yeah, I guess that's what I'm saying.

LEADER: Bill, sit here, be yourself. *(Bill moves to his original chair.)* What are you learning from doing this?

BILL: *(Slowly and thoughtfully)* Well, I never thought about what it's like to live my dad's life. I guess a lot of what he does he does for us. I just wish he wouldn't complain about it so much.

LEADER: *(Having taught TA last week, he uses that language because it seems to fit well with this situation.)* So he's in his Critical Parent a lot? *(Member nods.)* And you go to your Not-Okay Child rather than getting into your Adult? *(The member nods and smiles in recognition. The leader glances around the group.)* Does anyone feel he could play Bill's dad so Bill can get a chance at practicing staying in his Adult?

DON: I think I can play his dad.

■ ■ ■

■ EXAMPLE 4: Bringing the Past Into the Present

In this fifth group session of sexually abused women, the leader has conducted a fantasy exercise, guiding the members back into memories of childhood. One member is beginning to experience what she perceives as the "split" between the "good girl" part of her and the "bad girl," or abused part. The group leader is carefully encouraging this new awareness.

LEADER: Chandra, tell us about the good girl.

CHANDRA: *(Gazing off as if she is visualizing an image.)* She is very good.

LEADER: And what is the good girl doing?

CHANDRA: She is playing with her cousins in the front yard, having fun and then my 16-year-old cousin asks me to go with him.

LEADER: What are you feeling as you go with him?

CHANDRA: Scared. Wanting someone to help. Not wanting to go but not able to say no because I try to please everyone.

LEADER: And what do you see?

CHANDRA: Me being a bad girl and him threatening me.

LEADER: Now what is happening?

CHANDRA: *(Suddenly she sobs uncontrollably, then shudders and screams. She rocks back and forth in her chair.)* Why couldn't someone help me!! Why didn't I do something to stop it!!

LEADER: *(The leader motions to the member next to Chandra to relinquish her chair so the leader may be in closer proximity to offer her strength and support and also help the member come back from the pain she is experiencing.)* Chandra, I want you to hear my voice. We need to look at your pain now. That was many years ago. I want you to look up, look around. *(Chandra stifles a sob and looks around the group.)* There are people here who want to help you finish this unfinished business. *(Chandra nods.)* I want you to switch seats and sit in this chair, today's chair, and talk to the little girl who was abused in 1988.

This leader has the knowledge and courage to not be "freaked out" by her member's reaction. The leader stays with Chandra psychologically and helps her work through painful material. This ability is essential when using techniques that have the potential to deepen a member's awareness of past trauma. The leader must also be tuned into other members who may have past memories of abuse that could be triggered by Chandra's work.

■ ■ ■

■ E X A M P L E 5 : Use of Specific Language

In Passons's book on Gestalt approaches, he points out that the specific use of words can block our awareness and prevent us from making alternative choices (Passons, 1975). For example, clients may refer to "it" rather than "I" as a way of avoiding responsibility for their feelings and motivation. Some common statements that members might make are, "It's depressing to lose a job," rather than, "I'm depressing myself regarding losing my job." Or, "It's going to be impossible to get over her," rather than, "I find it hard to get over her." Or "It's scary in this group," rather than, "I'm scared being in this group." By using *it* or *you* rather than *I,* we tend to depersonalize our feelings and avoid responsibility. Another language barrier to becoming more aware of feelings involves the use of "can't" statements, rather than "won't."

In the following example, Odetta is dealing with a fear of failure that holds her in a low-paying job.

ODETTA: . . . Jobs are hard to come by. I can't quit my job.

LEADER: Odetta, try this. Say, "I *can't* quit my job." Then say, "I *won't* quit my job."

ODETTA: I can't quit my job. I won't quit my job.

LEADER: Which is more accurate?

ODETTA: I guess that I won't, that it's too scary. I'm still afraid I can't make it with all those smart people. They'll see through me and I'll be the laughingstock.

LEADER: Do others of you use the word *can't* to avoid taking responsibility for your choice? *(Heads nod.)* Any of you want to comment?

HENRIQUE: I always say I can't lose weight and I can't get up early to exercise.

LEADER: Let's spend some time on how our language affects us.

■ ■ ■

■ EXAMPLE 6: Focusing on Nonverbal Behavior

Perls recognized that members' nonverbal behavior reveals much about how they are feeling. In the following example, a member discusses the loss of his job.

LEADER: Ted, it sounds as if you were really surprised when your boss just let you go without any warning.

TED: *(Laughs)* Sure was. Boy, you just never know. I had that job for 3 years and, bingo, I'm out.

LEADER: Some people might feel angry under these circumstances.

TED: *(He smiles.)* Yeah, I'm angry.

LEADER: Are you aware that you are smiling even though you say you are angry?

TED: I said I'm angry. *(Smiling a tighter smile.)*

LEADER: *(Looks around the group and chooses a member he believes will respond well to his request.)* Jack, could you show Ted how he looks right now? Ted, just watch for a minute and tell us your reaction. *(Jack imitates Ted's smile.)* What is the smile saying?

TED: Friendly, safe.

LEADER: I'm going to ask you to try something. I'm going to ask you to be your friendly, safe smile. Will you do this?

TED: Like this? *(He forces a smile.)*

LEADER: That's right. Now I'm going to ask you to talk to us *as* your smile. Something like this. "I'm Ted's smile and I serve a good purpose for him when he's angry. The purpose I serve is . . ."

TED: I'm Ted's smile and I serve a good purpose for him when he's angry. The purpose I serve is to keep me from the rage I feel.

HAVIER: What is that about?

TED: My dad was a true rageaholic and I made a pledge to never act like him.

LEADER: Would it be helpful to express some of that anger here rather than keeping it in with a smile?

FRANCIS: I laugh to cover up my true feelings. This is good for me to watch.

LEADER: Let's finish with Ted and then maybe we can focus on that, Francis.

■ ■ ■

Cautions Regarding Gestalt Techniques

It is important to understand that Gestalt techniques, in particular, can tap quickly into deeper feelings. Members may experience painful or traumatic memories and emotions. Therefore, if you choose to use Gestalt techniques, you want to make sure that you are prepared to deal with deeper emotion.

Suggestions for More Reading

Gestalt Approaches in Counseling (Passons, 1975) is an excellent book for understanding different Gestalt techniques. *Gestalt Therapy Verbatim* (Perls, 1969) is an excellent book to read to find out how Fritz Perls led his "hot seat" Gestalt groups.

Other Approaches

Two other models for counseling that can be very useful in groups are solution-focused therapy and the transtheoretical model. Both are excellent models regarding how people change.

Solution-Focused Therapy

Solution-focused therapy is an approach to counseling that emphasizes the client's strengths and focuses on solutions (O'Connell, 2005). Solution-focused brief therapy is a very good model for school groups (Murphy, 2005) and many growth, counseling, and therapy groups because of its emphasis on solutions and positive coping. Numerous books and articles have been written about using solution-oriented principles with certain populations (with adolescents— Sklare, 2005; with parents—Zimmerman, Jacobson, Macintyre, & Watson, 1996;

substance abuse—Berg & Reuss, 1998; Pichot, 2001; assaultive behavior—Linton, Bischof, & McDonnell, 2006; anger management—Schorr, 1997).

Principles and Techniques Metcaff (1998) wrote a detailed book about solution-focused principles as they applied to groups. She outlines some principles that group leaders can use in their sessions:

- Focus on keeping the group discussions nonpathological.
- Change problems in a way that opens possibilities.
- Focus on exceptions to the problem.
- Comment on members' strength and coping.
- Avoid the tendency to focus on insight into the problem.
- Focus on positive coping behavior.
- View members as people with complaints about their lives and not as people with overwhelming problems.
- Assist members in finding "simpler" solutions.
- Encourage group members to ease into solutions gradually.

Solution-focused group leaders pay much attention to the climate of the group and make sure that the discussion follows these principles. Group leaders using these solution-focused principles concentrate the members on collaboration and solutions; that is, members try to help the working member see the possible solutions and opportunities instead of focusing on insight or the past.

There are also a number of excellent questions that group leaders use when working with an individual or the entire group. These questions get members to understand their goals and their strengths and help members focus on the possibility of and desire to change.

1. **Miracle question**. The miracle question is used to establish goals of a working member or for all the members. De Shazer (1991) describes the miracle question this way: Suppose that one night there is a miracle and while you were sleeping the problem that brought you to therapy is solved. How would you know? What would be different? (p. 113).

By using this question, the leader can get the member or members to clarify what it is that they want to be different and what that would look like. Group leaders using solution-focused techniques will frequently pose the miracle question.

2. **Exception questions**. De Shazer (1991) discusses the value of getting members to think about times when the problem is not a problem or when it is less of a problem. Linton et al. (2006) list a number of excellent exception questions for group leaders to use in a group for assaultive behavior:

- What is different about the times when you manage your anger effectively?
- What is happening during those times when you would expect you might lose your temper, but you do not?

- How often does that happen?
- What has to happen for that to occur more often?
- What would be a small step, something you could do this next week, that would help that happen?

Exception questions get members to think differently about their problems; the questions focus on making changes that will help members reach their desired goals.

3. **Scaling questions**. Berg and Reuss (1998) write about the value of having members use numbers instead of words, especially when members are having trouble expressing themselves in words. Linton et al. (2006) offer some sample questions that get members thinking about change:

- On a 1–10 scale, with 10 being the *most desirous,* how would you rate your desire to change?
- On a 1–10 scale, with 10 being the *most confident,* how confident are you that you will be successful for 2 weeks?
- On a 1–10 scale, with 10 being the *most confident,* how confident would your friends be that you will be successful?

These kinds of scaling questions help members to assess where they are in regards to changing and they tend to give members clarity.

Because a solution-focused approach is based on what *is* working rather than what isn't, the group leader will accept a lower number. For example, if a group member is asked how confident she is that she will be successful with an issue, and she responds with a 3 on the 1–10 scale, the leader might say, "That high," indicating that the member already has a start. This is in contrast to an approach that might focus on how to get the number higher. In other words, the member is seen as already doing or believing something that is moving her toward her solution or goal.

4. **Coping questions**. Linton et al. (2006) state that coping questions are helpful when attempts to elicit exceptions and future possibilities are met with negativity and a denial that anything positive is happening or could ever happen (p. 16). Coping questions would be something like:

- What keeps you going?
- What are you doing to keep things from getting worse?
- How do you get yourself to these group sessions?

The goal of coping questions is to heighten members' awareness of the effort that it takes to keep things the same or to cope with their problems. Coping questions also give recognition to the person's effort and highlight the fact that he is doing *something.*

Each of these questions is excellent and helps members focus on solving their problems rather than dwelling on them. Too, by using solution-focused principles as the primary approach in the group, the leader gets members to help other members both see possible solutions and emphasize their strengths instead of their weaknesses.

For those interested in using solution-focused techniques, we strongly encourage you to read articles and books on solution-focused therapy that pertain to the population in which you are interested.

Transtheoretical Model

In their theories book *Systems of Psychotherapy: A Transtheoretical Analysis,* Prochaska and Norcross (2010) present the *transtheoretical model,* which utilizes all of the theories and accounts for how people change. In the transtheoretical model, Prochaska and Norcross propose that people go through stages of change, and knowing these stages of change helps any counselor in both individual and group counseling. Much has been written about stages of change and we believe that *every* counselor and group leader needs to be familiar with these stages. Group leaders can use the information to understand group dynamics that arise because of members' stages of change. It is important for group counselors because members are at various stages of change and if leaders understand this, they will be more efficient and effective.

Stages of Change　According to Prochaska and Norcross, change takes place over a series of five stages: precontemplation, contemplation, preparation, action, and maintenance.

　　Precontemplation is the stage when the person has no interest in or desire to change. The member often does not see that there is a problem. Often members in a nonvolunteer group are in the precontemplation stage in that they do not see themselves as having a problem. Certainly in many addiction groups, the leader will be dealing with members in denial, which is the same as precontemplation.

　　Contemplation is the stage where members are aware of their problems and are seriously considering changing but have not yet made a commitment to change. It is important to understand that many stay in contemplation for a long time. Groups often help those in contemplation to move to preparation and action because the contemplator sees others making progress and changes— this often is quite motivating and is one of the benefits of being in groups. There will be times when a contemplator will fool a leader and the leader will spend far too much time with the member and thus the group will not be as productive as it could be. By understanding stages of change, the leader will make this mistake less frequently.

　　Preparation is the stage that combines intention and behavior. The member shows that he wants to change and in fact is taking some steps toward change, such as cutting down on drinking or smoking, or studying at least some each day. Other examples of the preparation stage are investigating different workout gyms or reading up on different diets.

　　Action is the stage in which members make changes. Often the leader will ask for "progress reports" and those in the action stage tell the different things that they are doing. Members who are in contemplation or preparation often are encouraged by hearing members who are in the action stage. It is important for leaders to remember that the goal of most counseling and therapy groups is to get members into the action stage.

Maintenance occurs in groups if they last long enough. This is the stage where people maintain their change, such as not drinking or not smoking or staying away from pornography. Members who have maintained their changes are an inspiration for those who are in contemplation, preparation, or action.

Use of Stages of Change   Leaders can use the transtheoretical stages of change model in many different ways in their groups. We recommend for any growth, counseling, or therapy group that the leader at the very least consider frequently the stage of change of each member as the group progresses or as a topic is introduced. By thinking about the stage of change of the members, the leader may not focus on a certain member because the member seems as if she is in precontemplation or stuck in contemplation. Often in groups, much time is mistakenly spent with members who do not want to change. This is unfortunate, especially if there are members who are in the preparation or action stages of change. Leaders who are always thinking about the stages of change of their group members will not be as inclined to make this mistake. They will focus on members who want to change.

Another way to use the stages of change in groups is to teach the stages to the members so that members can use this model when trying to help themselves or other members. Perhaps the best way to teach this is to have all members think of something they are interested in changing or a problem in their life and also something that they have changed, such as a bad relationship, losing weight, exercising, or quitting smoking. Then teach the stages and discuss which stage members are in regarding their particular situations. Also, get the members to reflect on the change process they went through in reference to the thing that they changed. By spending time discussing the stages, members come to understand them and the leader can use the stages in later sessions as members bring up issues to work on. *A skilled group leader is always thinking about the stage of change of any member who is working on some issue in the group.*

Concluding Comments

We cannot stress strongly enough the importance of understanding and being able to apply at least two or three theoretical models when leading counseling and therapy groups. The purpose of this chapter was to give you an overview of several counseling theories that can be used in group counseling situations. These theories were chosen because they are practical, effective, and, for the most part, easy to teach or share with group members. There are numerous others that could have been included but our purpose here was mainly to introduce some theories that we feel are particularly useful for many different kinds of groups.

TA and REBT are psycho-educational models that members can learn relatively easily and use with each other in the group and in their daily lives. Both models are effective with children and adolescents and offer considerable published materials that can be useful in working with those populations as well as with adults. Reality therapy is also a psycho-educational model that focuses on the here and now, with much responsibility placed on the member to determine her needs and to develop a plan to meet those needs. The Gestalt model provides strategies for deepening the focus in counseling and therapy groups. Several Gestalt techniques, such as the empty chair, can be combined with other theories. The Adlerian model is excellent for helping members gain a broad perspective on how family dynamics may have influenced their current behavior. This model can be used with REBT as members work toward disputing the irrational beliefs that support mistaken goals and guiding fictions. Solution-focused therapy is an excellent approach that focuses on possibilities and solutions. The transtheoretical model emphasizes the stages of change, which can be helpful to both the leader and the members.

■ ACTIVITIES

1. Imagine three critical moments in a group that you might be leading and then think of how you might use one or more of the theories described in this chapter to work through the various issues connected to the critical moments.
2. Discuss with fellow students or colleagues their use of theories in groups. Especially look for those who have used counseling theories in group settings.
3. Discuss the advantages and disadvantages of using just one theory in group sessions.

 GROUP COUNSELING SKILLS

View again the three segments using theories 13.1, 13.2, 13.3, and think about other ways to use these theories. Think of how these groups may have gone if theory was not utilized.

Chapter 14

Counseling and
Therapy in Groups

For most counselors, leading counseling and therapy groups is the most difficult and most rewarding of all the groups that we discuss in this book. Counseling and therapy groups are conducted in many settings, such as schools, psychiatric units, mental health centers, hospitals, college counseling centers, rehabilitation centers, prisons, addiction treatment centers, youth crisis centers, child abuse centers, women's shelters, and juvenile training schools. Counseling and therapy groups may focus on personal problems in general or on specific topics, such as anxiety, depression, cancer, AIDS, panic attacks, recovery, shyness, divorce, or relapse. School counselors are often not allowed to conduct "therapy groups," but they certainly do conduct counseling groups, where they are trying to help students with many different personal concerns. Throughout the chapter, we use the terms *therapy* and *counseling* interchangeably, with both defined as the process of helping members with insight into one's behavior. We are not saying necessarily that counseling and therapy groups are the same, but rather that the skills and techniques discussed apply to both. Many of the techniques that are valuable for therapy groups are also useful for support, growth, and experiential groups.

Goals of Therapy Groups

Behavioral researchers have identified two types of therapeutic goals for groups: *process goals* and *outcome goals*. *Outcome goals* are goals that pertain to behavior changes in the member's life such as obtaining employment, improving an interpersonal relationship, maintaining sobriety, or feeling greater self-esteem. Therapy groups that focus primarily on the members' concerns are usually much more beneficial than groups that focus primarily on the interactions among the members. Leaders who emphasize outcome goals get members to focus on their issues at a depth level of 6 or below on the depth chart. (To review the depth chart, see Chapter 7.)

The term *process goals* refers to goals that are related to the group process. For example, process goals can be to help members improve their comfort level in the group, to increase their openness in the group, and to learn to confront members in a more productive manner. Some educators teach that the focus of the group should mainly relate to what is happening in the "here and now" and that outside concerns are less important. With this approach, much time is spent on interactions, member feedback, and confrontation. Although focusing on process goals can be a valuable aspect of therapy groups, we feel this should not be the main focus for any therapy group. The focus usually should be on individual concerns and outcome goals.

Establishing Group Size and Membership of Therapy Groups

The ideal therapy group is composed of five to eight members, with the membership remaining constant once the group has begun. In the ideal group, the members attend voluntarily and share at a very personal level. In private practice, college counseling centers, schools, mental health centers, and various other settings, groups can be like this. Unfortunately, in many other settings, groups are not at all like this. We describe the less-than ideal group to prepare you for what may happen once you start working in the helping field. Less-than-ideal groups are often found in youth crisis centers, drug and alcohol agencies, residential treatment centers, prisons, and psychiatric hospitals. In these settings, leaders may be asked to lead groups with anywhere from 15 to 20 members and with an ever-changing group of members who are forced to attend. The leader regularly has to devote group time to introducing a new member or saying good-bye to a member who is leaving. In very large groups, it is difficult to involve all the members in any discussion or give individual attention to a member. In open-ended groups, sharing is often less personal because members do not feel the sense of cohesion and trust that exists in groups where there are the same five to eight members who want to be in the group.

Large, nonvoluntary groups are difficult to lead and are usually only minimally effective. In a situation where the members are very negative, resistant, or mentally disturbed, or in settings where a large group (12 or more members) is mandated by agency policy, the leader may want to try leading an education/discussion group for all the members and then a smaller therapy group for those who seem to have some commitment to personal change.

Screening Members

When establishing a therapy group, the leader should screen the members if possible. Screening can eliminate members who do not belong in the group because they are in too much pain or they are too emotionally unbalanced or they would fit better in a different group than the one being formed.

In many situations, the leader is selecting members from a caseload, or an agency may require all patients to be in groups. Each of these situations leads to the formation of a group of members with very different problems. In such a group, one member may express concerns about keeping employment because of aggressive behavior; another, about her marital troubles; another, about his lack of assertiveness; and another, about anxiety that prevents her from going places more than three miles from home. Screening can be helpful in trying to get the right mix of members. With experience, the skilled leader gets more adept at selecting members for groups. If possible, it is a good strategy to verbalize that the groups are not permanent and that members may be switched to other groups during the first few weeks.

When to Meet

There really is no specific number of times that a therapy group should meet. Some groups meet on a daily basis for 1 hour or more, and others meet once or twice a week for 1 to 3 hours. For different populations and settings, the leader should try various meeting schedules to determine the optimal number of meetings per week or month. In schools, counseling groups usually meet every week or every other week.

The Leader's Role and Responsibilities in Therapy Groups

The leader is the primary orchestrator of change within a group. The members are very important, but it is the leader who creates the therapeutic climate and is responsible for focusing the group. This does not mean that she does all the talking or counseling, but rather it means the leader is in charge, and has many different responsibilities. We discuss six such responsibilities.

1.   Knowing the subject or topic
2.   Providing the right atmosphere
3.   Directing the focus
4.   Being aware of individual members
5.   Watching the clock
6.   Apportioning the "air time"

Knowing the Subject or Topic

It is the leader's ethical responsibility to have a good grasp of the issues that may arise in a therapy group. For instance, in an Adult Children of Alcoholics (ACOA) group, the leader would need to know about trust, intimacy, and relationships. Too often, we hear of therapy groups being led by someone who does not know the issues or what to do when important topics are brought up. In groups for depression, eating disorders, sex addiction, or anger management, knowing the issues would enable the leader to introduce topics that are relevant and use exercises that are designed to get members to explore their inner thoughts and feelings.

Providing the Right Atmosphere

Creating an atmosphere where members feel safe to share their thoughts and feelings is the leader's responsibility. The members should feel that they will be heard. The leader should create a positive environment in which trust and respect are communicated and modeled. This requires cutting off comments that are negative, hostile, or insensitive. The leader uses certain phrases to remind members they are there to help each other. Some good phrases to use are the following:

- What ideas do you have that might be helpful?
- What is something you can say that may help?
- I appreciate the sharing and caring that you are exhibiting. With these attitudes, I know we can have a good group experience and people can be helped.
- We are here to help and support each other. Does anyone have a suggestion, thought, or reaction that they think may be helpful?

Another consideration regarding the right atmosphere is whether or not a leader should see a member of her group for individual counseling. In most cases, we feel this is not only appropriate, but often very useful, because the leader's responsibility is to be as helpful as possible. We disagree with some authors' positions that counseling a group member outside of the group session is detrimental to the performance of the group. We feel this rarely detracts from the atmosphere of the group.

Directing the Focus

The therapy group leader should always be aware of the focus and whether it should be held or shifted. If the group is focused on helping a member with a concern, the leader must assess if the concern being discussed has relevance for the other members and if the members can get involved in helping the member with her problem. For example, in a group for recently divorced women, it would be quite appropriate to discuss such issues as fears about dating or anger at an ex-spouse. However, if a member wanted to discuss the problems she was having with her neighbor over a new fence, the leader would probably want to shift the focus to something more relevant. She would offer to discuss the fence issue with the member after the session or some other time.

Being Aware of Individual Members

Another responsibility of the leader is to pay close attention to each person in the group, because at any moment a member may react emotionally to something being discussed. By watching all the members, the leader will observe different reactions and draw out certain members who seem ready to share.

If the group is made up of members with diverse cultural backgrounds, the skilled leader needs to continuously monitor the reactions to the different topics and problems. To completely understand, the leader may need to ask a member how his culture deals with the situation being discussed. This can be valuable in expanding members' cultural awareness and in understanding the specific members' reactions. It would be unethical to work intensely with an individual in the group if the leader did not understand that member's cultural frame of reference. In Chapter 17 we give an example of making a major mistake in a therapy group because of not understanding the person's culture.

Watching the Clock

Another responsibility is making sure that enough time remains in the session to cover an issue adequately. Sometimes leaders make the mistake of introducing a topic or allowing a member to begin discussing a very personal issue with only a few minutes left. For instance, much time would be needed to adequately cover topics such as death or rape.

Apportioning "Air Time"

It is the leader's responsibility to be aware of the amount of time that each member has had to address problems. Members should not necessarily have equal time, but it is important not to devote an inordinate amount of time to one or two members. If a member seems to need much of the group's time, it may be best to see that member individually or, in extreme cases, request that the member not remain in the group. The leader must realize that the group should not be dominated by one person's therapy needs. There will be times where the focus is on one person for 20–30 minutes, which is fine, as long as this person does not have the focus on him week after week. To avoid spending too much time on one person, a leader can find it helpful to reflect on the following questions:

- How long has the group been focused on the member?
- Is the discussion relevant for most of the other members?
- Do members seem annoyed at the amount of time being spent on the person?
- How much time in past sessions has been spent on this person?

The Process of Therapy in a Group

Getting, Holding, and Deepening the Focus

Therapy groups differ from other groups in that therapy groups are supposed to move to a deeper personal level. The skilled leader understands the value of trying to deepen the focus. Following are a number of examples that illustrate how the leader can be very instrumental in deepening the focus, which in turn makes the group more personal, more interesting, and more therapeutic.

■ EXAMPLES

This group consists of patients at a mental health center. The leader has introduced the topic of guilt for discussion. One member has described how she felt guilty about leaving her dog at home by itself all day; another felt guilty about not going to visit his grandfather more often. Neither of these members seemed too bothered by their guilt, but the leader senses that many of the members are, in fact, very much bothered by their guilt feelings. The leader decides to deepen the focus.

LEADER: I guess I am wondering if some of you have some guilt feelings that are hard to live with. That is, do you feel bad about something you did or are doing and do those actions cause you to think less of yourself? Guilt is often associated with doing something that runs counter to some value or expectation we hold for ourselves. Guilt is often involved with religion and sex. Let me ask this—is there something that you feel guilty about that would be hard to share? I'll ask you to say yes or no, but you do not have to share what it is.

TROY: No.

MARIA: Yes.

BOB: Yes.

BETH: No.

CINDY: Yes.

TED: Yes.

LEADER: What makes it hard to tell?

CINDY: I am afraid of what people would think of me.

LEADER: I think that is true for many people. More importantly, though, is how you feel about what you did or what you are doing. How many of you answered yes because of things that you are doing currently? (*Maria, Ted, and Cindy indicate that they did.*) Let me ask this question: How can a person quit feeling guilty?

TED: I don't see how I cannot feel guilty—it is wrong. I never thought it would go this far. (*Looks down*)

LEADER: Ted, perhaps if you talk about it, you will see it differently. I urge each of you to talk about what you are feeling guilty about, because there are solutions to guilt. You do not have to continually beat up on yourself. How much longer do you want to punish yourself?

TED: You're right about the punishment. I hate it, but I feel so rotten.

LEADER: From what you said earlier, Ted, my hunch is that it has to do with your marriage and possibly an affair. Others of you may have guilt over something in your marriage or your past that pertains to sexual issues.

TED: That's it—you see, at work ...

In this example, the leader asked members to be more specific. The leader also made some comments and asked thought-provoking questions in order to get members to personalize the discussion. The leader kept exploring the topic until one person was moved enough to want to work on his issue.

■ ■ ■

The members are all women in an eating disorder group. They are talking about their problems with food.

SALLY: When I am bored or upset I eat, and when I start eating I can't stop.

LORI: That's true for me. I like all kinds of food, but cookies and candy are my real downfall.

SARA: My downfall is ice cream. My favorite is chocolate chip.

NAJWA: Ice cream is one of my downfalls. Let's list our favorite downfalls. *(Everyone laughs.)*

LEADER: *(In a slow, deliberate voice)* Rather than focusing on your downfalls, I'd like each of you to think of how you lose control over your food intake. When does it occur and how do you cause it to occur? Think about that for a minute. *(Pause)* Any thoughts?

In this example, the leader shifted the focus to a new, more personal topic because she saw that the group could get focused on a "surface" topic. As a result of the leader's question, each member has to think about herself. Too often, leaders get caught up in the flow of the discussion and do not direct the members to more personal and meaningful dialogue.

■ ■ ■

The group consists of members who all experience frequent panic attacks when they are out in public (agoraphobia). Three different members have been sharing about their intense fear.

JOE: ... and as a result of those attacks, I have not been out of the house for longer than 4 hours in the last 5 years. I get out maybe once every 2 months. It's hell!

LEADER: I think Joe is right. It *is* hell, and because you are all here for the same reason, I know that most of you feel the same way. One purpose of this group is to help you realize that you are not alone. The other purpose is to reduce your fears. To do this, we have to look at the causes of panic attacks and what can be done about them. I want each of you to think about your panic attacks and the events and thoughts that occur right before they happen. Please comment on your understanding of what happens to you right before the attacks and during the attacks.

In this example, the leader is introducing a meaningful topic rather than just letting the members relate incidents from their lives. By focusing on what happens right before an attack, the members are more likely to share personal information and to get to pertinent issues.

■ ■ ■

The members are sharing events of the week without giving much thought to what they are saying.

LEADER: I'd like to say something that I think will be helpful to each of you. *(Using a soft, encouraging voice)* We have three sessions left, so I want to urge you to really consider what you want to talk about tonight. In the past few weeks, we have discussed a number of personal issues and I want to encourage you to look into yourself and see if there are other issues that you may need to talk about. What obstacles are in the way of having your life go the way you want it to? Are there some fears or unfinished business from the past that you need to talk about? Really stretch yourself in these last sessions. Are there some things that you would like to bring up in this session?

SANDI: *(After about 20 seconds)* There is something I would like to bring up. It has to do with me and my appearance....

■ ■ ■

Obtaining a Contract

The leader always needs to get a "contract" from an individual when the focus is going to be held on her for any length of time. By a *contract*, we simply mean that the member agrees to be the focus of the group's attention. When a leader senses that a member may benefit from being the focus, she might ask:

- Would you like to work on that?
- Would you like to discuss that for a few minutes?
- Would you like to understand that better?
- How can the group be of help to you?
- If we work with you on this issue for 20 minutes, what would be helpful?

The leader needs to be sure that there is a contract, because on many occasions leaders make the mistake of focusing on a person when that person is not ready or willing to work on the issue. Many times a member describes a problem or concern that appears to be severe enough to warrant help from the group. The severity of the problem or the emotional state of a member is not necessarily an indication of a desire to receive help. We have observed leaders who forego getting a contract and dive right into trying to help. As a result, suggestions are often met with a "Yes, but" response. Often this becomes frustrating for the other group members.

There are several reasons why members share their problems but do not really want to work on their problems. First, some members have a history of blaming or externalizing their problems. These individuals have little desire to take charge of their own lives. Second, some members are afraid to commit themselves to a plan of action in front of others. Third, some members tell a story to gain the sympathy of the group or to have others reinforce their position on some issue. The point is that there are many instances where members seemingly in need of help do not want to receive the help of the group.

GROUP COUNSELING SKILLS: Therapy in Groups

Go to segment 14.1 and watch the segment where the leader gets a contract and uses a therapeutic round and then engages all the members.

Use of Theories in Therapy Groups

Knowing and using counseling theories is a must for therapy groups. In the previous chapter we discussed the many different ways to use theories to guide therapeutic work. Because we devoted the previous chapter to the use of theories, we mention it here only as a reminder that no one should lead a counseling group without having at least one theory that he is able to use during the group session.

Techniques for Conducting Therapy in Groups

Techniques for Engaging the Members

In most situations when the focus is being held on one member, a skilled leader usually involves the other members in an active way. The leader does this because it keeps the members interested, it is therapeutic for members to be helpful to a fellow member, and members often have excellent ideas for the working member. Described here are a number of techniques that can be used when the group is focused on one member.

Members ask questions   Once a member has talked for a few minutes about the specific concern, the leader can use the technique of having the members ask the working member questions.

LEADER: I want you to think of a question that would be helpful for Ralph to answer. Who has one?

JUDY: I do. If your wife lost weight, would you feel more attracted to her? *(Ralph answers.)*

CARLOS: Why do you think you can't develop a long-term relationship with the other woman? *(Ralph answers.)*

SARAH: If you rid yourself of the notion that divorce is wrong, would that help you make a decision? *(Ralph answers.)*

Members guess what the problem is   Another way to involve members and cause the working member to stop and think is to have the members guess what the problem is. The leader would use this technique when the working member is being vague or acting confused.

LEADER: I want you each to try to guess what Ralph's problem is. I am not sure, and I don't think Ralph is, so perhaps our guessing will help.

JUDY: I think Ralph would really like to be divorced but is afraid of his parents' disapproval.

CARLOS: I sense that Ralph is afraid to get divorced because he fears he will be left with nothing.

SARAH: I think Ralph is feeling guilty about the thought of leaving his kids and wife of 15 years.

There are a number of benefits to having members ask questions or guess what the specific concern might be.

- It gets the members involved and prevents them from becoming bored or disinterested.
- It breaks up the member's storytelling (many times, a working member will ramble without really concentrating on what the specific problem might be).
- It causes the member to think about what she is saying.
- Good questions may be asked.
- The working member gets to hear how he might be feeling. This is especially true if some of the members are very good at pinpointing what the working member is feeling.
- The working member gets to feel understood if the other members are on target.

While the members ask questions or make statements, the leader has time to think about the direction in which he believes the therapy needs to go. It is important that the leader closely monitors the questions and guesses to make sure they are relevant and useful. Sometimes the guesses are projections of how members would feel based on their own values and past experiences.

Members role-play the working member A technique that is effective and also causes the members to be involved is to have the members role-play the working member. By *role-playing the working member,* we mean that another member acts as the working member. Here is how this may occur.

> LEADER: I would like someone to role-play Ralph, using his body language and voice pattern so that Ralph can see how he presents himself in the group. Be sure to speak in the first person singular, just as if you were Ralph. Try to feel what he is feeling based on what you have heard him say. *(After giving the members about a minute to think, the leader begins.)* Sarah, you look like you want to give this a try.
>
> SARAH: I think that Ralph—
>
> LEADER: *(Cuts in)* Sarah, see if you can speak as if you were Ralph.
>
> SARAH: *(Drops her head, slumps down in her chair, using a weak voice similar to Ralph's)* Okay. I'm Ralph and I'm real confused about what to do. I feel torn. Also, I feel guilty when I think about leaving my family. I'm not sure if this desire for a divorce will pass or not.
>
> LEADER: Are you tired of being so stuck? This has gone on for 2 years.
>
> SARAH: *(In a weak voice with head still down)* I just don't know what to do. I really fear my father's wrath.
>
> RALPH: Do I really look that pathetic?
>
> MEMBERS: Yes!
>
> RALPH: I had no idea that I was acting that way.

Creative use of members There are numerous creative ways that a leader can utilize members to make the counseling more concrete and have more impact. The following techniques are for specific kinds of problems and would be used only if the timing was right and the activity fits the problem being presented.

- Members are asked to stand in front of the working member, who sits on the floor and looks up at the standing members. This activity would be used when a member expresses feelings of "less than" or insignificance in comparison with others. By seeing the other members standing, the seated member experiences visually what he is expressing. This often stimulates further discussion.

- Members can play various ego states of the working member. This technique assumes that the members have been taught the theory of TA. For example, if the working member appears afraid to take risks, the leader might appoint another member to play the working member's Not-OK Child ego state. In essence, the other members act as different ego states of the member.

- Members are asked to talk about the working member in a kind, caring way while the member listens. (If the leader feels it would be helpful, the member may be told to close his eyes or face away from the group to facilitate listening.) This gives the member a chance to hear how others see him or the problem. To facilitate this, the leader can say, "Jeff, I want you to close your eyes and just listen as we talk about your situation." *(To the others)* "What do you think of Jeff's situation and how he is handling it?"

- If a member does not feel part of the group and the leader senses that the member would like to be but is not trying very hard, the leader may have the group stand in a circle holding hands and have the member walk around the outside of the circle with the option of asking or "fighting" to break into the circle. This can be very effective if the issue is feeling left out or not knowing how to be a productive member of the group. Some on the outside try hard to break into the group while some others need to be coaxed to try to get into the circle.

- An experiential technique could also be used with a member who feels held down by all of his obligations and responsibilities. To help the member experience this, the leader might have the member sit on the floor, with four or five other members holding him down. The leader instructs the member to experience the feeling and then decide on a course of action. Some members do nothing; others fight very hard to break free. The experience usually proves valuable to the member because he gets a sense of how he is handling what he believes is holding him down. This is valuable to the other members because they will reflect on how hard they are fighting to get to where they want to be and also on whether they are holding others back and what is holding them back. This exercise should be used only by an experienced therapist and must be used with great caution, because it often evokes the emotional release of some deep-seated pain from childhood or former relationships.

- Another effective way for experientially helping a member is to use drama to act out a scene that the member is worried about, such as a job interview or a conversation with parents (members would play the interviewer or parents). The person can get feedback and then try the scene again. In some cases, the leader may get another member to play the working member's role to give the individual a chance to view how the conversation could be handled more effectively.

- Psychodrama can also be used to explore in action not only historical events, but more importantly, dimensions of psychological events. Psychodramatic enactments are usually quite intense, because they often involve reworking traumatic experiences, memories, or unpleasant or puzzling events. Enactments are conducted using other group members to portray the different people in the protagonist's (working member's) life. Psychodrama is a valuable tool for therapy groups, but a detailed discussion is beyond the scope of this book. For a good background in psychodrama, we encourage you to read Blatner's book *Foundations of Psychodrama: History, Theory, and Practice* (Blatner, 2000).

- Another creative way that members can be used to bring about impact when a member is stuggling between two positions is to have two members take the working member's arms to symbolize feelings of being pulled in two directions. The following dialogue illustrates this example.

DAN: I just feel pulled, you know? A part of me wants to get married because ... *(States the reasons)*. Another part of me doesn't *(States the reasons)*. I just can't seem to make up my mind.

LEADER: Bill, you and Tom stand up. Dan, you stand too. Bill, I want you to stand on one side of Dan and take his arm. In a minute, I want you to tug on his arm, saying all the reasons why Dan wants to marry. Do this as if you were Dan—that is, in the first person. Tom, you get on the other side and pull on the other arm, saying all the reasons why Dan does not want to marry. Okay, begin.

Bill and Tom talk and pull Dan's arms simultaneously. Thus, Dan feels pulled in both directions. Dan is instructed merely to listen to each side and pay attention to the sensation of feeling pulled. He is also instructed to pay particular attention to whether one side of the issue emerges as more powerful or persuasive than the other side. Note that using such techniques requires that the leader make sure that everyone knows his part. The working member must not experience merely two people pulling on his arms but rather the mental struggle between two sides of an issue. This technique may also seem like a gimmick or a slapstick routine if the leader does not set the tone properly. The leader must explain the purpose of the technique and remain serious about conducting it, even if the members laugh or snicker.

GROUP COUNSELING SKILLS: Therapy in Groups

Go to segment 14.2 and watch the segment where the leader engages all the members when working with one member.

The Use of Therapeutic Rounds

A therapeutic round differs from the rounds described in Chapter 9 because in a therapeutic round, the working member is the one completing the round. The following descriptions of therapeutic rounds should clarify this point.

The in–depth, stationary round   This is a round where the working member says something to each member of the group while remaining in his seat.

The first type of in-depth, stationary round is one in which the working member makes the same statement to each member. The members serve as a sounding board for the working member by listening as the member repeats a belief that he has.

■ EXAMPLE

Ralph has been talking for about 10 minutes and one of his concerns is his parents' reaction to a divorce.

LEADER: Ralph, I would like you to turn to each member, starting with Sarah on your immediate left, and say, "I'm afraid to get a divorce because of what my parents will think."

RALPH: *(To Sarah)* I'm afraid to get a divorce because of what my parents will think.

LEADER: Now look at Carl and say the same thing. And then repeat it to Judy, Liz, and Asel.

RALPH: *(To Carl)* I'm afraid to get a divorce because of what my parents will think.

RALPH: *(Looks at Judy, obviously thinking)* I'm afraid to get a divorce because of what my parents will think.

RALPH: *(To Liz)* I'm afraid to get a divorce because of well, uh, this is nuts! I have got to live my life for me. My parents are not unhappily married, I am!

By saying the same thing over and over, Ralph gets a chance to listen to himself. It is important to note that in this type of round the members do not say anything. They merely act as listeners. By repeating something out loud, to others, a working member is usually able to gain some insight about his thoughts and feelings.

■ ■ ■

The second type of in-depth, stationary round is one where the working member turns to each member and completes the same sentence stem.

■ EXAMPLE

Kara has been talking about how she is not good enough.

LEADER: Kara, let's clarify what you mean. So far you are being kind of vague. Here's what I want you to do. I want you to look at each member and start with "I am not good enough because" and then complete the phrase. Start with Marj.

KARA: *(Looking at Marj)* I am not good enough because I am not pretty.

LEADER: Now look at Nan and start the same way.

KARA: *(Looking at Nan)* I am not good enough because I am not smart.

KARA: *(Looking at Dee)* I am not good enough because, uh, *(looks down)* my family does not have as much money as most of my friends. *(Tears up)*

LEADER: Is that what bothers you the most?

A member doing this type of in-depth, stationary round can be more specific about her concerns. It helps the group to understand her, and it usually helps the member to better understand how she is thinking and feeling. Using the members is more powerful than having her just talk to the group, and also the members feel more involved.

■ ■ ■

The third type of in-depth, stationary round is one where the working member responds to a repeated question from the other members.

■ EXAMPLE

LEADER: I want each of you to ask Charlie the following question: "Charlie, does being gay make you less of a person?" *(Pauses and sees that Bonita is ready)* Bonita, you go first and ask Charlie that question. Charlie, you look at Bonita and respond to the question. Then look at the next person.

BONITA: Charlie, does being gay make you less of a person?

CHARLIE: Everybody in my family thinks it does.

LEADER: Look at Meg. Meg, ask Charlie the exact same question.

MEG: Charlie, does being gay make you less of a person?

CHARLIE: I don't want to think that I am less of a person.

LEADER: Turn to Jenny.

JENNY: Charlie, does being gay make you less of a person?

CHARLIE: *(In a very thoughtful voice)* I thought I had resolved this, but it is clear to me that I haven't. I need to get clear as to what I believe.

■ ■ ■

A fourth type of in-depth, stationary round is one in which each member asks a different question of the working member, using the round format.

■ EXAMPLE

LEADER: I want each of you to think of one question that you want to ask Jesse in terms of what he is saying about his guilt. Try to make the question one that will cause him to really think about what he is saying and feeling. Who wants to start with a question? Jesse, make your answers brief. Faith, we'll start with you.

FAITH: Jesse, do you think you can ever be forgiven for the accident?

JESSE: No, I don't ever deserve to be happy given that I killed three people when I was drunk.

WAYNE: Do you think your guilt is helping anyone?

JESSE: Well, no, but I am not sure what you mean.

WAYNE: What I was ...

LEADER: Wayne, hold off. Let's go on.

JUSTIN: If you don't think you can ever get over this, then why are you here and why do you continue to go to church?

JESSE: *(Pauses, head drops)* I want to get over this pain.

JUSTIN: You can if you will let yourself be helped by us and by God.

ANNE: *(With a caring but irritated voice)* Why do you think you are the only one who has done a bad thing? In our own way, each of us here has plenty to feel guilty about, so why do you think you are so special?

JESSE: *(Somewhat taken aback, with a shaky voice)* I just haven't thought of it the way you are getting me to. *(Tears up)*

Often members ask good questions that cause the working member to explore the concern in greater depth. In addition, this allows the other members to be more involved.

■ ■ ■

The in-depth, movement round   In contrast to the in-depth, stationary round, the in-depth, movement round involves the member moving in front of each of the other members, thus intensifying the experience. This kind of round is one of the most powerful techniques for producing intense, in-depth exploration. Moving in front of the other members creates a potent atmosphere that often causes the working member to gain insight. During these rounds, there will be times when the leader will ask the members to sit silently as the person makes the round. Other times, the leader will instruct the members to ask a certain question or to respond in a specific way, such as, "No, it doesn't mean that." The role of the members will depend on the content of the specific round and the purpose that it is serving.

■ EXAMPLES

Sherry has been talking about not liking herself but has been vague.

LEADER: Sherry, sit in front of each member and say, "I don't like myself because...."

SHERRY: *(Moves in front of Pam)* I don't like myself because I am fat.

SHERRY: *(Moves in front of Kate)* I don't like myself because my teeth are ugly.

SHERRY: *(Moves in front of Beth)* I don't like myself because my parents never liked me. *(Starts to cry. Beth starts to reach out and take her hand, but the leader shakes his head no, because he believes Beth would be trying to "rescue" Sherry from her pain.)*

SHERRY: *(Moves in front of Patty)* I don't like myself, oh, I don't know if I can say it. *(Cries more and looks down)* I don't like myself because of what my father did to me when I was growing up.

LEADER: *(With a warm, caring voice)* Was it sexual?

SHERRY: *(Sobbing, looking down)* Yes!

LEADER: *(In a calm, firm voice)* Sherry, I want you to look up and see the others' faces. No one here thinks less of you. Look up—don't watch that movie that says, "Sherry's a horrible person." *(Sherry slowly looks up.)*

In this example, the round serves as a way to get the member into her feelings. The leader also used a couple of other skills. First, he continued to push the member even though she had begun to cry. Often in groups when a member cries, the other members and leader make the mistake of rushing to support the member, causing the work to cease. There are times when a person in pain needs to struggle with her pain.

Another skill was having Sherry look up right after she disclosed the sexual abuse. By doing this, the leader did not allow Sherry to reinforce her negative feelings by watching negative images in her mind. Also, by seeing the faces of concerned, caring members, Sherry could experience that they did not think less of her. This latter technique obviously requires that members in the group be empathic and sensitive.

■ ■ ■

Vicente has been talking about how he feels worthless because he was put up for adoption when he was 4. The leader has been challenging Vicente's irrational, self-defeating belief and thinks that Vicente may be about to give up this belief.

LEADER: Vicente, I want you to sit in front of each member and answer the question, "How does being adopted make you worthless?" Each of you asks Vicente that question. Vicente, start with Bonnie. *(He moves his chair in front of Bonnie.)*

BONNIE: Vicente, how does being adopted make you worthless?

VICENTE: Well, if they loved me, they would have kept me.

LEADER: Vicente, move to Donna. Donna, ask him the same question, and if he does not answer the question, try to get him to be more specific.

DONNA: Vicente, how does being adopted make you worthless?

VICENTE: If your parents give you away, you are worthless.

DONNA: You said that they gave you away because they just could not handle their own lives and they had no money! Now how does that make you worthless?

VICENTE: I don't know. I feel it.

LEADER: Go to the next person. Calvin, try to ask something that will challenge Vicente's thinking.

CALVIN: I don't believe being adopted makes you less of a person. My closest friend is adopted, and he certainly doesn't feel worthless, and I don't think he's worthless.

VICENTE: Well, uh, maybe I've been seeing this all wrong. I think I'm getting the point.

■ ■ ■

To reiterate, the use of in-depth, movement rounds can be very beneficial when they are used at the right time and with the right kind of problem. A leader should use the in-depth, movement round only when she is trying to get a member in touch with some intense feelings or thoughts.

Spinning Off

When the focus is being held on one member, the leader should always be thinking about ways to get others involved in either the member's work or in their own work. To get members involved in their own work, the leader will periodically seek comments from them while putting the working member on "hold." We call this *spinning off*. To do this, the leader might say the following:

LEADER: David, I want you to think about what you have said in the last few minutes while I hear from others. *(Looking at the other members)* What has this made you think about in reference to yourself?

This question serves a number of purposes: (1) members get to share what is on their minds (at this time, the leader would not focus on a new person because he has the other member on hold), (2) the leader gains information about how many others are ready or almost ready to work, (3) the sharing can be helpful to the working member, and (4) the working member gets some time to collect his thoughts before the leader comes back to him.

Another way that the leader spins off is by making a few comments to the group about what the working member is saying:

LEADER: Let me comment on what Joe is saying. Joe is talking about his part in weekly fights over household chores. Each of you may want to think about any routine fights that you have and the part that you play in those fights. It is really important that you understand your part in a fight. If you can see how you contribute to any fight, then I think many of you will choose to change. Joe, let's get back to you.

Spinning off to the members is *essential*. By making thought-provoking comments to the members and eliciting their comments about themselves, the leader can cause more members to think about themselves and thus to be ready to share when the current person's work is completed.

In the last few pages, we discussed many ways the leader can involve the members when the focus is being held on an individual. *Too often, leaders just conduct individual counseling and do not take advantage of all the possible ways to involve the members.* It is very important to realize that much of the help members receive in a counseling group comes from the sharing, caring, supporting, and challenging that takes place. Also, the leader has a much greater chance of keeping the members' interest when she involves the other group members while one member is working on a personal issue.

Techniques for Helping More Than One Member
at the Same Time

There will be occasions in therapy groups and even sometimes in growth and support groups where two members will need help at the same time, often concerning the same issue. For example, let's say the members of a therapy group are sharing about guilt. One of the members, Susan, gets in touch with some old feelings of guilt from an abortion. As she begins to talk about her abortion and her sense of guilt, another member, Donna, begins to cry and says that her tears are about an abortion she had 2 years ago. At this point the leader has several options:

- Ask Donna if she can wait until the work is completed with Susan.

- Ask Susan if it is okay to shift to Donna, because her pain seems greater.

- Work with both of them at the same time.

- Ask a co-leader or another member to go to another area of the room or somewhere else with one of the two members.

The first and second options require that the leader hold the focus on one member until her concerns have been alleviated enough to switch the focus to the other. In the preceding example, there may be no need to do this because their problems are similar. However, in an instance in which one person is talking about guilt over an abortion and another brings up guilt over her husband's suicide, the leader may find it extremely difficult to deal with these issues simultaneously. The skill required in this situation is knowing how to put one member on hold. This is done by being straightforward with the two members and asking if one can wait. If the leader feels both members need immediate attention, she may use the last option, which is to get help from a co-leader or another member.

In many instances, the concerns are so similar that it would save time and benefit the two members for the leader to work with both of them simultaneously. Sometimes the leader may have one or both of the working members complete an in-depth round and then have them talk about each other's round. Or the leader may have the two members give advice or suggestions to one another. The leader could have the working members complete a sentence stem, such as, "Because I had an abortion, it means I am _____." The leader could have the members answer to each other or to the other members. At other times the leader may do an in-depth, stationary round by having the members ask each working member the same question, such as, "Why does having an abortion make you less of a person?" When leaders work with two members simultaneously, each member sees another person in the same situation and most likely identifies with the therapy or recognizes her own faulty thinking by seeing the faulty thinking of the other.

 GROUP COUNSELING SKILLS: Therapy in Groups

Go to segment 14.3 and watch the segment where the leader works with more than one member.

Techniques for Working with Individuals Indirectly

At times in therapy groups, the leader will do therapy in an indirect manner with one or more members. Indirect counseling may be helpful for a member who does not feel comfortable being the focus of the group. Let's assume that Rita had a friend who died tragically 2 years ago. Although Rita has never mentioned this in the group, she did write about it briefly one time in the journal that she leaves at the end of each session. Rita has not participated much verbally and has never been the focus of the group. If the leader does not think Rita wants to work on the issue in the group, he has a couple of options for working with her indirectly.

- He can bring up the issue of death and grieving to get a discussion going and hope that this will be therapeutic and may even prompt Rita to share.

- He can work with another member who has a grief issue, knowing that the work will probably be beneficial to Rita.

If the leader chooses the second option, the group will focus on a member's pain over a death. While working with that member, the leader would observe any reactions from Rita in hopes that the work will trigger Rita to open up and request help. Or, using dyads, the leader could pair the working member with Rita. Both these methods may be successful in getting the silently working member to share.

If these methods are not successful in drawing out comments from the targeted silent member, the leader should keep in mind that members benefit from hearing others, whether or not they actively discuss their own personal concerns. Hearing the concerns and coping strategies of the other members can help the indirectly working member.

Therapy That Focuses on Process

Throughout this chapter, we have emphasized focusing on individual problems when conducting counseling groups. We do want to mention that there will be many times during a therapy group when focusing on group process will be therapeutic. By focusing on process, we mean focusing on what members are doing or feeling in the group. For instance, a member may constantly try to one-up everything that is said. Feedback from the members can be very therapeutic. Or a member may ramble and the leader or another member may point this out to the rambler in hopes that the rambler may get some insight on how he comes across to people. Some members can be afraid of what others will think, so the leader may want to focus on this as a topic. Feelings of being one down, not being part of the group, or fear of rejection are all potential material that is therapeutic to discuss. If handled well, the leader can turn conflict or tension among the members into therapeutic gains. The skilled leader always pays attention to process as well as content and will focus on group process when it seems necessary and valuable to do so.

■   EXAMPLE

It is the third session of a group of fourth-graders who have trouble making and keeping friends. The leader has observed that Ross has a tendency to interrupt people.

COREY: My dad is thinking of getting me a 4-wheeler. This means so ...

ROSS: *(Interrupting)* My dad said he's going to take me to New York this summer. I like...

LEADER: *(With a somewhat strong voice)* Ross, are you aware you interrupted Corey? Corey, you finish and then I want to focus for a minute on Ross.

COREY: I was just going to say this means so much to me because it will be something I can do with some of the kids that live by me. I think this will help me get some friends.

LEADER: Corey, that's great. Keep us posted. Ross, back to you. Are you aware that you interrupt people a lot?

ROSS: *(Angrily)* I just like to share. Isn't that what this group is about?

LEADER: *(With a nurturing voice)* Ross, I'm not trying to pick on you. The purpose of this group is about making friends, and I think this may hurt you in your effort to make friends. Ross, listen for a minute, okay? *(He nods.)* Do any of you think Ross has trouble in this area?

HANS: I tried to be your friend and you would never let me talk.

AHMED: You always butt in here in the group.

COREY: I don't think you listen or share very well.

ROSS: At home, I get interrupted all the time by my brother and father.

LEADER: I bet that doesn't feel good.

ROSS: No, I hate it.

LEADER: You are doing that in here and here at school. I think this is a big reason that people don't want to be your friend. Will you let us help you with that?

ROSS: How?

LEADER: By letting us point it out to you and you not biting our heads off. *(Ross smiles and nods okay.)*

By paying attention to the process (Ross always interrupting), the leader was able to make the group very beneficial for Ross and most likely for others.

■   ■   ■

Thoughts on Intense Therapy

In this chapter, we have discussed therapy in many ways—from helpful insight to deep therapy. Many counseling groups, such as those in schools, are not aimed at intense therapy. However, many therapy groups have as their goal deep, personal work; that is, the leader funnels the group to individual work at a level of 5 or below on the depth chart. In these groups, the leader usually directs much of the therapy, because the members are limited in their ability to be helpful. They can share and offer good suggestions or insights, but if the therapeutic process goes deep enough, the members will not know how to be helpful. For instance, in recovery groups from incest, rape, or abuse, we use a variety of techniques, including Gestalt, psychodrama, or in-depth rounds, to get at the deep-seated emotions. We then use REBT, TA, Gestalt, and other theories with some creative techniques to help the client work through the pain. Any leader who is getting members to look at their buried emotions has to know how to help the members get through their pain. Stated another way: *Do not unzip members unless you know how to zip them back up!*

If you plan to work in settings where you will be doing some intense group therapy, we strongly suggest that you become knowledgeable and skilled as an individual therapist. *Intense group therapy requires that you have good individual counseling skills.* We also suggest that you read some of the literature on psychodrama, because psychodrama includes many skills and techniques that can be used to help members get in touch with some deep-seated issues. It is these skills, coupled with counseling theories and the ideas in this book, that will make you a good group therapist.

Providing Therapy in a Nontherapy Group

At the beginning of this chapter, we mentioned that therapy may take place in nontherapy groups. Quite often in groups in which the purpose is something other than counseling, the opportunity arises to focus on one member's concern. Topics discussed in a support group or even a discussion or education group can cause members to get in touch with unfinished and/or painful issues.

The first thing that a leader must do when the opportunity for counseling arises in a nontherapy group is to decide if therapy would be appropriate. If the leader decides it is appropriate to focus on one member's concern (that is, the topic is relevant to the other members and there is enough time), she should ask the member if he desires immediate help. She would also want to ask the other members if they are willing to spend some time focusing on one member's problem. Once the leader has consent from the members, she will use many of the skills and techniques outlined in this chapter. The following are examples of when it might be appropriate to hold the focus on a member and do some brief therapeutic work in a nontherapy group.

- If a member of an education group for pregnant teenagers starts crying about how she hates being pregnant, the leader might choose to work with her for a few minutes, because, more than likely, others are having similar feelings.

- If a member of an experiential group that is doing the ropes course shares how bad he felt about himself when he was growing up, the leader might decide to funnel the group to a deeper level by focusing on this member.

- If a member of a parenting group discloses that she feels guilty because her baby was the result of an affair that her husband does not know about, the leader might want to take a few minutes and try to be helpful because the topic is guilt, which is something that most people can relate to. Working with the member from a theoretical base could prove to be valuable for all the members.

The benefits of conducting therapy in nontherapy groups are very much the same as for therapy groups. The main difference is that the therapy portion of the group is short-term. The focus is then brought back to the main purpose of the group.

Common Mistakes Made When Leading Therapy Groups

Several errors are common among leaders of therapy groups. These mistakes were discussed earlier in the chapter or in other chapters, but because they are so important, we want to review them briefly.

Attempting to Conduct Therapy Without a Contract

Many leaders attempt to focus on a member of the group without first getting agreement from that person. The result is that the member resists the leader's attempt to be helpful; time is wasted; and members become frustrated and even resentful.

Not Involving the Other Members

One of the most common mistakes made by beginning leaders is to conduct individual counseling with a member without involving the other members. It is a mistake to have members sit and listen while the counselor tries to be helpful to a member unless the leader is very skilled at taking the counseling to a deep level, using theory and a multisensory approach. By using this approach, the other members can relate to their own problems or become very involved in the intense work. Whenever possible, it is best to involve members in some way.

Spending Too Much Time on One Person

Some leaders make the mistake of spending week after week trying to help one member who is in pain or spending too much of the session on one member. It is important for the leader to realize that some members seek and/or need inordinate attention from the group. The natural tendency of the leader is to focus on those individuals, especially if other members are not as talkative. The skilled leader keeps a mental record of how much time is being spent with the various members and makes sure not to spend too much time with one member.

Spending Too Little Time on One Person

Many beginning leaders will be hesitant to hold the focus on one member when others also want to share. When this happens, one member shares for a minute or so, then another member, then another member. Sometimes this is helpful and valuable, but at other times this type of sharing is not as personal as when the focus is held on one member. Holding the focus on one member causes him to delve more deeply into his problem, which in turn often causes other members to look more closely at their own concerns.

Focusing on an Irrelevant Topic

Too often, a leader lets a member ramble on about a personal experience, even if the story has no relevance to the group. The leader might even ask the member questions about the story or have other members ask questions. A similar mistake occurs when two or three members are focused on some irrelevant topic and the leader fails to shift the focus. It is important to realize that if the leader does not cut off irrelevant topics, the session is likely to be much less meaningful for the majority of the members.

Letting Members Rescue Each Other

If a member begins to cry, it is often a mistake for another member or the entire group to rush immediately to the member's side, take his hand, and try to comfort him. The leader should discourage this type of behavior when it is antitherapeutic. Many times, the member needs to be with his pain instead of being "rescued" from it. The members should show support, care, and concern but should not rescue. The leader prevents rescuing by saying something like, "Let Mike be with his pain—I think he knows that we care. Mike, do realize that we care and want to help." As we discussed elsewhere, there are times when supportive touching is quite appropriate and very therapeutic—but leaders need to know the difference.

Letting the Session Become an Advice-Giving Session

Very often in groups, leaders make the mistake of turning the session into an advice-giving session. That is, a member brings up a problem, and then all the other members try to solve it by giving advice. This is *not* what a therapy group is supposed to be. Sometimes advice is given and is helpful, but by and large each member should work on her own concerns with the help of the other members. Advice-giving sessions often occur when the leader does not know theories and thus relies on the members' advice to be the agent of change.

Concluding Comments

Counseling and therapy groups are different from support and growth groups in that the leader focuses on the members in an in-depth manner. The main purpose of counseling and therapy groups is to help members alleviate personal concerns that interfere with quality living. Many of the techniques discussed for therapy may also be used in non-therapy groups. The approach we have described for leading counseling groups emphasizes the leader as being responsible for the therapy. The leader of a counseling group should be in charge, because she is more knowledgeable about counseling and therapeutic techniques.

When one member is exploring a problem in-depth, the leader can use a variety of skills and techniques. He can use his individual counseling skills to help the member clarify and work through the problem. He can also use the other members to play various roles, or he can use himself to help dramatize the problem. It is the leader's responsibility to establish a positive tone for the members and to get a contract from a member before focusing intensely on him or her. Once there is an agreement to work on a concern, the leader may need to help the member clarify the problem. Any of a number of techniques can be used, such as having the member engage in a clarifying round or having the other members ask the working member questions. A very valuable technique when working with an individual on a concern is the in-depth, therapeutic stationary or movement round.

When conducting individual therapy in a group, it is important to spin off to the group and hear members' personal reactions and get them involved in trying to help the working member. By spinning off and pointing out the themes, the leader keeps members more interested and this usually causes them to be ready to share when the focus shifts from the working member. We view the leader as the conductor of the group who orchestrates the focus on different members and topics. An excellent book with chapters on many different therapy topics is *Handbook of Group Counseling and Psychotherapy*, which is edited by DeLucia-Waack, Gerrrity, Kalodner, and Riva (2003).

■ **ACTIVITIES**

1. Think of five topics that could come up in therapy groups and then think of creative techniques that could be used to introduce and work with each topic. This can be very useful in helping you to develop the ability to think creatively about issues in counseling.

2. Think of three different topics and the different therapeutic rounds that could be used to deepen a member's work on that issue.

 GROUP COUNSELING SKILLS

1. View again segment 14.1. Ask yourself the following:
    a. How effective was the in-depth round for the working member?
    b. How did the round help to engage the other members?
    c. Why did the leader go to the members for comments and then come back to Lauren?
    d. Why did the leader focus on the topic of forgiveness with the other members?
    e. Did the use of props help? If so, how?
2. View again segment 14.2. Think about the following:
    a. Note how the leader got the other members involved. Why was it important to get the members to comment?
    b. Note how the leader used theory in the session.
    c. Observe the many ways that the leader involved the other members
    d. Was it good that the leader cut off the member's story when he said, "Stop, Stop," and then asked the members for comments?
    e. Was the round effective when the leader asked all the members, "Is she a terrible mother?"
    f. Listen to the narrator's comments and give thought to what he says in summarizing the session.
3. View again segment 14.3 and observe the many different techniques that were used. Also observe closely the different ways the leader handled the three members who had very heavy concerns. Here are some questions to think about:
    a. Why did the leader choose to focus briefly on the one member's issue about voting for herself?
    b. What did the leader do to focus on the heavy issues?
    c. Was the use of the chair helpful?
    d. What did the leader do to keep all the members involved?

Chapter 15

Closing a Session or Group

Two kinds of closing are discussed in this chapter: the closing of a session and the closing of the entire series of sessions. The *closing phase* is the period of a session when the leader wraps things up. The *closing stage* may be the last session of the group or the last few sessions, depending on the kind of group and the total number of sessions involved.

The Closing Phase

Every session should have a closing phase. The length of the closing phase will depend on both the length of the session and the kind of group being led. For a longer session, more time is usually required. For a 1-hour session, the leader may find 3 to 5 minutes sufficient; a 2- to 3-hour session may require 5 to 10 minutes for the closing phase. The closing phase of a discussion or task group may simply be summarizing the main ideas or decisions made. Because this is fairly straightforward, less time is required. In a support or therapy group where members share a range of thoughts and feelings, more time is required to pull together key points, clarify goals, check for unfinished business, and encourage reactions. With experience, the leader learns to judge the amount of time needed to bring closure to the session.

During the closing phase, the leader has the opportunity to encourage members to share their thoughts and feelings about the session. Members may share how they benefited from activities or discussion that occurred during the session. It is especially important for the leader to hear from those members who were less verbal in the session. The leader can benefit from hearing how they feel about what is taking place and whether they are feeling comfortable. Also, less active members may be perceived negatively, and their sharing can help link them to the group, causing other members to gain some better understanding of who they are and how they are experiencing the group.

It is important to inform the members that the session is entering the closing phase. This can be done by saying any of the following:

- We need to start winding down, so I want you to think about the session today and what it has meant to you.

- Because there are only a few minutes left in today's session, let's review what we have gone over today.

- I think we are at a good stopping point, so let's spend the next few minutes summarizing the session today, and then we'll talk briefly about next week's session.

- Let's begin the closing phase of the session, because we need to stop in about 10 minutes.

Purposes and Goals of the Closing Phase

The closing phase may serve one or more of the following purposes: (1) summarizing and highlighting the main points, (2) reinforcing commitments made by individual members, and (3) checking for unfinished business from the session.

Summarizing and Highlighting the Main Points   One purpose of the closing phase is to pull the session together by highlighting and summarizing important points. For example, in discussion or task groups, key ideas or decisions can be highlighted. In education groups, members may focus on what they learned and what impact this new information may have on their lives. Members of support, growth, counseling, or therapy groups can look back on what helped them. Pulling together salient points or experiences helps members remember them after the session has ended; the impact of the session can thus be increased. Having the group focus on key points also gives members a chance to hear what was important to others. This sharing often tends to build greater trust and cohesiveness among members.

Reinforcing Commitments   In many groups, members may commit to some task or change in their behavior. Reviewing such commitments in the closing phase is valuable. The following two examples show how a leader might clarify goals and strengthen commitments.

■ EXAMPLES

It is the end of the second session of a task group made up of members who work at a mental health agency. Their task is to develop a new residential program for adolescents.

LEADER: Let's review who is to do what. Joe, what are you going to do before the next meeting?

JOE: I am going to call those two agencies that have residential programs and find out what problems they have had.

LEADER: Good. See if they'll send you any material, too.

PABLO: I am going to draw up a tentative list of rules for the unit residents to live by.

LEADER: Be sure to get input from us, especially from Cindy.

CINDY: I am going to devise a list of personnel that would be needed to staff such a unit.

BILL: I'm going to try to get funding for the unit.

LEADER: Bill, I think we decided that you were to look into possible sources for funding and bring that list to the group next session.

■ ■ ■

It is the third session of a therapy group. Members have shared a variety of concerns during the session, and the leader wishes to clarify members' goals and reinforce their commitments to those goals.

LEADER: Each of you in today's session has expressed a desire to change an aspect of your life. Three or four of you worked on specific goals you want to follow through on before our next meeting. As we close today, let's take a few minutes to briefly hear from each of you about your goals.

CHANG: I want to go home this weekend and not fight with my mother.

LEADER: You sound pretty committed to that, Chang. I'd like to suggest you keep notes and report back to us on how that works. *(Chang nods.)* Who else feels they might try something different this week? *(Pause)*

JOHN: *(Looks around at the group)* Well, I know I've got to do something about staying out so late.

LEADER: What did you decide as a result of discussing it here today?

JOHN: I am going to ask my wife which days are better for me to stay out late.

LEADER: Didn't you also say that first you have to see if she will agree to let you stay out at least two nights and that you are going to ask her if she would like to come with you?

JOHN: That's right! I forgot that part, and it's important.

LEADER: You bet it is. You have it now, so what are you going to do?

JOHN: I'll talk to her and really try to be open with her.

■ ■ ■

In both of these examples, the leader increases the likelihood that the members will follow through on their commitments. A good closing phase is necessary to review and clarify decisions made during the working phase of the session. As in the preceding and following examples, the interaction may often be leader-member-leader-member in the closing phase, which is fine. You would not want to do this during the middle phase of a session, but it is appropriate during the closing phase. Sometimes members make commitments and plans that are unrealistic. Reviewing various members' commitments and plans during the closing phase allows unrealistic goals to be clarified. The following are two examples of a leader helping a member modify an unrealistic goal.

■ EXAMPLES

It is the third session of a personal growth group in a college counseling center. During the closing phase of the session, the leader asks various members about their goals.

LEADER: I think we've summarized what we covered today pretty well. In the next few minutes, it might be helpful if people share specific goals that they are shooting for this week. Betty, I know you decided to try a different approach with your boyfriend when he's late.

BETTY: Today I learned that yelling only gets us into a fight. When he is late, I'm going to calmly tell him that I'm disappointed and that I'm willing to wait for only 20 minutes. I feel better knowing I can be in control.

LEADER: Frieda, how about you? You said you wanted to set up a study schedule. Have you come up with any thoughts about how you might do that?

FRIEDA: I decided I'm going to study 6 hours every night. That should really help me catch up.

LEADER: *(Turning to the other members)* What do you think about Frieda's plan?

WILL: That seems like a lot. I'd get burned out in 1 day. *(Other members nod agreement.)*

LEADER: What do you think, Frieda?

FRIEDA: Well, maybe that is a lot. I guess I'll start with 2 hours and see how that goes. Anything will be an improvement.

By helping the member develop a realistic goal, the leader has increased the likelihood of the member experiencing success.

■ ■ ■

During the session, Al discussed his desire for a salary increase. With the help of the group, he role-played strategies for talking with his employer about the raise. Although he made progress, Al needed further assistance in increasing his assertiveness and in exploring ways to handle potential rebuffs and excuses from his boss. The group is now in the closing phase.

LEADER: Who else learned something from today's session?

AL: Boy, I did. That role-playing about asking for a raise really helped. Even though you don't think I am ready, I do. I think I'll go in tomorrow and ask for the raise!

LEADER: Al, if he says no, what are you going to say? We didn't get a chance to practice that.

AL: Oh, I didn't even think of that. All I was thinking about was how I now know what to say. I'm not prepared for a negative answer. Maybe I should wait until we talk about it next week in group.

If the leader had not clarified the member's goal during the closing phase, Al would probably have asked for a raise even though he had not developed the resources to cope with the situation. By reviewing Al's reaction to the session, the leader was able to discover his unrealistic plan and caution him about moving ahead prematurely.

■ ■ ■

Checking for Unresolved Issues (Unfinished Business)   The closing phase is also the time to check with members for any issues that are not fully resolved during the session. Sometimes issues are brought up that may need some additional closure as the session comes to an end. The leader may find it unproductive to focus for too long on a particular member or issue and thus bring temporary closure to the discussion. The closing phase may be used to refocus on that previous issue or concern, providing an opportunity for a member to express new thoughts or for the leader to help the member agree to continue to work on the issue in the next session. Occasionally, a member may have unfinished business that cannot wait until the following session, either because a decision is imminent or because the issue is causing considerable discomfort for the member. The leader could ask the members if they would be willing to extend the session to work on the issue. If this cannot be done, the leader may see the member individually as soon after the session as possible.

To find out if members have unfinished business from the session, the leader can say something like the following:

- Does anyone have something that was "stirred up" during the session that they want to mention? We'll either deal with it now, if it won't take too long, or we will deal with it at the next session.

- Is there any unfinished business from the session that you think needs to be discussed for a few minutes?

Because there are time constraints during the closing phase, the leader may need to carry unfinished business into the next session. However, by having members mention their unfinished business, the leader is able to either help them finish the issue or assure them that they will be able to discuss the matter at the next session.

■ EXAMPLES

During a counseling group at a rehabilitation center, John expressed some angry feelings regarding his parents' not visiting him often enough, but he was not able to see how he was upsetting himself by blaming his parents. After working with John for about 20 minutes, the leader chose to focus on another member. Now, during the closing phase, the leader wants to see if John has had any additional thoughts about his anger toward his parents.

LEADER: We'll spend the next few minutes bringing things to a close for today. I'd like each of you to think about what stood out for you. *(Pauses and scans the group. After a short silence, the leader makes eye contact with John.)* John, I felt there were more feelings you had to express about your parents. While we don't have time to work a lot more with those feelings today, do you have additional thoughts you would like to share with the group?

JOHN: I feel better after talking about it, but I still think they should visit more. I don't seem as angry.

LEADER: I guess I'd like you to keep thinking about this between now and our next session. I hope you'll bring it up at the next session. *(John nods in agreement.)*

Here the leader contracts with the member to work on the issue during the next session. He wants to make it clear to the member and the entire group that he is not forgetting the issue and plans to come back to it. He also wants to make sure that if there are any pressing feelings, they are handled before the session ends.

■ ■ ■

A group of divorced men and women are meeting for the fourth session in a support/therapy group. One member, Ann, worked on guilt feelings about giving the custody of her two children to her husband. During the session, Ann concluded that she did not have to feel guilty about her actions. However, when the focus of the group shifted to another topic, Ann continued to think about her decision. Now the leader is bringing the group to a close.

LEADER: Several of you worked on some pretty important issues today. It might be useful to review our session and see if you have additional thoughts about anything you discussed.

SUE: It was really helpful for me to see that even though my parents don't believe in divorce, that's their value and it's okay for me to have a different value.

LEADER: I'm glad that helped, Sue. What about other people?

ANN: *(Looking down and speaking in a weak voice)* I've been sitting here thinking about my kids. I know being without them right now is best for me. Yet, to be a good mother, I still feel I should be with them. I guess I'm confused all over again.

LEADER: Ann, it is apparent there is more we need to do to help clear up your concerns. Can this wait until our next session?

ANN: I think it can wait. I have to get this straight in my mind.

Had the leader not checked for unfinished business, Ann might have felt stranded with those feelings when she left the group. Also, the leader could have finished the session thinking that Ann had worked through a personal issue when, in fact, she was still struggling with it.

■ ■ ■

Formats for Closing a Session

There are several formats that can be used for closing a session. The choice of format for a particular session should depend on the kind of group, the purpose of the particular session, and what occurred during the session. To close a session, leaders can use rounds, dyads, written reactions, or have the members summarize. The leader may want to vary the closings of different sessions. In a discussion, education, or task group, it may not be important for each member to speak during the closing phase, because members have shared ideas and thoughts rather than personal feelings. In support, personal growth, counseling, and therapy groups, it is usually valuable for members to share their reactions and feelings about the session.

Rounds   Eliciting brief comments from members about what they learned or what stood out as they think back on the session is an excellent way to close a session. We most frequently use a round or series of rounds. The round provides a chance for every member to comment and encourages those who have talked less during the session to share their reactions. When setting up a round, the leader should instruct the members to limit their comments to a sentence or two. Longer responses defeat the purpose of the closing round, which is to highlight important points for each member.

■ EXAMPLE

LEADER: In a sentence or two, what will you take away from the session today? *(Pause)* Tim, let's start with you.

TIM: I learned that I am more nonassertive than assertive.

GUILLERMO: I learned that it is hard for me to be assertive. I guess I'm chicken.

Leader: I wouldn't say chicken. You simply have not learned to be assertive.

Bill: I learned that my parents are the cause of my being so aggressive.

Leader: Bill, let me clarify that for you and everyone here. We learn things from what our parents do and say. Often we tend to act like them unless we pay attention to our behavior. *(Turns to Bill)* In your case, from what you described, your parents are very aggressive. However, this does not mean you have to be aggressive, but you probably will be unless you monitor yourself. I hope the group will be a big help to you.

■ ■ ■

 GROUP COUNSELING SKILLS: Closing a Group–Use of Rounds

Go to segment 15.1 and watch the segment where the leader uses a round to close the group.

Dyads Followed by Comments to the Group   Starting the closing phase with dyads is a good way to involve all the members. Dyads are beneficial during the closing phase when much has happened in the group and the leader wants members to get a chance to share but does not have the time to hear all that each member has to say. In dyads, members can say out loud to another their thoughts and feelings. Dyads can also be used to energize members, especially if the energy level is low toward the end of a session.

■   **EXAMPLES**

Leader: Let's take the next few minutes to close. I'd like to form pairs composed of Phil and Pat; Roger and Paula; Ted and Ramón; Mike and Kay. What I'd like you to do is share with your partner one or two things that were particularly important to you about today's session. Then we'll come back to the large group and share any thoughts and feelings.

In this example, the leader decided to pair the members, but she could have allowed the members to select partners. If the leader decides to do the pairing, she should give special thought to anything that occurred during the session that might make it especially valuable for certain members to be together; for example, two members who expressed similar concerns or worked on similar problems could be paired. In the following example, the leader decides to participate in a dyad to encourage a member to share during the closing phase.

■ ■ ■

It is the second session of a support group made up of spouses of alcoholics. One member, Sally, has spoken only a couple of times during these first two sessions.

LEADER: As we're closing tonight, I'd like to take a few minutes to see how each of you is feeling about the group so far, what you think has been helpful, and what other topics or issues you'd like to discuss. To do this, I'd like people to pair up for about 2 minutes and then come back to share your thoughts. *(The leader pairs up the members, pairing herself with Sally. She learns that Sally is worried about how other members might view her because she has continued to live with her abusive, alcoholic husband. The leader reassures Sally that she will not let the members attack her and that it might be helpful if Sally shared some of her concerns before the session ended. Sally agrees. The leader ends the dyads and brings the group together again.)* I'd like each of us to share our thoughts about the group.

CARME: The group has been good for me to just get things off my mind.

BILL: Jack and I talked about what it was like to have alcoholic wives. I feel relieved just knowing other people are in the same boat.

LEADER: Sally shared some of her fear about talking about her family situation in the group. We both agreed it would be helpful for her to talk a little about that before we stop.

SALLY: It's real scary for me to be here. I feel I contributed to my husband's drinking by trying to cover it up.

CARME: I feel the same way—I hope we can talk about this at the next meeting.

The leader knew it was important for this quiet member to "break the ice" with the group before the end of this session so that she and the other members would begin to feel comfortable with one another.

■   ■   ■

Members Summarize   A simple way to close the session is to have one or more members summarize what has transpired. The leader can ask for a volunteer to summarize or may select a member who would do a good job. If one member summarizes, other members may also be given the opportunity to add what they feel is important. The leader may also want to add any important events that were overlooked by the members. During the closing phase, a summary should not be long or boring. The purpose is to give the members a brief review. Following the summary, members may wish to comment on particular points that were especially important to them.

Leader Summarizes   The leader may choose to summarize the session. By doing this, the leader can emphasize certain points and focus on certain members' comments. The disadvantage is that the leader may forget something that was important to one or two members; this may result in those members feeling hurt or resentful. To prevent this, the leader may find it helpful to let members contribute additional summaries following the leader's summary.

Written Reactions   There are several ways the leader can use written reactions during the closing phase (Riordan & White, 1996). The leader can begin the closing phase of a session by asking members to write their reactions to the session.

LEADER: It's about 8:45. Let's summarize and close the group. First, I'd like you to spend 2 minutes jotting down any reactions, thoughts, or feelings regarding the session tonight. We'll then share some of those thoughts and stop by 9:00.

Writing can be helpful for those members who respond more comfortably after having had a chance to put their ideas on paper. Members can also write for 5 to 10 minutes at the very end, when the group has completed the closing. The journal can be left with the leader, who then has an opportunity to read the members' reactions. The leader may choose to write encouraging or clarifying comments in the journals and then return them to the members at the next session.

The journal also provides each member with a lasting chronicle of the entire group experience from the first to the final session.

Helpful Closing Skills and Techniques

Clarity of Purpose   The leader needs to be very clear as to the purpose of the closing phase. A variety of issues and concerns may be raised by members during the closing phase that can take the group in unproductive or new directions. When members bring up new topics, the leader needs to explain the purpose of the closing phase and offer the option of bringing the topics up at the beginning of the next session. The important thing to remember during the closing phase of a group session is that the session is ending.

Cutting Off   To maintain the necessary focus on closing, the leader must be ready to use cutting-off skills. Members not only bring up new material during the closing phase but they often get into rehashing the session rather than highlighting or summarizing.

■ EXAMPLE

LEADER: What else did you learn from the session today?

LINDA: I'd like to know from the other girls if they have to go to church every Sunday. I do, and I hate it!

LEADER: *(In a warm, caring voice)* Linda, that seems like an important issue for you, but we really do not have time to get into a new topic right now. If you will bring that up at the next session, we'll certainly talk about it.

In this example, the leader stops other members from answering by speaking first. She does so to make sure that a new topic does not get started during the closing phase.

 GROUP COUNSELING SKILLS: Closing a Group–Preventing a New Topic

Go to segment 15.3 and watch the segment where the leader uses cutting off in order to prevent a new topic from being introduced during the closing phase.

■   ■   ■

Tying Together   The skill of tying together is especially beneficial during the closing phase of a session. By using this skill, the leader can create a sense of interrelatedness of themes, issues, and personal experiences. It is important for the leader to identify those points that relate to one another and then share them in such a way that the members see how patterns, issues, and people are connected. This is something the members are often unable to do themselves.

Drawing Out   Drawing out is also an important skill to use during the closing phase of a session because the leader usually wants to hear from as many members as possible. Several of the techniques for closing mentioned earlier—especially the use of dyads and rounds—facilitate the drawing-out process. It is especially important for the leader to draw out members who are less active during the session, both to help them feel involved and to get their reactions to the session.

Wishes   A useful technique for closing certain kinds of growth, support, and therapy sessions is the use of "wishes." This activity helps build positive and supportive feelings among members.

■   **EXAMPLE**

Leader: I think that pretty much summarizes the session. Any comments? *(Pause—no one seems ready to comment.)* Let's do this. *(Speaking slowly)* Look around the room and see if there is anyone you have a wish for. If there is someone, identify the person and then say, "My wish for you is...." For example, Joe, my wish for you is that you will call your parents and say those things that you want to say. You don't have to offer a wish and many may not receive a wish but I do think some of you will have wishes for other members.

Max: Don, my wish for you is that you get out at least twice this week.

Joe: Cherry, my wish for you is that you will stop blaming yourself.

■   ■   ■

GROUP COUNSELING SKILLS: Closing a Group–Use of Wishes

Go to segment 15.2 and watch the segment where the leader uses the technique of "My Wish for You."

Acknowledging a New Member   The leader may want to vary the closing slightly when a member is present for the first time. The leader might want to allow some extra time during the closing phase to focus on the new member if the member seems to feel comfortable enough but has been relatively quiet. Focusing on the new member gives that member a chance to share, which can help her feel even more comfortable. It also gives members a chance to know a little more about her. By hearing from the new member, the leader also has a better idea of how that person is feeling about being in the group.

■   **EXAMPLE**

Two members have finished summarizing the session, and others have commented.

LEADER: Connie (*The new member*), I hope this has been interesting and maybe even helpful.

CONNIE: Well, I was really nervous for the first 10 minutes, but I did relax. I am sorry that I didn't say more, but I really don't like talking in front of groups. I hope it will get easier for me.

LEADER: Was the session helpful?

CONNIE: Oh, yes. I already realize that others have feelings similar to mine.

LEADER: I hope that during the next session you will feel free to share. Anyone else have any closing thoughts before we stop?

■   ■   ■

Acknowledging a Member Who Is Leaving   There are occasions when a member leaves a group even though the group continues. In a closed group, members may drop out for any variety of reasons. More often, the departure of one member occurs in an ongoing, open-membership group, such as residential treatment programs in substance abuse or physical rehabilitation centers. Members leave the group because they are going home or somewhere else.

When a member is leaving, it is important that the leader allow some time during the closing to focus on that member. The leader may get the member to review his goals upon entrance to the group and the progress he has made, and have the members provide encouragement and feedback, and say good-bye. Although the exiting member is the major focal point, the leader may wish to use this experience to help other members think about when they will be leaving the group and what they still need to do to get themselves ready for leaving.

The amount of time that should be given to a member who is exiting depends on the length of time of the session, the purpose of the group, and the kind of member he has been. In open-ended groups, members may be exiting fairly often, so the time devoted to a leaving member must be monitored. It is important not to devote most of the session to the departing member because this could mean that every session or two would be focused on departing members rather than those who are in the group. To say goodbye to the exiting member, 5 to 10 minutes is usually sufficient.

■ EXAMPLES

LEADER: We have about 20 minutes left in the session, so I would like to begin to summarize the session. Also, I want to leave the last few minutes free to focus on Walt, who will be leaving the group after today.
I want each of you to think of the one thing that stood out for you today. *(Pause)* Mike, you seem ready.

MIKE: The discussion about the importance of not keeping our feelings inside was really helpful.

ANDY: The thing that stood out for me was ...

LEADER: *(After spending time completing the round and processing the session)* Okay, let's spend a few minutes saying goodbye to Walt. Most of you have known Walt for a while now. I want you to think of how you see Walt now compared to when he first entered the group. We'll share that and then we'll share any wishes that we have for him. How is Walt different?

MARIO: He is really different. *(To Walt)* When you first came into the group, you didn't talk or even look up. I really do think the program has helped you.

LEADER: I agree. You really have changed. I see you as a lot more open and that chip on your shoulder seems to be gone.

CARL: That's right! You did have a chip on your shoulder those first two meetings. It's gone.

LEADER: *(After others have shared)* If you had a wish for Walt, what would that be?

JEFF: My wish is that you have that conversation with your wife that you practiced in here.

BRUNO: My wish is that you don't let that chip come back. The soft, gentle side is much nicer.

LEADER: *(After two other members have shared wishes)* Walt, what thoughts or reactions or closing comments do you have for the group?

WALT: Well, I appreciate all your support. I also want to say …

In this example, the exiting member got a chance to hear some good and encouraging feedback.

■ ■ ■

There are times when a departing member has not really used the group or the treatment program that much. In this case, the leader may want to focus on feedback and wishes, in the hope that something might be said that will help.

LEADER: In saying goodbye to Sharon, I want each of you to think of what you believe will be the roughest thing for Sharon to handle when she goes home.

PAUL: I really think that Sharon is going to have trouble.

LEADER: Instead of talking to me, could you address Sharon?

PAUL: Sure. Sharon, I think you are going to have trouble with a lot of things, because you still seem angry at your parents.

BIFF: Sharon, I think you are fooling yourself when you say that you can make it without going to AA meetings. I hope your pride will not keep you from calling someone for help.

In this example, the leader wants to make sure that the member is not attacked, because she is leaving that afternoon. At the same time, he is hoping that someone says something that will be helpful, because Sharon really does not seem ready to leave the program.

■ ■ ■

Alerting Members to Reactions Outside of Group

Although the group experience can generate strong feelings among members, the leader should explain to the members that they will probably not experience the same kind of sharing with people outside of group (such as at home or with family), and this is normal. During the session, members often share at a very personal level, take risks, and experience warm, caring acceptance. They may go home and want to experience the same thing with their spouse, parents, friends, or coworkers. When this does not occur, some members become angry, frustrated, or resentful at the people in their lives and/or the leader of the group. Leaders should be aware that members may actually feel closer to other members of the group than a spouse, children, or long-term friends. The leader should always be sensitive to this occurrence and bring it up in group if it seems to be a problem.

LEADER: I want to say something now, and I will probably say it again in our last session. Many of you are really opening up and sharing with the group, and I think it is great. Also, the way you are responding to what is being said is terrific. I think nearly everyone is experiencing good feelings as a result of being here. For many of you, these feelings are unique, and I want to caution you about going home and trying to share like this with your spouse and friends. Remember, they have not been in this group and have not had this experience. If you want this kind of sharing, give them time. Don't expect them to be able to do this immediately. Also, realize that they may never be able to do exactly what we are doing here.

■ ■ ■

Handling Criticism of the Session

The leader should be prepared for criticism about the session or the group during the closing of the session. The leader must not be defensive. In most cases, the leader will not want the closing to be spent entirely on criticism unless he senses that the majority of the members are having the same feelings. The way the leader handles the criticism will depend on the kind of criticism, the merit of the criticism, and the amount of time needed for the actual closing. The following are several ways the leader can handle criticism during the closing phase.

■ EXAMPLES

Melvin is a member who has tried to dominate the group, and the leader has had to cut him off on numerous occasions. The leader has a strong sense from the members' nonverbal responses that they appreciate the fact that Melvin is not allowed to dominate.

MELVIN: *(In a hostile voice)* I have something I want to say. I feel you lead too much. In other groups, the leader hardly said anything—this is more your group than our group!

LEADER: *(To Melvin and the entire group)* I do hope you feel that this is your group. There are times when I direct what is happening simply because I am trained as a counselor and a group leader. And, as I said earlier, there will be times when I may cut you off to hold the focus on another issue or when it seems like you have gotten a little long-winded. Certainly, I do not want you to feel that I am dominating the group. Does anyone else feel that way? *(No one responds.)* Let's go back to summarizing the session. Other thoughts or reactions?

In this example, the leader briefly responded, got support from the members, and then went back to closing the group.

■ ■ ■

LEADER: Who else wants to comment on what stood out to them?

JAMES: I feel like the group gets too personal. When Troy was talking, I felt you really pushed him too hard!

LEADER: James, let me answer that. *(Looking at the entire group)* The group is personal, and I do push members hard because all of you have problems that need to be dealt with on more than a superficial level. Certainly, I try not to push you *too* hard, but do realize that not dealing with your problems is what got you into the hospital.

TROY: I'm glad you pushed. I think I understand why I get so angry.

■ ■ ■

The leader has been feeling that the group has not gone well the last couple of sessions.

JOSÉ: I don't mean to be critical, but the group has not been very valuable for me lately.

LEADER: How do others of you feel? I, too, think something is missing.

RUSTY: I would like us to be more personal rather than just discussing things. Does anyone else feel that way?

PAM: I do. The discussions about legal issues, custody, and so on are all good, but there are personal things that I think I am ready to share.

PAUL: I would like that better.

LEADER: So what you are saying is that you would like this to be more of a sharing group than a discussion/education group. How about the rest of you, how do you feel?

In this example, the leader decided to focus on the criticism because she felt that the group did perhaps need a new emphasis.

■ ■ ■

Final Thoughts on Closing a Session

The leader who successfully closes a group session enhances the value of the session considerably. Without an effective closing, many important issues discussed during the session may become blurred or lost. The closing phase requires thought and planning. If done well, members come away with a sense of completeness. Effective session closing can also help build cohesiveness, because members get to hear others' reactions.

The Closing Stage

Perhaps the most important point to remember when preparing for the closing stage of a group is that the group is not an entity in itself, but a collection of individuals. When the group is over, the individuals go away, taking with them new information, insights, decisions, or beliefs that make everyday living happier and more productive. The leader's task during the closing stage is to focus on these benefits.

Time Allowed for the Closing Stage

The amount of time allowed to complete the closing stage of a group depends on the kind of group, its purpose, the number of sessions, and the members' needs. As a general rule, the greater the number of sessions and the more personal the sharing, the longer the closing stage. For example, in a therapy group meeting for 2 hours weekly for 15 sessions, the leader might begin the closing stage toward the middle of the fourteenth session, because there will be a considerable amount to cover. In contrast, a task group working on improving a residential treatment program for drug abusers and meeting an hour each week for four sessions may require only 15 minutes of the last session for the closing stage. The closing stage of education and discussion groups would usually not take more than 10 to 20 minutes of the last session. Similarly, a children's self-concept group meeting for 40 minutes a week for five sessions may take only 10 to 15 minutes of the last session for closing. Although it is possible that the closing stage could take two or more sessions, the last session is usually enough time for closing.

Purpose and Goals of the Closing Stage

The purpose of the closing stage is to pull together the significant ideas, decisions, and personal changes experienced by the members during the group. This is a time for members to look at their progress in the group and to compare their goals at the start of the group with their accomplishments at the end. While the leader may focus to some extent on the dynamics of the group itself (such as how the members have interacted or how they have helped each other), the main focus for most groups will be on each member's growth and development. The following are the several tasks of the closing stage.

1. Reviewing and summarizing the group experience
2. Assessing members' growth and change
3. Finishing business
4. Applying change to everyday life (implementing decisions)
5. Providing feedback
6. Handling goodbyes
7. Planning for continued problem resolution

Reviewing and Summarizing the Group Experience   One of the first tasks during the closing stage of most groups is to review and summarize the significant developments of the group. The leader can accomplish the task of review and summary by: (1) summarizing the entire group, (2) getting members to summarize their experience, or (3) facilitating interaction that focuses on summarizing and reviewing. The first option can be used if there have not been many sessions and the leader remembers most of the significant events. If the group has met for a number of sessions, this might not be the best option because the leader may not remember some important topics or discussions. The second option, having the members summarize their experiences, can be valuable if the group is small and the summaries can be kept to 2 to 3 minutes each. If the group is large (10 or more), this is not usually a good option, because it would probably take too much time and become repetitive. The third option, which allows members to share what has stood out to them, is usually best.

■ EXAMPLE

It is the final session of a high school growth group.

LEADER: Because this is the last session, I want to spend the remainder of our time reviewing the group experience and how it has affected you. First, I want you to think of three things that stood out to you during the sessions. What discussions, exercises, or comments do you remember the most? *(Pause)* Sandi, you seem ready.

SANDI: The discussion about my mom and how I can deal with her better than I do. Focusing on the difference between being assertive and being aggressive was helpful. A third thing would be the discussion about taking risks to get more out of life.

PHILLIPE: The discussion concerning risk taking was the highlight for me. I think about that every day.

LEADER: Let me ask—was that a major insight for some others of you?

ARMAND: It was number one on my list, too. Whenever I am bored or afraid, I think over what risks I can take or remember that it is okay to be afraid when I am trying something new.

In this example, having members share what was important and periodically holding the focus on various topics is an excellent way to bring the group to a close.

■ ■ ■

Assessing Members' Growth and Change   This task applies to groups such as therapy groups, where the primary purpose is personal growth or change. By the time the closing stage rolls around, members should have experienced the implementation of some changes in their lives. One problem that members face when the group meetings end is that members may return to their former, less effective ways of living. It is important for the leader to highlight this potential problem for members and to reinforce their efforts to maintain positive change.

This can be done, in part, by getting members to evaluate their success in making changes. This assessment reinforces the changes and encourages members to pursue further growth and development.

■ **EXAMPLE**

The group is in the closing stage of a personal growth experience in a university counseling center.

LEADER: Since this is our last session, I think it might be helpful if each of you spent a few minutes looking at the changes you have brought about in your lives during these past 10 weeks. Some of you are more aware of your values and what you want to get from your life; others of you brought problems or concerns that you resolved through the group, and so forth. Take a minute and think about the important changes you've experienced in the group. When you are ready, I'm going to ask you to share those thoughts with the group.

This sharing can lead to feedback from other members, encouragement, and plans for continued work on issues following the end of the group.

■ ■ ■

Finishing Business   During the closing stage, it is common to have a few loose ends that still need to be tied up before the members can comfortably leave the group. It is important for the leader to allow time for this because unfinished business can interfere with the sense of closure and may leave one or more members with unresolved issues. Following are some examples of unfinished business that might come up during the closing stage:

- An issue or question that was brought up in a previous session but never dealt with
- Negative feelings about how the leader handled a particular situation during a session
- A question a member has for another member or for the leader
- A member needing to work on some unresolved personal issue

Although it is important to assess and handle unfinished business, the leader must be careful not to generate new business. For example, if a member expresses some dissatisfaction with how the leader handled a particular situation during an earlier session, the leader may simply want to accept the statement rather than get into a lengthy explanation or discussion. If a member wants or needs therapy on an unresolved issue, the leader may choose to refer the member for counseling or see the member after the session. Delving into new issues is seldom appropriate for the closing stage.

The following is an example of how a leader might introduce the topic of unfinished business.

LEADER: One thing that is important to do during this closing is to allow some time for any unfinished group business that needs to be dealt with. I am not asking for personal work issues because we are trying to close the group. If there is something that you want to say or ask, please do so. I urge you not to leave thinking, "I wish I had said this or that."

Applying Changes to Everyday Life
(Implementing Decisions)

Discussing how the members are going to continue to implement the changes that they have made is valuable. By talking about applying the changes in the group to their everyday lives, members can be reminded of how far they have come and what they still need to do to become the person they want to be. This applies especially to in-patient groups or treatment centers where they don't get to apply the changes to their "real" lives.

Providing Feedback During the closing stage, some final feedback to members is often helpful. Members should be given a chance to comment to one another about the changes each has made. Such reinforcement should be sincere and as specific as possible. The leader should monitor the type of feedback given to make sure it is on target.

LEADER: Let's spend a few minutes thinking of positive changes that you have seen in other members. I'd like you to pick three people who you feel have made some positive changes. I'll ask you to tell each person what the change is and how you think the change is helpful for the person. For example, Alan, I feel that you are much friendlier, and it is now much easier to talk with you.

■ ■ ■

LEADER: I want you to think about feedback that you feel would be helpful to give other members. You may want to think about changes that you have seen in members or thank them for something they said or did during a session.

■ ■ ■

Feedback can also be given to confront members who are still denying problems or who have not taken responsibility for their behavior. Such feedback, when given honestly and without anger or disappointment, can have an impact on a member who seems unwilling to face certain unresolved issues. Feedback may be given by the leader, the members, or both.

■ EXAMPLE

In a drug treatment group, a member who is still denying that his continued use of drugs is having a negative effect on his family life may benefit greatly from feedback sincerely given by the other members of the group.

SAM: Dave, even though you are fooling your family, your therapist, and even yourself by your continued use of drugs, you are not fooling us, because we've been there.

ANN: I agree, Dave, you really have to stop thinking that you don't have a problem. Face it, you have a drug problem! Even though this group is ending, I do hope you will decide to really get help.

In this example, the members can probably have more impact than the leader, because they are seen as peers who have struggled and dealt with a similar problem. In other situations, the leader is better able to give confrontive or negative feedback because he sees aspects of a member's behavior that the members do not see or because he knows the member better from having worked with him on an individual basis.

■   ■   ■

Handling Goodbyes   It is important for the leader to remember that for many members, the ending of a group is the end of a very special event in their lives. The relationships formed in the group may be the closest relationships some members have ever experienced. These members have especially strong feelings about the ending of the group. The leader should provide some time for those feelings to be expressed and for members to make final comments to each other. Members sometimes wish to exchange telephone numbers and addresses if they have not done so already.

Planning for Follow-Up Care   During the closing stage, it is the leader's responsibility to provide guidance, information, and the names and phone numbers of referral sources for any member who needs to continue working on personal concerns. For some, the best solution is involvement in another group experience. For others, individual, marital, or family counseling will be most helpful. Certain members may benefit most from joining a support group such as Alcoholics Anonymous.

Exercises to Use During the Closing Stage

Rounds   Rounds can be especially helpful during the closing stage. The round can be used to summarize key points, get overall reactions to the group or a particular experience, or check the degree to which members feel they accomplished personal goals. The leader might introduce closing rounds with one of the following questions:

- On a 1–10 scale, with 10 being *very satisfied,* how satisfied are you with your progress during this group?

- If you had to capture how you feel about your group experience in a sentence or two, what would you say? We'll do a round and hear from everyone.
- Because this is the last session, what is a word or phrase that expresses how you are feeling about the group ending?

Wishes   The wishes exercise provides a special type of feedback for members during the closing stage. We gave an example of this earlier for the closing phase, but it is also an excellent activity for the closing stage.

■ EXAMPLE

It is the last session of a support group for recently divorced persons.

LEADER: Let's take the next few minutes and see if there are any wishes you might have for one another. You may or may not have a wish. It's okay either way. I have a wish for Darlene. My wish for you is that you will be able to let go of your angry feelings toward your husband and get on with your life.

DARLENE: Thank you.

BILL: My wish for you, Jane, is that you realize your teenagers are old enough to help out around the house and that you can stop being their slave.

JOSEFA: I have a wish for you too, Jane. My wish for you is that you take a chance. You won't know whether you can build a new relationship if you don't try.

■ ■ ■

Reunion Fantasy   An excellent exercise to use in closing certain personal growth, support, counseling, and therapy groups is the Reunion Fantasy. The purpose of this exercise is to get members to project their lives into the future. Many members are startled to find that in their fantasies, they have the power to bring about significant changes. They are encouraged by this imagining process and gain confidence that their lives can change for the better. Conversely, members are also surprised to find that they are unable to imagine some of the changes they have worked for in the group. They realize the need for a greater commitment to change and that they must take more responsibility for their lives if change is to come about.

LEADER: I'd like you to relax. Close your eyes if that is comfortable for you. I want you to imagine that the time is 5 years from now; you have just gone to the mailbox and have received a letter from me inviting you back for a group reunion. In the letter, I explain that I have received a grant to cover all expenses. Now that you have

> decided to attend, I want you to think of what you will tell the
> other members about your life and any changes. Think about
> where you are living, with whom you are living, what you are
> doing, and any significant events that have occurred. *(The leader
> pauses to allow the members to experience the fantasy.)* What do you
> most want to say to the other members about your life now? In a
> minute, I am going to ask you to stand up and act like you are just
> seeing these people for the first time in 5 years, unless you
> remained in contact with some of them. Try to get into the role of
> having been apart for 5 years. *(Pause)* Okay, everyone open your
> eyes, stand and start milling and sharing.

This exercise can be very thought-provoking for members who have come to
know each other very well. As with all exercises, this one must be tailored to
the kind of group, its purpose, and the needs of the members as they experience
the group coming to an end. This exercise would be good to use during the
beginning part of the closing stage, because it would get members to think
about the group ending and the issues and changes they have talked about in
the group. (It can also be used during the middle stage of a group if the leader
wants to get members to focus on the future and possible changes.)

Members Writing About Their Experience   The leader may provide a chance
for members to write about some aspect of the group, either in their journals (if
journals were used) or on paper provided. The members may write on a variety
of topics: four or five things they learned, the most helpful experience for them
during the group, personal goals at the beginning of the group and the extent to
which each was achieved, and how decisions they made in the group will be
applied outside the group. The leader may then have members share their written thoughts in pairs, small groups, or with the entire group. If the topic the
members write about is lengthy or complex, the leader may ask each member
to underline two or three key passages to share with the entire group to save
time and maintain the focus. When using journals, members may also review
their journal entries from all the previous sessions and write a summary paragraph
that pulls together the key points of the group for them.

Using the Flipchart or Handouts   An excellent tool for reviewing, summarizing, and consolidating information is a flipchart or whiteboard. The flipchart can
be used to list points during the review and can be referred to as those points are
discussed. It also serves as an excellent focal point for the members, as they continually gaze at the flipchart and thus stay focused on the review. Writing on the
flipchart also gives members a chance to have direct input into the review and
summarizing process.

Handouts are a variation on the flipchart technique. They differ primarily in
that the leader has already summarized the key points. The advantage of the
handout is that it saves time and gets the members focused on the discussion
immediately. A handout may be particularly useful with discussion, education,

and task groups, because the leader can often easily summarize the various key points.

Additional Considerations for the Closing Stage

As the leader plans the closing stage of the group, there are a number of points to think about. Not every kind of group requires consideration of all these factors. It is the leader's responsibility to determine which of these considerations are relevant.

1. Dealing with feelings of separation
2. Guarding against ending with strong emotions
3. Helping members in their transition
4. Conducting exit interviews
5. Holding follow-up sessions
6. Evaluating the group
7. Ending with a party

Dealing with Feelings of Separation   Members need to say their goodbyes as the group comes to a close. For most members, this will go smoothly. However, for some, the ending of the group will elicit anxiety over separating from the others. The positive effect of the group may be lessened if the leader does not identify and deal with those feelings. Clues to such feelings might be found in statements from members like these:

- I couldn't sleep last night because I knew today would be our last meeting.
- I feel like this is my second family, and I don't want to leave it.
- I don't think I can make it without this group.

When the leader hears these comments, the first task is to help members realize that these feelings are normal and allow them to express their feelings of sadness or loss. Second, the leader might want to point out that the kind of sharing and closeness members feel toward one another need not be unique, although the positive sharing may have been a new experience. Also, if the leader knows that some members are going to have a tough time with the ending of the group, he may allow additional time during the closing stage to work with those members.

Guarding Against Ending with Strong Emotions   When closing a group where members have gotten very close, the leader will want to pay close attention to the emotional tone. The members may experience the ending as a very sad, intense, or extra-special event. If possible, these kinds of feelings should be avoided. Members should ideally see the ending as a new beginning, feeling positive about the group experience and excited about their future. The first example that follows depicts a leader talking about sad feelings regarding the ending of the group. The second example depicts a leader talking about the possibilities of ending on a "high."

■ EXAMPLES

LEADER: When we stop today, I know you might feel sad since this is the last group session. I hope you will realize that you can continue with the things you have learned in this group. I purposely will try to have us end with good feelings and not sadness, because I feel the group really has been a good experience for all of us. It has helped members to share and care, and I hope you have already started to create the same kind of sharing with significant others in your life.

■   ■   ■

The leader can prevent the false high phenomenon by presenting a positive, yet calm, attitude. To avoid ending on the "high," with much hugging and joyous crying, you might try to end groups that have been very close and personal by saying something like this:

LEADER: *(In a soft, rather neutral voice)* We are going to stop now. I do think the whole experience has been good, and the closing has been very good. I think you have had enough time to say what you wanted and to start a new beginning for yourself. If I can ever be of help, please feel free to contact me. I certainly have found the experience to be a good one. I think it is time to end.

■   ■   ■

Helping Members in Their Transition   A third consideration during the closing stage is the importance of helping members make a transition back into the "real world." Members must learn to employ their new information and knowledge about themselves with people in their daily lives. This is especially important for group members who have been clients in a residential treatment program for a period of time. Some members, such as those who have had addiction problems, need continued support and monitoring in the community. Many communities have a variety of support groups available either as independent organizations or through mental health centers, hospitals, or rehabilitation programs. The leader should include a discussion of the value of these groups during the closing stage.

In some types of groups, members may form support networks of their own to ensure continued reinforcement of one another, and they may plan "booster" meetings periodically to report on their progress. The need for this type of follow-up should be assessed by the leader in conjunction with the members. The entire group may be involved in the network, or members may choose one or more persons with whom to network. For members who ordinarily have difficulty developing and maintaining relationships, networking is very beneficial. Networking may also be a temporary measure for members who are new to a community or who have simply lost social contacts because of addictions or other problems. In some groups, time may be provided during the closing stage to develop individual plans for each member.

Conducting Exit Interviews   Earlier in this book, we discussed the value of interviewing potential group members before a group begins to establish rapport and exchange expectations about the group experience. There is also value in conducting exit interviews with members as the group enters the closing stage. Exit interviews are not needed in all groups; the leader must consider the value of such interviews with regard to the kind of group and the needs of individual members. If exit interviews are conducted, they should last from 10 to 20 minutes. We suggest that they take place either before the final session of the group or very soon after the last session. The reason for meeting before the last session is that the leader can suggest how the member might use the closing stage to her benefit, such as requesting additional feedback from other members. The exit interview can also be a time for the leader to reinforce the gains a member has made, as well as to focus more individual attention on ways the member can apply those gains to everyday living. The interview further gives the leader a chance to ask for feedback about the group and various aspects of his leadership. Depending on the kind of group, some members may feel more comfortable giving the leader feedback on a one-to-one basis.

Holding Follow-Up Sessions   The leader may consider holding a follow-up session of the group several weeks or months after the final regular session. The decision to have one or more follow-up meetings depends on the kind of group and the members' needs. For example, members of a task group who work together in the same organization may wish to have a follow-up session to assess how things are going. With some support or counseling groups, follow-up sessions give members a chance to share how they are doing and lessen the anxiety of separation. The leader may set up a formal follow-up program where members are notified and encouraged to return for a meeting. Occasionally, members decide they want to plan for a reunion in 6 months. This decision usually arises from the good feelings members have toward one another during the closing stage.

Experience suggests that these reunions are usually not very successful, because the feelings fade as time passes and members become involved in their own lives. If a reunion is planned, the leader should not feel disappointed by a small turnout, and members should be prepared for the experience to be very different from when they were meeting regularly.

One unique follow-up procedure that we use is to have members write themselves letters in which they assess their goals, give themselves feedback, and list plans for the future. The letters are given to the leader in a self-addressed, stamped envelope and are then mailed several weeks or months after the group has ended. Members have reported that this technique is powerful.

They say that writing the letter is thought- provoking, and knowing that it will come in the mail someday causes them to keep working even after the group has ended. Others have said that often their letter arrived at a good time, because they needed a "booster shot." The letter exercise is designed for use in a personal growth, counseling, or therapy group, but it could also be used with a task group as a way for members to check on the degree to which they have followed through on their decisions.

Evaluating the Group   When any group ends, the leader must decide how she will evaluate the experience. Groups can be evaluated formally, with a question-naire, or informally, with the leader asking specific questions during the closing stage. No matter how the evaluation is done, the leader should seek answers to the following questions:

- How valuable was the experience? (The leader could use a 1–10 scale.)
- What did members like about the group?
- What did members dislike about the group?
- What did members like about the way the leader led the group?
- What did members dislike about the way the leader led the group?
- How could the group have been better?

These are just the basic questions that should be asked. Certainly a more elabo-rate questionnaire could be devised that asked about specific topics, exercises, and events that occurred during the group. We encourage leaders, especially begin-ning leaders, to evaluate any group they lead. The responses and comments from their members can be very helpful in leading future groups.

Ending with a Party   Often members want to end the group with a party. They may suggest meeting at someone's house or meeting for pizza. The leader should give a good deal of thought to such a request; often, when the group meets in another setting, a group session never really takes place and thus no real closing occurs. If the leader and the group decide to meet in a setting like this, the leader will want to tell members ahead of time that the first hour or so will be devoted to closing the group.

A variation of this is for the group to plan a party to be held after the group has officially ended. Sometimes this type of party works fine, and other times it does not work out very well. We suggest that the leader at least prepare mem-bers for the possibility that the party may not go well.

Concluding Comments

The *closing phase* is a very important phase of a session and is often mishandled because the leader has not managed the time of the session very well. The clos-ing phase serves the purpose of reviewing a session and ensuring that members leave feeling reasonably "finished." When a leader fails to plan for the closing phase, closing is either hurried or skipped, causing the members to leave with no closure. It is very important to have a closing phase to each session.

The *closing stage* of a group is the last stage—it is when the group is winding down and preparing to stop meeting. The closing stage is usually a portion of the last session, the entire last session, or perhaps, the last two sessions. Its purpose is to bring closure to the experience.

The closing phase and the closing stage are each very important aspects of a group because they allow members to review what has happened and to commit to what they are going to do in the future. Also, closing is an important time for reflecting on the group, and giving and receiving feedback. During the closing stage, it is important for the members to assess their progress, evaluate the experience, and discuss follow-up support.

There are a number of skills, techniques, and exercises that are useful during closing. Rounds are very helpful because they tend to get everyone to speak, and it is important to hear reactions from the quieter members. Writing as a part of closing has proved to be quite valuable for many different kinds of groups. Cutting off is essential because members tend to tell stories or bring up new topics.

■ ACTIVITIES

1. Think back to group experiences or classes that you had where there was no time for closing. What did it feel like to have the experience just end? What would have made the ending better for you?
2. List the skills and techniques you plan to use in the closing phase and stage of groups that you will be leading in the future.

GROUP COUNSELING SKILLS

View again the three segments (15.1, 15.2, 15.3) showing closing in a group, and think about different directions the group could have gone if the leader had not had closing skills. Also think of some other ways these groups could have been closed.

Chapter 16

Dealing with Problem Situations

When leading groups, a leader must be prepared to deal with any number of situations. In this chapter, we identify many of the most common problems that arise and provide examples to illustrate some skills and techniques for handling these situations. We have identified the following 13 common problems:

1. The chronic talker
2. The dominator
3. The distracter
4. The rescuing member
5. The negative member
6. The resistant member
7. The member who tries to "get the leader"
8. Dealing with silence
9. Dealing with sexual feelings
10. Dealing with crying
11. Dealing with mutually hostile members
12. Asking a member to leave
13. Dealing with prejudiced, narrow-minded, or insensitive members

It is important to remember that the behavior of all these types of group members has a goal. That is, problematic behaviors of group members hold true to the Adlerian concept that all behavior is purposeful (Sonstegard, & Bitter, 2004). Typically, the behavior is attention seeking, seeking power, seeking revenge, or a display of inadequacy. If the leader can work to understand the purposefulness of the member's behavior, she can more easily decide the most appropriate avenue for dealing with the difficult situation.

The Chronic Talker

It is not difficult to spot the chronic talker. He is often characterized by persistent rambling and repetition. When a chronic talker is present, other members who have concerns that they would like to discuss are prevented from doing so. Soon the group members either tune out the chronic talker and lose interest in the proceedings or get frustrated and angry with both the talkative member and the leader. Depending on the reason underlying his talkativeness, the chronic talker falls into three different types: the nervous member, the rambler, and the show-off.

1. *The nervous member* talks to hide his feelings of nervousness or as a means of self-control. Easily recognized, the nervous member is often the first one to answer questions posed by the leader and the first to volunteer for some task. Because the nervous member is talking to alleviate anxiety, he will talk frequently and for as long as the leader lets him.

2. *The rambler* dominates discussions because she is simply a talkative person and is unaware of the effect her rambling has on others. She is also easily recognized because she tells long, drawn-out stories and sometimes repeats herself. The stories are often trivial and are not usually meaningful to others.

3. *The show-off* is a talkative person because he is insecure and wants to impress the group leader, other members, or both. The show-off seems to be attempting to show others what he knows. In doing so, he answers all questions, asks irrelevant questions in an effort to grab the leader's attention, and may offer unsolicited advice to other group members. The other members often resent this and grow to dislike this type of member. The problem with the show-off is that he can quickly divert the group from its intended purpose.

Handling the Talkative Member

To determine whether or not a member should be seen as a chronic talker, the leader should consider the following questions:

- For how long has the member been talking?
- How many comments has the member made compared with other group members?
- Are the member's comments in line with the intended purpose of the group?
- Is this member preventing others from talking?

- Are others becoming bored or irritated with the member's comments?
- Does the member seem to be talking because of nervousness or a desire to impress others?

There are several ways to handle a talkative member. For example, upon recognizing such a member, the leader could have members form dyads, making sure she pairs herself with the talkative member. In the dyad, the leader could attempt to speak to the member about his "talkativeness." The advantage of this strategy is that the talkative member receives the message about his talkativeness from only one person, thus causing less embarrassment.

There are a couple of strategies that involve the whole group. One is to address the group with the hope that the talkative member hears the message. The other strategy involves seeking feedback from the members.

■ EXAMPLES

It is early in the life of the group, and the leader wants to curb the rambler's talking but at the same time not seem critical of the member. Therefore, the leader decides to deliver the message to the entire group by looking at everyone as she speaks.

LEADER: It is important to keep in mind that the purpose of the group is for *everyone* to share thoughts and feelings. If any one member gets too long-winded, the focus of the group changes from sharing to listening to one member. Please be aware of how much you are talking and whether or not you are dominating the discussion.

■ ■ ■

In this example, the leader introduces a feedback exercise because she believes members want to confront the talkative member.

LEADER: As I stated in the beginning of this group, one of the most potentially helpful aspects of a group such as this is for members to receive feedback about themselves from other members of the group. In effect, this feedback acts as a mirror, letting you know how others in the group see and react to you. Is there anyone here who would like to give another member some feedback?

The leader would use this kind of opening to a feedback exercise only if she were confident that members wanted to share their feelings about a member's excessive talking. If the leader felt that members would not speak up unless the leader did, a feedback exercise could be devised in which the leader could also give feedback to the rambling member. Sometimes members will offer feedback without being prompted to do so. When this happens, the leader merely needs to make sure that the member receiving the feedback doesn't feel attacked.

■ ■ ■

If the leader is about to ask the group a question and is sure that a talkative member will again speak up and attempt to dominate the discussion, the leader might say something like, "I'm going to ask a question, and I would like to hear from some of you who haven't talked yet." The leader should say this while avoiding eye contact with the talkative member. These techniques may stop the dominating member and draw out comments from members who have been silent. At times the leader unknowingly perpetuates a particular member's talking by maintaining eye contact with him and nodding her head as that member speaks. Maintaining eye contact usually reinforces the member's talking.

One direct way of intervening with the talkative member is to speak to the member immediately after the session or sometime before the next session about his excessive talking.

■ EXAMPLE

LEADER: *(Talking to a member after the session has ended)* Wanda, tell me if I'm wrong, but you seemed a bit nervous during the group tonight. You were repeating yourself a lot as you talked, and you talked very rapidly.

WANDA: Yes, you're right. I was hoping that no one would notice. I just get uptight every time I'm around a new group of people. It is something that I definitely want to work on.

■ ■ ■

Another strategy that could be used if the leader were having the members turn in any kind of written reactions to the group would be to give the member feedback in writing. (In therapy and growth groups, members often write a brief reaction at the end of each session.) For example, the leader might write the following feedback at the bottom of the member's reaction:

> Tom, I sense that you are uncomfortable because you talked quite a bit and at a very rapid pace. I am hoping that you will be a little more comfortable and thus talk a little less. Let me know if there is anything that I can do to help you feel more comfortable.

Members usually receive this message very well and become more cognizant of their talkative behavior. In addition, a note such as this often helps members feel more comfortable about talking to the leader outside the group. This is a non-threatening way to offer feedback; however, there is no guarantee that the member receiving the feedback will respond favorably to it, and if the member reads it somewhere outside the group, no one will be there to help process the feedback.

 GROUP COUNSELING SKILLS: Dealing with a Talkative Member

Review segment 8.2 and watch how the leader has to twice deal with the very talkative member.

The Dominator

The dominator is a member who tries to rule the group. This member is different from the chronic talker because this person wants to run things and be in control. This kind of member is fairly common in residential treatment settings and in school groups. In education, discussion, or task groups, a dominator is often present. The leader should try some of the different techniques suggested for dealing with the chronic talker; however, the leader quite often needs to meet with this kind of member privately to discuss his behavior in the group. Sometimes this kind of member can be used as a helper or be given a role that makes him feel special. Other times, the behavior is such that he has to be asked to leave the group because he is not willing to give control to the leader.

The Distracter

The distracter is a member who is either seeking attention or is avoiding looking at herself. To accomplish this, she tries to get the group off task by bringing up unrelated subjects or asking questions that are not relevant. Some distracters make noises or move around as a way to distract members. This person is often found in school or residential groups, and in groups that are not voluntary. Sometimes this member is very difficult to deal with because she is not intentionally trying to distract the group. Talking with the member and then ignoring her comments or behaviors often helps to minimize the effects of the distracter.

The Rescuing Member

Rescuing is the attempt of a member to smooth over negative feelings experienced by another member of the group. When a member becomes upset, often other group members attempt to soothe the member with such statements as, "Now, don't worry, it will be all right" or "Everything has a way of working itself out if you just give it time." This is usually not helpful, and such comments often sound patronizing. Rescuing can prevent the member in pain from problem solving.

■ EXAMPLES

One of the members, Judy, cries as she tells the group about her upcoming divorce. As she does so, another member, Karen, attempts to rescue her.

KAREN: Don't worry Judy, everything will be okay. I went through a divorce myself, and you just have to make the best of it. I think...

LEADER: *(Interrupting Karen in mid-sentence)* Judy, you are in a lot of pain right now, and if you would like, we can listen and try to be of help. By sharing, I think you will at least get some of your thoughts out, and I think that you will feel our support. *(Judy nods that she would like to.)*

LEADER: *(After Judy has discussed her divorce and using a kind voice)* I'd like to say something to all of you here. Usually when a member is struggling with some issue like a divorce, she doesn't need our sympathy or advice as much as she needs to be listened to and supported.

Members often think they are being supportive when, in fact, they are trying to rescue the member. Teaching members how helping and sharing differ from rescuing is important as the group progresses. In the early life of the group, the leader may need to intervene quite often, because group members are not aware of their rescuing behaviors. In the preceding example, the leader decides to convey the message about sympathy being unhelpful to the entire group so that they could observe her modeling the correct method of being therapeutic in the group.

■ ■ ■

This group is a stress management group composed of first-year teachers. One of the members, Vivian, is upset with her husband. Another member hears this and gives her sympathy and pity.

VIVIAN: It is so stressful being a first-year teacher and juggling all the things with the kids and the house. My husband is always on me about the house and the kids, but it is hard to get it all done. I am trying but sometimes I just can't get to the laundry or the cleaning, and then he doesn't have a shirt to wear. I feel so bad. I feel so lucky to have met such a good person who doesn't drink or yell that often. I just feel like a failure on all fronts—I am not pleasing him and I am not being a good mom or a good teacher. *(Starts to tear up)*

ROSE: Vivian, things will get better. The school year is nearly half over and we all will know so much more about teaching next year. I think you're doing a good job. I like teaching with you when we have those joint classes. Don't the rest of you think Vivian is a good teacher?

LEADER: *(With a slow, kind voice)* Wait just a second. I don't think this is really about whether Vivian is a good teacher, but more about the self-talk that is going on in her head. Vivian, would you like to understand more about where your stress is coming from?

■ ■ ■

The Negative Member

A negative member is one who constantly complains about the group or disagrees with other members of the group. Negative members are particularly troublesome because their attitude and behavior counter the leader's goal of maintaining a positive working tone. If one or two members are negative and begin to complain, other members will sometimes join in and also become negative. The group sessions may become gripe sessions, and very little is accomplished.

There are three possible strategies for dealing with the negative member:

1. Talk to the person outside the group and attempt to establish why he is so negative. The leader can even ask for the member's cooperation in making the group productive. Sometimes such members simply want the leader's attention or a role to play in the group. By talking to the member, the leader can offer a positive role to the negative member.

2. Identify the allies (positive group members) in the group and direct questions and comments to them. Getting these members to talk more than the negative members can help to establish a more positive tone in the group.

3. When asking the group a question, avoid eye contact with the negative person so that you do not draw her out.

Leaders should usually avoid confronting a negative member in front of the other group members. This confrontation can turn into an argument between the leader and the negative member, which would not be productive for the other group members. If the leader finds herself in any kind of argumentative situation, she should shift the focus to another person or topic and then talk to the negative member at the end of the group.

It is important to remember that groups will at times have one or two negative members. This is especially true at the beginning of a group and particularly so if the group is a mandatory one. Many times negativism diminishes as the group becomes more interesting. However, there will be times that, no matter what the leader does, a member will remain negative. In extreme cases, it may be necessary to ask the member to leave the group or to sit quietly. Leaders often devote far too much time trying to work with a negative member while ignoring those members who are interested in the group.

GROUP COUNSELING SKILLS: Dealing with Negative Members

Review segment 1.1 and watch how the leader dealt poorly with negative members. Then watch 1.2 and see how the leader better handled negative members.

The Resistant Member

Some members are resistant because they are forced to be in the group. Sometimes these members will work through their resistance if they are given a chance to express their anger. This situation is difficult for the leader, because he does not know whether allowing the member to express anger will be of benefit or if the member will merely complain and set a negative tone for the group. However, it is essential for the leader to pay attention when a member is seemingly working through her resistance.

Four examples of resistant members would be:

1. The member who, during the first meeting, says he does not know why he has to be at the meeting and does not see how the group can be helpful

2. The member who comes and sits with her arms crossed and does not contribute unless forced to—and then says as little as possible

3. The member who always tries to focus the group on topics not relevant to the group, such as movies, sports, or the latest fashions

4. The member who is not resisting the group but is resistant to changing something about himself

Some members have negative expectations about the effectiveness of a group. These members believe that the group will not be helpful, and therefore, they refuse to participate cooperatively. If the leader is faced with a resistant member, her two primary strategies are to let the member share his feelings in the group or to talk to him in a dyad or after the session and try to help him work through his resistance. If neither of these works and the member has to remain in the group because of the setting (such as a residential treatment center), the leader will want to be sure *not to focus* on that member. A common mistake of leaders is to devote as much as half of each session trying to break down members' resistance.

Sometimes a resistant member appears to be opposed to the leader's attempt to be helpful but not to the members' attempts. If this seems to be the case, the leader may want to set up situations in which the member can share with other members of the group. This can be done through the use of dyads, triads, and small-group discussions without the direct participation of the leader. Or if the member is the focus of the group, the leader lets the members do the majority of the helping.

Conversely, the resistant member may oppose the attempts of the members to be helpful but not the leader's attempts. If this is the case, individual counseling within the group or privately may be the best way to help the member.

It is important that the leader distinguish between the member who is resisting the group process and the member who is resistant because she does not want to change something about herself or her situation.

■ EXAMPLE

Angela has been discussing being a mother and having a career. She has stated that she wants to continue her career but doesn't know what to do with her children during the day.

JACKIE: Could you leave them at a day care center?

ANGELA: Yes, but I'm not so sure that is a good place for them.

TODD: Does your company have a program for taking care of employees' children?

ANGELA: Yes, but I don't like some of the children and workers there.

FRANCES: Do you have relatives nearby who would be willing to care for them?

ANGELA: Yes, but I hate to impose.

In a case like this, the leader should realize that the member is resistant to or hesitant about hearing suggestions. One way to deal with this resistance would be to say something like the following:

LEADER: Angela, I think we understand the concern, but I am not sure how we can be of help here in the group. What would be helpful to you?

■ ■ ■

Another way to handle resistance in many groups is to focus on the resistant member in an indirect manner, as described in Chapter 14. That is, the leader may work with a more willing member with the intent of helping the resistant member learn something by watching. Conducting therapy in this manner takes the direct focus off the resistant member. The important thing to remember is not to spend too much time with the resistant member if it takes productive time away from the other group members.

The Member Who Tries to "Get the Leader"

When leading a group, a leader needs to be prepared for what we call "get the leader." This occurs when a member attempts to sabotage what the leader is saying or doing in the group. Get the leader can take the form of disagreeing with the leader, not following through with instructions given by the leader, asking unanswerable questions to make the leader look bad, or talking to others while the leader is talking. This member is different from the negative member in that the member is truly after the leader.

There are a variety of reasons for members to want to get the leader. Often the reasons can be traced to something said or done by the leader that caused the member to become irritated or embarrassed. The following is a list of some leader behaviors that might cause members to want to get the leader:

- Putting a member on the spot in front of the other members
- Cutting off a member inappropriately (or even appropriately)

- Not giving a member the chance to talk or failing to recognize when a member wants to speak
- Telling a member that the group will come back to his issue or concern and then failing to do so
- Allowing the group members to offer too much negative feedback to a particular member
- Not being skilled enough to control the group
- Allowing the group to be boring because of the leader's lack of skill

Although the leader is often the cause of get-the-leader behavior in the group, there are other possible causes.

- Members who are not self-referred sometimes take out their frustrations and anger on the leader.
- Members sometimes project their fears about being in the group onto the leader.
- Members who have struggled in their relationships with authority figures might attempt to spoil the leader's efforts.
- Members sometimes want to be the leader's "favorite" and react angrily when they don't feel that they are.

Probably the first thing a leader should do when she realizes that a member is trying to get her is to shift the focus away from any power struggle between the member and herself.

■ EXAMPLES

LEADER: I'd like us to begin today's session by talking about how drinking has affected your family life.

JOE: Why do you always pick the topics? I thought this was *our* group. Tell me!

LEADER: *(Speaking in a calm voice while making eye contact with all the members, using no extra eye contact with Joe in order to try to discourage Joe from additional comments)* Let me explain to all of you how I decide on the topics. Also, be aware that if there is a topic or something that you would like to discuss, you can let me know. There are a number of topics that I feel we should cover....

■　■　■

LEADER: I would like each of you to close your eyes and try to imagine that...

LYNN: *(Interrupting)* Are you going to do another one of those stupid fantasy exercises? What good are they?

LEADER: Lynn, feel free to sit quietly. *(To the other members)* I want you to close your eyes and imagine that you are an animal....

■　■　■

Once the leader has sidestepped the member's attempt to get him, he should try to understand why the member has targeted him. Often, the leader knows why it happened, and if the problem can be corrected by such techniques as paying more attention to the member, going back to the member's issue, or making sure not to put the member on the spot, then the leader should make the correction. If the leader does not understand why the member has targeted him, he might choose to pair up in a dyad with the member or talk to the member at the end of the session to see if he can gain some information. He might say something like, "Something seems to be going on between you and me. Is it anything I said or did that upset you?"

If the member does not want to share his thoughts, the leader might be able to gain some insight from talking to other members. Often a member will share disgruntled thoughts with a fellow member but not with the leader. If the leader seeks information from other members, he must be very careful to ensure that the members do not feel any pressure to share something they feel they should not share. This may happen in school or residential settings where the counselor interacts with the members on a regular basis.

If a member persists in trying to sabotage the leader and the leader has talked to the member, the leader may get help from the group by asking for feedback about the member's complaints or behavior. The leader would do this only if he knew he had the support and understanding of all, or nearly all, the other members. The leader could ask the entire group, "Do you like the way the group is going and the activities I ask you to do?" Or he could be more specific: "I would like some feedback. Whenever I suggest anything, Cleve always wants to argue with or question me. How do the rest of you feel about Cleve's doing that?" Assuming the leader receives a favorable response from either of these feedback questions, the member should see that he is alone in his attacks or that the other members are annoyed with his behavior.

We hope this discussion has alerted you to the existence of this phenomenon and has given you some ways of dealing with it. Too many beginning leaders fail to recognize "get the leader" and misread it as resistance or negativism, when in fact it is something that they either caused or can change with a slight adjustment. However, there are times when there is almost nothing the leader can do to stop the member other than removing that member from the group.

Dealing with Silence

There are both productive and nonproductive silences in a group. Productive silence occurs when members are internally processing something that was said or done in the group. Nonproductive silence occurs when members are quiet because they are confused about what to say, fearful of talking, or bored. When the group is silent, the leader should ask herself if the silence is productive.

The leader can usually tell by observing the members' reactions as they are sitting there and also by considering what has just occurred in the group. If the members seem deep in thought as a result of someone's intense work, the silence should be allowed. Sometimes the leader may allow the silence to last for 1 or 2 minutes if it appears to be productive. The leader may choose to wait until someone else breaks the silence, or she may choose to break the silence by saying something like, "Many of you seem to really be thinking about what just happened. I'd like you to briefly share your thoughts." However, if the members are silent because they are not interested, then the silence should signal the leader to change the focus or address the group about their lack of interest.

Sometimes members are silent at the beginning of a session because they are not yet warmed up to the session. It can be a mistake to let silence occur at the beginning of the session, because what the members really need is some discussion or activity to get them started. This goes back to what we have said about the importance of leading the group rather than waiting for the members to take charge. Sometimes the wait is very long and not productive.

If the members have nervous or blank looks on their faces, wondering who will start, we suggest that the leader break the silence after 15 or 20 seconds to get the group started. Some experts feel very differently about this and let a group sit in silence for 5 to 10 minutes in the belief that the members should be responsible for what happens in the group. For the most part, we have found this to be counterproductive. In groups where this has occurred, many members have reported that they were confused about what was going on and were bored sitting there waiting for something to happen. It can also promote verbal attacks among members. We feel that in situations where the members are not really thinking, the group time usually can be better spent when the leader breaks the silence with a question, a round, or an exercise that is relevant and productive.

When the leader feels the silence is being very productive and a member starts to speak, the leader can say to the member, "Let's wait just a few more seconds. People seem to really be thinking."

Dealing with Sexual Feelings

Sometimes group members are sexually attracted to other members, especially in therapy, growth, and support groups where members share on a personal level. Certain group dynamics may emerge when this occurs. Members may try to impress each other; they may hold back sharing because of another; or they may become jealous, hurt, or angry at what another member is sharing. These kinds of dynamics can be detrimental to the group process, but a leader must keep in mind that sexual attraction can and will occur. There is nothing the leader can do about it, and, in fact, leaders will not want to act as moral legislators. Some leaders set a ground rule that members cannot relate to one another outside the group. Our observation is that members are going to do this regardless of the rule, so a better strategy is to talk about how this can become a problem.

At times members form relationships that do not interfere with the group; other times outside relationships do cause problems. If a situation has arisen that is hindering the group (such as two people dating or one person being interested in another member who is not reciprocating), the leader may choose to talk privately to the person or persons involved about possible solutions to the problem. Other times, the issue can be brought up in the group, especially if other members feel that the relationship is disrupting the group in some way. This may not be easy to handle, but the leader should not ignore these situations. Sometimes, having one of the members drop out of the group is the best solution.

Dealing with Crying

Members may cry at any time during the group. They may cry when they or someone else talks about topics such as low self-esteem, abuse, the death of a loved one, a divorce of their own or of their parents, the loss of a job, an illness, or moving from one place to another. The tears may range from moisture in the eyes (tearing up) to uncontrollable sobbing and may indicate a range of emotions from sadness to fear, anger, depression, emptiness, confusion, anxiety, and even happiness.

Some leaders who notice that a member is starting to cry immediately try to help the member with the pain before getting a contract to do so. Often, members are not ready to discuss what they are feeling, so when the leader tries to help those not ready to share, the member feels pressure, which may lead to resentment. The leader should always be sure the member wants to work on the problem and that there is enough time to adequately deal with the emotions of the member. A common mistake that beginning leaders make when they notice a member tearing up is to focus on that member without considering how much time is left in the session. They then find themselves having to cut short the work with that person in order to end the session at the designated stopping time. Naturally, if someone is in pain, the leader will want to be sensitive to that person, but he also needs to be aware of the time.

If time is not a factor, the leader may pair up with the member in pain to find out more about the pain. To occupy the other members, the leader would have them get into dyads and process what they were just discussing or some other topic that the leader thinks is relevant. The leader could also acknowledge the pain and suggest to the member that they talk after the group.

Another important consideration when a member is crying is whether the crying is a result of some struggle or painful event or is an attempt to gain sympathy. Some group members naturally feel sorry for the person and reach out and touch the person who is crying. Members can usually not distinguish who is genuinely struggling with some painful issue and who wants to be rescued. Often, it is appropriate to ask a member not to touch or hug another member who is feeling sorry for himself or playing a "poor-me" game. Hugging or touching that member would not be therapeutic.

In some groups, such as educational or discussion groups or even some experiential groups, dealing for any length of time with a member in psychological pain is not appropriate. If the leader observes that someone is beginning to cry, he may want to shift the focus away from that member and then seek her out after the group. Or the leader may want to say something like, "Martina, I can see that you are in some pain. Let's talk after the group." When leading education, discussion, or task groups, beginning leaders often make the mistake of holding the focus on the person in pain, thus creating confusion in the members who are expecting a different kind of group. In a therapy group where crying is appropriate, the leader may say something like: "I notice you are tearing up/crying; is there something you would like to work on in group today?"

■ EXAMPLES

This group is composed of cancer patients. One of the members, Wanda, is discussing her failing health.

WANDA: Some days are better than others. I try to keep a positive attitude about the whole thing, and I succeed if I feel good that day. Today, I've felt bad. *(She begins to cry.)* It's on these days that I wonder if I'm gonna make it.

JERRY: *(Sitting next to her, he puts his arm around her shoulders and attempts to comfort her.)* Wanda, let it out if you need to. I don't think it helps to always try to keep up a positive image.

In this example, Wanda was genuinely struggling with a life-and-death issue. It is perfectly acceptable for Jerry to touch her.

■ ■ ■

LESLIE: *(In a little girl voice)* They just never let me grow up. Just like this past Christmas. I wanted to go to the mountains to ski, but my mother said that I should come home because my grandparents were going to be there. They make me so mad. *(Starts to cry)* And they also hurt my feelings. My dad said that I was selfish and that I only think of myself. I just wish they would learn to accept me and stop trying to make me a clone of them. *(Carey starts to put her arm around Leslie.)*

LEADER: *(In a calm, soft voice)* Carey, don't do that. Leslie, I am wondering if we can get the thinking part of you to deal with this issue? Right now, I sense that you are coming more from the hurt, angry part.

■ ■ ■

One of the biggest mistakes that leaders make when a member begins to cry over some painful issue is to allow the other group members to ask a series of irrelevant questions. In the last example, some members might have responded to Leslie's statement in the following ways:

- Where do your parents live?
- How many grandchildren do your grandparents have?
- How often do you visit?

Those of you who have led groups know how group members can divert the central focus of the group by asking such irrelevant and untimely questions, often out of discomfort and a desire to stop the crying. When this occurs, the leader must step in and cut off the questions.

A member may also start to cry during the first or second session, before the group is ready to deal with an intense emotional concern. Many times a member will be ready to delve into his concern. However, the leader needs to be careful in this situation, because sometimes members become frightened by the emotional intensity and do not return. During the first and second sessions, a leader should be cautious about how much pain and emotion she lets members express. If the majority of the group seems ready, then it can be valuable to let a member get into his intense pain.

Dealing with Mutually Hostile Members

In any kind of group, there is the possibility of a member disliking another member. This dislike may manifest itself in arguments, disagreements, and silence between members. Sometimes members begin the group disliking each other because of something that happened before the group began. If possible, this should be checked out by the leader during the screening interview by asking, "Is there anyone whom you dislike and would not want to be in the group with you?" However, this is not a foolproof method for preventing members from disliking each other because even members who do not know each other at the beginning of the group can quickly grow to dislike each other as the group progresses. When this occurs, the leader may want to address the issue in the group if she feels that such a discussion would be beneficial. Often members' behavior within the group is indicative of their behavior outside the group. Thus, focusing on the process of how members came to dislike each other can be one of the most beneficial discussions for them in terms of helping them become more accepting of others in their daily lives. Helping members come to terms with each other can also potentially be one of the most productive processes for solidifying the group and building group cohesion. However, there will be times when, no matter what happens in the group, members will not overcome their personal dislike for each other. Rather than getting members to like each other, the goal is to get the members not to let their dislike for another completely interfere with their benefiting from the group experience.

If the leader decides to focus on a major conflict between two members during a group session, we suggest that the leader meet privately with each of the conflicting members to identify the issues clearly and explain the reason for wishing to deal with it in the group. This individual contact between the leader and each member should also be used to build additional rapport and enlist the cooperation of the members. Without getting a commitment from each member to work toward a resolution of the issue, the leader is setting the stage for a potential disaster. If the leader confronts the members unexpectedly, either or both members may use the group as a major battleground.

■ EXAMPLE

Two members of a group in a residential treatment center for adolescents are in a power struggle over control issues in the center. The leader has the option of switching either member into another therapy group, but decides to try to help them work on their issues. The leader meets with each member individually and then opens the session as follows:

LEADER: Today I'm hoping we can spend some time dealing with an issue that's important to all of us. As you know, Jack and Phillip have had some problems with each other. I talked to each of them and got them to agree to try and work some things out in the group. *(The leader then turns to the two members to get confirmation.)*

JACK: Yeah, I agree to try.

PHILLIP: It's okay with me.

LEADER: Okay, I guess I'd like to start by asking the rest of you what you see as the cause of the problems between Jack and Phillip.

MOE: They each think they are right and can't stand it if the other is right.

PETE: They are always trying to one-up each other. Jack is a pretty good listener when anyone but Phillip is talking. When Phillip talks, Jack, you don't listen to him at all.

JACK: He doesn't listen to me. When I was talking about my dad, he said I was stupid!

LEADER: So wait a minute. Some of your anger, Jack, is over the thing Phillip did when you were talking about your dad? How do others of you deal with someone who has done something upsetting to you?

In this example, the leader chooses to allow the other members to provide feedback and will gradually involve these two members as the discussion continues. Instead of focusing on specific complaints, focusing on the general topic of conflict resolution and ways of dealing with anger may be the most productive direction. Later in the session, examples provided by the two members in conflict may be used to demonstrate how differences can be handled. The leader is not avoiding the conflict between these members by this approach. On the contrary, the leader is assuming they lack good techniques for resolving their power struggle and must be taught such techniques before their efforts can be successful.

■   ■   ■

When members don't like each other, the leader may be able to prevent any further growth of animosity by using dyads and exercises. Placing members who dislike each other in pairs or having them complete an exercise together may only serve as a battleground for their dislike toward one another. On the other hand, forcing antagonistic members to work together may help them bridge their differences. Sometimes leaders find it effective to pair the two members who dislike each other and then join the dyad to help them talk through their dislikes.

If the dislike is so great that it is interfering with the group, one or both members should be removed from the group if possible and placed in a different group. In addition, if this type of behavior seems to be a pattern for a particular member, perhaps the member is not ready for a group and would benefit more from individual counseling.

Asking a Member to Leave

Although asking a member to leave the group is not a regular occurrence, it is an option that leaders need to understand and be willing to implement. There are several reasons a leader would ask a member to leave, such as being very negative, hostile, or resistant. A leader may also ask a member to leave the group because her needs may be so contrary to the purpose of the group that she would receive no benefit from it. For example, if a member of a parent education group kept bringing up personal problems dealing with her self-concept, marriage, and weight, it would be best if that member were not a part of that group. After determining that a member should not be a part of the group, the leader must next consider how and when to tell that member. Sometimes the task can be quite easy. For example, the leader could meet with the member after the group and say something like the following:

LEADER: Teresa, it seems that the things you really need from a group are not what this group is about. Maybe you have even wondered whether or not this group could be helpful to you. Given that your needs will not be served by this group, I think it might be best if we found you another alternative. Perhaps we could locate a more appropriate group for you or refer you to someone whom you could see on an individual basis. What do you think?

Another reason for asking a member to leave is that he has been very disruptive. Certainly there must be attempts to bring the disruptive member under control before asking the member to leave. However, if the member continues to disrupt and intrude on the rights of the other members, the leader should ask that member to leave the group. Ideally, it is best to do so at the end of a session or during a dyad. This prevents a power struggle from occurring in front of the other members. For example, at the end of a session, the leader could say, in private, something like:

LEADER: *(Calmly)* Patty, I must speak to you very frankly for a moment. Whether or not you are aware of it, you are disrupting the group to the point that I'm afraid the other members are not receiving any benefit. All attempts to halt your disruption have been to no avail. I think it would be best if you did not return. It is my responsibility to refer you to another group or to an individual therapist, and I will be glad to do so.

If the disruption is so severe that waiting until a break or the end of the group is not possible, the leader must act immediately so that the session may resume and be of benefit to the other members. In this case, the leader must explain the action to the entire group and then say something like, "Steve, I must ask you to leave," or "Steve, you have disrupted the group too much; please leave."

Of course, the strategies mentioned here apply to group situations where the members can be removed; that is, they are volunteers in the group or the setting, which gives the leader the freedom to remove a member if necessary. In a setting where the members must attend and there is no freedom to remove a member, the leader may ask that the member sit in silence or sit outside the circle of working members.

Dealing with Prejudiced, Narrow-Minded, or Insensitive Members

Occasionally, a leader will have to deal with a member with a very narrow or prejudiced view of the world, one who tries to act as a moralist or preacher. This is a difficult situation, because one purpose of most groups is to hear different points of view and learn to be tolerant of others. However, there is a point when a member who cannot refrain from preaching and judging others may need to be removed from the group. It is not good leadership to always let members have their say. For instance, if a woman is talking about having an affair and another member starts in about how evil and wrong it is, the leader should quickly cut off that member. In a case like this, the leader must politely ask the member to try to understand that others have different views. If this does not work and the member insists on being heard, the leader may need to ask the member to leave the group. The leadership rule is to be tolerant of members' differences and intervene only when a member's comments are so prejudiced that they could be harmful. In the following example, the leader did not hesitate to quickly cut off the member who was not being sensitive.

■ **EXAMPLE**

SUSAN: I know I am young and all, but for the last year or so, I have been really questioning if there is a God. I am not sure how others of you feel, but I don't think I believe in God. This has me worried and I end up often fighting with my mom about this.

DONNA: *(Angrily and with a condescending voice)* How can you not believe in God!

SUSAN: I am confused and it does not feel good because all my life I have thought of God as an important part of my life, and now, I don't know what to think. It just doesn't make sense to me, especially when I talk with these friends of my brother who are in college and studying world religions.

DONNA: That's crazy. What do they know compared to what older people know! Where do you think we came from?

LEADER: *(In a calm, caring voice)* Donna, try to be helpful to Susan. Tune in to her.

DONNA: Maybe you are just going to the wrong church. You should come to my church! I just can't believe you are questioning if there is a God. My father says that anyone who doesn't believe in God is . . .

LEADER: *(Firmly)* Wait a minute. Donna, if you cannot tune in to her pain, then you need to not talk. Your comments are not helpful. Susan, I want you to look at other members and realize that we do understand how hard this is for you. *(She looks around and sees very concerned faces; Donna is staring down.)* I feel that we can help you. Are you willing to talk about it some more?

SUSAN: Yes.

In this example, the leader had to intervene quickly because the member was being insensitive to the situation. If the member persists, the leader may have to talk with the member or even ask her to leave the group if she is not open to viewpoints different from hers.

■ ■ ■

Concluding Comments

As a group leader, you will be faced with many difficult members and many difficult situations, such as the chronic talker, the dominator, the distracter, the negative member, the resistant member, the crying member, or the member who is out to get the leader. For each of these situations, there are different skills and techniques that can be helpful. For resistant clients, it is important to distinguish whether the member is resistant to being in the group or to changing.

For crying members, the leader has to know when the tears should be supported and when they should be ignored. A very important thing to understand is that there will be times when you will have to ask a member to leave the group because of the dynamics that he is creating. When faced with these situations (and you will be faced with them if you lead groups), we suggest you refer back to this chapter. And remember, these problems are not unique to your group or a reflection on your leadership.

■ ACTIVITIES

1. Think of at least three different situations you have been in where there was a problem member or student. What would you have done if you had been in charge of dealing with that person?
2. Consider the problem situations of a crying member, a dominator, or a member who is out to get the leader. Which one of these will be hardest for you to handle? Why? Talk with your fellow students or colleagues about this and hear which one would be hardest for them.

 GROUP COUNSELING SKILLS

View again segments 3.2 and 8.2, and watch how the leader deals with these difficult members. Try to picture what would happen if the leader did not intervene.

Chapter 17

Working with Specific Populations

Group leaders often work with specific populations. For each population, there are some unique leadership considerations. In this chapter, we have selected 10 populations that we feel present some special challenges. We realize that there are a number of other populations that we could address, but we think these are among the most frequently led groups or populations. This chapter should be of great interest for beginning students who are just learning about groups and may be asked to lead all kinds of groups. This chapter may not be relevant for an experienced counselor who is looking for help with specific groups that are not addressed here.

The purpose of this chapter is to explore some of the group counseling issues concerning these 10 selected populations. It is important for you to understand that this chapter is meant only as an overview to these specific groups and that you would want to read much more than we present if you were asked to develop a group program for these or any other populations. For each population, we give some resources; but with the availability of the Internet, you can find books and resources that can help you with almost any group. An excellent resource is the Self Esteem Shop, which carries many books and materials that would be helpful in the groups described (800-251-8336; www.selfesteemshop.com). This Web page is an excellent place to start if you don't already have some favorite Web sites for resources.

In this chapter, we discuss mainly support, growth, counseling, and therapy groups within each of the following populations.

1. Children
2. Adolescents
3. Couples
4. Addiction groups
5. Older clients
6. Clients with chronic diseases or disabilities
7. Survivors of sexual abuse
8. Divorce groups
9. Adult children of alcoholics
10. Multicultural groups

Children

For this book, we define children to be under the age of 12. Groups for children take place mostly in schools, although some agencies conduct groups for children dealing with specific concerns. According to Shechtman (2004), "There is a consensus among professionals, based on research evidence, that group intervention with children is effective" (p. 7). School groups are conducted by the school counselor or by a counselor from a mental health center who is assigned to the school. Most of the groups for children deal with values, building social skills, self-concept, and building academic skills.

For some children, groups can be much better than individual counseling because groups allow children a place to learn and practice new skills. Counseling and support groups for children are extremely valuable children get to hear that they are not alone in their feelings. Groups also provide good information, support, and counseling for children living with an alcoholic, children whose parents are going through a divorce, children who are beginning to live in a stepfamily, or children who are facing other difficult situations. For groups with young kids (below the age of 7), we suggest that much of the group time be spent in play time (drawing, toys, sand tray) with some sharing and processing, or in group discussion regarding a book that is read to them. Effective groups have been conducted with 4- or 5-year-old children, where they play with one another and talk about their play.

There are now many excellent, helpful resources for anyone who is leading groups for children. In the exhibit area of any state or national counseling conference, one can find more than 30 books that have activities and ideas for leading children's groups. If you are just getting started, seek out material that can help you with the specific groups that you are leading. One of the best overall resources is the Self Esteem Shop mentioned earlier. If you are planning to lead groups with children, we suggest that you read Rosemarie Smead's book *Skills and Techniques for Group Work with Children and Adolescents* (1995), in which she describes setting up and conducting groups with children. She also discusses such aspects as working with principals and teachers, obtaining permission from parents, confidentiality, and how to prepare for the group. Ann Vernon (2010) provides another outstanding book for children, *More What Works with Children and Adolescents,* with activities coming primarily from an REBT perspective.

Confidentiality with groups of children and adolescents has to be understood by any group leader. School counselors should become familiar with the American School Counselor Association's ethical standards for their stance on confidentiality in school groups. In most schools and treatment settings for children and adolescents, files and case notes are open to parents, so confidentiality is limited.

Kinds of Groups

Many different groups are available for children. They often deal with specific topics or on skill development. The following is a list of some of the groups that are currently being led in schools.

Self-concept or self-esteem	New-to-the-school
Anger management	Dealing with bullies
Getting along with siblings	Dealing with name calling
Shyness	Grief support (after some tragic event)
Friendship	Study skills building
Divorce	Building social skills
Living in a stepfamily	ADHD children
Living with a chemically dependent parent	Improving academics

The following issues are addressed in some of the agency-led groups for children:

Severe behavior problems

Divorce

Alcoholic parents

Abused children (upper ages; need a very skilled leader)

Screening

Leaders must carefully screen in groups for children because a group situation is very difficult for some children. Often teachers serve as an excellent referral source. However, some referrals from teachers or self-referrals from children are not always appropriate for groups. Individual counseling may better serve children who demand an inordinate amount of attention, who just can't seem to be able to focus for any length of time, or who can't share time well with others.

Leaders should think of the first session of a children's group as a time for screening. Children should be told that the first meeting is for learning how they like being in a group and how they do in a group situation. (See *Screening* in the index for additional information.)

Group Size

Children's groups are usually smaller than adolescent and adult groups because the attention span of a child needs to be considered. When there are more than six members, it is hard for most children to stay focused. Four is a good number, but often one or more are absent and then the group is small. For groups where the members have trouble paying attention or interacting with others, the leader may want to have a maximum of four children. A group size of three children in an ADHD group or a group with severe behavior problems is not uncommon.

Length of Session

Most children's groups last around 30 minutes, although some may be as long as 40 minutes or as short as 20 minutes. Each leader has to decide what length is the best, given the ages of the children, the topic or purpose, and the members in the group.

Number of Sessions

Some groups for children last for only one or two sessions because they are more psychoeducational or deal with a specific topic that can be covered in a couple of sessions. Other groups may last for eight or more sessions, such as dealing with divorce, making friends, or living in a stepfamily. School counselors may want to structure the number of sessions around the number of weeks in the school term or quarter.

Special Skills

There are a number of important skills that are necessary for leading groups with children.

Use a leader-oriented model as opposed to a facilitator model   One of the main differences in leading groups with children is that the leader usually needs to take more responsibility for the group than in a group composed of adults. Picking good books and activities is a must for children, because they do not usually come prepared to discuss any topic. There are numerous books on many subjects that may arise in counseling for children. Search catalogs and bookstores and ask other experienced counselors for material on subjects you want to cover in a group.

Vary the format and use a multi-sensory approach   Exercises, short stories, skits, and the use of puppets, drawing, and other props all are helpful tools for the leader. If the proper tone is established, children usually are more than eager to talk.

Cut off and hold the focus   A primary skill in leading children's groups is holding the focus on a given topic long enough so that there is some impact. In fact, the leader may frequently need to cut off members to let others share. Often, other children will change the subject and the leader will need to bring the group back to the topic of discussion. Leaders have to be prepared to gently redirect discussion and not let a member drift into other topics before completing the first discussion.

Use an enthusiastic voice   When working with children, the leader's use of his voice can be an effective tool. It is very important to show enthusiasm and excitement about the subject being discussed. This gets the children interested and focused. Leaders who have a dull voice rarely are able to have successful groups with children.

Clarity of purpose—get children to think, but understand that much of the counseling will be done privately   In workshops for elementary school counselors, participants have commented that they had too much "fluff" (fun and games) in their groups and not enough depth. Granted, with young children it is sometimes hard to take the group deeper, but if the leader is clear about the group's purpose, she can have a productive session. By using props, creative ideas, and good leadership skills, the focus can be held and taken to a level that is meaningful for the members. Usually the counselor will not do individual work for any length of time, because the other children would probably become restless, but the focus on a topic can go to a 7 or a 6 level on the depth chart. Often, a group session can lead to an individual follow-up session.

Special knowledge   For each different kind of group, the leader needs not only group leadership skills, but also knowledge of specific topics such as the effects of divorce on children, problems when entering a new stepfamily, how to improve school performance, or living with a chemically dependent person.

Comments from Practicing Counselors

We asked four counselors who work with children to write about what skills they feel are important in leading groups with children. In their own words, here is what they said.

> Cutting off is extremely important. The kids are constantly interrupting each other. I find that if I go around the circle and give each a turn to talk and then go back around again, this works better for many of the younger kids, instead of skipping around like you would with adults. Kids respond a little more to the structure of knowing when it is their turn to talk. Also, keep tables away from kids. Definitely work with them in a circle with no table in the middle. They are more open with each other this way, tend to get less distracted, and tend to look down less. Keep extra chairs in the group. Kids like to slide over to an empty chair next to them. For ADHD kids, this gives them movement opportunities without being disruptive. Have books, pencils, and paper on

the floor—not on their laps—because they fiddle and doodle too much. Having them repeat what someone said in their own summarizing way and having them give advice to each other are good techniques. Also, have one student tell his or her story and then ask another student how they would feel if that had happened to them. In other words, they talk for each other on the tough stuff. In schools, allow 20–30 minutes for a group session. Less is not enough, and you lose their focus more easily with much more than 30 minutes. They like movement exercises. They love to act out things, so drama works well for kids in groups.

Shelly

In children's groups, you absolutely are going to lead 95% of the time if you want kids to get anything out of the group (and I am speaking elementary levels), because developmentally, they can easily get off the subject. Movement exercises are very important. More teaching tends to take place than with adolescents or adults. I use smaller member numbers than in adult groups. Six is definitely enough in elementary groups even when the kids can focus individually for longer periods of time—four members in ADD groups.

Chris

Kids are often thinking really hard about what they want to say when they are called on to talk. They want to contribute to anything that is talked about, but then they forget to listen carefully to what others are saying. I am constantly trying to make connections between group members to keep them focused and to help them learn something from the other members. For example, I often comment that two members are going through a similar situation, or ask for members to make a comment or suggestions about what someone else said.

Sometimes kids come in and aren't ready to do work, so I may give them 1 or 2 minutes to talk about whatever they want before opening the session. Then they have to be ready to talk about real issues. This strategy is incredibly effective! Kids have a shorter attention span, so you have to change the activities and format more frequently from talk and games, to books, and so on.

Behavioral strategies also work really well. For example, every 5 minutes, everyone who is on task gets a sticker. At the end of the 40-minute session, everyone who has six stickers gets a prize. This is better for grades K–2. Unfortunately, kids sometimes have to be extrinsically motivated to pay attention. Hopefully, the topic and activities are relevant and captivating, but it doesn't always work that way.

Give them things they can take back to class or home, such as pictures or a card with things about themselves written on it, and so on.

This provides a means for them to share with their parents and reinforce what was discussed in the group.

Dana

I have recently been working in groups with children ages 4–6 and I have found that an understanding of holding, shifting, and deepening the focus, a clear purpose, and being creatively flexible have been the keys to successful sessions. Children at these young ages, they're not developed enough yet to express themselves through words. They speak through their actions and interactions. Lots of time is spent in play.

A clear purpose is imperative when leading groups with children. Children will mentally float, daydream, and get excited—that is part of the experience of being a child. My job is to point and guide these free spirits towards a common goal. When I work with children I am always prepared to validate their contributions and use them to further the purpose. For example, I was working with a group of six four- to six-year-old children, all in foster care. The purpose of the group was to normalize their experience in foster care and break their emotional isolation. We were working on an exercise to identify the job description of a parent. As we were listing the "dos" and "don'ts," one 5-year-old boy picked up a doll and began banging the doll off of the table. With a big grin the boy stated, "The daddy doll is making noise." Using this boy's expression and focusing the contribution to the purpose, I used a round to ask the other children "whose parents make noise?" The children giggled, and then each explained how their parents act around them. This assisted the children with accepting that other children's parents behave similarly to theirs, and provided the opportunity to release emotional discomfort. Without understanding how to manage the focus, clarity of purpose, and being creatively flexible, a young children's group probably will be a struggle.

Earl

Adolescents

Adolescence (ages 12–19) can be a difficult period in a young person's life. Groups can help with identity problems, sexual concerns, and problems with friends, parents, and school. Groups for pregnant teenagers, drug users, teenage parents, potential school dropouts, and runaways can be extremely helpful. Other valuable groups are those for adolescents who are having problems because of their parents' divorce, remarriage, or alcohol abuse. Many experts have said that teens listen more to their peers than to adults, so groups can serve as a great source of learning and exploring. As was mentioned in the previous section, there are many activity books on working with different adolescent groups. Check with the Self Esteem Shop or your favorite resource for books pertaining to the topics in which you are interested.

Kinds of Groups

Groups for adolescents are both voluntary and nonvoluntary. The voluntary groups usually take place in schools, churches, or mental health settings, whereas the nonvoluntary groups are conducted primarily in treatment centers, residential settings, or mental health centers. Voluntary growth, discussion, education, counseling, and therapy groups can be quite valuable during adolescence.

The following is a list of many groups that may be found in a middle or high school setting. Most of these groups would be voluntary, although some may be mandatory.

Self-esteem or self-concept	Friendship
Assertiveness	Divorce and stepfamily issues
Anger management	Grief and loss
Study skills	Sex education
Drug education	Dating
Drug abuse	Gay and lesbian issues
Post high school planning	Teenage pregnancy
Teenage fatherhood	Teenage motherhood
Dropout prevention	Living with an addicted person
Improving Academics	

The following are groups that would take place at a mental health center, treatment center, or detention center.

Drug abuse	Pregnancy
Survivors of sexual abuse	Teenage motherhood
Living with an addicted person	Teenage fatherhood
Probation or parole	Self-esteem building
Gay and lesbian issues	Cooperative living (for residential treatment centers and group homes)

Screening

For school groups, it is important to screen members to make sure they are appropriate for the group that you are forming. The best way to screen is to conduct a brief interview and find out why the potential member wants to be in the group. Young students often will sign up for group just to get out of class or to be with their friends. For a more in-depth discussion of the various aspects of recruitment and screening of minors for group counseling in both schools and agencies, see Ritchie and Huss (2000).

Depending on the group's purpose, the leader may want to lead all males, all females, or a mix of the two. Because there is a lot to learn about the opposite sex during the adolescent years, a coed group can be beneficial. The disadvantage of mixed groups is that members may be inhibited when members of the opposite sex are present.

In an ideal situation, the leader always has a chance to screen members, but this is not how things are in many counseling settings. Any discussion of adolescent groups would be remiss if it did not touch on the nonvolunteer adolescent group that the leader does not get to screen. These groups may be school ordered, court ordered, parent ordered, or agency ordered. Many schools have mandatory groups for those caught with drugs, those with too many absences, those with poor grades, or those who want to quit school. Courts sometimes order teenagers to participate in group therapy with an agency. Many residential settings have mandatory group attendance.

Group Size

For best results, there should be no more than 8 members in growth, support, counseling, or therapy groups, with 6 being ideal. If the group is more psychoeducational, then as many as 12 members may be appropriate, although it is usually best to keep the number to 10 or fewer.

Length of Session

Sessions with adolescents should last between 40 and 90 minutes. Groups in schools usually last one period, which is around 40 to 50 minutes. In residential settings, sessions may last longer, especially if some time is spent on "house business." In mental health centers, groups usually meet at least 90 minutes.

Number of Sessions

The number of sessions depends on the kind of group and the members. Some will meet for only one or two times. Others, such as drug and alcohol groups, groups discussing gay and lesbian issues, and probation groups may meet for 10 weeks or even an entire year.

Special Skills

A group leader working with adolescents should like and respect teenagers, want to learn more about their immediate world, and understand the kinds of struggles they go through while trying to grow up. Teenagers are very aware of phony attempts by the leader to be one of them or of a one-up attitude that suggests "the adult knows more." Adolescents will often test the leader's level of acceptance of their values. Unfortunately, it is common for group leaders of teens to sound like parents. Students can quickly spot hidden agendas, such as wanting the members to study harder in school, stop using drugs or drinking, or behave better in class. This can cause the members to lose respect for the leader. Leaders of adolescent groups are often confronted if they are dishonest or not open about their intentions.

Three important skills are (1) take charge, (2) use structure, and (3) make it interesting.

1. ***Take Charge.*** It is very important with teenagers for the leader to establish that he is in charge and that he will lead the group. If the leader does not take charge, one or two of the members will, and the group will most likely go in a nonproductive direction. If the leader takes charge and makes the group interesting, the adolescents will not mind. Remember, *people don't mind being led when they are led well.*

2. ***Use Structure.*** Because adolescents often do not come prepared to discuss issues, planning activities or topics is usually the best way to structure the group. Leaving it up to adolescent members to come up with things most often leads to irrelevant and shallow discussions.

3. ***Make It Interesting.*** Any group leader who does not make her group interesting will be asking for trouble, because teenagers are used to computer and video games, TV, and so on. It is the leader's responsibility to make the group interesting by introducing stimulating topics, using relevant and interesting activities, and using a multisensory approach that keeps the members engaged. This is especially true for nonvolunteer groups, because they are extremely difficult to lead. The leader will have to be creative and innovative to turn the negative energy around. With adolescents, especially in the initial sessions, the leader must plan interesting and relevant activities. The use of role-plays, moral dilemma exercises, sentence completions, and common readings is helpful for getting members interested and involved. Starting with a formal presentation of the rules is *not* the way to start a nonvolunteer group—this sets a negative tone for members who are already negative.

During the first couple of sessions of a nonvolunteer group, the leader should expect negative behavior, both verbal and nonverbal. Sometimes it is a good strategy to allow members time to complain during the initial session. One counselor we know started her after-school group for adolescent drug users by dealing with their anger at being in the group.

LEADER: I know you do not want to be here, so we can take 10 minutes to complain about it, but after that we'll get focused on what we are doing here. If you want to complain, I am going to put this trash can in the center of the group. In 10 minutes, after you have dumped much of your anger, I'll remove it and we'll get started.

Problems with confidentiality can often occur in groups with adolescents. Sometimes the leader can avert these problems by carefully screening the members to avoid placing members who do not get along in the same group. Because confidentiality is so important, the leader must make clear to the members the consequences of breaking that confidence. Leaders should also make members aware that confidentiality cannot be guaranteed. The consequences of breaking confidentiality may be discussed and agreed upon by the entire group, or the leader may simply state the consequences, such as removal from the group. The leader also needs to inform the members that she may have to tell parents about certain things that are said, if she feels the person is in danger of hurting himself or is engaging in behaviors that are very harmful or self-defeating. Agency or school policy, plus state laws, may dictate what a leader can and cannot keep confidential.

Comments from a Practicing Counselor

Adolescents are an exciting breed. Their search for "self" and desire to belong can make group counseling quite a challenge. Most importantly, in my view, is the strong need to build a trusting relationship within the group. Activities that build rapport and trust are an absolute. Confidentiality issues also appear to be of extreme importance to this age group. It is important to offer private counseling for your members when you recognize that certain issues may best be addressed outside the group.

Cutting-off skills are crucial. As the group's leader, it is imperative to possess skills to be able to halt the domineering adolescent member. I've seen this type of child begin to exaggerate or fabricate stories and situations once they've realized they have the members' attention. To protect this member's acceptance by the others, it is important to recognize this and come to their aid by using effective cutting-off tactics. Effective planning is an absolute must for leading adolescent groups.

Wendy

Couples

Several kinds of groups involve couples: marital enrichment groups, groups for abusive relationships, premarital counseling groups, gay and lesbian couples, interracial couples, and interfaith couples. Other beneficial groups include those for parents of children who died suddenly and couples who are caring for a physically or mentally ill person or someone with Alzheimer's disease.

The value of these groups lies in hearing what other couples are dealing with and doing about various issues in their relationships. Partners can often hear what other members are saying much better than what their spouses are saying, and the group format allows for this. Also, hearing others helps to stimulate thought and discussion in the group because members bring up topics that couples have either avoided or of which they have not been consciously aware.

Couples' groups are usually conducted at a mental health center, treatment center, or church. The church groups are mostly enrichment-type groups, whereas the other settings focus on enrichment, support, or therapy groups.

Kinds of Groups

Below is a list of the kinds of groups that are frequently offered to couples. Note that, as stated above, the kinds of groups can be dictated by the setting in which the leader is working.

Enrichment and Support Groups:

Communications

Living with differences

Living with religious differences

Living with racial differences

Dual-career marriages

Surviving the loss of a child

Living with a parent with Alzheimer's disease

Living with a chemically dependent child

Living with a mentally ill parent, child, or other person

Living in a prejudiced world

Living as a gay or lesbian couple

Therapy Groups:

Abused spouses

Healing from an affair

Healing childhood wounds

Stage II Relationships   beginning a new relationship after recovery

Weekend intensive work

Screening

Because the needs of couples wishing to participate in a group experience can vary considerably, it is important for the leader to be clear about the purpose of a group. Through screening interviews, the leader can inform couples about the purpose and assess their individual and mutual needs. By meeting with the couple and each partner individually, the leader may get a broader perspective on the relationship. If one of the partners is not committed to working on the relationship, the leader may suggest couple counseling before or in addition to the group experience. Often, during screening, it will be evident that one of the partners needs some intensive therapy rather than a couples' group experience.

Group Size

The size of a couples' group varies, depending on the format. Some are conducted in large groups of 10 to 12 couples. For the more personal groups, usually no more than 5 couples is best to allow enough time for each person to share his or her thoughts and feelings.

Length and Number of Sessions

The format for couples' groups can vary. Many enrichment groups are held on an extended basis, for a full day or a weekend, the idea being that this allows time for partners to more fully explore the dimensions of their relationships and to work more intensely on issues (Corey, Corey & Corey, 2009). Full-day or weekend sessions also allow more sharing with and learning from other couples. A drawback to this format is that couples may leave the session with a group "high," feeling renewed and excited about their relationship, only to

reenter the real world of kids, work, traffic, money, and in-laws. Their enthusiasm and renewed commitment may carry them for days or weeks, but long-
standing, underlying problems can surface again for some couples under the
pressure of everyday living. Many leaders who conduct such marathon couples'
groups hold follow-up meetings to support the couples' changes and to help
strengthen areas they have worked on.

A weekly or biweekly group session format can also be used with couples.
However, couples—especially if they are parents—may have a problem finding
time to attend a 2- or 3-hour group session on a regular basis for several weeks
or months. If couples are willing to make this commitment, much can be done
to help them look at their relationship. Couples can work on improving intimacy, handling disagreements, decision making, and so forth. They also have
the opportunity to discuss and handle daily issues that might arise for them,
such as parenting, money, personal time scheduling, sex, in-laws, and vacations.
Weekly or every other week sessions allow couples to try out communication
and problem-solving techniques over an extended period of time; if they run
into snags, the group is there to help work them out. This format takes into
consideration that personal change, especially when two people are involved, is
often slow and erratic, requiring continued reinforcement to be lasting.

Special Skills

Groups for couples offer some special challenges to the group leader. If at all
possible, couples' groups should be co-led, and often are led by leaders who are
partners themselves. The leader is not only dealing with the dynamics among
six or eight members but also with three or four relationships that have their
own dynamics. Couples' groups, therefore, are very complex and are usually
difficult to lead. We briefly discuss some of the special skills for leading couples'
groups.

1. *Understanding of the kinds of problems that may arise.* In a therapy group for
   couples, members may have different agendas. One member of a couple
   may be coming to the group hoping that the relationship can be improved or saved, whereas the other is perfectly satisfied with the status
   quo or wishes to negotiate a divorce. Groups of this nature can become
   quite intense, because the two members often air their differences in the
   group. Sometimes this is very painful for the couple as well as for other
   group members who are watching.

Other problems that may arise during the group itself include the following:

- One or both partners may be reluctant to share personal feelings in front
  of the other.
- One partner may feel the need to conceal an affair.
- Couples may use the group to vent powerful negative feelings they have
  held in for a long time.

- One or both partners may try to use the group as a jury to justify their behavior in some way.

- One member in the relationship may try to enlist the group to change the partner's behavior.

- One partner may use the group to search for a new relationship.

- Members may compare themselves or their partners with others in the group and feel bad because they do not compare favorably to the others.

2. *Knowledge of the counseling theories.* Counseling theories are important to teach because so often couples are looking for information about why they do what they do to each other. Along with other theories, we always use Transactional Analysis because TA is excellent for understanding and explaining transactions between couples.

3. *Knowledge of many different kinds of couples' exercises.* It is useful to have activities for the couples to share with each other as well as with the group. Such exercises are helpful because they encourage couples to look at the broader issues that many people in relationships share, rather than to focus only on their own specific disagreements. Exercises help couples examine such areas as sex-role problems in the relationship, dependency, the need for innovation to keep relationships interesting, the need for separate identities, games that interfere with intimacy, and the role of childhood experiences in shaping values about relationships and marriage. Hearing other couples discuss their reactions to the exercises is very valuable for the members. Excellent exercises can be found in various sources available for leaders working with couples' groups (Corey, Corey & Corey, 2009; Jacobs, 1992; Stevens, 1972).

4. *Use of drama and psychodrama.* In many couples' groups, drama and psychodrama are used to get at the deeper emotions that exist. By seeing other couples work on issues and situations, other members find that they can relate to scenes being acted out.

5. *Working with couples who have special needs.* For gay and lesbian couples' groups, the leader must know and understand the particular issues facing these couples. This knowledge comes from reading and from interacting with those living this lifestyle. It cannot come from one's own imagined ideas as to what this is like, and it is unethical to lead these groups without knowledge. Often someone who is lesbian or gay leads these groups. Other kinds of couples' groups include parenting groups and groups for parents with children who are addicted or who have special needs. Much literature can be found on leading these groups.

In summary, couples' groups are exciting, dynamic, and challenging. Couples' groups call for an in-depth understanding of relationships as well as the ability to handle complex dynamics that often arise. Group leaders working with couples need to have strong leadership skills and extensive experience in individual and couples' counseling.

Comments from a Practicing Counselor

It is so important to be clear as to the purpose of any couples' group. Marriage education is about teaching skills to couples, whereas therapy groups deal with specific issues of couples. Screening is key for all couples' groups. In my therapy couples' groups, I made sure the partners were functioning well enough to be in a group setting rather than just couple counseling. You have to cut off and redirect a lot because partners try to blame, shame, and focus attention on their partner. If a member talks about his or her partner, I throw it back on to the person doing the blaming. This tends to stop attempts to put the partner in the hot seat. Facilitating ownership is an important skill.

Pat

Addiction Groups

Many different groups exist for people who are addicted to some substance or activity. We took the liberty of putting many different and unique populations into one category, but we feel that in this condensed discussion, the reader can get a sense of the challenges of working with anyone who has an addiction. The groups discussed in this section could apply to any addiction, be it overeating or not eating, shopping, gambling, sex, or drugs and alcohol.

Many groups are available to the addicted individual. Twelve-step support groups that are usually not led by a professional—such as Alcoholics Anonymous, Narcotics Anonymous, Overeaters Anonymous, Sex Addicts Anonymous, and Gamblers Anonymous—have benefited millions of people. For each of these populations, education groups led by a trained therapist can provide valuable information. Also, therapy groups are beneficial for those who are in denial or are still struggling with their addiction and its consequences. Excellent books can be found on almost any group. A search of the Internet can lead you to Web sites for the topic in which you are specifically interested. These Web sites contain references to books and materials that can get you started with ideas for leading groups for those with eating disorders, crack addiction, or for those trying to break a gambling addiction. Our discussion is only meant to give you some overall understanding of these groups, but you will definitely need much more information than is provided here.

The value of addictions groups cannot be overstated. Addicts need to hear from other addicts, especially those who are struggling and those who are doing better than they are. Much support and help can be given because members feel a strong bond with those who are living what they are living. Also, other addicts can call each other on their "stuff."

Kinds of Groups

Any discussion of an addiction group has to be divided into two groups: nonvoluntary and voluntary.

Nonvoluntary Groups Nonvoluntary groups for addicts consist of those who were caught driving under the influence or those who were mandated to attend by their employer, school, parent, or some other outside authority. These groups may be strictly educational or they may serve the purpose of breaking the addicted person's denial that nothing is wrong. These groups take place in mental health centers or treatment centers and should be led only by persons who have extensive knowledge of the addiction they are addressing.

Voluntary Groups There are many voluntary groups for those who have some addiction that greatly affects their lives. Those addicted who want help often volunteer for recovery, therapy, and relapse-prevention groups. Any such leader must be well versed in the specific addiction to lead these groups, because the power of the addiction is so strong that much manipulation, pain, and struggle will be present.

Screening

Ideally screening is done for all groups, but with addiction groups this often is not possible, because the members are mandated to the group or are confined to a residential treatment center that requires everyone to attend a group. For volunteer groups, leaders should screen for commitment to change. Too often, people come to appease a spouse, parent, or boss. These members can mean trouble, especially if they try to sabotage the group process. For those groups where attendance is mandatory, some leaders use an inner circle/outer circle concept for each session. They have those who want to actively participate pull their chairs to the center, and those who just want to "listen" sit on the outside. Theoretically, this keeps those on the outside from offering distracting comments, and it allows other members a chance to go deeper with the session.

Group Size

The ideal size is 6 to 10 members for a therapy group, depending on the members and the purpose of the group. Educational groups can be larger and AA type groups can have 30 to 40 or even more members, because they are open to the public.

Length of Session

AA groups and other similar groups usually last 1 hour. Groups led by a therapist usually last 1½ to 2 hours but may be longer in some residential or treatment settings. In some treatment centers, groups meet daily, so the leader has to have a tremendous amount of knowledge and excellent skills to make it interesting and valuable every day.

Special Skills

1. *Dealing with anger.* The initial sessions of any nonvoluntary group for addicts are difficult to lead because the members do not see themselves as

having a problem. The leader must be prepared to deal with the members' anger at being forced to be in the group and the anger members feel when the leader refers to the fact that their addiction is creating problems in their lives.

2. *Use of a multi-sensory approach.* There are no easy answers to the problems of working with nonvoluntary addicts. Quite often the use of interesting movement, writing, or prop exercises can be very helpful in "hooking" the nonvoluntary member. Leaders who use a multi-sensory approach are almost always more successful than those who rely on just talking.

GROUP COUNSELING SKILLS: Therapy in Groups

Go to segment 14.1 and watch the segment where the leader uses multi-sensory techniques (the hammer and the large beer bottle) when working with one member.

3. *Handling confrontation.* Besides having a thorough knowledge of addiction and group leadership, the leader has to have the courage to be confrontive and be comfortable with members confronting each other. The leader must always remember that effective confrontation involves the leader or another member confronting a member about inconsistencies. Too often, inexperienced leaders either attack the member or let other members viciously attack the person. This is usually not effective and can be quite harmful. Leaders can easily become frustrated with members who deny their problems and may use confrontation in a punitive way. Punitive confrontation is inappropriate confrontation that attacks, belittles, and/or humiliates the member. If a leader finds herself feeling anger toward a member, she should examine her own expectations for the member and perhaps talk with a colleague about her frustration. Constructive confrontation is valuable and often necessary. It involves statements such as, "You tell us you are going to get sober, yet you have no real plan for how you are going to do it. That's why none of us believes you." The use of confrontation requires skill and sensitivity.

4. *Planning.* Careful planning must be done for most groups of people with an addiction, especially in the beginning. For any nonvolunteer group, the leader should realize that the members are often defensive about their addiction and hesitant to talk about any of their issues. The leader has to plan relevant, interesting exercises and discussions to get members involved and committed to trying to benefit from the group.

5. *Cutting off.* One other skill that is absolutely essential when leading groups for addicts is cutting off. The leader needs to use cutting-off skills because addicts, especially alcoholics, often want to tell their story over and over

again. Many leaders who have worked with alcoholics have said that cutting off the long-winded stories has proven very valuable in allowing for more sharing and interaction, and in focusing on a topic in depth without having to listen to one story after another.

6. *Patience.* Leaders must be patient and understand that they will not see quick and dramatic results. Always keep in mind that this is an extremely difficult population with which to work. The success rate is not as high as group leaders might find with members who have other types of problems. Group leaders in the substance-abuse area should not expect rapid, large-scale behavioral change. Leaders should be especially careful to avoid burnout by having realistic expectations and not leading an excessive number of groups in a given day or week. Leaders want to make sure their psychological worth is not attached to clients getting better, because many addicts relapse or simply don't work any kind of recovery program. It is important not to feel personally unsuccessful as a leader or counselor when members return to the treatment program for the same problem.

Comments from a Practicing Counselor

The need to be creative is extremely important. This is especially true with those clients mandated into treatment. I use a lot of movement exercises.

Cutting off and drawing out are essential tools when working with substance abuse clients. Oftentimes, members get stuck in "telling their story." Although this can be very beneficial, I have found that I need to be attuned to their tone of voice and their purpose for sharing. Other members are reluctant to share and will try to hide in the group. This is especially true for women, specifically when the group is made up of considerably more men than women. Breaking members into dyads or triads has proven to be very effective. Also, written exercises often focus members. I have done an exercise prompting clients to reflect and uncover their ritualistic behaviors as they relate to their alcohol or drug use. This has been very helpful, not only in breaking denial, but also in having members identify with one another.

Trish

Older Clients

As with other special populations discussed so far, there are some special considerations to be aware of when working with groups of older persons. Although we speak of "older persons" or "the elderly," these labels cannot possibly accurately describe those over a certain age, because many people in their 80s function as well as those in their 50s. As group leaders, we must be aware that the needs of the elderly are similar to the needs of us all; that is, their needs are very diverse. Older persons may feel they have less personal power and impact than they had previously in their lives when they were employed, had children who sought their advice, or had friends who relied on them. This may lead to feelings of lowered self-esteem or alienation. Older people may have less contact with family members, siblings, or children than in previous years. They may also have fewer social contacts, their friends having died or moved away. This can lead to feelings of isolation and depression. Older people, having realistic concerns about physical and mental infirmity and death, can benefit greatly by being in a group where they can talk about these feelings. The group leader must be comfortable with dealing with thoughts and feelings about death.

Older people are often preoccupied with past events. They tend to reminisce and tell stories from the past. Although such storytelling may become boring for other members, it is often a healthy way for people to process their lives and feel good about themselves. A very common activity in groups with older clients is reminiscing about different aspects of their lives. For example, the leader might allow a certain number of minutes for each member to recall his most memorable holiday, a particularly happy moment with a spouse or friend, or the most rewarding experience she can recall. These exercises can elicit memories that might lead to the member's wanting to do some personal work. These groups for older adults also serve the purpose of fulfilling social needs that they have but have few outlets for meeting these needs.

Goals and Kinds of Groups for Older Persons

Although older persons can benefit from personal growth and counseling groups, the leader may find as much interest and response among older members for task, support, and education groups. A recent development being tried is to bring older people together to teach them about computers and to show them how they can communicate with others around the country. So far, this has been very successful.

Following are five possible goals of groups involving this population.

1. *Providing information.* The first goal involves providing information about various matters such as finances, health and medicine, housing, or insurance. The leader can either present the information or arrange for guest speakers.

2. *Making things happen.* Another goal is what we call "making things happen." Older people, especially if they are living in a residential facility, often do not have the resources or the influence individually to make things happen, such as changing a schedule, planning a holiday party, improving living conditions, and so forth. A task group may take on such goals to improve the general quality of life. Such a group can also provide an opportunity for members to learn or relearn effective assertiveness skills.

3. *Working through personal issues.* A third goal involves working through personal issues. A personal growth or counseling group can help members

deal with unfinished business from the past, such as guilt about not being a better parent or spouse, anger at a former friend or employer, or sadness at not having accomplished something during their lifetimes. Issues such as their treatment by children or other family members or their concerns about the future, infirmity, or death are also potential areas for personal work. Members also benefit simply from sharing these concerns and finding support within the group.

4. *Developing and maintaining social contacts.* The fourth goal for groups with older persons is developing and maintaining social contacts. As people grow older, family contacts may be less frequent because of distance or their family's preoccupation with their own lives. Friends move away or die, neighbors change, longtime neighborhood hangouts close, and the opportunity for continued social contact seems to diminish. Making new friends can seem difficult, and therefore some older people tend to become more introverted and preoccupied with themselves and the past. This can lead to diminished social skills and diminished initiating behavior. A support group can provide a place for members to socialize—to regain former social skills—as well as to meet others with whom they may form more lasting relationships.

5. *Explore new goals in life.* Finally, we have found that groups can be very useful in helping older persons explore new goals in life. Such a group may have characteristics of an education group, a support group, and possibly even a growth group, as members shift their preoccupation from the past to focus more on the present moment and the future. The leader and other members may provide information and ideas for specific projects, such as arts and crafts work or community activities such as joining a foster grandparent program. New goals may involve writing to old friends, establishing closer ties with other family members, or pursuing goals formerly abandoned, such as writing or taking college courses. Members can learn that, whatever their medical or health restrictions, it is possible to generate a new and continuing interest in life.

Settings

There are four primary settings where groups for older persons might be held: (1) the community, (2) minimum-care residences or retirement facilities, (3) nursing homes, and (4) institutions. We briefly discuss the implications for each of these settings.

The Community   There are older persons in most communities who do not have contact with family or friends and who may live rather isolated lives. Some may be in touch with local social agencies. A group program may be developed for such persons to pursue any or all the goals discussed before. Such groups may be sponsored by the community mental health center, schools or colleges, local churches, or senior citizen centers.

Minimum-Care Residences   Standard living facilities designed for older persons also provide a setting in which such groups might be held. Although such facilities may have professional staff qualified to lead groups, it is more likely that a group leader from the community will provide this service.

Nursing Homes   Nursing homes need some kind of group program. The severity of a person's physical illness obviously places some constraints on involvement; however, the need may be just as great. Members should be screened for both their physical ability to participate and their mental status.

Institutions   There is a great need for groups for older persons in institutional settings. Many of the goals discussed here can be pursued effectively in such a setting. Institutional living can be very difficult and, coupled with medical and psychiatric problems, can lead patients to become depressed and socially isolated. A group program can go a long way toward helping with re-socialization, developing a support network, and providing information and guidance. Corey, Corey and Corey (2009) provide a warm description of the contributions Marianne Corey made to a group of older residents in an institutional setting.

Screening

Screening groups for the elderly is very important and will depend on the purpose. If the purpose is to teach something new or have members focus on some task or topic, then it would be important to select members who have the ability to learn and focus. For groups where focusing on memories of the past is a primary component, the leader will want to make sure that selected members are able to access their memories, which is a difficult task for certain older people.

Group Size

The size of the group for the older population depends on the kind of group and its purpose. If it is more for social interaction or education, 10 to 12 members is fine. If the group is more for support and sharing, 4 to 6 members usually works best.

Length of Sessions

Sessions usually should last between 1 and 1½ hours, depending on the level of functioning of the members, the group size, and the purpose of the group.

Special Skills

The following three skills are just a few that leaders should possess in group counseling for older clients.

1. *Patience.* Probably the most important skill in working with the older population is patience. Things tend to move at a slower pace, and the counselor needs to understand and adapt to this.

2. *Energy.* A skilled leader will have lots of positive energy in hopes of energizing those who are not so enthusiastic. An upbeat, positive attitude will usually help the group go more smoothly.

3. *Knowledge of certain issues.* The leader working with older persons must be sensitive to relevant issues, such as concerns with aging and death, as well as to real constraints, such as waning physical health and vitality, and fewer social outlets. The leader should develop a group program that will meet a wide range of member needs.

Clients with Chronic Diseases or Disabilities

Groups for persons with chronic diseases or disabilities can be formed on a community basis or in hospitals or rehabilitation centers. Such groups are especially important in light of the stress generated by the onset of a disability or long-term or terminal illness. Clients are often uncertain of the course or prognosis of their condition. They must deal with a change in lifestyle, the feelings of loss of control, and the physical separation from family and friends because of being in a medical setting, perhaps in a different city. The focus of their lives for many weeks or months shifts from the day-to-day business of making a living or attending school, socializing, and being involved with family and recreation to medical examinations, treatments, and waiting with some degree of uncertainty.

Kinds of Groups

Given the uncertainty of medical factors, the need for emotional support, and the struggle of working through lifestyle changes, different kinds of groups with this population can be quite beneficial. Groups can provide education and information on health-related issues and help clients deal with psychological issues such as loss of identity, anger, and the grieving process. Groups can also provide support and help with problem solving.

Two populations where groups are quite prevalent are AIDS and cancer patients. Many excellent support groups are being led for these populations. If you are planning to lead these kinds of groups, you should be aware that much literature discussing different approaches to each is available.

Screening

It is usually best to form homogeneous groups based on one particular illness or disability, because the illness or disability is the common denominator about which patients have concerns. There will be times, however, when this is not possible or when it is helpful to involve group members with different medical concerns. The leader must give a great deal of thought to who is let into the group and must be especially sensitive to the intense anxiety, depression, and anger that people may experience following the onset of a long-term illness or disabling condition. It is important for the group leader to understand the grieving process that people go through when faced with a long-term illness or disabling condition, both in terms of selecting members for a group and also in terms of actually leading the group. Members who are dealing effectively with their medical condition can provide information, lend support, and serve as role models for those who are still in the angry or depressed stages.

Groups with members who have a chronic disease or disability are led both as open and as closed groups. Most hospital groups are open because of the need to accommodate new people arriving in the unit who are suffering from the same illness or disability. Groups for family members of people with certain illnesses are also being conducted with great success.

Group Size and Length of Sessions

The size of these groups varies according to their purpose. Educational groups can be large. Support and therapy groups should probably have no more than eight members, with six often being an ideal number. These groups usually meet for 1½ to 2 hours because members usually have many thoughts and feelings to share.

Special Skills

1. *Dealing with powerful feelings.* Leaders of groups that deal with a disease or disability need to be prepared for many different dynamics. Because of the sense of injustice members feel at the onset of a chronic or terminal illness or disability, they often have a strong need to express powerful feelings—frustration and anger, in particular. For this reason, group leaders must feel comfortable handling hostility, some of which will be displaced onto them. The anger often takes the form of finding fault with the medical staff, nurses, schedules, and so forth. It is important for the group leader to recognize this anger as an important aspect of the grieving process and to help the member work through it.

2. *Getting members to focus on other aspects of life.* Members often become intensely focused on their medical conditions to the exclusion of other aspects of their lives. They may need to be encouraged to look beyond their medical condition to the possibility of future employment, socializing again with friends, regaining a role in the family, and so forth. It is important to use effective cutting-off skills along with exercises that structure how the members share. For example, sentence-completion exercises are helpful, because the leader can focus members on certain aspects of their lives and illness by the sentences he uses.

3. *Letting members be experts.* Leaders, especially beginners, need to understand that clients with a chronic disease or disability often become quite knowledgeable about their condition. Rather than be threatened by the members' knowledge, leaders should try to learn from them.

4. *Cutting off.* Certain members may try to use their superior knowledge about their condition to manipulate the leader, attempting to dominate

the discussion or discount the leader's effectiveness because of lesser knowledge. The leader may need to use cutting-off skills to make sure that such members do not sabotage the purpose of the group.

5. *Being knowledgeable.* Having as much knowledge as possible about the disease or disability is always helpful. A few illustrations may help to emphasize this importance. For example, when working with young men with spinal cord injuries, sexual dysfunction is frequently a major topic that members wish to discuss. Often there is a high degree of misinformation about sexual problems that circulates among such patients. The leader will need to have—or make available through medical staff—sound information on the disability and sexual dysfunction. Also, he needs to anticipate the anxiety surrounding this topic. Group members who have had a stroke may experience mood swings caused by their physical condition, depending on the nature and extent of brain damage. It is important for the leader to be aware of the cause of such mood swings, to make sure the affected member knows the cause, and to ensure the other group members understand. Stroke patients may also experience difficulty expressing themselves at times or fully comprehending others' ideas. Much support and encouragement must be given to such members to keep them involved in the group. Cardiac patients may develop a preoccupation with death and a concern about how much physical energy they can expend safely. Again, misinformation is common; even accurate information is often not fully comprehended because of these patients' high anxiety levels. Education, along with support and encouragement, is important when working with cardiac patient groups.

6. *Understanding the psychological ramifications of being in a residential treatment center.* A final consideration in working with group members with problems of chronic disease or disability in a residential treatment program is the effect the setting may have on members' outlook and behavior. Most hospitals and rehabilitation facilities regiment behavior and foster dependency. Patients are frequently told when to get up in the morning, when to eat, what activities to attend, when, if, and how often they may use a telephone, and so forth. Patients may even develop a belief that their lives are literally in the hands of the medical staff. Regimented thinking and dependency may lead to apathy on the part of such group members. Leaders may find the need to work with both staff and group members in countering this apathy.

Survivors of Sexual Abuse

Sexual abuse of children and adolescents is a significant mental health problem. To help people heal from the abuse, groups for survivors are being conducted for teenagers and adults in such places as mental health centers, abuse shelters, and drug and alcohol centers.

Value and Kinds of Groups

Survivors of sexual abuse are likely to benefit from one of two kinds of groups: support or therapy. Most of these groups are therapy groups because the content relates to painful events and memories. Groups provide an opportunity for survivors to speak of their pain, perhaps for the first time, with others who have also been victimized as children or adolescents. These discussions can be empowering because they validate the abusive experiences and cut through the veil of secrecy that most survivors were subjected to as children. The chance to speak openly in a supportive, confidential setting often helps survivors gain courage to work more productively in their individual therapy.

Screening

When establishing a group dealing with abuse, the leader must consider the maturity level of potential members. We feel that the minimum age should be 12, although in most cases, 13 or 14 is a better age. We usually recommend that a potential member become involved in individual counseling before joining a survivors' therapy group. Individual therapy gives survivors a chance to gain an initial understanding of what happened to them. It is not unusual for survivors to deny or rationalize their abuse or to feel overwhelmed with shame. Survivors can benefit more from a therapy group when they have passed beyond their denial and are firmly committed to healing from their abusive experiences.

An individual interview with the leader before the first group session is especially important in a survivor's group. Members should be informed of the purpose of the group, its goals, the frequency and length of sessions, the group rules, and the techniques that will be used to help members work therapeutically on their issues. The interview should serve as a time for potential members to decide whether they feel ready to be in a therapy group. A member who is not ready for open discussions or is ambivalent about being in the group may feel too vulnerable to participate and may want to continue with individual therapy.

Size of Group

Most of the time, these groups are quite small. We recommend no more than six members and often as few as three or four, depending on the members, their ages, and their stage of healing.

Length of Sessions

Sessions should last 2 to 2½ hours to allow time for members to go to a deeper level and have ample time to come out of the pain. Sessions shorter than 2 hours may leave members feeling "unzipped."

Number of Sessions

Survivor work in groups may take many sessions. However, because of the pain and distress survivors may experience, it is important to keep members motivated to work on issues. We suggest setting up groups on a time-limited basis – 6 or 8-weeks. Although the group will likely continue for many months, these benchmarks allow members to assess their progress and decide whether they wish to continue or take a break. It is especially important to avoid leading an ongoing group where the members and the leader become comfortable with meeting but are not doing the work that is needed.

Special Skills

Leaders of survivors' groups should have considerable knowledge of the issues surrounding incest and sexual abuse. Classes, readings, workshops, and leading under the supervision of a more experienced leader should be aspects of the leader's preparation. If the leader is also a survivor of sexual abuse, she should consider the progress she has made in her own healing. As is true in leading any group, personal issues that the leader has yet to resolve could interfere with the leader's role or effectiveness.

Therapy groups for survivors focus in-depth on the pain of the individual members. However, this does not mean that the members must discuss details of their experiences in the group setting. The extent of detail discussed will depend on the comfort level of the members and the therapeutic needs of each member.

Because of the potentially intense reaction of individual members when exploring their abuse, we recommend that the group leader work with one member at a time rather than, as might be true in other kinds of therapy groups, attempting to take the entire group to a deeper level. Even the most skilled leader will be ineffective in trying to deal with the severe pain of four or five group members simultaneously. Leaders will soon discover that most members of survivors' groups can benefit greatly from watching other members explore their issues.

We support the idea that those in a survivor's therapy group either remain in individual therapy or, at least, maintain periodic contact with their therapist. In many instances, the individual therapist will be the group leader. It is important for members to have a "safe person" with whom to process their experiences if the group experience becomes overwhelming.

Divorce Groups

For many people, getting a divorce is one of the hardest periods in a person's life. Many mental health centers and churches offer groups for those going through a divorce. Groups for those divorcing fall into two major categories—recovery groups and starting-over groups. Recovery groups help people feel that they are not alone in their pain over their divorce. Hearing and helping others with similar issues can be quite therapeutic, and groups can help the members not focus so much on themselves. Also, sometimes the pain is such that a member may feel there is no hope until she sees other members progressing through the stages of grief. Recovery groups are usually short-term groups, lasting 6 to 8 weeks. Recovery groups can also be either open or closed. Ideally, they would be closed, but because clients at an agency may need such a group, having the group be open might work best for the population being served. Many people who complete a recovery group go on to a starting-over group.

Starting-over groups help members to do just that—start over. Support, sharing, caring, and risk taking can be experienced in a starting-over group. Often feeling a sense of belonging is quite helpful for those who do not have a local support system, because family and friends are either far away or nonexistent. If they are closed, starting-over groups can last for several months, or they can be open and last indefinitely.

A third category of divorce groups is the parenting group, intended to help divorcing parents with single parenting and the shared parenting process. Groups for single parents and non-custodial parents are being conducted in churches, mental health centers, and schools.

Screening

When setting up a divorce group, the leader must be clear about the group's type and purpose. If the leader is not clear, then the composition of members may be such that the group cannot be successful. Divorce recovery groups consist of members who are currently going through a divorce or are recently divorced and are still very much grieving the loss. For these groups, the leader wants to make sure the member is not in so much pain that he would not be ready for the group. Some people need time with an individual counselor before joining a recovery group. Starting-over groups are for people who have worked through the initial pain and loss on their own, with a therapist, or in a group, but who are still looking for help and support in fully letting go and getting on with their new life.

Group Size and Length of Sessions

These groups should not have more than eight members, because there must be time for each person to share. Often these groups end up having only three or four members, which is fine, because the members are usually willing to talk about their issues. Sessions usually last between 1½ and 2 hours.

Special Skills

A leader of a recovery group must have a thorough knowledge of grief counseling and not be afraid of the emotional pain that will be exhibited. Also, the leader must be skilled at individual counseling, because the leader often works with one member at a time. Working with one person at a time is usually quite effective if the leader uses theories that the other members can apply to their own situation.

Rational emotive behavior therapy (REBT) or cognitive behavioral therapy (CBT) is quite useful in recovery groups because most of the members are telling themselves a number of irrational sentences about approval, failure, and unhappiness. Many say to themselves that they don't think they can live without their partner or that they will never be happy again. Also, they may feel much anger and blame either themselves or their partners; this needs to be discussed and challenged. The skilled leader can use REBT or CBT to dispute these ideas. It is important for the leader to be strong in theory; she cannot rely heavily on the members for helpful input, because they all are telling themselves many of the same things.

The leader's role in a starting-over groups is to make sure that members discuss important issues, such as dealing with an ex-spouse, anger, issues with children, meeting new people, and dating again. The leader has many options in the way this kind of group is conducted. She can let the members direct the focus of the group by letting them bring up topics that are relevant for them, or she can use a format where she brings up relevant topics at each session. Some leaders who prefer the latter model use one of the many books or workbooks that have been published about divorce. One excellent book we have found is *Rebuilding* by Bruce Fisher (2005).

Leaders of parenting groups need to have a good theoretical base such as Adlerian, TA, or behavioral. They should also have experience in dealing with the different issues that arise in parenting after a divorce, especially a divorce where the spouses do not get along and see the world quite differently.

Adult Children of Alcoholics (ACOA)

Adults who grew up in alcoholic or addicted families often have problems stemming from all the chaos and craziness that occurred during childhood. Groups provide an excellent place for people to hear that they are not alone and that others have some of the same feelings, fears, and habits that they do.

Kinds of Groups

There are three basic kinds of groups for adult children of alcoholics: leaderless support groups, leader-led support groups, and therapy groups. All these groups are valuable and have helped millions who have been involved with one or more of them. Our discussion will focus on leader-led support groups and therapy groups.

Screening

Leaders of support groups for ACOAs want to make sure the members are ready to be in such a group. If screening is not conducted, leaders may find they have members who actually should be in individual therapy rather than a support group. A support group can come early in a person's recovery and can help the person become aware of the issues that he has, or it can come when a person is in a later stage of recovery.

Leaders definitely should screen for a therapy group to make sure the members are appropriate. The leader will want to make sure that any potential member is able to function in a group. In addition, potential members should not be in such great need that individual therapy would be more helpful than group therapy.

Group Size and Length of Sessions

For leader-led ACOA support groups, 8–12 members is good because you mainly want members to share and support each other. ACOA therapy groups should not have more than 6 members and may be as small as 4 because members are often working on painful, emotional issues. We recommend that ACOA groups last at least 2 hours because usually most members have much to share.

Number of Sessions

ACOA support groups are often open groups, so they last indefinitely. Closed therapy groups last anywhere from 8 to 15 sessions and can be extended if the leader feels more time would be beneficial.

Special Skills

Any leader of ACOA groups must have extensive knowledge about alcoholism and its effects on family members. A leader definitely needs to understand issues such as trust, intimacy, shame, guilt, and abandonment that plague most ACOAs. The leader must be prepared to deal with much emotional pain and anger. The Gestalt technique of talking to an empty chair that represents the alcoholic or addict has proven very effective. Using TA seems to give members a better understanding of themselves now and when they were living with an alcoholic parent. Activities such as family sculpture or psychodrama are extremely valuable if led by a skilled leader who can deal with the emotional material generated.

If you plan to lead these groups, be sure to get the necessary skills and knowledge. Too often, we hear of mental health workers leading ACOA groups when they do not have the knowledge or the individual counseling skills essential for leading such groups.

Multicultural Issues in Groups

In thinking about multicultural groups or diversity in groups, leaders need to be aware of some specific situations. In the second part of this section, we discuss multicultural groups that are formed for the purpose of exploring and understanding differences. First, we focus on what most often occurs regarding diverse populations.

Frequently, leaders need to be prepared to deal with differences such as race, religion, and sexual orientation. Members of different cultural and social backgrounds will likely have different perspectives and values, and the leader needs to be prepared to deal with these differences if the differences cause tension or confusion among the members. If tension arises between or among members *because* of cultural differences, often the main purpose of the group cannot be dealt with until these issues are resolved.

When differences are obviously present, the leader has to decide whether to focus on the differences that have arisen. The decision to point out cultural differences among members depends greatly upon the purpose of the group. If a counselor is working with a group of volunteer students on the task of planning a student party for a favorite retiring teacher, and the members are from various cultural backgrounds, cultural differences may surface in terms of suggestions for the celebration. The leader would probably not focus too long on the cultural differences, because they most likely would not play a major role in the planning of the retirement party. However, in a school group focusing on friendships that includes diverse cultural points of view, the leader may want to point out cultural differences that influence interpersonal styles and facilitate an exchange of cultural perspectives.

■ EXAMPLES

This group consists of new students, both girls and boys, in a middle school setting.

LEADER: Now that we've gotten acquainted and spent time last week talking about your first several weeks in a new school, I thought we might talk about how you are doing making friends here. Any thoughts or comments on how you are doing with friendships?

AMY: It's really hard coming to a new school. My mom thinks a party for some of my classmates would help me make some friends. I don't think anyone would come.

LEADER: That's a good topic. We'll come back to that.

PETE: I have been mostly hanging out where the guys play basketball. The other day, I just grabbed the ball and tried a basket from the side. I missed, but right away they asked me to play. I got two new friends already.

LEADER: So Pete, you found that by being assertive, you were accepted. How about someone else?

KAMEKO: I could never do that. In my country, we were taught to be patient. Wait and friends will come to you.

PETE: But you could wait a long time. Sometimes you have to show you want to become a part of their group.

LIAN: I am like Kameko. My parents have taught me that I may offend people by being too pushy, so I also wait until someone seeks me out.

LEADER: It sure seems that for Lian and Kameko, the way you were raised may be playing a part in your not making friends. Maybe some of you can share your thoughts on how the American culture works in regards to making friends.

In this example cultural differences have definitely emerged. The leader decides to focus on these differences, because it may help Lian and Kameko.

■ ■ ■

In this example, the leader, a pastor trained in counseling, is leading a premarital values exploration group for his parishioners in a large urban setting. There are five couples from various cultural backgrounds. The leader has spent time privately with each couple discussing their plans for marriage and what they might wish to gain from participating in six sessions of the group. It is 10 minutes into the second session.

LEADER: Joe, you seem like you have something to say.

JOE: Sally and I talked about how important it is for us to figure out how to have kids at an early age and still have both of us working. I don't think that's going to be easy. We both have careers to build, yet we don't want to wait to have kids because we want to be young parents.

PHIL: I'd actually like to stay at home and let Peggy work after her leave is up. I can set up a home office and be very productive. She has a much higher earning potential than I do.

ABDUL: But why wouldn't Sally and Peggy stay at home to care for the children? That's what Kamilah will do. Children need their mothers. That is their work.

LEADER: Abdul, your point of view is very interesting and I think probably comes from your cultural upbringing.

ABDUL: Most definitely. *(In a rather dogmatic tone)* The role of a woman is to be there for her husband and children. She should . . .

LEADER: *(In a calm, soft voice)* Abdul, let me interrupt. I think there are obvious differences here based on cultural values. Rather than presenting your view as law, I think it would be better and helpful to hear how your culture views women and children, and then you can hear how Phil, Joe, and others here see the role of women based on their cultural upbringing or desires or what have you.

Here, the leader quickly intervenes when members express differing cultural views and decides that focusing on the differences will be beneficial. The leader also wants to prevent any tension by trying to get Abdul to understand that others in the room have values very different from his.

■ ■ ■

It is the second session of a group of high school senior girls talking about their plans after graduating from high school.

LEADER: Where do you plan to go to college?

MARQUITA: I'm going to room with my sister who goes to the University of Texas. She loves the university, so I figured why not go there? I want to get away from home but not be by myself.

SUSAN: I'm going to go as far away as I can so that my family won't bug me.

DARLENE: I'm going to go to a college in Florida because I want to be near the water.

FATIMA: I will stay here since I'm not married.

HEDAYA: Me too. My father would never support me going away to school.

SUSAN: You two ought to live a little. There's nothing here in this town for you.

MARQUITA: What in the world does married have to do with it? I think maybe you are afraid....

LEADER: *(In a kind, forceful voice)* Hey, hold on just a second. I think we need to consider that what Fatima and Hedaya may be saying may have to do with their culture. Is this right?

FATIMA: For sure. I'd love to go away but my father would not think of it unless I was married. It is hard sometimes for me to listen to others in here who have so much more freedom than I do. Is it hard for you, Hedaya?

HEDAYA: Yes. I don't think all of you understand our culture.

LEADER: Why don't you two take a few minutes and tell us about it?

Here the leader sees the importance of pointing out the cultural differences, and how different values may be operating. Focusing on the differences may clear up some confusion.

■ ■ ■

We believe that in most group situations members should neither be allowed to nor encouraged to argue with one another about cultural or diversity differences. Usually little is accomplished by arguing. This is a group at a mental health center and members are talking about the holidays.

BRIAN: ... I think it is wrong that my parents won't let me bring Eric, my lover, home for Thanksgiving.

RALPH: I understand why they don't want you to do that. I would not let my child do that. I think it is wrong.

BILL: Oh, Ralph, get off of it! Open your mind up.

RALPH: What do you mean, open my mind up? You need to read the Bible.

LEADER: Wait, guys. We're not having a discussion about homosexuality. We're talking about the holidays. Let's focus on issues you have, and I want people to try to listen and be helpful and understanding.

In this example, the leader decided not to focus on the differences, because the purpose was to focus on Thanksgiving; it was a week away and the leader knew that a number of the members had some issues regarding the holidays. In a later session, the leader may decide to focus on the different views, especially if the leader feels that the differences are causing tension in the group.

True Multicultural Groups

As we mentioned earlier, some leaders form multicultural groups or lead groups of people from a different culture than their own. The following examples should give you some ideas about how these groups should and should not be conducted.

■ **EXAMPLES**

The group is a multicultural group on a college campus led by a professor of religious studies from the Middle East and a campus minister. The purpose of the group is to discuss cultural beliefs derived from several religions, and their impact on the members. In recruiting members, the leaders stressed that the intent of the group is more than a simple exchange of information—it will involve personal sharing. Ten students from various cultural backgrounds and religious beliefs volunteered for the five-session group.

The members were asked to get into pairs and discuss how their religious and cultural beliefs have been formative in their lives. They are told that when they return to the large group, each will be asked to introduce their partner and talk about the impact of their cultural and religious beliefs on their lives.

LEADER 1: Now that we're back, I'd like to start with asking one of you to introduce your partner to the group.

JENNIE: I'll start. This is Daya. He is 19 and comes from Pakistan, where, in his family, he was not allowed to date as a teenager. When he came to this country, his family tried to fix him up with the daughter of a friend from a neighboring village over there, but Daya saw there were opportunities to meet all kinds of people here and didn't want to date this girl. And this has been a problem between him and his family.

DAYA: This is Jennie. Jennie grew up in what you call the suburbs here. She was into every kind of thing, like soccer and ice-skating and ballet. She feels the suburb where she lived had kind of its own culture and if you didn't do a lot of things you were not very much liked. She is a Christian but is studying Zen Buddhism now because she wants to make her life more simple and quiet her mind.

LEADER 2: That's interesting. Both of you are trying to break from some of the way you were raised. Who will go next?

TANI: Yolanda was my partner. She was raised a Christian till she was 12, when her mother married a man who followed Islam, so that's what she believes now. She feels Islam gives her more structure to her life but doesn't like some of the ways that women are treated by Muslim men.

JENNIE: *(In an inquisitive voice)* Yolanda, you are not wearing one of those things that cover your head. Why not?

YOLANDA: I don't usually dress in with a hijab and that bothers many Muslim men. I have been reading this wonderful book by this liberal-thinking Muslim woman, Asra Nomani, and it has really gotten me to think about courage and how I want to be as a Muslim woman.

LEADER 2: Let's finish hearing from everyone and then maybe we can hear more about your thoughts on being a Muslim woman.

LEADER 1: *(Having seen Daya's head nodding as Yolanda was speaking)* Daya, it'll be interesting to hear what your thoughts are about Yolanda's views.

This is a multicultural group that is going to focus mainly on cultural differences. The leader's role is to facilitate discussion, to help members learn about other cultures, and to challenge their way of seeing the world through just their own eyes.

■　■　■

When leading a group made up of people from a different culture or different cultures, you need to understand their culture and ways of being in a group. We close this section with a brief account of how not understanding the culture can really create problems for the leader.

In 1989, I (Riley Harvill) was fortunate enough to be invited to conduct a series of group counseling workshops as a visiting professor at the University of Hong Kong. Unfortunately I responded to my good fortune with both ignorance and arrogance. I went there thinking that the vast store of knowledge I possessed was going to "WOW" them! After all, they had never—by their own admission—seen live demonstrations of counseling.

Because the participants were eager to see it rather than hear about it, I had no trouble pulling together a demonstration group, and because the participants were well acquainted with each other, we got right down to business.

Touted as a therapy group workshop, one of the women in the group—who had studied in America—quickly shared that she was distant from her mother because of recent arguments, the gist of which centered on old Chinese traditions and family loyalty versus independence and individualism. It seemed evident to me that she wanted to break free of the long-standing cultural bonds of her upbringing and gain the kind of independence that we Americans are so proud of.

If there is such a group-counseling skill as "going for the jugular," I demonstrated it. I was not going to let such a value as desire for independence slip through my therapeutic fingers. Not only was it my fervent intent to help this woman think for herself and break free of archaic obligations, but I was also going to artfully demonstrate to the class how to lead a group member to insight and change.

Like a stage play, the emotional pitch rose in a kind of dramatic crescendo; my client's emotions were palpable as she wept with anguish over the choices that lay before her. The remainder of the group was transfixed on the counseling work like medical students watching surgery for the first time. I was certain they had never seen anything like this before. I remember thinking that they would certainly anoint me as the next counseling guru, and, when the dissection was complete and my client had been skillfully sewn back together, I looked up with puffed chest only to find that at least one-half the class had left and the other half was considering the same. Furthermore, my group members were looking at the floor as though someone had just died. And although I wasn't sure if the death was mine, the woman's, or the group's, something had gone terribly wrong.

Some time later I discovered that I had caused this poor woman to lose face. I had facilitated not only her crying, but her criticism of her family as well. Furthermore, I had shamed her entire family by encouraging her to reveal the existent riff between all of them. "Her ancestors would not be pleased," someone offered. Great, I thought. I've not only offended this woman but probably her entire lineage extending back to the Xia dynasty. Needless to say, an attempt to offer an explanation of my extremely American-like actions seemed rather trifling in comparison to 3,000 years of shamed relatives.

In the end, it was another one of those dreadful learning experiences and, of course, as these things go, a valuable lesson indeed. Values are powerful and exist within the context of culture, nationality, ethnic practices, and family and life experiences. Not only did I not share her values, I didn't understand them either. The independence that was valuable to me was not valuable to her.

In summary, we believe that effective leaders must give much thought to the individual needs of members. The issues of diversity and multiculturalism you deal with as a leader will be determined by the purpose of your group. At times, these issues will affect the dynamics of your group (Jacobs & Schimmel, 2009). On other occasions, they will be the focus. Although it is unrealistic to expect that group leaders can know every dimension and nuance of a given culture, we hope you will continue to read and discuss these issues, broadening your understanding and awareness and expanding your frame of reference.

Concluding Comments

In this chapter, we discussed considerations and skills involved when leading groups for ten different client populations: children, adolescents, couples, addicts, the elderly, the disabled, survivors of sexual abuse, those who are divorced, ACOAs, and multicultural members. Leading groups for each of these populations requires specialized knowledge. Our comments here are meant to introduce you to the issues and considerations involved. You will want to do additional reading and attend workshops on the specific groups that you will be leading.

We want to reiterate that there are many populations that we omitted or just touched upon. We did not stress specifically gay and lesbian groups, eating disorders, anxiety disorder groups, or women's groups. Each of these, along with so many other populations, could have been covered here and can be explored through books, journals, and the Internet. For example, a good starting point for women's groups would be the September 1999 issue of the *Journal for Specialists in Group Work*.

Chapter 18

Issues in Group Counseling

In this chapter, we cover issues that have been briefly touched upon in previous chapters. We discuss coleading, evaluation of groups, legal issues, research, training, and future trends. We believe each of these areas is important, though you may find some areas more important than others. The section on evaluation is essential for conducting productive groups because all leaders should consider how to evaluate any group that they lead. The sections on research, training, and future trends should be of special interest to doctoral students and anyone who plans to teach or work with groups extensively.

Coleading

Advantages of Coleading

Coleading is a luxury that many counselors will never get to experience because the setting in which they work does not have the staff to pay for two leaders. We did not focus on coleading. We wanted to prepare you for leading by yourself because that will likely be your experience. In this section, we discuss the benefits, disadvantages, and models of coleading.

Leading groups with one or more colleagues can be very advantageous, especially for a beginner. A major advantage of coleading is that it is often easier than leading a group alone. A coleader can provide additional ideas for planning and can provide support, especially when working with intense therapy groups or with difficult groups. Coleaders often bring different points of view and varied life experiences to the group, providing members with alternative sources of opinion and information on issues. Differences in the interpersonal style of each coleader can also create variations in the flow or tone of the group that make it more interesting. There may be occasions when a coleader with more specialized knowledge about a given population is needed. For example, in an educational group for pregnant teenagers, a coleader with a thorough knowledge of prenatal care can add valuable, relevant information to the group.

Coleaders can serve as models for members of the group. Coleaders who work well together demonstrate effective interaction skills and cooperation. Even though this would seem like a major advantage, limited research of coleading actually does not indicate that modeling is an advantage. McNary and Dies (1993) found that few leader-to-leader interactions actually occurred in the context of group psychotherapy. Opposite-sex coleaders may serve as role models and may be particularly effective in working with couples groups or with marital concerns. In certain kinds of groups, male and female teams can also serve as parental figures in helping members work through unresolved family issues. It should be pointed out that it is not essential that coleaders be of the opposite sex. Many groups are led successfully by coleaders of the same sex. Alfred (1992) found no gender differences in how group members perceived female and male coleaders.

When coleading, leaders also get a chance to get feedback from another leader. Additionally, leaders learn from watching each other handle various situations. *For maximum awareness of nonverbal cues, coleaders should* **sit across** *from each other in the circle.* This provides an opportunity for them to easily maintain eye contact with each other while viewing the members from different vantage points.

We especially feel that coleading is valuable in training a person who is going to be leading groups he has never led before. By coleading a few times with a good, experienced leader, a new leader can then lead on his own and feel reasonably comfortable. Even though Dies (1994) states "there is no evidence that the presence of two therapists enhances the quality or efficacy of the therapeutic outcome," we believe coleading can be advantageous when it is done well. More research needs to be done on the advantages of coleading.

Disadvantages and Problems of Coleading

A number of disadvantages and problems may occur because of coleading. One disadvantage for some agencies and settings is that coleading takes time away from other counseling duties and can add stress to an already demanding work schedule. Therefore, coleading may not be a good use of staff's time.

Problems with coleading groups arise mainly from differences in attitude, style, and goals of the leaders. Coleading becomes a disadvantage when two leaders do not see group leading the same way. Dies (1994, p. 141) states that "limited findings suggest that coleadership may complicate group process unless the leaders manage their relationship effectively within the sessions." As Corey, Corey, and Corey (2009, p. 29) state: "The choice of a coleader is important. If two leaders are incompatible, their group is bound to be negatively affected." Incompatible leaders can confuse the members because each leader wants to take the group in her own direction.

■ EXAMPLE

Ineffective Coleading

LEADER 1: To get started this evening, we'd like each person to share how the week went. I think it is important to start with comments about your week so that everyone is aware of how you are progressing.

LEADER 2: You might also have some questions from last week's session. We'll be glad to answer them, too.

STACY: I had a good week. I exercised three times at the track!

LEADER 1: That's great Stacy. John, you were going to visit your dad. How did that work out?

JOHN: Great. When he asked me if I had decided if I was going to medical school, I just said I was still thinking about it instead of arguing with him.

LEADER 2: That's something we talked about last week, not arguing with parents. Instead, it is often better to simply acknowledge what they have said. Let's talk some more about arguing with parents.

SALLY: What about teachers? Can we discuss them?

LEADER 2: Sure.

In this example, Leader 2 is working at cross-purposes with Leader 1. Leader 1 is looking for self-reports about significant events that occurred during the week, but Leader 2 shifts the focus to handling authority figures. Although the focus of Leader 2 is not necessarily wrong, it is poorly timed. The members were sharing events of the week and then were forced to shift their thinking. Leader 1 has a difficult decision: to abandon the original goal and allow Leader 2 to pursue this new direction or to try to get back to processing the week and risk a power struggle with the coleader in front of the group. These coleaders are not working well together and will need to correct this problem if they are to continue to share the leading.

■ ■ ■

If either or both coleaders feel a need to compete or dominate, coleading will be difficult and the members will suffer. Coleaders must work as a team. The process of coleading should add to rather than detract from the group experience. Coleaders should be secure in their relative position in the group. To have a good working relationship, coleaders must like and respect each other.

When two leaders have distinctly different styles of leading or opposing views on how to proceed in the group, coleading is not recommended. Differences can be valuable, but totally different styles usually will cause friction, frustration, or both. For instance, if one leader is trained to focus mostly on process and the other, to focus mostly on content, each leader will be frustrated by the other's style of leading.

Coleaders must also be willing to set aside time to plan each session and share feedback. The advantage of coleading breaks down if the coleaders are unwilling to take the necessary time for planning. Experience suggests that coleaders who try to go to the sessions without having prepared jointly run the risk of not flowing well together. This may lead to conflict and bad feelings. Coleading requires the joint commitment of leaders to work together for the benefit of the members.

Coleading Models

Three models of coleading are presented here: the alternate leading model, the shared leading model, and the apprentice model. Each of these models assumes that the coleaders are committed to discussing goals and activities for each session. The model used will depend on the purpose and goals of the group, the experience of the two leaders, the individual styles of the coleaders, and the degree to which the coleaders feel they can coordinate their efforts.

The Alternate Leading Model   The alternate leading model is one where coleaders alternate taking the primary leading role. Alternating roles are usually decided upon during the planning of a given session. For example, one coleader may be responsible for this week's session and the other coleader for next week's, or one coleader may be responsible for the first half of the session and the other leader for the last half. With experience, coleaders who work well together find that shifting roles goes smoothly.

Coleaders may want to use the alternate coleading model if they differ somewhat in their approaches and find themselves pulling the group in opposing directions. By alternate leading, one coleader has primary responsibility to direct the group for a specific period of time, without worrying about interruptions from the coleader. This does not mean that the second coleader is inactive. On the contrary, the coleader may offer supporting comments, clarify, or summarize when it seems to be helpful to the group.

The Shared Leading Model   The shared leading model is one where coleaders share the leadership, with neither designated as the leader during a specific time period. Leaders flow with each other and lead jointly. Although in this model they lead together, at times one coleader will take charge, such as when conducting an exercise or working with an individual. Also, the other leader is ready to come in at any appropriate point and continue in the same general direction.

■ EXAMPLE

LEADER 1: Maybe to get started with the group this evening, we'll ask for people to report on how the week went. *(Pause)*

LEADER 2: John, you were going to visit your dad. How did that work out?

JOHN: It was great. When he brought up my going to medical school, I just told him I was still thinking about it instead of arguing with him. We got along a lot better.

LEADER 2:   I'm really glad you found avoiding an argument helpful. What happened with other people?

AMY: I went ahead and told my mom I was going to work at the beach this summer. She took it pretty well, but I know she'll bring it up again.

LEADER 1:   I'm glad you went ahead and took that risk. Maybe we'll talk more about how you'll handle your mom if she brings it up again.

LEADER 2:   Amy and John had a chance to handle some important issues for them this week. Did others of you do something similar?

In this example, the coleaders are actively working together, drawing out and encouraging members. Both leaders have a common goal in mind, getting members to share events that happened during the week in the expectation that a worthwhile topic or some individual work may emerge. If this does not happen, the leaders will move on to an activity they have planned for the session.

■   ■   ■

When using the shared leading model, coleaders should be careful not to echo each other's words; that is, one leader will say something and then the other leader will say something that is very similar to the first leader's comments. Also, it is important for the leaders not to get into one commenting, then the other, then the first leader commenting again, thus creating a dialogue with each other to the exclusion of the members.

The Apprentice Model   In this model, one leader is much more experienced than the other; the group is led mostly by the more experienced leader. The coleader is present to learn by watching and by trying her hand at leading at various times. This is beneficial because the less experienced leader knows someone is there to help out if necessary when she is leading. The more experienced leader benefits by having someone to plan and to debrief with after the sessions. Also, most skilled leaders enjoy teaching others how to lead groups effectively.

Closing Thoughts on Coleading

In summary, choosing to colead will depend on a number of factors. Among the most important are your style of leadership, the needs of your group members, and the availability of a compatible coleader who is willing to make the commitment to plan and cooperate in this joint venture. Regardless of the coleading model selected, it is important for coleaders to maintain a consistent tone in the group and work toward common goals. This requires careful listening to each other, along with an awareness of each other's nonverbal cues. In addition to paying attention to each other, coleaders should watch the members for clues regarding the impact of their coleading styles. If members seem confused or if momentum fails to build, the coleaders should consider their interaction as a possible cause.

Legal Issues

Group leaders can become involved in lawsuits if they do not use due care and act in good faith. Therefore, as a leader, you will want to be sure to practice within your limits of expertise and not be negligent in performing your duties as a group leader. A leader who uses techniques and practices that are very different from those commonly accepted by others in the profession may be considered negligent. It is your obligation to make sure members are not harmed by you, the other members, or the group experience. Paradise and Kirby (1990) list the obligation to protect the client and other members as one of the main legal issues in group work. We have heard stories of members being harmed by the leader's inappropriate use of exercises or the use of very powerful exercises when members were not ready for such experiences. We have also heard of groups where members were allowed to viciously attack other members. These practices are not considered ethical, and the counselor could be brought up on charges of malpractice if a member felt harmed by such experiences.

The most important point to remember regarding legal issues is to know the laws in your state regarding counseling, clients' rights, and the rights of parents and minors. Also, it is important that you do not practice outside your level of training and that you at all times demonstrate care and compassion for your group members (Corey, William, & Moline, 1995).

Evaluating Groups

Most group leaders do not evaluate their groups either because it takes extra time or it forces them to look at the outcome of their professional work. Professionals can more easily believe that their work with clients has been helpful when they lack data to the contrary. Although group leaders should not become preoccupied with evaluating their groups, periodic evaluation can give them useful feedback about their approach to groups, as well as information on the kinds of experiences that are most helpful in meeting the goals of their members.

Three kinds of evaluations are possible: (1) evaluation of the changes that actually occur in members' lives, (2) self-evaluation by the group leader, and (3) evaluation by the members. There are advantages and limitations to each, and each type of evaluation serves a particular function.

Evaluation of the Changes in Members' Lives

Perhaps the most important type of evaluation is the evaluation of how the group experience has impacted the members' behavior. Do students get better grades in school or have fewer reported incidents of misbehavior? Do spouses communicate more effectively? Do teen mothers provide better care for their babies than they would have if they had not been in the group? Do unemployed workers from the group get jobs sooner than those not in the group? Do members who experience much guilt and anxiety cope with life better after being in the group? Some of these questions are rather easy to answer and some are difficult to answer, but there is an increasing demand for outcome-based evaluation. Agencies, schools, and institutions want to see data showing that the group work is effective in bringing about changes.

Some groups easily lend themselves to outcome-based evaluation, whereas with others, it may be difficult to quantify changes in members. Members' self-reports are one method of determining if they are actually changing. Throughout the life of the group, the leader should ask members to comment on changes that they are making. Of course, such responses are not always accurate, but the leader can often get some idea of the impact the group is having on the members. Another method of evaluating behavioral change is to have other people in the members' lives give a more objective evaluation. These outside evaluators may be teachers, employers, parents, spouses, friends, probation counselors, primary care medical treatment staff, or individual therapists. The leader may receive informal comments or anecdotes, such as, "Yes, Billy is definitely paying more attention in class," or more formal feedback through the use of a written behavioral checklist. Presuming that Billy's behavior in class had a negative impact on his academic work, checking Billy's grades at the end of the next full marking period would also be a way to evaluate the influence of the group. School counselors can also review data such as referrals for discipline issues for former group members and school attendance to determine if the group experience was successful for students.

To produce data measuring the outcome, the leader must follow a procedure that includes these steps:

1. Determine the outcome goals of the specific group (for example, students stay in school, students reduce the number of days of skipping school, grades increase, members stop smoking, members have fewer panic attacks, members get jobs). For some groups, the leader may need to determine goals for each member.

2. Collect pre-group data (for example, the number of panic attacks, number of days skipped, number of fights at work, number of work days missed).

3. Focus the group sessions on the desired outcome goals. Allow members to work on their goals.

4. Develop an appropriate form for members to complete regarding their progress toward the established goals. It is very important for the form

to contain questions that allow measurement of the outcome of the group.

5. Determine whether people other than the members can be involved in evaluating outcome and, if so, obtain permission from the members and contact those people.

6. Collect data periodically, using a form.

7. At the end of the group, collect data, using a form.

8. Plan for follow-up data collection by either mailing forms to the members (and others if appropriate) at certain intervals or giving members extra forms and asking them to send the completed forms at designated intervals. Collecting data at 3 months after the group ends, then 6 months, and then 1 year is an excellent way to evaluate the group based on lasting changes in the members.

The Leader's Self-Evaluation

Many leaders do a self-evaluation after each session. Usually a self-evaluation is simple and straightforward. The leader will want to recall any interactions or dynamics that seemed especially important and evaluate her role in the group. For example, "My instructions for doing the 'Family Sculpture' exercise were confusing" or "I could have cut off Dan earlier and kept the group from getting so restless" or "Sarah attacked Bill and I didn't do anything about it." The leader can ask herself these questions:

- How closely did I follow my plan?
- When I deviated from my plan, was it because I thought of a more appropriate strategy at the moment or because I felt lost or overwhelmed by the group?
- How closely was I able to meet the needs of the individual members?
- Did things happen in the group that I did not plan for or anticipate?
- Could I have predicted these with more forethought?
- What have I learned from the session that I can implement next time?
- On a 1–10 scale, how would I rate my overall satisfaction with the session? What can I do to improve the rating?

The leader should keep these self-evaluations and periodically review them to observe the progress that he is making. If there are areas where the leader feels he is not improving, he may wish to give them special attention or ask a fellow group leader or supervisor for help.

The Members' Evaluations

The leader will find it helpful to have members evaluate the group. An informal evaluation can be done as part of the closing of any session. The leader might say: "What happened in the group during this session that was particularly valuable for you?" A more formal evaluation can be done a third of the way or halfway through the group. This might involve a check sheet with questions about the process that takes place in the group, as well as its content, and ways in which the group has been helpful. An evaluation that is done midway through the group allows the leader to make changes that seem desirable based on the members' feedback. A final written evaluation is also helpful for the leader in planning future groups.

A useful evaluation form for the end of groups could contain the following questions, plus some additional ones that are specific to the given group.

- What were the most important things you gained from being in this group?
- What activities, discussions, or topics stood out for you?
- What did you like most about the group?
- What did you like least about the group?
- What would have made the group better for you?
- What could the leader have done differently that would have made the group better for you?

A leader should exercise caution when reading member evaluations. Some members may not like her and thus give inaccurate feedback, or members may have a need to please and therefore give only positive feedback. Some members give dishonest feedback because they feel threatened by or concerned for the leader. For example, if the leader continually asks members if they like the group or if it is being helpful to them, members may conclude that the leader is fishing for positive feedback and may be reluctant to offer constructive criticism. Some members develop what can be termed a "groupie" mentality; they identify so strongly with the power of the leader that, no matter what happens in the group, they believe it is for the good of the group. Because it is natural to look for positive feedback, such feedback may lull leaders into thinking that their groups are terrific, when in fact there are problems that should be corrected.

We cannot sufficiently stress the benefit of evaluating your groups. Much can be learned from evaluations, using any of the preceding methods of evaluation. The ultimate evaluation may lie in experimental research, with experimental and control groups. Research of this nature is difficult to design because accurate assessment of outcomes is not easy.

Research

Horne (1996, p. 66) states that during his tenure as journal editor for ASGW: "... there was little or no increase in research-based, evaluative studies in group work." Gladding (2008, p. 420) sums up the research section in his recent book by saying, "Overall, research on the effectiveness of groups needs to be greatly expanded to reach the level of sophistication that has been established on the effectiveness of individual counseling." Editorials have been written on why group research is difficult and why there is so little quality research in the group field (Asner-Self, 2009; Rubel & Villalba, 2009). Lack of time, lack of money, and lack of interest are cited as reasons. Another major reason for the lack of research is the difficulty of designing a research project where the variables can be controlled enough to study different aspects of group counseling. Corey (2008) states;

> the general consensus among experts is that the current knowledge of the effects of specific group treatments is modest at best. Researchers know little about how group processes mediate change in participants, how members influence group processes, and what dimensions of psychological functioning are most amenable to change in small groups (p. 41).

Although there have been many articles published encouraging group research, no one has come to the front with ongoing quality research, regarding either the training of group leaders or the effectiveness of group work. DeLucia-Waack (1998), the former editor of the *Journal for Specialists in Group Work*, has an excellent editorial regarding group research. She states that, "It is essential that we begin to understand both the content and process of how groups work. We must know what kinds of groups are effective with what kinds of populations" (pp. 235–236). In her article on research, DeLucia-Waack (1997) discusses some measures for evaluating group work and instruments for measuring both leaders' and members' behavior, and post-group assessment.

In our last edition, we wrote, "With greater emphasis being put on group therapy, we remain hopeful that more research will be conducted both at the university level and in the private sector." We can say for this edition that more research is being done, but still much more is needed in so many areas of group counseling. We agree with DeLucia-Waack that good data-based research is needed on the effectiveness of what leadership style is best for specific groups. It is our belief that research with school, mental-health, and drug and alcohol groups would show that an active, multi-sensory leadership approach would be more effective in most situations than one where the leader is more of a facilitator, focusing on group process and letting the members set the pace and tone. Unfortunately, no definitive research has been done to verify this belief. We do know that the predominant model taught in most graduate programs leans more toward the facilitator/process model, yet there is no data that justify this. We hope that researchers will empirically study different ways that students are taught to lead groups and what ways are more effective.

Training of Group Counselors

We have been group educators for a number of years and currently conduct workshops throughout the United States and Canada on group counseling. We are especially concerned about the training of school counselors when it comes to leading groups. Too often, they are taught a model that assumes that groups last 60 to 90 minutes, when in fact school groups usually last anywhere from 20 to 40 minutes. At workshops with school counselors, inevitably we hear comments about being taught a much more passive, time-consuming approach to groups. School counselors need group leadership skills that equip them for leading groups for a short period of time with non-volunteer members, very active kids, very shy kids, bullies, and potential dropouts.

Another major deficit in training that we have identified is that trainees do not get to practice using specific skills such as cutting off, drawing out, holding and shifting the focus, deepening the focus, and introducing and conducting an exercise. Many beginning counselors report that their group course consisted of being a member of a group, with part of the class time spent on processing the group. Being a member of a group does not prepare someone to lead groups. Some workshop participants reported having had courses with a practice component consisting of leading a group with their peers. It is definitely beneficial to practice, but unfortunately, this kind of practice usually does not accurately simulate what counselors will be doing in work settings when they graduate. Usually the students get to practice only once or twice during a semester. Much practice with classmates role-playing members of various kinds of groups in different settings is needed to prepare students for the kinds of groups that they will be leading when they graduate.

Our belief is that group skills can be taught like individual counseling skills; that is, the skill is described, demonstrated, and then practiced. We believe that effective training should include delineating specific skills, practicing those skills, and practicing leading groups similar to those the student will be leading after she graduates. Toth and Stockton agree: "This tends to indicate that the education of group leaders may well be enhanced, encouraged, and perhaps even accelerated through the development of certain skill-based approaches that use didactic, observational, and experiential methods" (1966, p. 107).

Another concern regarding training has to do with the ability to plan effective groups. As we said in Chapter 4, good planning is essential for good leading, and yet, at our workshops, many counselors comment that they did not learn how to plan their groups. The planning of quality sessions can and should be taught to anyone leading a group.

Our last concern about training at the university level deals with requiring a group experience during a graduate program. If a group experience is required, it should be productive, and the leader should model some of the skills necessary for leading groups in various settings. Too often, we hear workshop participants describe a boring or bad group experience at the graduate level. They complain of "just sitting there with the leader doing nothing." Workshop participants have said that a combination of lack of practice leading and their poor graduate group experience turned them off to groups.

Probably our biggest training concern is for those leading groups who have no training. Often, helpers in prisons, residential treatment centers, and group homes are asked to lead groups even though they have no training in group counseling or in counseling theory. It is important for anyone working in these settings to speak up about how no one should lead a group without proper training. If you are ever in a work setting where groups are being led, please try to make sure that all the group leaders are properly trained.

The Future

Most experts seem to agree that group work will continue to be a major force in the field of counseling. Gladding is very excited about the potential for groups: "There is little doubt that in the future, group work will be robust and permeate almost all segments of society" (2007, p. 17). Corey, Corey, and Corey (2009) have listed the increase in short-term structured groups for special populations as one of the major trends of the last decade. We are finding more and more professionals seeking training in leading specific kinds of groups where the leader takes much responsibility for what happens in the group. Many school districts are requesting training in group leadership because of the need for many different kinds of groups in the schools. Teachers are also being trained to lead support and academic advisement groups.

We believe that the future of group work lies in the integration of counseling theories with an active, multi-sensory, intrapersonal model of leading. More training in specific group leadership skills is essential if leaders are going to be prepared for all the different kinds of groups that will exist in the next 10 years. We also believe leaders need to learn more ways to involve the members in the therapeutic process while using counseling theories and the intrapersonal model. Therapists will need and demand better training as they become more aware of the legal and ethical issues surrounding group work.

Advocacy

Trained group leaders must speak out when untrained helpers are asked to lead groups. Unfortunately, some administrators view group work as something anyone can do, like washing dishes or sweeping a floor. Group work is a very demanding and skilled activity; whenever possible, trained leaders and experts need to keep spreading the word that no one should lead groups unless he or she has training to do so. Far too many groups are led by people who have little or no training.

Social Justice

Social justice has become a major area of emphasis in the field of counseling during the last few years (Singh & Salazar, 2010). The editor of *The Journal for Specialists in Group Work* in 2010 invited two leaders in the field, Anneliese A. Singh and Carmen F. Salazar, to serve as coeditors for two special issues that are devoted entirely to social justice (Singh & Salazar, 2010). These two special issues have a wealth of information regarding the history of social justice and examples social justice applied to group work. One article by Hays, Arredondo, Gladding and Toporek (2010) addresses the integrating of social justice in group work in the next decade.

Marketing

Nonvolunteer, reluctant people make up a large portion of members in groups in the United States. Residential centers, treatment centers, prisons, and schools often have mandatory groups. Too often, leaders do not show much enthusiasm for leading mandatory groups; thus the members tend to not get much from them. Counselors have to do much better at marketing the idea that groups can help people to change. Counselors have to sell this to the members. With nonvolunteer groups, leaders must be excited about what they are doing. In our workshops with the Federal Bureau of Prisons, we are teaching the leaders how to market change in groups with inmates. We have also done this in numerous workshops for drug and alcohol group leaders.

Groups in Prisons

The prison population in the United States is growing at a tremendous pace, which is forcing prisons to run more groups. Many jobs exist now, and the need for group workers will continue to grow in the prison system because one of the major therapeutic modalities is group counseling. We see this as an emerging area for group workers, and the workers need to be well trained, because the majority of prisoners are not highly motivated.

Groups in Medical Settings

Groups continue to be popular with health care providers. Many kinds of support groups now exist for various illnesses and for family members of people with devastating illnesses. Medical facilities will continue to recruit group workers to provide groups in the medical setting and in the community.

Groups for the Elderly

This population is growing and with the baby boomers getting older, there will be an even greater need for groups with the elderly. Activities, social, support, and therapy groups are all needed for this population. More attention is going to have to be given to training helpers to work with these groups.

Multicultural Groups

Throughout this book, we have mentioned the need to be aware of multicultural issues that may arise during a group session. The recent push to heighten counselors' awareness surrounding multicultural issues has been valuable (Salazaar, 2009). There now exist many articles pertaining to groups that focus on different cultures. A debate may arise regarding working with groups from the same culture (subculture) versus working with groups from the population at large. Both kinds of groups are valuable. Research will have to answer questions regarding which kind of group is best for various populations. Certainly, groups can serve as a way to gain greater understanding of the diverse population that now exists in North America.

Online Groups

At recent national conventions, workshops have been given regarding online groups. Given the current trend of using the Internet for almost everything, we would imagine that more and more online groups will be conducted. Page et al. (2000, p. 134) state "The extent of online group work is revealed by an online search for a support group conducted by the first author in March 1999, that resulted in 873,370 listings." We feel that whoever is leading these groups is doing something different from what we have written about here in this book, and the "leader" will need some very special skills to make this experience helpful and meaningful. With more and more people having video capabilities on their home computers, we most likely will see groups online using this technology. This can add to the experience and make the experience more personal, but certainly this has great limitations when compared to a face-to-face group. Page et al. (2000) present an excellent article with some additional references regarding online groups and software that is available to make the groups run quite smoothly. When asked if we think these groups may work for some people, our answer is *probably*. We simply do not have enough information to make any definitive statement about the benefits or harm that such an experience may cause.

Final Thoughts Regarding Leading Groups

Now that you are at the end of this book, we hope that you feel much more prepared to lead groups and are excited about trying to master the skills presented. At the beginning, we commented that we thought this book would give you an understanding of group dynamics and the skills necessary to allow you to lead almost any kind of group. We hope the book has been thorough enough to provide you with the basic tools for leading a group. We enjoy lead-ing groups and have enjoyed the challenge of writing about what we do. We would like to hear your comments. Please contact us if you have any questions, comments, or reactions to share (Ed.Jacobs@mail.wvu.edu or for groups in schools, Chris.Schimmel@mail.wvu.edu).

References

Adler, A. (1927). *Understanding human behavior*. New York: Greenberg.

Adler, A. (1964). *Social interest: A challenge to mankind*. New York: Capricorn.

Akos, P., & Martin, M. (2003). Transition groups for preparing students for middle school. *Journal for Specialists in Group Work, 28*, 139–154.

Alfred, A. R. (1992). Members' perception of co-leaders' influence and effectiveness in group psychotherapy. *Journal for Specialists in Group Work, 17*, 42–53.

American School Counselor Association. (2003). *The ASCA national model: A framework for school counseling programs*. Alexandria, VA: Author.

Anderson, D. (2007). Multicultural group work: A force for developing and healing. *Journal for Specialists in Group Work, 32*, 224–244.

Asner-Self, K. K. (2009). Research on groups. *Journal for Specialists in Group Work, 34*, 195–201.

Association for Specialists in Group Work. (2008). Guidelines for best practice. *Journal for Specialists in Group Work, 33*, 111–117.

Association for Specialists in Group Work. (1999). Principles for diversity-competent group workers. *Journal for Specialists in Group Work, 24*, 7–14.

Banks, V. (1999). A solution focused approach to adolescent group work. *The Australian and New Zealand Journal of Family Therapy, 29*, 78–82.

Bauman, S. (2009). Group work in the economic downturn. *Journal for Specialists in Group Work, 34*(2), 97–100.

Berg, I. K., & Reuss, N. H. (1998). *Solutions step by step: A substance abuse treatment manual*. New York: Norton.

Berne, E. (1964). *Games people play*. New York: Grove Press.

Blaker, K. E., & Samo, J. (1973). Communications games: A group counseling technique. *The School Counselor, 21*, 46–51.

Blatner, A. (2000). *Foundations of psychodrama: History, theory, and practice* (4th ed.). New York: Springer.

Brown, N. (2009). *Becoming a group leader.* Columbus: Merrill.

Campbell, C. A. & Dahir, C. A. (1997). *Sharing the vision: The national standards for school counseling programs.* Alexandria, VA: American School Counselor Association.

Capuzzi, D., & Gross, D. R. (2009). *Introduction to group counseling* (5th ed.). Denver, CO: Love.

Carroll, M. R. (1986). *Group work: Leading in the here and now* [Film]. Alexandria, VA: American Counseling Association.

Conyne, R. K., Harvill, R. L., Morganett, R. S., Morran, D. K., & Hulse-Killacky, D. (1990). Effective group leadership: Continuing the search for greater clarity and understanding. *Journal for Specialists in Group Work, 15,* 30–36.

Corey, G. (2008). *The theory and practice of group counseling* (7th ed.). Pacific Grove, CA: Brooks/Cole.

Corey, G., Corey, M. S., Callahan, P., & Russell, J. M. (2010). *Group techniques* (4th ed.). Pacific Grove, CA: Brooks/Cole.

Corey, M. S., Corey, G., & Corey, C. (2009). *Groups: Process and practice* (8th ed.). Pacific Grove, CA: Brooks/Cole.

Day, S. (2007). *Groups in practice.* Boston: Lahaska Press.

De Shazer, S. (1991). *Putting differences to work.* New York: Norton.

DeLucia-Waack, J. (1996). Multiculturalism is inherent in all group work. *Journal for Specialists in Group Work, 21,* 218–223.

DeLucia-Waack, J. (1997). Measuring the effectiveness of group work: A review and analysis of process and outcome measures. *Journal for Specialists in Group Work, 22,* 277–293.

DeLucia-Waack, J. (1998). What is the relationship between therapeutic factors and group work effectiveness really? *Journal for Specialists in Group Work, 23,* 235–236.

DeLucia-Waack, J. (1999). What makes an effective group leader? *Journal for Specialists in Group Work, 24,* 131–132.

DeLucia-Waack, J., & Donigian, J. (2004). *The practice of multicultural group work.* Pacific Grove, CA: Brooks/Cole.

DeLucia-Waack, J., Gerrity, D., Kalodner, C., & Riva, M. (2003). *Handbook of group counseling and psychotherapy.* Thousand Oaks, CA: Sage Publications.

Dies, R. R. (1994). Therapist variables in group psychotherapy research. In A. Fuhriman & G. M. Burlingame (Eds.), *Handbook of group psychotherapy: An empirical and clinical synthesis* (pp. 114–154). New York: Wiley.

Dyer, W., & Vriend, J. (1980). *Group counseling for personal mastery.* New York: Sovereign Books.

Egan, G. (2010). *The skilled helper* (9th ed.). Pacific Grove, CA: Brooks/Cole.

Ellis, A. (1962). *Reason and emotion in psychotherapy.* New York: Lyle Stuart.

Fisher, B. (2005). *Rebuilding* (3rd ed.). San Luis Obispo, CA: Impact.

Gazda, G. M. (1989). *Group counseling: A developmental approach* (4th ed.). Boston: Allyn & Bacon.

Geroski, A., & Kraus, K. (2002). Process and content in school psychoeducational groups: Either, both, none? *Journal for Specialists in Group Work, 27,* 233–245.

Gladding, S. T. (2000). *Counseling: A comprehensive profession* (4th ed.). New York: Merrill.

Gladding, S. T. (2008). *Group work: A counseling specialty* (5th ed.). New York: Merrill.

Glass, J. S., & Benshoff, J. M. (1999). PARS: A processing model for beginning group leaders. *Journal for Specialists in Group Work, 24,* 15–26.

Glasser, W. (2000). *Reality therapy in action.* New York: HarperCollins.

Hackney, H., & Cormier, L. S. (1994). *Counseling strategies and interventions* (4th ed.). Englewood Cliffs, NJ: Prentice-Hall.

Hagedorn, W. B., & Hirshhorn, M. A. (2009). When talking won't work: Implementing experiential group activities with addicted clients. *Journal for Specialists in Group Work, 34,* 43–67.

Hansen, J., Warner, R., & Smith, E. J. (1980). *Group counseling: Theory and practice.* Chicago: Rand McNally.

Harvill, R., Masson, R., & Jacobs, E. (1983). Systematic group leadership training: A skills development approach. *Journal for Specialists in Group Work, 8*(4), 16–20.

Hays, D. G., Arredondo, P., Gladding, S. T., & Toporek, R. L. (2010). Integrating social justice in group work: The next decade. *Journal for Specialists in Group Work, 35,* 177–207.

Herlihy, B., & Corey, G. (1997). *Boundary issues in counseling: Multiple roles and relationships.* Alexandria, VA: American Counseling Association.

Hershenson, D. B., & Power, P. W. (1987). *Mental health counseling.* New York: Pergamon Press.

Hopkins, B. R., & Anderson, B. W. (1990). *The counselor and the law* (3rd ed.). Alexandria, VA: American Counseling Association.

Horne, A. (1996). Ending—or beginning somewhere else. *Journal for Specialists in Group Work, 21*(2), 66–68.

Hulse-Killacky, D., Killacky, J., & Donigian, J. (2001). *Making task groups work in your world.* Upper Saddle River, NJ: Prentice Hall.

Hulse-Killacky, D., Kraus, K., & Schumacher, B. (1999). Visual conceptualization of meetings: A group work design. *Journal for Specialists in Group Work, 24,* 113–124.

Humphrey, K. (2009). *Counseling strategies for loss and grief.* Alexandria, VA: American Counseling Association.

Jacobs, E. (1992). *Creative counseling techniques: An illustrated guide.* Odessa, FL: Psychological Assessment Resources.

Jacobs, E. (1994). *Impact therapy.* Odessa, FL: Psychological Assessment Resources.

Jacobs, E., & Schimmel, C. (2004). Small group counseling. In C. Sink (Ed.), *Contemporary school counseling* (pp. 82–115). Boston: Houghton Mifflin Company.

Jacobs, E., & Schimmel, C. J. (2009). Processing multicultural exercises. In C. Salazaar (Ed.), *Leading multicultural groups.* Association for Specialists in Group Work. London: Taylor and Francis.

Jacobs, E., & Spadaro, N. (2003). *Leading groups in corrections: Skills and techniques.* Lanham, MD: American Correctional Association.

Johnson, D. W., & Johnson, F. P. (2009). *Joining together* (10th ed.). Boston: Allyn & Bacon.

Kees, N., & Jacobs, E. (1990). Conducting more effective groups: How to select and process group exercises. *Journal for Specialists in Group Work, 15*(1), 21–30.

Lakin, M. (1969). Some ethical issues in sensitivity training. *American Psychologist, 24,* 923–928.

Lanning, W. (1992). Ethical codes and responsible decision making. *Guidepost, 35*(7), 21.

Lefly, H. (2009) A psychoeducational support group for serious mental illness. *Journal for Specialists in Group Work, 34*(4), 369–381.

Linton, J. M., Bischof, G. H., & McDonnell, K. A. (2005). Solution-oriented treatment groups for assaultive behavior. *Journal for Specialists in Group Work, 30*(1), 5–22.

Maslow, A. (1962). *Toward a psychology of being.* New York: Van Nostrand Reinhold.

Masson, R., & Jacobs, E. (1980). Group leadership: Practical pointers for beginners. *Personnel and Guidance Journal, 58*(3), 52–55.

McNary, S., & Dies, R. (1993). Co-therapist modeling in group psychotherapy: Fact or fiction? *Group, 15*, 131–142.

Metcaff, L. (1998). *Solution-focused group therapy: Ideas for groups in private practice, schools, agencies, and treatment programs.* New York: The Free Press.

Moreno, J. (1946). *Psychodrama: Volume 1.* New York: Beacon Press.

Moreno, J. (1964). *Psychodrama: Volume 1* (Rev. ed.). New York: Beacon Press.

Morran, D. K., & Stockton, R. (1985). Perspectives on group research programs. *Journal for Specialists in Group Work, 10*(4), 186–191.

Murphy, J. (2005). *Solution-focused counseling in middle and high schools.* Upper Saddle River, NJ: Prentice Hall.

Newlon, B. J., & Arciniego, M. (1992). Group counseling: Cross-cultural considerations. In D. Capuzzi & D. R. Gross (Eds.), *Introduction to group counseling* (pp. 285–307). Denver, CO: Love.

O'Connel, B. (2005). *Solution Focused Therapy.* Thousand Oaks, CA: Sage.

Ohlsen, M. M., Horne, A. M., & Lawe, C. F. (1988). *Group counseling* (3rd ed.). New York: Holt, Rinehart, & Winston.

Okech, J. E. A. (2008). Reflective practice in group co-leadership. *Journal for Specialists in Group Work, 33*, 236–252.

Page, B. J., Delmonico, D. L., Walsh, J., L'Amoreaux, N. A., Danninhirsh, C., Thompson, R. S., et al. (2000). Setting up on-line support groups using the Palace software. *Journal for Specialists in Group Work, 25*(2), 133–145.

Paradise, L. V., & Kirby, P. C. (1990). Some perspectives on the legal liability of group counseling in private practice. *Journal for Specialists in Group Work, 15*(2), 114–118.

Passons, W. R. (1975). *Gestalt approaches in counseling.* New York: Holt, Rinehart, & Winston.

Perls, F. (1969). *Gestalt therapy verbatim.* Lafayette, CA: Real People Press.

Pfeiffer, J. W., & Jones, J. E. (1972–1980). *A handbook of structured exercises for human relations training* (Vols. 1–8). San Diego, CA: San Diego University Associates.

Pichot, T. (2001). Co-creating solutions for substance abuse. *Journal of Systemic Therapies, 20*(2), 1–23.

Posthuma, B. W. (2002). *Small groups in therapy settings: Process and leadership* (4th ed.). Boston: Allyn & Bacon.

Price, G. E., Dinas, P., Dunn, C., & Winterowd, C. (1995). Group work with clients experiencing grieving: Moving from theory to practice. *Journal for Specialists in Group Work, 20*(3), 132–142.

Prochaska, J. O. & Norcross, J. C. (2010). *Systems of psychotherapy: A transtheoretical analysis* (7th ed.). Pacific Grove, CA: Brooks/Cole.

Project Adventure 1992 Workshop Schedule. (1992). Hamilton, MA: Project Adventure.

Riordan, R. J., & White, J. (1996). Logs as therapeutic adjuncts in group. *Journal for Specialists in Group Work, 21*(2), 94–100.

Ritchie, M. H., & Huss, S. N. (2000). Recruitment and screening of minors for group counseling. *Journal for Specialists in Group Work, 25*(2), 146–156.

Robison, F. F., & Ward, D. (1990). Research activities and attitudes among ASGW members. *Journal for Specialists in Group Work, 19*(4), 215–224.

Rogers, C. (1970). *Carl Rogers on encounter groups.* New York: Harper & Row.

Rohnke, K. E., & Tait, C. M. (2007). *The complete ropes course manual.* Dubuque, IA: Kendall Hunt.

Roland, C. B., & Neitzschman, L. (1996). Groups in schools: A model for training middle school teachers. *Journal for Specialists in Group Work, 21*(1), 18–25.

Rubel, D., & Villalba, J. A. (2009). How to Publish Qualitative Research In JSGW. *Journal for Specialists in Group Work, 34,* 295–306.

Salazaar, C. (2009). *Leading multicultural groups.* Association for Specialists in Group Work. London: Taylor and Francis.

Schorr, M. (1997). Finding solutions in a roomful of angry people. *Journal of Systemic Therapies, 16,* 201–210.

Shechtman, Z. (2004). Group counseling/psychotherapy with children. *The Group Worker, 32*(3), 7–9.

Shulman, I. (1984). *The skills of helping: Individuals and groups* (2nd ed.). Itasca, IL: F. E. Peacock.

Simon, S., Howe, L., & Kirschenbaum, H. (1978). *Values clarification.* New York: Hart.

Singh, A., & Salazar, C. (2010). The roots of social justice in group work. *Journal for Specialists in Group Work, 35,* 97–105.

Singh, A., & Salazar, C. (2010). Special issue: Social justice issues in group work, Part I and II. *Journal for Specialists in Group Work, 35,* (2) and (3).

Sklare, G. B. (2005). *Brief counseling that works: A solution-focused approach for school counselors and administrators* (2nd ed.). Thousand Oaks, CA: Corwin Press.

Smead, R. (1995). *Skills and techniques for group work with children and adolescents.* Champaign, IL: Research Press.

Sonstegard, M. A. (1998). A rationale for group counseling. *Journal of Individual Psychology, 54*(2), 164–175.

Sonstegard, M. A., & Bitter, J. R. (2004). *Adlerian group counseling and therapy.* New York: Brunner-Routledge.

Stanley, P. H. (2006). Using the 5 P relay in task groups. *Journal for Specialists in Group Work, 31,* 25–35.

Steen, S. (2009). Group counseling for African American elementary students: An exploratory study. *Journal for Specialists in Group Work, 34,* 101–117.

Steen, S., Bauman, S., & Smith, J. (2008). The preparation of professional school counselors for group work. *Journal for Specialists in Group Work, 33*(3), 253–269.

Stevens, J. (1972). *Awareness.* Lafayette, CA: Real People Press.

Stewart, I., & Joines, V. (1987). *TA today.* Chapel Hill: Lifespace.

Stohr, M. K. & Walsh, A. (2009). *Corrections: A text/reader.* Thousand Oaks, CA. Sage.

Strumpfel, U., & Goldman, R. (2002). Contacting Gestalt therapy. In D. J. Cain & J. Seeman (Eds.), *Humanistic psychotherapies: Handbook of research and practice* (pp. 189–219). Washington, DC: American Psychological Association.

Sue, D. W. & Sue, D. (2003). *Counseling the culturally diverse: Theory and practice.* New York: John Wiley & Sons.

Toth, P. L., & Stockton, R. (1996). A skill-based approach to teaching group counseling interventions. *Journal for Specialists in Group Work, 21*(2), 101–109.

Trotzer, J. (2006). *The counselor and the group* (4th ed.). Philadelphia: Taylor & Frances.

Van Velsor, P. (2009). Task group in the school setting: Promoting children's social and emotional learning. *Journal for Specialists in Group Work, 34*(3), 276–292.

Vernon, A. (1995). *Thinking, feeling, behaving: An emotional education curriculum for children grades 1–6.* Champaign, IL: Research Press.

Vernon, A. (2010). *More what works with children and adolescents.* Champaign, IL: Research Press.

Vorrath, H. (1974). *Positive peer culture.* Chicago: Aldine-Atherton.

Walen, S., DiGiuseppe, R., & Dryden, W. (1992). *A practitioner's guide to rational-emotive therapy* (2nd ed.). New York: Oxford University Press.

Ward, D. (2006). Classification of groups. *Journal for specialists in group work, 31*(2), 93–97.

Wilde, J. (1992). *Rational counseling with school aged populations: A practical guide.* Bristol, PA: Accelerated Development.

Worden, J. W. (2009). *Grief counseling and grief therapy.* (4th ed.). New York: Springer.

Wubbolding, R. E. (2000). *Reality therapy for the 21st century.* New York: Brunner/Mazel.

Yalom, I. (with Leszcz, M). (2005). *The theory and practice of group psychotherapy* (5th ed.). New York: Basic Books.

Yontef, G. (1993). *Awareness, dialogue, and process: Essays on Gestalt therapy.* Highland, NY: The Gestalt Journal Press.

Zimmerman, T., Jacobsen, R., Macintyre, M., & Watson, C. (1996). Solution-focused parenting groups: An empirical study. *Journal of Systemic Therapies, 15*(4), 12–15.

Web Sites

American Psychological Association Division 49 Group Psychology and Group Psychotherapy:
http://www.apa.org/about/division/div49.html

The American Society of Group Psychotherapy and Psychodrama:
http://www.asgpp.org

Association for Specialists in Group Work:
http://asgw.org

Impact Therapy Associates:
http://www.impacttherapy.com

The International Association of Group Psychotherapy:
http://psychnet-uk.com/psychotherapy/psychotherapy_ group_therapy.htm

Index